CRS

THE OWL OF MINERVA

THE AUTHOR WITH A MEXICAN IDOL

The Owl of Minerva

The Autobiography of
GUSTAV REGLER

Translated from the German by
NORMAN DENNY

The Owl of Minerva spreads its wings
only with the falling of the dusk.
HEGEL

RUPERT HART-DAVIS
SOHO SQUARE LONDON
1959

Printed in Great Britain by Richard Clay and Company, Ltd.,
Bungay, Suffolk

To Mary Lloyd

Contents

CONTENTS

BOOK FIVE

BOOK SIX

Illustrations

*The photographs facing pages 204, 232, and 238
are reproduced by permission of Fred Stein*

BOOK ONE

1 . Gruesome Fables

IN the beginning was fear, and fear was in me and I was a part of it. I was five years old. Twelve men stood beneath the outside stairway of the old hunting-castle where the rigorous Burgomaster of my native town exercised his functions.

He had his office in the west tower, from which he could see all ways. I was seated at the edge of the road on a clean sheet of newspaper which I had myself put down, but which I would certainly not leave lying about. Of the men concerned the only ones I knew were the lean, light-hearted tailor and the policeman, who smelt of leather. All men were giants in my eyes. I understood nothing of what they were talking about until the policeman made a gesture, striking downwards with his open hand, while he glared at the tailor and said, "Off with his head!" They all laughed, and one of them looked towards the Burgomaster's window and said, "Not too loud!" Then the clocks began to chime and the midday-whistle of the brewery joined in. The policeman sprang at the tailor, gripped him by one ear, pulled his head a little sideways and forced him, squealing like an animal, up the steps. The tailor made no attempt to resist; he behaved as though he was done for.

I jumped to my feet, grabbed my sheet of paper and ran in terror along the High Street towards the stream that divided the town in two. To cross the bridge was in itself a relief. I turned, still running, down a side-street where the blacksmith was shoeing a horse, and he raised a pair of terrifying, red-hot pincers as I passed. In renewed panic I ran on, knowing that I must pass through the saw-mill, where they slowly thrust tree-trunks against the screaming teeth of the circular saw. I jumped over a trunk destined for this treatment and came out into the Bauerngasse, with ploughshares and hoes outside the doorways, and looming over me, enclosed by high walls and trees, the stark shape of the synagogue. I ran up the steps to its porch, saw the teacher and the singers standing in the doorway, and cried, "Good day, Herr Tannenberg." I had grown calm at once.

I never asked anyone what happened to the tailor. I did not like asking questions and it was useless in any case.

The grown-ups knew very little about us children. They did their best to explain their world to us but revealed only fragments. I wanted more than this. Hence the darkness in which I groped my way.

A priest followed by a choir-boy walked gravely along the High Street; it was evening and the people were seated on chairs outside their doors. The boy, in red-and-white vestments, was ringing a bell as he walked, and the people rose and knelt for a moment beside their chairs. "Someone is in need of the Sacrament," my mother said. They all sat down again and waited. If when the priest returned the boy was no longer ringing the bell, it would mean that all was well; but if the bell was still being rung it would mean that the priest had arrived too late. "Too late for what?" I asked, but there was no reply. Ten minutes later we heard the sound of the bell again, approaching from the end of the street. Mother crossed herself and a woman ran off crying "Oh, my God!" and I repeated "Too late for what?" but only to myself.

No one gave sufficient answers. Our snub-nosed maidservant came squealing out of the cellar and thrust an unusually large trap of rusty wire under my nose, with a plump rat inside it, twisting back and forth. "What are you going to do with it?" I cried. The girl laughed and said, "I haven't decided yet." She seemed to be considering numerous possibilities. As she bent over the wash-tub I saw her bare, round calves and forgot the rat.

I do not know whether I already guessed that the grown-ups' answers skirted round the truth. The darkness grew deeper with every day that passed. And it was dark in our house, where there was no electric light. This inconvenience brought me closer to my grandparents, but it peopled the house with ghosts in every corner, considerably shortened the day and stimulated my lively imagination to the danger-point.

Our home was made up of two attached houses with stairs on either side of the central wall. About halfway up, at the darkest place, the wall was pierced, and here all the powers of darkness lay in wait for me, no matter how quickly I hurried past to reach my grandparents, who occupied the whole of the top floor.

I devised a method which shows the extent of my childish terrors. I would grip the stair-rail at the foot of the stairs and run with my eyes closed, going at full speed as I turned the curve of the half-landing, bursting into my grandparents' sitting-room with a bang on the door, and not opening my eyes until I had come within the light of the oil-lamp, breathless but safe again. Grandfather was fond of reading aloud, and I would cross the room on tiptoe and sit on the foot-stool by the stove. On one occasion he read to us about Sternickel, the murderer, and how he was beheaded in Berlin, thus plunging me from one terror into another. But the terror on the stairs was by far the greater of the two, and I sat motionless listening to every detail of the painful business, the whole thing written in a rather stylised fashion, with the murderer "very composed"—I still remember those words. Grandmother laughed shortly as the blade descended, and Grandfather polished his glasses, visibly delighted that the fellow was dead. "Now he won't be able to keep pigeons any more," said Grandmother, and chuckled. There was an ironical allusion in this.

I knew that Grandfather, before he was pensioned off, had worn a stiff red cap and stood on the platform of the main railway-station in Saarbrücken, waving the trains out; or he had sat high up on a platform above the lines, causing signals to rise and fall, and the puffing, whistling locomotives had obeyed him. A mighty man, in short. His other attribute was of a more problematical kind: he had been a soldier, and a real fighter, what was more. Nobody explained to me what this entailed, but I was told the facts. He had served under three Kaisers for a period of more than thirty years, had stormed the *Düppeler Schanze* in 1864 and captured Danish soldiers, had captured Austrians at Königgrätz in 1866 and had helped to capture an Emperor at Sedan; and before this, at St Quentin, he had, as Mother always solemnly emphasised, dragged his wounded captain "out of the firing-line." For all this he had received many medals which Mother cleaned once a fortnight and then returned to their velvet cushion in a glass case.

When he put aside his red cap for ever and came from Saarbrücken to live with us, I went in great excitement to the station to meet him. He was wearing an ordinary blue suit, and as he gave up his ticket he said, "That's the last." It was the only time I heard him make a remark about himself. Then he picked up two tall baskets in which his carrier-pigeons were cooing and bickering.

Mother had already had a pigeon-cote installed in the back-yard of our house, and I was watching when the great warrior thrust his symbols of peace one by one through the trap-doors. "They won't stay," said Grandmother, but he only grunted.

The next day he opened the doors and they all came out. Some of the male birds preened themselves and curvetted, executing love-flights; but then they followed the females, who were already soaring high in the air to fly in a straight line back to Saarbrücken, as Nature had taught them.

Half an hour later Grandfather went after them, and returned in the evening with his basket full again. Grandmother whispered to me, "He forgot to put any aniseed in their corn." "You and your aniseed," Grandfather said. "They weren't shut in long enough."

They went on arguing for a little while. Both came of peasant stock, but they were poles apart in their views. He believed in authority, even over animals; she in kindness, persuasion and appetising food. Thus did they come to live above us, inhabiting their own world, caring for their birds and having their favourites among them, which they pointed out to me and which I learnt to love in order to please them. But one morning I came upon Grandfather standing by a big block of wood in the yard, holding his favourite bird of all (I knew it by a white spot on its neck) and thrusting a small pair of scissors in among its throat-feathers. There was a sound of snipping; the pigeon beat its wings; then red blood flooded through the feathers while the fist of the old soldier held the bird with its head hanging limply down. Before long all was quiet, and Grandfather carried the bird into the house.

This happened on the day after he read us the account of Sternickel's execution. I saw the blood on the block, I remembered Grandmother's chuckle and nothing made sense to me any more; only the horror stayed rooted in my hair. In the evening I went up to their room. There they sat in the soft light of the lamp, and Grandfather was cutting the cooked entrails of the pigeon into small pieces, to feed the ones left alive. Grandmother sat in a corner of the sofa, her glasses on her hooked nose, and read us that day's instalment of the serial in the morning paper. I was afraid it would be something bloodthirsty; but it turned out to be a story about a Count who seduced a girl with pretty speeches so as to steal her only gold ring, and Grandmother broke off reading to exclaim in delight, "He talks just like a count!" and it sounded as though she were reminded of some similar adventure of her own youth. Grandfather scraped little stones out of the pigeon's crop and grunted, "You go on reading. He's sure to be another imposter." He spoke as though, old campaigner that he was, he could not fail to see through all the frauds of love.

The less I understood them, the more I loved them. If only there had not been that darkness on the stairs! But the darkness was made even worse for a time, when Mother took to telling us three children fairy-tales after we were in bed.

She sat gazing through the window at the gathering dusk. A cuckooclock ticked on the wall above us, and near its swinging pendulum a stuffed squirrel sat on a round bracket, gnawing a hazel-nut. When I looked past my brother to where Mother sat spinning her story as though it were a spider's web, I could see her wedding-garland of myrtle in a glass case, and beside it were Grandfather's medals on the tallboy, flanked by little china figures which we never ventured to touch.

Mother told the story of Red Riding Hood, and I liked to lie hidden under the blue eiderdown. She told the story of Tom Thumb, the tiny boy no bigger than a thimble but cunning as a dozen foxes. I could well understand the danger he was in when he and his brothers arrived by night at the ogre's castle—but was there no other way out except to change the nightcaps, so that the father cut the throats of his own children? Without ever saying anything, I secretly rebelled. Why did the witch want to roast Hänsel when her store of gingerbread was overflowing? Fairy-tales were stories you couldn't explain, said Mother. I kept silent, gazed at the squirrel and told him everything.

There were two worlds; I soon realised it and thought I was the only one to know it. I daily discovered the real world for myself.

One evening, peering through the curtains of our "good room" into the dimly lighted street, I saw a small girl standing by our window. I knew her at once; she was one of the many children of the red-bearded drunkard who lived under permanent police supervision. No one was allowed to sell him drink, and so he sent his children out separately in the hope that the inn-keepers would not know them all. The little girl was visibly screwing up her courage, knowing that she would be beaten if she returned home with the bottle still empty. She must have repeated the message he had taught her and gone on murmuring it to herself as she crossed the street; but then, when she reached the other side, her brain had refused to work and she forgot what she had to say. Now she stood there looking towards me as though at a possible rescuer, and I was as distressed as she because I could offer no help—I was not allowed to open the window or even to stand on one of our plush-upholstered chairs.

That this moment should have stayed in my memory is to me a revelation of how deeply I must have felt the little girl's plight. And that same evening Mother told us the story of Cinderella, in which, in the old German version, the sisters lose a toe and a heel in trying to force their feet into the glass slipper. I pictured the blood running, and admired their courage and wished they might succeed; but then it all came to a happy ending in which I did not believe. The thought of the drunkard's child returned to me, rendered the more vivid by my bedtime sleepiness; I saw the dark hovel in which they lived and the red-bearded father punishing the little girl over his knee. I must have burst into tears, because years afterwards Mother was still telling as a joke the story of how, when the prince went off with Cinderella, I cried in great agitation, "Now he's beating her!"

I came to hate those fairy-tales, derived principally from the brothers Grimm. They nearly all took place in the woods, which became in conse-quence terrifying to me. Our town was surrounded by royal game-forests. In them, it seemed, giants lived and witches flew on broomsticks, children were inveigled into strange houses, the pathways were beset by wolves and no one might drink from a stream without incurring some dire penalty. All this made nonsense of the happy endings. The sufferings in the stories afflicted me like knife-thrusts, but finally there would always be some such sentence as, "The wicked stepmother was rolled down the hillside in a barrel pierced with nails, but the others all lived happily; and if they have not died they are doing so to this day."

One evening, after Mother had left the room and when the loud ticking of the cuckoo-clock was keeping me awake, I derisively mimed this concluding sentence; but very unexpectedly, and rather like one of those shadowy terrors

B

harboured by the woods, my brother Franz fell upon me and beat me with his fists—he was not going to be robbed of his happy endings. Thereafter I called him "step-brother" in my heart, but obeyed his orders even more faithfully than before, secretly concluding that all his actions were further proof that life is hard and cruel.

A group of us played a game in which I was supposed to dig up a buried treasure in an empty arm of the mill-stream. The others showed me where to dig, warning me that I might be caught by the water if the sluice were opened, but saying that I could get out of the way if I was quick enough. While I dug feverishly in the mud they kept watch higher up, near the tannery. I saw a little water trickle through, but when the full flood overtook me I was afraid to move. Realising the trick that had been played on me, I stood as though paralysed with the water up to my knees, while the others jeered at me from the bank. They were quite right to jeer. I had been dreadfully stupid; I ought to be ashamed of myself, and my punishment for getting my clothes wet would be no more than I deserved. Standing there confronting my grinning playmates, with rusty tins floating round my legs, in the filth and stench of water that was like a stream in the underworld, I felt myself to be one with all the tormented and the persecuted, in fairy-tales and in the town.

But Mother now turned to a different kind of fairy-tale; she felt that the time had come to introduce the Bible into her bed-time stories.

She took me with her to the church, which I thought terribly high and secret. It was an old Gallo-Roman building with tranquil lines; it had three naves and a raised altar, in front of which an oil-lamp hung. Mother showed me everything and then embarked upon a new course of decidedly doubtful instruction. I learned, following this visit, that the red lamp never needed to be filled, but that angels tended it so that it would go on burning for ever; also that the water in the font by the left-hand nave had been brought straight from the River Jordan. The cross that was placed against my forehead (it was Ash Wednesday) was, so Mother said, made of the dust of leaves gathered in the Garden of Gethsemane, where "Our Lord sweated blood and tears."

I am convinced to this day that Mother believed all these things. For her the love of story-telling was something that might be turned to any purpose, and she was not to be shaken by fanatical, narrow-browed priests. Plenty of these were to be found, the sons of small peasants, as healthy as they were direct of speech. No sooner were they vested with apostolic authority than they began to exercise it; but their imaginative scope was limited, so Mother thought, and she bettered their teachings with a lavish and fond good-will. She believed that the church bells did not ring on one day in the year, the eve of Golgotha, because they had truly flown to Rome to confess all the sins that during the year had been wafted up to them from the town. When she suspected that her belief in legends was perhaps a little excessive she would confess, and what was not forgiven her in the confessional she would confide to the bells. She had a faith as immovable as the mountains.

One day she came hurrying out to me in the garden, where I was watching Grandfather fork poultry-droppings in among the beetroots, and told me that tomorrow the Lord God Himself was to pass by our house. She meant the Corpus Christi procession, and she said that we must decorate the house with an altar because this would greatly please Him.

I at once offered to help. The single carpet in our parlour was laid out from the front door so that it just reached the edge of the pavement. While I fetched flower-vases Mother set up a framed copper-engraving of John of Patmos with his eagle, which was to adorn the background. Then Father, not without misgivings, brought out the greatest treasure the household possessed—presently it was taken indoors again, because this was only a rehearsal. The treasure was a round-bellied Chinese vase decorated with pictures of mandarins and beautiful women in alluring garments, its handle shaped like a gilt dragon.

Later I went with Louise, our maid-of-all-work, to the town meadows where we surreptitiously gathered long grass; we were afraid the meadow-keeper might see us. When we had got the grass safely home and scattered it over the pavement everything was again legal, and we made a second excursion for more. Mother made us strew some outside the house of our Jewish and Protestant neighbours—"Everyone must join in," she said. By evening the whole town looked as though the meadows had overflowed.

The next day she showed me the Lord God, but I did not see Him. A cannon-shot from the nearby Kreuzberg heralded the start of the procession. We stood with my grandparents at the first-floor window, beside the empty wooden pedestal from which Father had taken the vase. As the echoes of the shot rolled over the valley Mother went down on her knees, pulling me beside her, and took my hand and with it made the sign of the cross on my breast. "The whole town is kneeling now," she said, as though the words were a song. I felt a shiver run down my spine; something uncanny was happening. Glancing sideways, I saw that my grandparents were also kneeling. We were all doing the same thing, yet all had become strangers to me because none looked at another. I was afraid; and then another cannon-shot sounded and we all stood up again.

It was the biggest of all the communal events: unity flowed over us like a warm tide, and at the same time each was rendered solitary: there was nothing in it to delight the heart. Out of my fear arose the wish to see what was happening in the street, and Mother lifted me up after shutting the window.

I first saw the Chinese vase, and then in the house across the way the figure of the protestant chemist's wife standing behind a half-drawn curtain; and next door I saw the wife of the Jewish doctor leaning full-bosomed out of the window on an embroidered cushion. I saw a canopy adorned with ostrich-feathers come swaying down the street, and beneath it a masked man in the garments of masquerade bearing close before his face a sun, mounted on a handle, with a pane of glass in its middle; he was trudging straight ahead as though he were blind. "That is *He*," said Mother, and she and my grandparents knelt again. This time she forgot to pull me down with her, and I stared at the man under the canopy; he was walking on our flowers. I realised that all mother's preparations had been intended for this moment. I wanted so badly to understand, but there was a void in me which I remembered long afterwards, when much else had been rounded and filled in. All I know now is that I found the man comical because of the circle he had cut in the hair on the top of his head.

"Did you see him?" asked Mother; but then, as Grandfather rose creakily from his knees, she corrected herself: "Of course, one is never really allowed to see *Him*." This was even more perplexing to me. I looked again along the street, where the procession was somewhat untidily dissolving, and then I saw that the chemist's wife was drawing back her curtains and opening all the windows, as though to air her house.

2. *Day of Atonement*

I COULD never bring myself to undeceive Mother, although perhaps I should have had the courage to do so. For a long time I went on pretending to believe the German myth of the Easter hare, although I had watched the eggs being coloured. I went on pretending to be surprised by St Nicholas, the Christian saint, when I was long past the age; and I did not tell her that I knew what happened to the ashes for the first day of Lent and the bells on Maundy Thursday. Why tell her that I had seen the sacristan fill the "Jordan font" with tap-water? And I was sure that if I confessed to having seen a choir-boy fill the Eternal Lamp on Saturday nights it would only cause her to shake her head. I protected her because for so many years she had woven her brightly coloured tapestry over the grey face of reality, although to me this came to represent a double life of rather doubtful aspect, only to be unified by drastic means. But life itself supplied the means in the person of the chaplain who initiated me into the mysteries of the confessional. He allowed no evasions and was astoundingly intolerant. He seemed to have grasped from his earliest youth how easily one may be led astray by the joy of life. I remember him most clearly because of the annual fair that was held in our town. As a rule he avoided the gaily-decorated square where the stalls, set up round the church in accordance with tradition and with perfect propriety, waited dutifully until that which was God's should have been rendered unto God, before themselves opening for business. In the afternoon, instead of the wheel of life oiled by a Divine Providence, it was the merry-go-rounds that went spinning, those platforms for children's laughter, the starting-place of all our conscious journeyings. The booth-wrestler came out of his tent as though emerging from a world of giants, and none could overthrow him. Kasperle, the clown, appeared with his healthy hatred of uniforms and the big stick that went with them. An organ played outside the first travelling movie-shows, but not to accompany devotional singing: a white plaster figure of a lady with a quivering baton conducted its piping, enriching the lively tunes with drumbeats and the clash of cymbals.

I was watching her jerky movements and revelling in the performance, already able to anticipate the moment when she would cause the drum to boom, when I felt a heavy hand on my shoulder. Before I could even look round I had caught the scent of incense and knew that the Chaplain was standing behind me.

His hand was an accusation. He had undoubtedly paused only to rescue me from the "stew of iniquity." I had heard his sermons on the "licence" of the carnival, and although I did not know what the word meant there had grown up in my child's mind an increasingly clear conception of the limits which he sought to impose on life. Now that he had caught me in the act of rejoicing in this other world I had no choice but to go forward, for I could deny my plaster lady only at the cost of betraying my first true love. It was too strong and pure for that. I twisted away from under the heavy hand and said, turning boldly to face him, "She's beautiful!" Then I ran.

This, as I may now venture to put it, was my break-out from the Gothic twilight into the Renaissance. From that day I listened to the tale of my friend Max Hanau's amorous adventures and secretly read the forbidden parts of the Bible that lay in Grandmother's bedroom. Grandfather had marked some of the alluring passages with bookmarks, and others were illustrated, so that I had no difficulty in finding them. The new maid-of-all-work, Käthe, taught me the mysteries of her body in my own attic bedroom. She also taught me something about feminine presence of mind when at a crucial moment my mother called to her from downstairs and she answered, hugging me tighter to her breast, that she would come in a minute but had still not quite finished her work up here. I admired her with a slight feeling of outrage which did not, however, much impair my youthful delight.

But despite these goings-on, there still remained the problem of the two worlds. The Chaplain was to be encountered in the streets and the school corridors. He even intruded into my room, although only as a menacing spirit. He insisted that everything must be measured by his yardstick, and for him there was only white and black—the blessed and the damned. He hung El Greco's *Last Judgment* in our classroom, but then changed it for that of Michelangelo, a fairly authentic instance of the misuse of great art in the service of petty morals, but which had the advantage that it looked more impressive. Provincial Savonarola that he was, he had never an instant to spare for organ-princesses or light-hearted serving-wenches, and he cared nothing for the erotic engravings in the Bible or the love-stories my grandparents read. He averted his eyes from the love-making cocks and hens and the sense-drunk pigeons which I watched with pleasure from my attic window. When the cinema posters were too daring he got as excited as we, but in the opposite sense. He impressed upon me that in admiring the organ-lady I had been guilty of an act of frivolous rebellion calculated to weaken the giants of abstinence.

It was after this fair that I heard him for the first time go into details. He described hell-fire with a dramatic exactness. A clock was suspended over the flames saying, "Ever—never," which meant, "For ever shall you remain here and never shall you escape." I sat in the front rank of the bare school benches while for the benefit of us boys he enacted the swing of the pendulum with the swaying of his own body. "Ever—never." A sort of reflex caused me to kick out at him with my foot. I apologised at once, feeling instantly relieved by the gesture, but he took hold of me, laid me over a bench and beat the stuffing out of me with the flat of his hand. My only feeling was one of humiliation that the whole class should have a view of my behind; but I got over this pretty quickly, because that kick had done me far more good than I realised.

I was sent to Trier for the *Exerzitien*, devotional exercises in the Bishop's hostel which always ended with Confession and Communion and a galafeast in the refectory. I confessed in all sincerity. It was as though someone had taken a heavy pack off my back, while at the same time I was escaping the flames over which the clock hung; it was like a new beginning, a new, unsullied life. The enemies of Catholicism say that confession is a self-indulgence, a sort of garbage-can which positively demands that garbage shall be collected to fill it. But I have never felt this. I took this catharsis very seriously, although it posed a fatal problem. "Absolute repentance" must be attained, so the words said; and I subscribed to this and longed never again to fall, never again to come so near to eternal damnation. But then the doubts crept in and grew until they had the force of dynamite. Oppressed by the constantly growing burden of my sins, I went over the list and found that there were some which I must leave out. For instance, Käthe. Käthe was life, she gave like a goddess and was the only friend I had. She belonged to another world; she helped me over the uncertainties borne of so many contradictions, the gulf between myth and reality which I myself had discovered. I returned enchanted and radiant from our stolen, secret moments to the thinner light of every day. There was no hypocrisy in our parting kiss under the sloping roof of my attic. Was I to sacrifice this laughing, warm-hearted creature to that strange man in his little house that reminded me of death?

I confessed other matters with a youthfully defiant honesty. But after a year or so it occurred to me that I always turned up with the same bundle of sins. There was something suspect in this repetition. Was my repentance no more than lip-service? Why did Evil so regularly overcome me—or was it perhaps not evil at all? Was it a part of my nature to become involved in moral complexities, or was there something wrong with the scale of values? For weeks on end I would weigh my soul in the balance; but when this process had gone on too long I began to miss the benefits of purification. So then I would go to church again and use methods of auto-suggestion to induce in myself a properly contrite frame of mind.

I would kneel on a low praying-stool in front of the altar, close to the small brown confessional with its green curtains; I would bury my face in my hands, invoke the blessed and the damned, set my whole body quivering until my heart beat furiously, and thus bring my soul to the prescribed state. But one day the stool fell over and I banged my head against the pillars of the altar. Looking round, I saw that the Chaplain had drawn back the green curtains. He gazed at me as I lay sprawled on the floor and burst into loud laughter. That was my last confession, at least in the sense of a voluntary catharsis. Thenceforth I gave up nearly all my soul-searching and repeated the avowal of penitence as though it were a litany. I abandoned the rarefied airs of strict thinking for that more comfortable climate in which one simply obeyed the rules.

But could this state of affairs last? I began to ponder over other problems. There were so many.

There were our strange Jewish neighbours. They invited me one Saturday to their house. When I arrived there was a man with a wallet in the hall, come to collect some money. He was asked if he could not call some other day, but he said that it was impossible. So Frau Sarah Kaufmann, my hostess, asked me to fetch the cash-box and get the money out of it and give it to him. Another time I was passing the Bonnems' shop. A customer had gone in to ask for a litre of olive oil, and the Bonnems stood confronting her across the counter as though paralysed. They called to me and asked if I would mind . . . The shop smelt of herrings and lard and spices, all the odours of *delicatessen*, and I went in and poured the oil into a jug, took the money, which fortunately had been counted out exactly, and offered it to Frau Bonnem. She drew back, but smiled as she did so. I laid the money on the counter—the notes were no dirtier than any others. What went on in these houses? My friend Max explained it to me, but without making it any more clear or reasonable. From that time on I became an indispensable assistant in a number of Jewish households.

It still seems to me that it is asking a lot to attribute any sense to customs brought from the wilderness into modern towns, with all their scientific paraphernalia, without making any greater change in them than is permitted by centuries-old disputation in synagogue courtyards. My duties, as they were explained to me although I did not understand them, were not the outcome of any feast-day recoil from money, but arose simply out of the absurdly exaggerated rule of Sabbath-day repose, on which day no hen might lay an egg, no man blow his nose, no woman turn on the gas, without technically sinning against laws laid down for a nomad tribe three thousand years ago, after a volcano had erupted. But Father said that we must respect the customs of minorities. "All minorities are under God's special protection," he concluded.

I often encountered strange faces at the tables of these new friends. They were wandering beggars, displaying an impressive knowledge of the Bible, who were honoured as though they were the emissaries of distant kings. Max Hanau's father once said: "Every beggar is a reminder of poverty and of what we may become if the Lord should abandon us. If they did not exist we should have to invent them."

"They're something you couldn't possibly invent," said Max cheekily, probably referring to the uncleanliness of the guests. His father made a movement as though to box his ears, but he ran away. In a Prussian household this would have led to severer reprisals later on, but old Hanau simply smiled and gave up the attempt, thereby displaying a notable difference of outlook.

Such differences cropped up all the time, and I was increasingly fascinated by this curious religion which laid claim to an especial God who yet stood in some never wholly avowed relationship to our own. Max compared his Bible with mine. We found that they had much in common, but now and then we exchanged glances, wondering which had lost contact with the other. Should *his* forebears have followed the Child into the temple, or was it we who had gone astray, while the man of the burning thorn-bush, at the head of the Chosen, followed the true path through the centuries, never giving us a glance?

I heard of *Yom Kippur*, the Feast of Atonement. Max told me about it, unconsciously endowing the proceedings with an air of grandeur. I begged him to take me with him and offered bribes. He hesitated, saying that it was almost sacrilege; but then he remembered the women's gallery in the synagogue, which had its own private stairway, and agreed. He was attracted by the thought of having his religion judged from outside. Even as a youngster he was opposed to all forms of orthodoxy.

In the midday break (permitted to the children) he crept with me up to the women's eyrie, and at the door he gave me a bar of chocolate with a friendly, half-mocking smile. I told him that I had fasted since morning. "I want to do the same as you," I said, but I took the chocolate, resolved not to eat it.

I hid in a corner behind a plank in the balustrade, but with a wide slit in front of me through which I could see everything that went on down below. The building was full. Men, all known to me, stood at their prayer-desks, on which lay many books and writings. Indeed, it might have been an assembly of book-keepers, had it not been for the white smocks they wore. I knew that these were the garments they would be clad in when they died, and the morbid humility of the gesture was at once clear to me. It was indeed the more impressive inasmuch as there was nothing else to be seen—no service before the altar, where the Ark of the Tabernacle containing the Scrolls of the Pentateuch stood open, no procession, no clouds of incense or illuminated walls, and no organ. Yet they sang throughout the afternoon, until the *Widderhorn* was blown, denoting the forgiveness of sins.

I listened to the singing with a sort of fearful wonderment, thinking instantly of Jacob and his lamentation when they brought him the blood-stained garment of his best-beloved son. I thought of Job too, and his quarrel with God. The singing was a cry of protest, a stifled question; it was as though each one of these men were recalling the forty years' journey through the wilderness. They stood in that bare room as though the desert lay about them, the endless void abandoned by God.

I do not know when I first fell asleep. My head sank against the balustrade and drowsiness overcame me. But I was aroused time and again by the voice of the leading singer, the one standing nearest the chest containing the scrolls.

It was a dark voice of disquiet, and it sounded wonderful in my ears. This was how I wanted to sing, now that I had begun to doubt. The *Te Deum* of my own church had come to seem to me nothing but an expression of complacency, a strident invocation of Heaven, loud and without humility; it contained no questions. But the white-clad men below me in the synagogue were all asking questions. Their bodies swayed as though the building were a ship rocked by a heavy sea. Near the Rabbi stood old Rauner, the Mazzoth-baker, and his son who was always full of jokes—but they had serious impersonal faces now. I noticed Max's father as dusk was beginning to fall. He sang in a deep voice, so musically that it brought tears to my eyes.

I stoutly resisted the temptation of the chocolate melting in my trouser-pocket, and towards evening I fell asleep again from sheer exhaustion.

I was awakened by the sound of scraping benches and crept out of my hiding-place. An old man was sweeping the gallery. He stared at me in astonishment and then seized hold of me. "What are you doing here? Did you come to steal?"

I smiled in embarrassment. "I've fasted all day," I said, and pointed out where I had been hidden. He released me and made a motion towards the door, but I stood my ground. "I've fasted all day," I repeated. He put down his broom, took me by the hand and led me downstairs to the courtyard that was now filled with dusk. Then he said as he turned away from me: "That doesn't make you a Jew. You'll never be one. Perhaps a Sabbath-Goy"—he laughed—"but a Jew?" He shook his head with a finality that was suddenly humiliating, and went back into the empty synagogue.

The reason why I never paid the Lutherans a similar visit is a chapter in itself.

I knew little about Luther. Our religious instructors had warned us that he was a heretic who had escaped burning only through the weakness of princes, and now roasted eternally in Hell.

Although he had been a monk he had married, and what was more, he had married a nun. "Nun–monk," said one of my schoolfellows. "Minus times minus is plus, so what more do they want?"

It was perhaps the most apt way of disposing of that trivial defamation, but in those days I did not understand jokes. I sought further enlightenment, but the Protestants, from an arrogance which will be explained, kept silent. I had no notion of their evangelical faithfulness to the Bible or their passion for a morality without Jesuitism, and I knew even less of Luther's thirst for Grace and the stubborn battle he fought. His "revelation on the tower," his contention against Paul's letter to the Romans, his whole vehement intellectual rejection of the banality of the epistles, all this was never mentioned. The Chaplain only told us the legend of the devil's appearance in Wartburg Castle, and from the account he gave us it seemed clear that Luther had hurled the ink-pot at one of his own kind.

But there was another and conclusive reason why I kept aloof from our sister religion.

In that western and overwhelmingly Catholic part of Germany the Protestants stood for the Prussian Government: Mayor, Town Councillor, Military Commander, all were the representatives of Berlin, by which they undisguisedly meant the Kaiser and his Officers' Corps. They conducted themselves in a manner appropriate to their "mission" and disdained their fellow-citizens. On taking up office they paid ceremonial visits only to their own kind, riding in elegant carriages which, however, were merely hired for the occasion. On the Kaiser's birthday the gentlemen all wore their regimental uniforms.

They foregathered at exclusive skittle and card parties. They had their own carnival, differing in its stiff formality from that of the easy-going Catholics, although it was once rumoured that "the pastor positively let himself go a little." The relatively small group was, in short, a fraction without a local denominator, a self-ordained diaspora or dispersal of reserve officers.

Its local chieftain, noteworthy for his exceptional height, was Mayor Thiel, a retired regular-army captain. He had a good deal of animal-tamer's blood in his veins, that peculiar mixture of love of the whip and retrospective tenderness for the whipped. He fussed to everyone's sorrow about everything. He bore his stately person like a flagpole through the streets on tours of inspection of the gutters, for the cleanliness of which he made the adjacent householders responsible.

He turned the whole town into a barracks, reminding all and sundry that, as he said, the human species began only at the officer level. I remember him personally beating some of my schoolfellows whom he caught smoking in the park. The town was cleaned of dog-messes, but it stank of his prohibitions. I once saw the old pastry-cook, Thewes, come blushing out of his pleasant-smelling shop and sweep up some newly dropped horse-dung beneath the gaze of that censorious eye and the grins of the neighbours. On patriotic occasions Mayor Thiel saw to it that the town was beflagged from end to end. His letters to the townspeople were Bismarckian in manner, sometimes of a blatant effrontery, sometimes disarming in their naïveness and sometimes shaming, like the one he wrote to my father, which cast a shadow upon my youth, for never again did I see Father in such a state of helpless rage. "I have guaranteed the mortgage on your house which you have taken out with the Town Bank. I now learn that you want to send both your sons to High School. How can you afford to do so?"

This letter was the more humiliating in that it bore upon an unhappy state of affairs, a sluggishness in the budget of the Regler family that was at times very upsetting.

Father himself was never greatly put out when the books did not balance. He would thrust the bills aside as though they came from undeserving suppliants for charity or were indecent anonymous letters. "People are so importunate," he would say, a phrase that delighted me but caused excessive indignation in my serious-minded brother (he later became deservedly well-to-do, having pursued a quite other philosophy and methods).

When the bailiff's man, a small, plump fellow who wore a leather cape over his best jacket, entered our shop, Father would leave the customers standing while he told him with the utmost politeness how sorry he was that he should have had to come so far for nothing. "He probably finds it very painful," Father said to me. "Once he didn't even bring the piece of paper giving him the right to attach the furniture. An optimist, you see. Do you know what an optimist is?"

Father had a little reserve cash-box in which he always kept a few marks, and he would produce these on occasions so that mother could buy cake to go with her midday coffee. She ate very little and enjoyed an improvised luncheon of this kind.

His chief anxiety was to protect her, and so he would sometimes go of his own accord to the bailiff's man's house when he had reason to fear that this functionary would otherwise be turning up again in the shop. "Mother doesn't like the gossip," he would say reassuringly to me when I went with him. The truth, as I have reason to believe, is that Mother regarded these frequent crises as social setbacks dishonouring to us all. Wrenched abruptly out of her fairy-tale world, she was inclined to exaggerate their importance, feeling herself exposed to the mocking gaze of the neighbours as though they possessed a magic mirror of which they could inquire, like Snow White's stepmother, "Mirror, mirror on the wall . . . what did Herr Regler pawn today?"

I once heard her protesting vehemently to the Supreme Being when she

THE AUTHOR'S FATHER

thought herself alone in the garden. "I don't deserve it," she said, plucking at a shining cluster of currants. I was pretty sure to whom the words were addressed, and I knew what she meant. Hidden behind the tangled vine-leaves of our arbour I asked myself the same questions—Why should her own story not have a happy ending? Why did they persecute her knight? Why was that toad of a bailiff's man allowed to come hopping into our house? (Fairy-tale pictures ran riot in my mind: the ogre who had meant to cut the throats of Tom Thumb's brothers was among them.)

When Mother happened to meet the disturber of our peace she crossed over to the other side of the street. She seldom saw him in our house because we children organised a warning system of which I shall have more to say in a moment. I think she would have liked to see him done to death in that nail-pierced barrel, although he was only carrying out his dismal duties.

But Father remained tolerant, involving neither God nor Devil in his tribulations. When on one occasion a child came in to ask for something that was not in stock, he gave him a sheaf of transfers; it was midday, and there was still not a penny in the till.

He enjoyed the visits of my chaplain, who came every month to search the shelves for sinful literature. Father would set up a pile of suspect books in front of him. When it reached a great height mother would find that she could not bear to contemplate this pillar of perdition and would vanish into the kitchen. Father would then start to argue. Only once did he let a book go without defending it. It was Bierbaum's *Prince Cuckoo*, a chronicle of the lives of university students in the reign of Wilhelm I, their drinking orgies and their brothel adventures. I now suspect him of having deliberately thrust it under the pious man's nose so as to give him a restless night.

At Easter he led us over the fields and hills and taught us what he called "important matters." He showed us the sharp, nervous tracks of deer, the fox's lair and the thrush's nest; the flight of the buzzard, the runs of the wild boar, the fresh-tasting sorrel, the bark of fir and beech, the course of the streams, water-lilies and animal and tree preserves. When we had thus been taken back to the root of things, where political geography had no meaning, he would lead us to the much-disputed frontier between Germany and France, and let us pick flowers in certain places or taste the windfalls from the fruit-trees. He would ask abruptly, "Which apple is French?" and with the half-eaten apple at our mouths we would stare down the long, planted rows that seemed to go on for ever. We were quick to grasp what he meant: he did not believe in frontiers. We loved his picture of a world in which all things merged into one another, just as we loved his quiet humour; and we closed our ranks the tighter to protect him from the hateful onslaught of the world we lived in. Without much discussion we three children had constituted ourselves a sort of bodyguard for that gentle and kindly man.

Whenever we had warning that the bailiff's man was likely to appear we would resort to all kinds of stratagems to keep Mother out of the way. One of us, for example, would discover an urgent desire to know how the tulips were getting on, and Mother must be dragged out into the garden, as far as possible from that menacing figure, who might at that very moment be sticking labels on our plush furniture.

When such diversions did not answer we had promptly to think of something else. We invented scandalous stories about the chemist and the furrier's girl, or about the drunkard on the island and our wealthy neighbour, the wife of Kaufmann the horse-dealer: we were ready to slander anyone if by so doing we could keep Mother in her room. But generally she would stand in the midst of our gabbling circle and exclaim, "So *he's* here again!" and march out like a prophetess of doom.

So it happened that one day we anxiously awaited her return from the market while the bailiff's man was conducting negotiations with Father in the best room. "I haven't any ideas today," my brother said. "We mustn't tell any lies," said my sister. "I'll go to meet her and pretend I've sprained my ankle," I said. And then Mother appeared in the doorway.

We were all bad liars. She looked at us and asked where Father was.

At this moment the door of the shop was shadowed as four figures entered and went towards the back stairs. They were four students lodging in our attic rooms, whom Mother looked after and for whom her charges were quite modest. It occurred to me for the first time that she had some right to complain, since she so often bridged the gap in our finances with her hardwon earnings. But even at this critical moment my sympathies remained with Father, the dreamer. That any notion of dishonour might be associated with poverty did not enter my head. So far as I was concerned our neighbours, all honest shopkeepers, had no right to turn up their noses at us; it might as easily happen to them that their customers would not pay and their finances be reduced to chaos.

As luck would have it, one of the students stopped to tell Mother a piece of good news: he had heard that morning that he had passed an examination and was to be promoted to a higher class. I ran across the street to the house of Kaufmann, the horse-dealer, whose son I helped from time to time. It was the prosperity of the house that attracted me. No round-bellied little man ever came in here to stick labels on the furniture! The curry-combed mares whinnied in the stalls, a stallion snorted and a dozen hens pecked at the scattered corn round my feet. An exasperating prosperity that made me feel sad and helpless. I wanted to be a part of it, and bending down, I picked up a few grains of corn and offered them in my open hand to a handsome cock, without any other thought in my mind. The cock approached suspiciously, but I made myself relax, which always gives an animal confidence, and with a swift peck he took one of the grains. I looked at his graceful tail-feathers, the high comb, the taut thighs and the comical dewlaps hanging below his beak; and suddenly I had the notion that he could be useful to me. I could see no one in the yard. There was not a second to lose. Without feeling the smallest twinge of conscience I grabbed the cock and ran out through the gateway of the house back to our shop, where I found to my relief that nothing had changed except that my brother Franz, who always hated this business of the bailiff's man, had vanished. Mother was still talking to the student, glancing nervously from time to time at the closed door of Father's room. I held the bird high above my head and cried, "Look! A good, fat cock!"

The immediate effect was excellent. Mother positively smiled. Then she asked, "Who gave it to you?" But she did not have to wait long for an answer. The bulky Frau Kaufmann was close behind me. "Nice children you have, I must say!" she cried, and expertly took the cock out of my hands. At the same moment the door of the best room opened and Father appeared with the detested, plump little man.

The ground seemed to rock beneath my feet, and then Heaven itself intervened. Someone came along the street ringing a bell. We all looked out and saw him opposite our door. It was the town-crier proclaiming in a voice of high excitement: "The Kaiser is coming!" The words rang out like a tocsin, as though the royal coach must be on his very heels. "The Kaiser is to visit the Rhineland. He is coming to open the new Kaiser Wilhelm bridge in Trier!"

Father, who, as I had already begun to suspect, did not greatly esteem the Kaiser, looked very taken aback, not because of the bailiff's man, who "couldn't help his job," but because of this conjunction of his own painful situation and a public occasion announced with so much ceremony. The cock got free and, fluttering to earth, ran out through the door as though it wanted to pursue the crier and hear further details.

Frau Kaufmann went after it, doing her best, although she was not built for speed. My sister clung to my mother's skirts. The bailiff's man put some papers back in his brief-case and said in a horribly condescending voice: "We'll leave things as they are for a week." He looked about him. "His Majesty might pass this way, and it would make a bad impression." Until that moment I had only despised him, but now I hated him. No one had the right to look condescendingly at Mother, or in a voice of sarcasm to confer favours that were not favours at all. But then I glanced at Mother and was amazed. She was standing lost in a dream, no longer seeing anyone. I realised that she was already picturing the day of the royal visit, the Hussars of the Guard, the coaches with their liveried coachmen, the throng of people lining the streets; she was hearing the trumpets sound. "Rome," she murmured. "The Porta Nigra." And suddenly she whistled the notes of the imperial motor-horn, which were well known to her—*tatu-tata*! She was looking like a bride—indeed, one so young that she would have had to be fetched from school by the fairy prince . . .

It was this particular crisis in our affairs which caused the Mayor to write his scarcely tactful letter. Nevertheless, despite his semi-feudal prohibition, we went to High School, that is to say, to the *Gymnasium*. In the Germany of those days this was the stepping-stone to a social status held high in traditional esteem. After six years of the *Gymnasium* a youth was entitled to enter the Army as a candidate for a Commission. Imperial Majesty seemed to attach particular importance to the education of its officers; although one might marvel, none the less, that the Prussian educational system should be so directly aimed at the Army. As the Mayor said, "The human species begins only with the officers."

We rejoiced in six Kaiser's Birthdays, upon each of which we High School boys received a gift of a sugared cake. This was the somewhat scanty relic of mediaeval largesse, when the Prince had caused an ox to be roasted in the market-place and wine to flow from the fountain. I always gave my cake to Mother, who kept it until it was either mouldy or as hard as a rock.

Those years were filled with a running dispute, never a quarrel but obstinate on both sides, between Father and Mother about the ruler of Germany.

Father maintained that this man, invested by the accident of birth with such vast powers, was in the moral sense a usurper. There was something positively demonic in Father, so gentle in other respects, when he criticised Wilhelm II. He denounced his fondness for uniforms and his two-faced intervention in the Boer War; he jeered at his pilgrimage to the Holy Land and his passion for having monuments erected to himself. From natural delicacy he refrained from ever referring to the Kaiser's tragic disability, the partial paralysis of one arm; but he used very unchristian language in his account of how the youthful monarch had so cavalierly dismissed Bismarck.

He considered the influence of the big eastern landowners on Berlin to be a disaster, having theories regarding the difference in character between the people of northern and southern Germany. He believed that wine makes men easy-going and friendly, whereas beer makes them heavy-handed and quarrelsome; which may serve to account for the northern craving for corn-spirit, that inducer of melancholy, but does not explain the good-nature of the beer-drinking Bavarians. Father, in short, was not very logical in this. He himself was a beer-drinker all his life, and the Kaiser was born in the south, in Sigmaringen!

But these contradictions did our unfortunate monarch no good in Father's eyes. As he put it in moments of exasperation (but only privately, to me), he regarded him as nothing but a puppet.

In public he dealt with the Kaiser much more gently so as to spare Mother's feelings; he had for her a very shy but profound reverence. Mother clung to her fairy-tales. There was a glossy weekly paper, the *Leipziger Illustrierte*, which published pictures of all the Court festivities. On the occasion of the Tsar's visit to Berlin it contained a group, spread over two pages, of all the more exalted guests, together with a transparency with their names printed on it over the positions they occupied, so that each could be identified. Mother pored over this until she knew it by heart. No secret was hidden from her, despite her boundless respect for Court circles, which to her were composed of enchanted beings fallen from Heaven.

Until everything collapsed in the first World War I had my own fairy-tale figure, as I may justly describe him. He was a religious paranoiac who should in virtue of his calling have been catching fish in the Saar, but he had become instead a "fisher of men." Such was the richness of his fantasy that he identified everything he saw and did with the events of the New Testament. He deserted his family and cultivated his abundant beard. He wore a fluttering garment like those in the pictures of Guido Reni. The River Saar was for him the Sea of Galilee, and our parish church a most dubious resort of money-getters. When I first met him he was standing upright in his boat, preaching. He pointed to a dog of which some man ("Can he be called a man?" he cried) had put out one eye, and which he had adopted. He was answered with laughter, and this so infuriated the dog that it sprang out of the boat, swam ashore and cleared the river-bank of his deriders. It bit me on the leg several times, and the prophet shouted at it, "That's the wrong one, you silly animal!" He came ashore to inspect my wounds and exorcise them in the most eloquent language.

We came to be friends, although I never knew whether he really believed all the things he said. He restored to me something of that sense of the marvellous which, to my loss, I had not been able to carry with me into adolescence.

His air of conviction was astonishing. He talked of the brook of Bethesda and how he had merely dipped the sick in it and they had taken up their beds and walked. He talked of the wedding-feast at Cana, and the amazement of the guests when the pitchers were refilled.

I liked him because he provoked opposition among the heedless church-goers and the official priesthood. He was admonished by our fanatical Chaplain when once he went to confession. But the admonition was in very uncertain terms. He told me in triumph that the Chaplain had admitted that he was doing nothing wrong, since the imitation of Christ was the duty of all men.

c

After this his preaching became even more vehement. The Chaplain summoned him again, and again admonished him. "But in the end he understood," said my fisherman. I was profoundly interested in this duel. It seemed to me that they were both cheating. The Chaplain was a bad priest, he lost his temper too easily. He was probably impressed by the fisherman's gift of rhetoric, and it was this that brought about the astonishing partial reconciliations between them. Neither went so far as to accuse the other outright of being a charlatan, and once it even seemed that the Chaplain was half-afraid he might himself incur the Divine wrath, if he behaved too much like a doubting Thomas. This was on the occasion of one of those floods, after the melting of the snow, which devastated our meadows. The fisherman might have made a rich haul, for a great deal of trout and carp had been swept down by the tributary streams, but he chose to regard the disaster as a trial visited upon him by God, and he rose and "wrestled" with the storm. The wind did in fact drop for a whole night, and in the town the women whispered to one another, "He can work miracles!" The Chaplain was to be seen next morning at the water's edge. The sun had broken through, and on higher ground, near the town gaol, a crowd of people stared at the boat of the miracle-worker as it rocked in the turbulence of midstream. The extraordinary event was talked about all day, but in the evening the storm broke out again and everything reverted to normal. I went secretly through the stinging rain and found the fisherman standing on the river-bank. He did not see me. He had eyes for nothing but the water splashing at his feet. I think he was fighting the greatest battle of his life.

"Be still and cease from troubling!" he cried to the water, speaking in educated German, which was the more surprising since he always preached in dialect. I was very soon soaked to the skin and decided that I had better go home. But then I saw him seize two fish-baskets, swing them high in the air and bring them down with a smack on the surface of the water. In fact, he was beating the water, a most heathen manifestation, and I gazed at him in admiration. We were alone with the waste of waters, and never was I closer to him than at that moment. I only wished he had not set his heart on so great a miracle, for what good were his fish-baskets against that vast, grey, desolate expanse?

Soon afterwards he was put in an asylum.

With a gloomy countenance Father read his daily paper and *Die Zukunft*, the review edited by Maximilian Harden, whom he greatly admired. His chief cause for concern was the Kaiser, who had sent a warship to Morocco, to demonstrate the might of Germany to the world. "He's in Austria again," he said to me, adding that he mistrusted these constant meetings with the Habsburg Crown Prince. He suffered all the torments of a patriot who sees the coming of disaster and knows that he can do nothing to prevent it. He often poured out his heart to me, a fifteen-year-old youngster, and he would break off in the middle and run a hand through my hair as though in a gesture of apology which was also an avowal of defeat, because he could talk frankly to no one but a boy. And one June day he came up to my attic, breathing more heavily than usual, to tell me that the heir to the Austrian throne had been assassinated. The only question now was whether Germany would accept this as a *casus foederis* bringing into effect her military alliance with Austria.

August the First. We were sent home from school at midday.

The *casus foederis* had been accepted and Germany had declared war on Russia. That evening the tall figure of the Mayor stood on the steps of the Rathaus, where, many years before, I had seen the policeman drag the tailor in to face some tribunal about which I never knew anything. Seeing him stand there, facing the citizens of the town, I realised that this was his hour. A school-teacher named Sonntag brought forward his son, who was to volunteer for the Army, so his father had decided. The parents embraced in the evening light. Helmar, the Mayor's son, who was also going to volunteer, embraced the schoolmaster's son, who had a gloomy expression. Everyone understood that class-distinctions had been abolished. There was an unusual solemnity in the air. It was reported that the Kaiser, speaking from the palace balcony, had said that he no longer saw any political parties but only Germans.

"Only Germans," I heard Father repeat many times that day.

3. The Narrow Wall

It was spring in the year 1915. A troop-train was pulled up in the station as I went by with Father. The following doggerel was chalked on the walls of the coaches; *"Jeder Schuss ein Russ', jeder Stoss ein Franzos', jeder Tritt ein Brit', alle Serben müssen sterben"*—which may be roughly rendered, "At every shot a Russian falls, at every thrust a Frenchman bawls, at every tread a Briton's dead, the Serbs all must soon bite the dust."

The soldiers laughed as I read it, inviting me to laugh with them. Father led me past and they began to sing. The song travelled down the train from coach to coach, a resounding martial ditty with the refrain, *"Zum Rhein, zum Rhein, zum deutschen Rhein . . ."*

Father's moustache twitched and his shoulders rose and fell as though he had been overtaken by a fit of asthma. Then the train started again and the singing soldiers were borne away.

"Well?" I said defiantly.

"Nothing," said Father.

But that evening he returned to the subject.

"All you need do is look at their silly faces. What was it they said? 'At every tread a Briton's dead.' They've got a long way to go before they're across the Channel and can start treading on them! And what does that word 'every' mean? Only one bullet in sixty hits anyone. Can't you see that they're just inventing rhymes? 'The Serbs all must soon bite the dust.' Why the Serbs, particularly? And then that patriotic song—'A call that sounds like thunder!' Whose call? And—'Zum Rhein, zum Rhein, zum deutschen Rhein . . .' They crossed over the Rhine five hours ago! Don't you see how witless a mob is? Look at their faces! There's nothing else to be learnt from war."

I was called up a year later. The major in the Pioneer Barracks at Königsberg asked me my age. I answered in alarm, "Eighteen and a quarter."

We practised the goose-step and marching for hours with packs. I collapsed once and was ashamed of myself. We marched for miles over icy roads, constantly slipping and falling with a clatter to the ground like old cab-horses. When we had struggled to our feet we were warned that if it happened again we should be made to carry our rifles above our heads, to protect them. Our finger-tips burned, our ears were frozen blue, our socks blistered our heels and our eyes streamed tears in the biting wind. Sometimes we had to turn our heads away so as to breathe. At the end of one such march we did rifle-drill, lying on our stomachs on the frozen ground to shoot at an enemy line represented by targets. We shot badly; it was the first and only time we used live ammunition before being sent to the front. Apart from this we did guard duties.

I was on duty on the parade-ground when a van with barred windows drove past. An unshaven man was peering out of it, seeming to gasp for breath. I presently heard the sound of a volley from the rifle range, and after a time an ambulance drove past. Lastly some soldiers appeared, walking very slowly, and they told me that they had shot a spy.

I did sentry-duty outside the signal-tower. Everyone approaching it had to be challenged, and if he did not reply to the third challenge he was to be shot. Water squelched in my boots and dark clouds covered the moon. I heard footsteps approaching and challenged. They came nearer and I challenged again. I challenged a third time, raising my rifle, and then got a reply in the familiar voice of my lieutenant, giving the password for the night. I stood to attention and he came up to me. "Well done," he said and vanished into the darkness like a ghost. I wondered, would I really have shot him? The clutch of the war was tightening round my throat.

Another time I was on duty at the back of the barracks. A snowstorm drove me to shelter in the sentry-box, and before long nothing was to be seen of the buildings I was supposed to be guarding. The snowflakes melted on the lamp above my head. I got out a pocket edition of Goethe's *Werther* and began to read. Suddenly a voice said, "What are you doing?" It was the lieutenant. A hideous shock passed through my benumbed body; the penalty for negligence on sentry-duty in time of war was death. The book had fallen in the snow. The lieutenant picked it up and looked at the title. He gave it back to me. "You'd better forget all about that sort of thing for the present," he said. "It must be hard for you, this sudden change. . . ."

I clicked my heels, "*Jawohl, Herr Leutnant,*" with quite other feelings warming my heart, and he went off again into the snow.

On my first and only day of leave, Max Hanau, my former schoolfellow, came to fetch me. We went to a performance of *The Czardas Princess.* In the middle of a chorus by the "girls of the Café Chantant" a comedian came to the footlights and announced that Captain König had safely entered New York harbour in his U-boat and would be bringing back all kinds of treasures. The audience, already suffering under bread-rationing, applauded with an enthusiasm that was eloquent.

"I prefer my own treasures," said Max, and took me to his barracks, where we ate things which I had not seen since I left the Saar. Max had three girl-friends in Königsberg, one of whom kept him supplied with sausages, another with rolls and cakes and the third with tobacco. He did not believe in victory and saw no good in being a soldier.

But I thought there was some sense in it, at least for two weeks during the spring. In March 1917 we were taken into a flooded area in the Samland. I saw houses collapse in the flood; I heard the frantic lowing of terror-stricken cattle and saw the drowned bodies of pigs floating on the water. The thought of my fisherman kept recurring to my mind, but then a new cry for help from some rooftop would give me other things to think about. We rescued the peasants from the thatched cottages where they were clinging to the chimney-stacks. We waded through a dangerous swamp to rescue a horse from a wrecked stable. We rowed children over the unnatural sea, singing to them as we did so. For me these were the happiest days of the war, and I said so when I wrote to Father.

His reply, which I found awaiting me when I got back to barracks, dealt only with politics.

"I will give you a brief outline of the situation. In November 1916 we got the Auxiliary Service Bill (*Hilfsdienstgesetz*). This makes every German a soldier, which henceforth is to be his chief aim in life. It was also a way of disposing of the tiresome trade unions. Old father State has now taken their place, and strikes are as good as abolished. In December 1916 the German Chancellor made a peace offer. He did not, however, say anything about terms, as everyone was expecting him to do, so we can be quite sure that nothing will come of it. The real intention was to get the credit for being the first to talk peace. Then in January 1917 Wilson made a peace offer, but who can trust him? We're sinking more ships than ever, and America with her new armies and all her industry is against us. 'The more enemies, the more honour,' as the Kaiser says."

I could understand the note of irony, but I had no time to dwell on it. We were sent to the French front. I was all of nineteen years old.

As we detrained in a village near Soissons a party of ten soldiers came along the street. They were caked with mud, having come straight out of the line. Some of us went over to them as they stretched themselves on the floor of a shed, after putting aside their rifles and gas-masks. "It's hell," one of them said, wiping the sweat off his forehead. He rolled over and closed his eyes, as the others had already done. We stood staring at the ten recumbent bodies, and now we knew—it was hell.

The distant mumble of artillery-fire answered the thoughts in our minds.

The German line lay along the northern ridge of the Chemin des Dames, and communication with the valley was maintained by means of a tunnel through which the wounded were carried to the rear. I went along this tunnel on the first day not knowing anything about the recumbent figures I passed and marvelling that they should lie so quietly. But just as I was about to mount the steps a hand gripped my arm. "Shoot me," a voice said out of the darkness, and as though everyone in the tunnel had only been awaiting these words a sound of groaning arose, the more appalling since we had to walk bent double and, dazzled by the light breaking in at the entrance, could see very little. I wrenched myself free of the restraining hand, which was like the hand of death itself, and climbed up into the trench, over which shrapnel was exploding at that moment. This was my baptism of fire and it was almost a relief.

It rained for a fortnight. The company lived in mud, a relentless mud that at every instant reminded us what we were. It sucked at us, clinging tightly to our boots, and it swallowed up the hands of anyone who fell. We strove against it, but even when at nightfall we laid planks on the squelching earth and relapsed into unquiet slumber, the mud was still there; sometimes a hand slipped off the plank, to be gripped round the wrist as though by a handcuff.

Every seventh day we were sent out to an advanced post from our position in a wood. We walked looking neither to right nor left, but once I found a destroyed ammunition-cart in my path. The wheels had tried to get away, but had been brought up against the steep banks of the lane. The horses were stiff already, and in a last, heart-rending gesture of tenderness had crossed their necks the one over the other; worms were writhing in their burst bellies. The dead driver of the cart lay in a dark puddle and looked as though he were drinking. "He's drinking his own blood," I thought, and went hurriedly on, as though someone had pushed me from behind.

It was not so much that they were all dead, the wheels, the horses and the man, but that they looked so terribly deserted. Mankind had abandoned them.

On the same day I had a new view of Gabens, a youth of my own age who came from Berlin. We scrambled up a muddy hillock, with Gabens in front of me. Watching him as he plodded on, a shudder ran through me so that I had to pause for a moment and rest. It seemed to me that I had suddenly grasped the truth of what was happening to us.

He looked, in his uniform, like a child in fancy-dress. The whole thing was such an evil joke. The churned-up, rat-grey earth around us, where for years nothing would grow, was like an indictment. The child in fancy-dress had hand-grenades slung round his waist which he would detach to fling in the faces of strangers. Back in the wood Gabens had always been full of poetry; he was like an aeolian harp amid the trees, moved to song by every puff of wind. Now, however, he was like a damned soul, with lice in his shirt, gases in his entrails, sores on his toes, a strayed, eighteen-year-old Job.

"Who sent us here?" I thought, and started up in panic. I was suddenly afraid of the earth on which I had been sitting; it seemed to be smouldering under the palms of my hands. I followed Gabens, wanting to catch up with him so that he could recite me a poem. It was a strange impulse, but it arose out of a real need. I called to him, but a shell whistled over us, drowning my cry, and I gave up. Gabens plodded on. That evening a messenger told me that he had been killed by a stray bullet.

We lived in a lunar landscape, quite inhuman, carved up in the fear-inspired geography of the trenches, strewn with the rotting fragments of corpses; a neutral territory with which no divine spirit could wish to have any further dealings. But then, did any such spirit wish to have dealings with us? I doubted it; there was too little sense in the things we did. At night we crept out between the lines, scarcely knowing one from the other, and flung grenades at random into the shell-holes. We sat in dug-outs shored up with timber and killed rats. We repaired telephone-lines and dug saps deep below the ground by means of which we hoped to blow up the French dug-outs. When our listening apparatus told us that the French were up to the same game, but digging even deeper, we ran for it. Soon after this the French gave up, and we were just as relieved as we were sure they were.

Neither side wanted to attack. When anything of the kind was ordered, from far behind the lines, we delayed matters for as long as we could. If Battalion Command insisted on an assault we stuck out for an artillery barrage. When this came we had to follow behind it. Quite often we over-ran the enemy trenches opposite. Two days later would come the counter-attack. We would be forced back to our original positions, having lost a few men whom we were unable to bury, and everything would be as before.

The worst trial to the nerves was sitting underground. The earth crumbled softly in the dug-outs and sometimes a timber broke. I often went up above at the risk of being cut to bits by the flying, jagged lumps of metal. Once a rat came up the steps of the dug-out, sniffed the sulphurous air uneasily with its pink nose and then ran off unconcealed along the lateral trench. I let it run.

We were ordered into the Aisne valley to repair a wrecked bridge. The site had to be inspected by daylight to see where we could lay down a corduroy road. A stray shell came whistling our way and exploded near us. As we moved forward again our captain stumbled over a headless man who must have been one of our advance party. I saw nothing but the wound, which reminded me of the pictures of martyrs painted by the mediaeval masters, and the care with which they depicted the anatomical details of a truncated neck.

The captain leaned against a tree and vomited. Then he ordered the man be buried, and said that that would do for today.

We spent a week laying a corduroy road over the swampy river-bank, and another week repairing the bridge. The next day a French reconnaissance plane spotted the change, and that evening our work was destroyed by an artillery bombardment. The bombardment lasted half an hour.

After I had been in the line a month I began seeking to redeem myself by deeds of desperation. Whenever a volunteer was called for, for some especially dangerous task, I stepped forward. It even happened that I crept out of our cavern into the light of day and shouted in the direction of platoon-command to ask if I was wanted.

This had a grotesquely calming effect on me. There were often things to be done that not everyone could be expected to undertake. I took them all on. It was a form of flight—running away by running forward.

I crept out between the lines and listened to conversations in the enemy trenches, and reported them to our company commander. When the foreign idiom reached me through the murky air, I felt, "That is the wall!" The idea seemed to stifle me. There were times when I was so oppressed with this feeling of a wall that I forgot what the Frenchmen on the other side had been saying.

I was looked upon as a hero in those days. The sergeant-major gave me a whole bagful of flare-cartridges. The enemy was nervous, so he said, although the truth was that he himself was tormented with fear. He talked in the friendliest way. "Loose off as many as you can," he said. "Just don't let it be dark. I hate the dark."

I nodded drowsily. I knew all about the business. The sap from which these flare-cartridges were generally sent up was a death-trap. No one came back from it alive if he had faithfully carried out his orders. After a period of observation the other side knew perfectly well where the lights were coming from, and if they preferred darkness they brought their trench-mortars to bear.

I shot to left and to right. The cartridges burst into green stars which sank slowly down over the black expanse of shell-holes. Without paying any attention to the crump of the mortars, I shot off my whole supply.

Suddenly someone called to me. I was listening to the enemy in front. "*Chargez!*" I heard a voice say. "*En deux minutes.*" Then I heard the voice from behind, calling to me again. I turned and saw a runner from my company, bringing me a fresh supply of cartridges. "The sergeant thinks you're doing a splendid job! Here are some more." He thrust the bag to the edge of the sap. "But don't shoot till I've got back—please!"

This unaccustomed politeness shook me to the core. Soldiers are not in the habit of saying please. I leaned out over the edge of the sap and pressed the man's hand; it was damp with the sweat of fear. "Go on," I said. "But hurry. They're going to attack."

At this moment machine-guns opened up. The man raised himself suddenly, his eyes opened wide with terror, and then sank silently back to earth. He was now no more than a part of it. The bullets were whistling round me like venomous wasps, and I realised that they came from our own lines.

But it was not this that distressed me. Suddenly it dawned on me that to volunteer for dangerous exploits simply to allay the anguish of my own mind was a form of self-indulgence. This man had died because I had wanted to distinguish myself. He was one of those forced into battle who had wanted to have nothing to do with the shooting and the killing; a man with a right to a peaceful life, which I had caused him to lose.

Since then I have sinned often enough in the same way, in that I have forced my ideas upon those, without ambition, whose only desire was to live in anonymity. But ambition is the wrong word. I was just as unhappy in this sea of mire, and among these terrified human animals, as the messenger whose death I had brought about. Being unable to see any way out of the dilemma, I went further still in the direction of frenzied courage. All heroes are born of moments such as these, and it is this that makes them suspect.

I dropped down into the sap again, pulling the bag of cartridges after me. I shot them off with a suicidal calm. The field of view ahead of me was no longer dark. During a lull in the machine-gun fire I heard a French voice. The man was evidently shouting into a field-telephone. *"Impossible . . . ils sont alertés . . . suicide . . . je ne prends pas la responsabilité . . . merde!"*

I was startled by the nearness of the voice, and then, peering over the edge of the sap, I saw the enemy's telephone-wires for the first time. They lay behind me! The sap had been driven so far forward that in the chaotic maze of trenches I was behind the enemy lines.

I was now perfectly calm. I lay on my back and shot off more cartridges.

The machine-guns were rattling away all round me, and now and then a mortar-shell exploded and spattered me with earth. And then all the shooting died down. The attack had been thwarted by my lights!

I ceased to contemplate the heavens and left the sap without worrying about the mortar-shells, which at once began exploding again. I thought I had better go right back to Battalion Command, but when I reached our front-line trenches the sergeant-major appeared at the entrance to his dugout. "I've reported what you did," he said, wiping his forehead, and he added benevolently: "You'll see what they think of it. You'll see!"

A few days later one of the ambulance-men brought me a little book which had been found on Gabens's body. My name and the number of my company were inscribed on the title-page. It was Rainer Maria Rilke's *Book of*

Hours. So this was what Gabens had been quoting when he sought to uplift my spirits in the evenings!

I was turning to go down into the dug-out when a lance-corporal came up the steps and laughingly thrust two fat rats under my nose. "These won't eat any more army bread," he said, holding them up in the sunlight. I gazed down into the hole and decided to stay where I was. Leaning against the muddy wall of the trench, I began to read Rilke's fevered and humble verses until I came to a passage which Gabens had underlined. I paused in amazement, scarcely able to believe that this message should have been left for me:

> Between us there is but a narrow wall,
> and by sheer chance; for it would take
> merely a call from your lips or from mine
> to break it down,
> and that all noiselessly.[1]

I closed the book. The verses were an insidious poison, and I felt it coursing through my veins. At that time I knew almost nothing of Rilke's music. I could relate it only to the moment and my own dilemma, and it was deeply exciting. The coincidence of the underlining and the constant invocation of God in terms of the familiar *du*, which could mean so much, seemed to make all things possible; also that the name of God should have been spoken here, in this landscape of human madness.

I stood upright in that field of murder with the stray bullets whistling here and there. The world, which had seemed as harshly cramped as a prison-cell, was suddenly extended beyond the rat-infested trenches with their stink of corpses into a boundless space. I had suffered to the point of complete sleeplessness from the compulsions of this unworthy existence, inwardly protesting whenever I ducked my head, feeling humiliated by every movement of precaution. Death had seemed to me the wall which no man dared to breach. But now Rilke spoke of the wall. It had been a facile image, but now a poet had ennobled it. It was a message addressed to me in person, the voice from the burning bush, and now nothing more was needed but an immediate pretext to urge me on to even greater heights of lunatic daring. The wall was trembling; it should be made to fall by "a call from my lips."

I read the passage again, and as I repeated the words "and all that noiselessly" the voice of the sergeant-major came bellowing out of the depths of the earth. I did not answer, listening to the noise he made; there could be nothing very pressing in what he had to say to me. I was lighter in heart than I had been for months. "Old coward," I murmured as the voice came

---

[1] English translation by Babette Deutsch.

again, hollow and uncertain from the dug-out, "are the rats biting you?" I was positively gay. Then he came stamping up the steps, blinked in the daylight, saw me and greeted me in a friendly voice. I was standing upright, but he kept his head well down for safety. He saw that I had been reading. "Letters from home?" he said in East Prussian dialect; but his smile vanished as a mortar-shell exploded, spattering us with earth.

When he had recovered from this he said with an unpleasantly ingratiating smile:

"I've got a job for you, Regler. We want to blow up the pillbox at Aleman—make a breach in the wall, see? What do you say?"

I felt as though a prayer had been answered. I remember my hands clutching the mud of the trench-wall while I turned slightly giddy—I was encountering too many unnatural coincidences!

"Of course," I said, and felt the grit driving in under my finger-nails. "Of course."

"I knew I could count on you," said the sergeant, and he went so far as to stand upright for a moment while he patted my arm.

The pillbox was a concrete stronghold in a salient, situated at the exact spot where the Chemin des Dames abandoned its east–west course to turn abruptly north; the ideal point to force a breach and enfilade the enemy line.

But thus far neither side had ventured to attempt anything of the kind. A break-through at this point might set the whole front in motion, and at that time—Autumn 1917—neither side seemed to desire this.

In April 200,000 workmen in Leipzig and Berlin had gone on strike, clamouring for peace, coal and bread. In July the Reichstag had passed a resolution advocating peace without annexations. Perhaps, after all, it would all be over by Christmas. Russia had already capitulated. So for Heaven's sake no "rolling up" of the front. A "Blighty one," a minor wound that would get them out of danger, was what half the men in the trenches were praying for.

It seemed like the jest of a crazy general that a single man should be sent out to blow up that blockhouse. But, far from troubling me, this merely spurred me on. A superhuman task was what I wanted as a way of escape from my own flickering insanity. Or so it appears to me now, and I wonder how many deeds of heroism arise out of the same need. Unfortunately they serve to keep the notion of the "hero" alive.

"*Zu Befehl, Herr Feldwebel,*" I said, and thrust the envelope containing Gabens's little book safely into my hip-pocket.

I crept out of the most advanced sap into the pitch-black night. The carefully packed explosive charge was secured to my back with the aid of a strip of wood. From my belt hung a knife with which I was to cut the cords when I had got close enough.

Death creeping through the darkness? In reality it was nothing but a half-crazed youth of nineteen. Or was I the only one to see clearly, in all that endless network of mud-filled ditches?

When I had crawled far enough, and the fortress was no more than a stone's throw away, I got up and ran the last few yards. I cut the charge loose, thrust it against the concrete wall and covered it with stones. Machine-guns were rattling over my head. I pulled the fuse-lanyard, ran back and flung myself into a shell-hole. Then the earth rocked with the explosion.

A few hours later I was lying somewhere on the edge of a damp field amid a litter of dead bodies. They were scattered all round me, that day's harvest, and a man was busy digging a grave for us. I watched him bend down now and then and carefully remove a worm from the earth, as gardeners do when they dig the soil in spring. Sometimes he gazed at the worm before tossing it away in the direction of a burnt-out tank.

I looked at the tank and the flying worms, and suddenly I understood. The man was not *against* the worms. Rather, he loved them, and he picked them up so that the sensation of life writhing in his palm might help him to forget what lay about him. Perhaps he also wanted to save them from a diet of corpses. The thought pleased me. "But we aren't all corpses," I murmured, and tried to get up, but found that I was too weak. So I crawled slowly towards the grave-digger and drew near to him without his seeing me. The moon hung above us with its cold, empty gaze, and frogs were croaking.

I felt that I was in danger of losing consciousness again. The gas which I had swallowed during the attack on the blockhouse was choking me. I had to give a sign of life before it was too late, and I hastily gripped the man's ankle with both hands. "I'm alive," I said, but my voice was drowned beneath his unearthly yell. I felt his boot in my face, and then I heard him run off whimpering like a dog that has been whipped.

I managed to stay conscious until other help arrived. Then I sank back into oblivion, to reawaken hours later in Laon Cathedral.

I had a vision of pillars soaring upwards to join in a brotherly embrace. It was like a motet by Palestrina; a world of which one had caught glimpses long ago in concert halls.

This time I had a sense of having come home; and however affected the claim may seem, cathedrals have given me the same feeling of security ever since. I lay gazing upwards to where the pillars joined. Light poured through a rose-window; light flooded through the hearts of the saints; light caressed the flowing garments of Mary and Elizabeth. From the chalices of the flowers light streamed, and I was thankful as a child at Christmastide.

There was constant propaganda in the hospitals, building us up for the great spring offensive which was to bring the war to a victorious end. I was given immediate promotion, and the Iron Cross which I had been awarded was sent to me. The sisters went skipping through the wards, and the doctors manipulated joints and listened to lungs with greater care than ever. It was whispered among us that two million shells had been stockpiled behind the lines and that a new weapon had been devised. (This last the panacea that should always be interpreted as a herald of approaching defeat, but which always achieves the opposite effect: we believed in it, lying in our beds).

Then came a letter from Father, and that afternoon I rubbed the thermometer for the first time to send up my temperature.

"More than a million munition-workers are on strike," Father wrote. "Don't you know this in your rat-holes at the front? I'm sending you The Book of a Pacifist. Try to understand him!"

The book never reached me, but the news of the strike had its effect. So the workpeople wanted no more of it! They were no longer ready to bestir themselves for the Kaiser. Well, then, why the new offensive? What point was there in shooting off a million shells if the people in the rear were not going to send us any more? Why blow off more heads, rip open more bellies, tear out more eyes? Next to me was a blind man, his head completely swathed in bandages, who lay hoping, day in and day out, that presently they would take the bandages away and he would see again.

All my memories stirred to life—the man drowned in his own blood, Gabens, the runner who had brought the flare-cartridges, the headless man. I hated the smiles of the nurses. What did they know of that lunar landscape to which they were so anxious to send us back?

With a little practice I became so skilful at rubbing the thermometer that I had got the column of mercury up to the danger-point by the time the nurse had reached the next bed. I would then stick it back in my mouth before she saw what I was doing, and smile up at her with an air of suffering when she took it out. She studied it, shaking her head, and then patted my hand, while I closed my eyes in relief. She knew that I was a "hero," and so she believed in my fever. She was quite sure that I would presently report for duty at the front.

But one morning a number of men in the neighbouring beds did not awake. The big, black heating-stove had spread carbon monoxide over their slumber and they had unconsciously breathed themselves to death. I awoke out of a frenzied dream. The Great Offensive was sweeping over my bed, and it was an endless flight of silent, blue dragons with green, human hands.

I turned my head to the side where the blind man lay motionless, only the thick bundle of bandages showing above his pillow. I screamed for a gas-mask and knocked over the table by my bed. An orderly came running, a nurse came, and I hit out at both of them and they shouted in their turn. The fight with my real enemies had begun. So I thought, and tore the sister's blouse when she tried to reason with me. Then I felt as light as a bird.

Somebody hit me under the chin. "He's gone mad!" someone shouted in my ear. I heard him pouring out a glass of water and then I lost consciousness.

When I woke again I was in another bed. I did not know that I had been taken back to Germany as a hopeless case. There were numerous dark heads around me, and I turned my own head sideways, the better to see them. Then I noticed the windows. They all had iron bars across them. Snow was falling outside.

My neighbour on the left suddenly stirred. He pulled the coverlet over his head with a jerk and then lay quiet, as though confident that the shells which he had heard coming could no longer find him.

I waited for him to reappear. I wanted to say something to reassure him, but I could not utter a word. I tried again and again, but I had lost the power of speech. Perhaps my hand could help him; I raised it, but it was too weak.

Then he pulled the covers over himself again, and this time I saw his bare legs. "Like an ostrich," I thought, and at this moment a hospital orderly appeared at his bedside and everything was changed. I examined this new-comer with a quick glance. He had red hair and one of his eyes was coloured a milky white, which accounted for his being exempt from service in the field. But he had to justify himself in his present duties, which was why he behaved so abominably to the victim in his charge. He ripped the clothes clean off the bed, and I saw that the patient, haunted by the fear of shells, was lying huddled with his hands over his genitals. The wretched man's whole posture cried out for help, for covering; in spirit he was still at the front.

The orderly emitted a sort of braying bellow, like that of an animal. He intended it for laughter, but it was only the sound of braying, and all I understood was the words that accompanied it—"Naked as an idiot!" It was like beating a pack of deaf-mute children with a cudgel.

I sprang up and pounded the orderly on the back of the head with my fists. It gave me a feeling of sensual pleasure; I was sure I had killed him. For a moment I continued to stand there, and then my knees gave way and I collapsed on to my bed, a spent force. I shall never fight for you again, I thought. Then I was dragged up and three newly arrived orderlies beat me and forced me into a strait-jacket.

I lay like this for many hours, watched by the red-headed dwarf, who now had a rubber truncheon in his hand.

When I opened my eyes I saw a white flower lying in front of me. I tried to move but seemed no longer to possess a body. I was light as at the beginning, no cataracts, no dragons. Had I dreamed it all?

"You were very brave," a voice near me said. I could not roll over because of the straight-jacket. "They all got bloody noses," the voice went on. "But don't worry, next time you'll beat their brains out."

I managed to turn my head. My neighbour had changed. He now had a beard, and he looked like an El Greco saint, burning with an inward fire, unreal. He pointed to the flower. "Anda made it," he said, and then pointed to the bed opposite, of which the foot nearly touched my own. In it lay a man with a very small head who was spinning a red apple between his two index fingers with extraordinary speed.

"Anda," said my neighbour, introducing him. Then he bent towards me again and said, "My name is Brill—librarian. I've been here since yesterday, since they beat you." He looked hastily round and then whispered, "They're Chinese brigands. From the mountains. The ones in white jackets, you understand. We've got to stick together." He crumpled a silk handkerchief tightly in his right hand, and went on: "They get money for keeping us locked up. And they're eating my sheep, one after the other." He pursed his thin lips grimly. "But when you come to visit me we'll eat camel-butter. Tibet is rich." He raised his voice in a singing note. "You'll see how rich it is—you'll see . . ." He let the handkerchief fall from his hand and it fluttered over his dark eyes.

I gazed in sudden rapture at his pale, bearded face. Why had he said that he was a librarian? In the Dalai Lama's library? Or the Emperor of China's? A fragrance of Tibet was wafted over me. Did war make the nose more sensitive to these scents of fantasy?

Brill closed his eyes.

"It is a country like a giant cradle. In the broad valley there is peace, and you can hear the camels chewing the cud as you lie under the stars. You forget the robbers, who can exist only in the shelter of the mountains. They don't all wear white jackets. Some are clad in skins crawling with lice."

He nearly laughed, but checked himself with his hand, glancing across the room at the orderly. I wanted to ask him to tell me more, but then I remembered that I had lost the power of speech and I spared myself the fruitless effort.

Brill got off his bed (I saw that he was fully clothed), stood up and bowed to a tall man, who responded with a military salute.

"This is Sergeant Brant, the head camel-driver," said Brill, and bowed again and went out.

Sergeant Brant was a handsome man with dark, amiable eyes under bushy brows. As his lids half-closed in a smile one might indeed take him for an Oriental. He had a calm, sensitive face and a full mouth. Head camel-driver? I smiled. He dragged up a stool and sat down beside me, and as though it were required of him, like a child repeating a lesson, he began to tell me the story of his life. I closed my eyes and let the words flow over me.

Brant had been an architect in a small town in central Germany. He hoped soon—"after we have won the war"—to go back and resume his work there. The town would certainly need him.

He talked in a disturbingly normal way. I wondered why he had been brought here.

He had saved the town from the danger of a serious epidemic by discovering that the drainage from the church cemetery, on a hillside, was seeping through into the drinking-water system. He said, snapping his fingers:

"When I saw the geological plan of the valley I thought to myself, 'So that's the trouble!' The dead were poisoning everyone's diet, you see—meaning the water. So I put the men to work digging, you understand, digging and digging. Digging trenches. No one thought when I was in my cradle that all my life I should be concerned with digging trenches."

He doesn't really come from Tibet, I thought; he's just wearing a Tibetan head.

He gave me a friendly pat on my limp hands, and a sudden, almost imperceptible change crept into his voice.

"But the work had to be stopped when war broke out. It wasn't my doing, mark you. The corpses wouldn't have it. They signed a petition saying that it was an irresponsible waste of public money. They said the money should be put into war-loan, which meant that we should be certain to lose it when the war was over. . . ."

He started to laugh, but looked round quickly and went on in a lower tone:

"They were simply scared, the rats—afraid the enemy would come just when they were being moved. Those corpses are cowards, not real Germans. But I'll have them all shifted!" He squared his broad shoulders; all the kindness had now vanished from his eyes. "Sergeant-major Brant has always known how to spot twisters. I've got all their names written down here."

He pulled a fat notebook out of his jacket-pocket and tapped it.

I saw the grin of sensual cruelty on his lips and wanted to turn my head away. I had had enough of the sergeant-major. But then he startled me with a vision which may be termed the apotheosis of the barrack-square. He leaned forward and whispered in my ear:

D

"I shall go up there the evening I get back. There's a way through the chestnut avenue, with a little rusty gate that only the grave-diggers know about. I'll creep in and shout at the top of my voice, so that it fairly echoes over the graves, 'Attention!' And then I'll read out all the names, just like a roll-call. After that they won't dare to run away!"

He uttered a hoarse laugh of triumph.

Brill sat beside my bed telling me of his caravans.

"In one particular part we have to use yaks. They know the paths better, and they can sniff out the trail of the monks in whose cells we spend the night."

He gazed past me at the barred window, talking in a soft voice, and I thought: when such a man talks of the wilderness it really is a wilderness.

Brill said:

"The yaks can also eat and drink snow. The Dalai Lama watches us from his castle, perched high on a mountain. It has a thousand eyes, and in every eye the swallows nest, and below, at its foot, is the lake. The swallows sometimes pluck hairs from the monks' beards to build their nests, and the monks let them do it and watch the nests grow under the eaves. Presently there are six little yellow beaks in the nests, and one day you will see the parents carrying the little ones down on their wings to drink from the water of the lake."

Brill smiled slyly.

"Or rather, you *won't* see it, because they choose a time when everyone is asleep. But the owl told me of it, the one that lives in the highest pagoda. We can eat the nests, but only after the swallows have left them and flown to Ceylon; the owl does not allow it until then. The owl keeps watch over the whole palace; it has eyes that shine like carbuncles, they light the Dalai Lama when he has to get up in the night. Sometimes the stars will not let him sleep. They shine with a cold light in those skies, like icicles, as my yak-man says. But when the owl flies slowly round the palace the Dalai Lama is warmed again and he can sleep."

Brill closed his eyes, swaying his body from the hips.

"Sometimes I see the owl," he said. "Once when I was in a pass where there was nothing but ice and snow he flew down at midnight, almost brushing the tent. Now I'm waiting for him to come here, because if he doesn't come it will mean that this is a bad place."

I too closed my eyes as I lay listening. It was pleasant to wander with Brill over the Himalayas. He presently fell silent, but I did not open my eyes. And then another voice spoke:

"I'd like to draw you. Stay just as you are."

I nodded in a half-dream. The voices were like a symphony, one dying away as another broke into the silence. Disharmonies were resolved by the play of chance. A single fiddle might rise above all the deep and stifled questioning, to be followed by a groan sounding like the note of a tormented bass, and then a shrill voice would be raised in a quiver of loneliness. And And now came this voice that pleaded with me, soft as the striking of a harp.

He was seated in Brill's place. Brill had vanished. "Off on an owl-flight," I thought, and studied the newcomer's face.

It was pale, enlivened by two eyes black as misfortune, probing stars, almost beseeching.

"I am David," said the man, and rested a sketching-pad on his knee.

He looks like the boy Joseph, I thought; as though all night long he had watched the stars from the spring: and by daytime too, for one may see them from the depths of the spring. His skin was white as lotus-petals. Did he draw sparrow-hawks? I saw how the youthful David devoured me with his eyes.

"Is there still enough of me to be worth looking at?" I wondered; and passed a finger softly over my benumbed hand. Why did his gaze seem to give me strength? "He's setting a frame round me, a barrier against endlessness," I thought.

But suddenly David sprang up and flung the pad on my bed. He shook his head, and as though racked by some deep inward pang he pressed his fist holding the pencil against his heart, turned and ran towards the far door, where the orderly stopped him and forced him to the ground. I did not see this, and did not see how they got a strait-jacket on him and took him away; the ward was so long that these dreadful sounds were lost beneath the groaning, singing and laughing of the others.

I picked up the pad with a weak hand and saw an enchanted garden— butterflies that grew out of marble pillars and the bodies of women half-covered by their feathered arms. And there was my name and what must be my portrait, a half-moon out of whose craters my face grew, with sad and staring eyes; but at the edge of the sheet there was a heart encircled by vine-leaves, bleeding and possessing a mouth in which all my doubts could be read. I was sure that this was what he had intended.

Why is he here? I thought; but then the door of the ward opened and the doctor in charge of the hospital entered with his staff. They were closely followed by a giant in uniform; a member of a war tribunal, one of those dreaded beings who sat in judgment on deserters.

But no one in this place feared him. The men in the beds gazed blankly past him, absorbed in the contemplation of their private worlds, which had nothing more to do with discipline and heroism.

"How many fakes have you got here?" the officer asked as the doctor paused at the foot of my bed.

I looked at the doctor's pallid, narrow face, so different from that of the soldier. Could they really belong to the same nation? It was the old, agonising question asked by all who study the many-featured face of Germany.

"You may judge for yourself," said the doctor and sat down on my bed. I understood him at once and closed my eyes. He gently stroked my forehead; then he opened a case and began to stick needles into my face. He had done this once before and had found a fairly generalised state of anaesthesia. He thrust other needles into my arms, driving some right through so that the points emerged on the other side.

Finally, he glanced up at the bulldog countenance of the visitor.

"One of my fakes!" he said ironically.

The officer was staring at the drawing which I still held in my hand.

"What about those?"

The doctor picked up the pad and examined it with care.

"You mean, he couldn't have done these in his condition?"

The officer nodded, now no less ironical.

The doctor again swiftly stroked my forehead, and I gazed up at his pale face.

"Did you do these drawings or didn't you?" the burly soldier demanded in a voice that made me feel weak. It was a voice demanding obedience—obedience of the bad kind.

"I was at the front," I wanted to say, "and I don't talk to hangmen." But my tongue refused.

"Don't be afraid to answer," said the doctor; but then another voice joined in, that of Brill.

"I collected poems in Tibet," said Brill's voice. "Poems with foreheads. Don't let them take your forehead from you, Gustav Regler! They want to brand it with the mark of Cain, but you must put your own mark on it. I demand that your forehead remain unsullied. I cannot bear unclean foreheads. I smashed one . . ." He broke off, and then cried: "Where was it that I smashed one? God help me, I don't remember where it was that I smashed the forehead of a man!"

His words ended in sobbing, and the doctor nodded to the orderlies, who led him away.

"Was that the man Brill?" the officer asked.

"The same," said the doctor, and stood up.

"And the man David—he's here too?"

The doctor nodded.

"They're taking all my friends away," I thought, and I wanted to cry out in protest. But my tongue still refused its office, and presently I fell asleep. Helplessness is very tiring.

They are all executioners, I thought.

When I awoke stars were hanging from the branches of the tall ash-tree in the garden. I looked slowly round and saw Brill in the next bed. A man in a doctor's overall was sitting on a stool beside him. I heard his voice and knew that it was Dr Schomburg, whom I had seen that morning, the doctor in charge.

"It's no use trying to fool me," he said. "You were in full possession of your faculties when you knocked down the young lieutenant. You knew what you were doing. Now you're pretending. I know it perfectly well. You'd do far better to admit it."

A long pause ensued. I was expecting the doctor to turn to me and say the same thing, but he didn't move.

"Tomorrow we're going before the tribunal in Cologne," the doctor went on. "They'll condemn you to death. They won't believe the tale that you're a donkey-driver. Your wife wrote a clever letter. She asked how you were getting on, and whether you'd had any more homicidal outbursts. She described your previous attacks."

The doctor had been speaking in a matter-of-fact tone, using the familiar, or contemptuous, *du*. Brill now interrupted him. His voice was cold and dignified.

"I have not given you permission to address me as *du*. I deserve to be treated with the deference due to a lama. I have never ridden a donkey and shall never ride a donkey. This was determined at my birth."

"You're a remarkably good actor," said the doctor, making a little bow. "I am the psychiatrist of this establishment, Dr Schomburg. I warn you that tomorrow I shall stand with you before your judges, but I don't intend to get into trouble on your account. Your wife's letter was written on your instructions. You had a message smuggled through to her from France, by Army Transport. You told her what she was to say. It was a good trick, but it hasn't worked with me. Your victim, the young lieutenant, is dead. He died during the shelling of the hospital, certainly, but that won't make things any better for you. I know those judges, they have hearts of stone."

I was now sure that the doctor was only testing Brill. He could not really be so cruel.

Brill looked steadfastly at him and said:

"I hear what you say, but that is not how we talk in the Himalayas. You are a false monk; probably you eat raw meat."

"Excellent!" I heard the doctor murmur. Then he stood up and said: "You will probably be shot tomorrow night."

He did not wait to observe the effect of his words. Brill lay gazing in silence at the ceiling.

I woke up when they came to take Brill away next morning. Two orderlies came, bringing David, who was in a strait-jacket. They left him by the wall, where he remained quietly standing. Then they went over to Brill's bed and said that they had come to fetch him. Their civility made it clear that they thought he was going to his death. They did up his boot-laces and asked if they had tied them too tightly. I watched as they knelt in front of him and was again conscious of my utter helplessness. This was not Germany, and certainly it was not the land of my father. These were impudent, self-assured murderers in uniform.

Brill perceived my agitation and smiled at me.

"We'll visit Peking together," he said in a friendly voice. "You'll like the Royal Palace. It has so many courtyards that you'll probably get lost in it." He laughed, while one of the orderlies set him on his feet and the other went over to loose David from his bonds. "Just suppose," said Brill, "that the Emperor himself were to get lost, and that they were to search for him for a hundred years!"

He bent down meaning to kiss me, but the orderlies, fearing that at the last moment he might do something rash, dragged him back.

All day I seemed to hear the shots of the firing-squad. It'll be better for him, I thought. We should all be shot once a year.

I thought these thoughts in an attempt to find refuge in some kind of unreason. But it didn't help; I had to go on thinking and was back at the Front again.

The senseless spring offensive had begun. Hindenburg and Ludendorff had been awarded the Grand Cross of the Order of the Iron Cross. The prisons had been emptied to furnish more men for the drive on Paris. The wounded were dragged out of their hospital beds and no longer asked if they wished to report for service. "*Kv*" was the password of the day—*Kriegsverwendungsfähig*—fit for military duties. It was pronounced *kafau*, and it had the sound of a bad word, one whose ugliness was to be felt when generals had lost their battles and sought to save themselves. Such was the present state of Germany.

"*Kafau*," said a man near me. "I'm *kafau!*" he repeated as though it were a lament. I looked up and saw that it was one of the orderlies, the one with only one good eye. He had just heard the news. He was pacing up and down between the ranks of the mentally deranged with a clenched fist pressed to his blind eye, running in torment as though a wasp were buzzing in his brain. The patients stared at the ceiling. For a time I followed him with my eyes, but then I remembered Brill. I had a sudden picture of Brill falling, slowly falling, like a tree. I could bear it no longer. I staggered up from my bed, overwhelmed by the idea that I must help Brill, prevent him from falling.

I fell flat on my face. So then I was Brill.

The orderly had picked me up and given me a shot in the arm. When I woke again it was night. A shaded lamp stood on the orderlies' table. The patients were asleep; but then someone stirred in the bed next to mine.

I shut my eyes quickly. I wanted it to be Brill, even if it was only his ghost.

But the ghost spoke, and it was Brill's voice, that low, soft voice that passed over one like a hand smoothing all distress away.

"I've come back. They didn't condemn me. Schomburg got me off—although he knew. They were a lot of idiots sitting up there, with duelling scars on their cheeks. Arses with noses—and the scars like creases in the arses. Is there any other country in the world where men take pleasure in disfiguring themselves?"

I listened in a growing wave of happiness. Brill had come back, and now he was openly a rebel. He had no need to play-act any longer, he could talk from his heart. Oh, there was sense after all in this house over which Schomburg presided!

"They sat there," said Brill, "as though they were chewing human flesh. They ordered David to the front. He spat at them, and they had him taken away. 'A tough customer!' one of them said, and they laughed. Then Schomburg told me to stand up. I wanted to spit too, but David had been a warning to me; I could still hear the sound of his yells as they dragged him out. Schomburg spoke for half an hour. He said that, far from being opposed to officers, I regarded their insignia of rank as something to be held in reverence, but that I had frequent brainstorms in which everything was transformed into its opposite, so that the officer's shoulder-straps became for me the mark of Germany's enemies. This caused the gentlemen to exchange hurried glances, and they whispered in each other's ears. Then Schomburg read out my wife's letter, all about how I smashed all the crockery every month and bit off her ear-lobes and beat her black and blue. It was all I could do to stop myself laughing. Finally, the fattest of the gentlemen hammered on the table with his gavel and announced that I was to be released from the army and sent home, to be a burden to the civil authorities."

I lay listening to this, and to me the sound of Brill's voice was like the murmur of the sea when the evening breeze plays over it. But then something happened. The waters suddenly became troubled, dark as blood and bitter as gall.

Brill said without any change of voice:

"If only things were not going so badly for the *owl*. It has red eyes. The orderly with one eye has shot himself. He didn't want to go to the front, he wanted to keep his one eye, and now there is no one to carry away the dead. The offensive has started. They're shooting already; they have a hundred thousand guns. Who can talk in that pandemonium? No one listens to post-cards. We can't even hear our own words."

He put his fingers in his ears and for a little while he stood thus. I lay breathless and near to tears. I knew that now he had been stretched to break-ing-point. "I can hear you!" I wanted to cry, but my voice was still not there.

Instead, it was Brill who cried out, and it was like the cry of a wounded animal.

He ran to the window, thrust his arm between the bars and succeeded in smashing the pane. But before he could grab a splinter of glass, presumably to open his veins, an orderly came and dragged him to the floor.

I never saw him again. There was a rumour that he beat himself to death in solitary confinement.

Dr Schomburg came and sat beside my bed.

"I would like to send you home," he said, "but you don't want to go. If you did you'd be able to speak. You want to go back to the front because you think you're a deserter. And you want to stay here because you know what the world looks like outside. You want to leave and not to leave. But you won't admit this to yourself, and so your tongue is crippled, because you can't say two such different things at the same time. I am not forcing you to do anything. I only want you to know that there is one person here who knows all about you."

He left me without saying another word. During the night I had an hysterical crisis. I fought the orderlies and shouted for Brill and then for Gabens, so they told me afterwards. I struggled for two hours.

The next day Schomburg again came and sat by my bed.

"There's no way back to the front for you," he said. "This is a place from which one goes to a new life or else into total darkness. You will go out into another day. The offensive has started and the nation will bleed heavily. Why do you want to be a wasted drop of blood? Because you don't want to be a deserter? We are all deserters, all shams, more or less, throughout our lives. We lie to ourselves. Only one part of you despises war. I have read your diary. You will volunteer for other wars as senseless as this one. But so long as you remain here with me there is no war, and no laurels either. Only donkeys eat laurels." He smiled. "Did you know that you talk when you have these attacks? There's nothing the matter with your tongue, only with your spirit, which is stronger than any material thing and does not lie. Your dumbness is in itself an avowal."

Abruptly he seized hold of my hands.

"There are many people in this country who would hate me if I talked to them like this. The young always hate the truth, they need to discover it for themselves. But you're old enough. You can see the two rails of the line. Your train can travel on both, it's simply a matter of having the points properly set. But there's a lot of mist over the track, so you must be careful. And you must stay with me a little longer; I don't want to lose you as I lost Brill. If you go out now you will lose yourself. It doesn't look like it at first. Danger hammers a man together, but it also damages him. The Prussians believe that this is the way to become a man. Others chafe their knees bloody with prayer. But one cannot find oneself by merely keeping one's eyes fixed on a figure of greatness, such as Christ. Nor can one make any other person suffer in one's place. There can be no salvation through another's sacrifice."

I shook my head, I did not want to hear any more. The man talked as though he had wrested all the secrets from my heart. It was like theft. I began to cry, but he went on remorselessly:

"I know that you understand something of this, and yet you want to go back to the front. So you still don't know enough. You must seek further in the depths of your spirit. But you must not plough that field too much; you must leave a corner unploughed. Your eyes must grow calmer. They are turned inward. Try to give them a little rest; we cannot see everything at once. And there is one other thing. Until you recover your speech nothing can be solved. Don't forget that. I'll send you a meal today from my own kitchen."

He got up quickly and left the ward.

The meal came—chicken soup with rice and a little pot of preserve. The orderly set it before me with a servile inclination of his head. I sniffed it, and then I made signs to him indicating that he should offer some to the man from Westphalia in the bed across the ward, who was refusing all food. I thought that he must be tempted by anything that smelt good.

But when the orderly offered him some of the soup he spoke in a cavernous voice:

"The Lord Jesus said to me, 'Hermann, don't eat! Then the fighting will soon be over.'"

I lay motionless for a long time. I felt that I was guilty. All that Schomburg had said to me seemed no more than the talk of a selfish father to a selfish son. The Westphalian with his hunger-strike was putting us both to shame. He was a better man even than Brill, who after all had only been a rebel.

I felt the admonishing presence of the Westphalian towering over me like the shadow of a mountain. If only Schomburg would come, I thought; and the door opened at the end of the ward and he appeared.

He passed me by and stood beside the Westphalian's bed. The Westphalian did not look at him.

Schomburg stood studying the sick man with something like admiration in his gaze. He himself was undoubtedly no Christian. He believed in the gods of Greece, in chicken soup and venison stew. He found room in his own dwelling for girls driven out of their villages by the manifest consequences of a love-affair. He sought out pretty, full-bosomed nurses for the casualty-wards of the hospitals and allowed a soldier leave when he fell in love. Now he stood in the presence of a man who challenged him with a stubborn asceticism.

He gazed at him for a long time, and then seemed to come to a decision. He turned and went out, without so much as glancing at me.

He came back on the day when the rumour had gone round, even penetrating to our madhouse, that the western offensive was not going as well as had been hoped. There were photographs of newly decorated commanders in one of the newspapers. That they should be thus extolled in defeat was a bloody farce. Whole mountains of shells had been poured over the enemy lines; a fresh lunar landscape had been created in France; and now the Americans were counter-attacking through it with tanks, and over-running one battalion after another.

A wounded man brought the first news, but that night a train of ambulances arrived, and most of the occupants were destined for our part of the hospital.

"Nothing but shell-shock cases," I heard Schomburg say, and his eyes, as he gazed at the trembling victims of the barrage, were filled with compassion.

He appeared again in our ward at about ten, like an avenging god, bringing with him the Westphalian's wife, a sturdy young woman who had with her a basket of food. Schomburg led her without warning to her husband's bed-side.

She had evidently been told nothing of her husband's state of mind. She greeted him affectionately and, as though she knew exactly what he needed, began to display the good things in her basket—ham and fresh butter and home-made bread.

"We still have everything," she said, cutting the loaf and offering it to him with a thick slice of ham. He sat bolt upright against the pillow. She smiled, leaning forward and displaying a full, firm bosom in her low-cut cotton blouse. But he remained staring into the mists of his own fancy while

Schomburg stood watching in the background. The young woman raised the bread to his lips and he spat on it. Then he repeated in his deep voice:

"The Lord Jesus said unto me, 'Don't eat, and the fighting will soon come to an end!'"

She stared at him, startled, and once again offered the bread to his mouth. Many of the other patients were watching, and she now became aware of the circle of hungry, staring eyes. Then Anda came and stood by her, clapping his hands together in a gesture of supplication.

She began to plead with her husband, praising the things she had brought him. Schomburg moved forward to bring himself within the man's line of sight, and he at once repeated his words.

But now the young woman could bear it no longer. Picking up her handbag, she hit him with it on the face, making a small wound over the temple, which began to bleed. She took no notice of this. She had set out to do battle with the demon, and she meant to finish it in her own peasant way.

"It's not his fault," said Schomburg and nodded to the orderlies, who came and dragged her off him, still in a frenzy of rage.

"He really is the stronger," I heard Schomburg murmur.

An hour or so later a man suffering from locomotor ataxy fell out of his bed. He lay on the floor close to the Westphalian, who was still sitting upright, now with a bandage round his head.

The orderlies came and put the man to bed again, examined him briefly and then went to fetch a screen. They set it up round him, which was a sign that he was dying.

After another hour had passed the priest came. He asked to see the doctor but was told that the doctor was busy and that death was certain. So the priest went to work at once.

He went behind the screen and began to address the heavily breathing man. He talked to him of the torments of Hell and the screams of those who repent too late, and he asked him repeatedly if he heard what he was saying and if he repented.

According to church doctrine advantage must be taken of a lucid moment on the part of the dying to pronounce the remission of sins. But the dying man answered with nothing but a rattle in his throat which sounded as though he were already roasting in the flames the priest had so graphically described.

The priest had great faith; he stood there for a good hour. I lay listening to the sonorous murmur of his voice, like the buzzing of a swarm of bees that have strayed into a vast drum.

The rattling ceased.

The whole ward seemed to feel the stillness. Anda ran to his bed and hid under the blankets. The orderly rose from his chair and went slowly towards the screen.

After a while the priest emerged. He was sweating, but there was a smile on his face. He seemed assured that at the last instant he had wrested a soul from Satan's grasp.

I watched him as he drew nearer. What a terrifying faith it is, I thought, that confers so much simple strength; and for the first time since I had lain beside the grave on the Chemin des Dames I was afraid. But another released me from the fear that had overtaken me.

The Westphalian, opposite me, raised himself in his bed. He had ripped the bandage from his head, and he cried out so that his voice echoed down the ward:

"Father, father, why hast thou forsaken me?"

It was no dream. The Westphalian repeated his cry of suffering.

The orderlies ran on tiptoe to the corner where the man had died, and fetched the screen and put it round the Westphalian's bed. The ritual gesture enhanced the horror of the scene, and as though the setting up of that isolating wall marked the final phase of the drama, the voice of the Westphalian rose with the full poignance of his enforced solitude, that was now so nakedly made manifest.

Schomburg had me brought to his office.

"I just wanted to tell you that the offensive has failed. A hundred thousand more mutilated men, ruined for life. What's more, the scoundrels knew they couldn't bring it off. If only this nation would stop following its generals! But the Germans love order, groats and army bread. They're all masochists; they can't live without their barrack-squares. And so they end up in mud and blood a thousand miles from home."

He turned to his assistant:

"Get the syringes ready. Tonight we shall have fifty more to calm down while they're asleep."

When I was back in the ward the orderly pointed to the screen. The Westphalian was dead. I approached his bedside.

He still sat upright against the pillows, only his head was lolling a little to one side. By the light of the candles I could see a faint smile on his lips; but it was only the grin that accompanies the onset of *rigor mortis*: he had not died happy.

I bowed my head. A feverish agitation ran through my body. I saw Dr Schomburg enter and halt in mid-stride. My stick fell from my hand, but no one moved to give it back to me. I must trust to myself. A warning voice said this to me, and I felt new powers grow in me as though a spring had been tapped. No more surrender, no more fog, no more fooling with death, no more adventures!

I nodded at Schomburg and spoke without effort, pointing to the dead man:

"I owe him a great debt of gratitude. And you too, doctor—especially you."

I said it quietly and without a mistake.

Two days later Dr Schomburg discharged me with all his good wishes. He advised me to sign a declaration stating that I made no claim to any pension, adding, with that realism that had so bracing an effect: "Otherwise they'll have you back in the slaughter-house in two months."

They did not call me back. I was admitted to the University of Heidelberg. My suit-case contained two old shirts and one new shirt-front, three pairs of socks and four handkerchiefs.

Mother was ashamed as she looked over this scanty outfit, but Father laughed. "At least there's nothing from the Kaiser in it," he said, and then added: "Well, God has rescued you from the war—now for God's sake try to steer clear of politics!"

He guessed what was coming.

BOOK TWO

4. The Labyrinth of Utopia

I WAS on the River Neckar with Hanna from the Baltic. She let me lie with my head in her lap while she steered the boat with one hand. We were gliding downstream.

"At last I've managed it," she said fondly. "This is the first time we've been out together that you've noticed that there are such things as trees."

I gazed at the autumn-tinted river-banks.

"Tease me if you want to. 'A young man came out of the wood with a book . . .' End of quotation from *Wilhelm Meister*. But do you realise that everyone who comes back from the war has the feeling that he must recover things that have been lost, and that he knows nothing about his own time or his surroundings?"

"That he certainly doesn't know," she said. "Or do *you* know how this war will end?"

I attempted the idle tone proper to lovers.

"Our beloved Kaiser will draw his sword and challenge the charming Monsieur Poincaré to a duel in Paris, in front of Notre Dame; and the victor will have mercy on the loser and send all the soldiers home."

"And who will pay the bill?"

"There won't be any bill. Everything will be as it was before. We're all defaulters, but for the first time no one will ask us to pay, and so this will be the last war."

I arranged my head more comfortably in her lap. I wanted to seem perfectly relaxed. For once it must be made to last more than a fortnight—perhaps even the whole eternity of a month. And this would cure me. Hanna was like a haven in which one takes shelter, although not without resistance on her part. Like all Baltic people, she had curious intuitions. She was uncompromising in her judgments and, moreover, although she did not readily admit it, she possessed the gift of second sight.

"These last two days I've been hearing sounds that I don't like," she said, "just like at the beginning of the war, only worse. There are too many spirits of the dead in the air, unhappy dead who have found no true rest. It's like a clinging fog, and one can easily go astray when the roads are all so darkened—you especially."

"Why am I in such particular danger?"

E   65

She did not answer, but I felt her hand grip my hair and then saw it suspended in the air above me. Without moving, I looked in the direction she was pointing. High above us was the great façade of Heidelberg Castle, rising dramatically against the gold- and brown-leafed trees of the wood. The ancient feudal magnificence, the tilt-yard, the courtly self-assurance, all as solid and actual as it must have appeared in olden days. It was not hard to picture the trumpeters on the broad terrace, and the fluttering standards, when some illustrious guest arrived.

But instead of this one of the many windows had opened and a head was looking out. A man's hand appeared, fumbling on the window-ledge, and then a red flag was unfurled and hung flapping in the breeze.

"There it is!" cried Hanna, and lifted my head off her lap and turned to seize the oars. I knew at once what had happened, although we had avoided politics. But now politics had arrived, even for us. The revolution had broken out. It was like the announcement of a death, long awaited, which the mind had sought to evade, but about which there could no longer be any doubt.

As we crossed the university square we passed a party of sailors wearing brightly-coloured armbands, such as were destined to dominate the German street-scene for months to come. They looked very out of place, there in the heart of the town, but they were the more resolute in consequence, their eyes ignoring us as they marched past. Suddenly we heard a cry like that of an animal scenting its prey. We turned and saw that the sailors were attacking a young officer. He made no attempt to run; he hit out at them and then covered his shoulder-straps with both hands. They quickly overpowered him, and he stood in their grasp like a condemned man catching his first glimpse of the guillotine towards which he is being dragged. His head was rigidly thrust forward, his eyes wide, and there was a sound like the plucking off of wings. They were tearing the shoulder-straps, the insignia of rank, off his uniform. They did not hit him again but let him go. He stood there drooping and helpless as though his life-line had been cut.

"Come on," said Hanna, but I couldn't move. I knew that an innocent had suffered, punished for things that were not of his making, humiliated in the name of a republic which now he would hate for ever.

To my left stood the graceful buildings of the university, where there were philosophers, historians, philologists. Although I had put my name down for their lectures, I had scarcely gone to any, and now I knew why. It was pointless to sit scribbling in notebooks, filling them with facts and dates from the past, while one knew nothing of this world in which Germans ripped away the shoulder-straps of other Germans as though they were a part of their bodies, and where hatred paraded in the neat dress of sailors, assailing the wrong people.

Hanna waited patiently, and then she said:

"Let's go to Oncken. He's sure to have something to say about what's going on."

Oncken was the Professor of History. I had heard him lecture on Bismarck. He had brilliantly analysed the mixture of cunning and ruthlessness that characterised the Iron Chancellor, the use he had made of the weaknesses of Prussia's neighbours, the victories on the frontiers—Düppel, Königgrätz, Sedan.

Although I had thought myself absurd for doing so in the middle of his epigrammatic but convincing lecture, I had suddenly found myself thinking of the notable part my grandfather had played in these matters—Düppel, Königgrätz and Sedan had been *his* victories, too.

In an access of family pride, although not without irony, I had written about this to Mother, and she had replied in delight, "Now you know all about Grandfather!" It was like a cry of triumph, and I was ashamed of my veiled sarcasm and did not attend any more of Oncken's lectures.

Now events were driving me back to him. "I knew it!" said Hanna, when we found his lecture-room densely packed.

I gazed about the low-ceilinged room, lit with primitive lamps. His audience was almost entirely composed of discharged soldiers, twenty-year-old youths like myself, mutilated, disillusioned, who had returned to school to forget the war and everything of which it had robbed them. Now the war was at an end, but still it was like a flood bursting its dykes and pouring over their hardly defended land.

But all was not yet lost. There was expectation in their faces. The man with the neatly trimmed beard and the lucid, incisive speech could tell them what had to be done.

Someone near me shouted, "Bravo!" an unusual cry in that place, but then it was an unusual day. Feet were stamped in approval. I looked round and saw a torn uniform. Near me stood the boy who had been so brutally degraded in the square. There was sweat on his forehead, his lips were grimly compressed and his eyes were fixed on Oncken as he followed every word the old man uttered.

Oncken was saying:

"A week ago I referred to the Chancellor's proud assertion, 'We Bismarcks were in the land *before* the Hohenzollerns!' Today I would like to add something to this. The Bismarcks will *remain* longer in the land, that is to say, in our memory!" The professor raised his reedy voice. "If it is true that His Majesty today crossed the Dutch frontier without making any struggle, then all our sympathies must go to that handful of officers who have barricaded themselves in the royal palace in Berlin, resolved to resist the mob to the last and"—his voice sank in genuine grief— "prepared to die at their posts rather than shamefully surrender."

This was followed by a thunderous stamping of applause. I saw how Oncken clung to the speaker's desk as though needing its support; his slender hands were trembling.

Father would not have suffered from this distress, I thought; but then I forced myself to be fair. Throughout his teaching career Oncken had been an honourable guide to Germany's Valhalla. When he used the word "Majesty," this was truly what he meant. He subscribed to the lofty remoteness of royal palaces—Sans Souci, Windsor, Fontainebleau, the Quirinal. The gardens of the Hofburg were more to him that a mere flowery adornment, and never would he have called the Escorial an arrogant fortress or referred to the splendour of Versailles as a provocation. His conservative mode of speech was proper to his chivalrous habit of thought; and from the things which he courteously refrained from saying emerged the spell of the symbol which was monarchy. He had an almost Shakespearian concept of the pride of kings. The "magic of the anointed"—in all humility Oncken acquiesced in this.

It was a bitter sense of disillusion that now spoke from his lips. I felt and respected it, despite the fact that Father had brought me up to attach no great value to the Hohenzollerns. But Oncken's utterance was born of pain; it was one man's private palace revolution. The other listeners perceived this just as I did, and perhaps their applause frightened him, for it rose in tumult, the rowdy stamping and clapping of the students as they listened to these words of renunciation from an historian passing through his own tragic hour of history.

"Idiotic!" said Hanna amid the clamour. "Treating a few sentimental fools in a cellar as though they were heroes!"

"It's a re-grouping," I said, and marvelled at myself as I spoke the words. "The palace means something to them—can't you see that?" The people near me pricked up their ears. Oncken was on his way out of the room, thrusting a passage through the applauding crowd. I don't know what got into me, but I said more loudly: "We've all got to re-group, form up in new ways!"

"Come out in front!" shouted my neighbour, the one who had lost his shoulder-straps, and in a moment I was standing behind Onckens' desk, meeting the gaze of all those eyes which now expected something of me. I was utterly at a loss; I stammered something, and the things I said were incoherent vapourings; but this, nevertheless, was my entry into political life, which never let me go again.

I think I said that we must go back to the trenches, but our own trenches; we must dig in our own selves like moles, until we reached daylight.

I recalled a children's tale of how the mole, as he thrust his way out of the earth, had been blinded by the dazzling sunshine. "But *we* will not let ourselves be blinded!" I shouted in conclusion, and then forced my way back into the seething crowd, of which, if I remember rightly, one part was applauding while the other part jeered wildly at my babblings.

I met Hanna on the bridge over the Neckar. "You were terrible!" she said. I leaned over the stone balustrade and stared down at the stream.

"People like Oncken and his reactionary students," she went on remorselessly, "are the unteachable part of your race. They can be called to account now, and they feel it, but it only makes them more stubborn. In 1917 Oncken was agitating against a compromise peace. He's one of those responsible for the fact that now you'll get no peace at all."

"I'm not concerned with day-to-day politics."

"But the day is here now, the grey, filthy, threadbare day with all its wretchedness!"

"All I meant was, how much we're all groping in the dark."

"They'll make your words mean whatever suits them. You must get the fog out of your eyes—everything you said was foggy. I should like you to know a friend of mine, a sort of prophet; I'm meeting him tonight on the Schlossberg. Oh, God, you've got so much to learn!"

I listened as she went away, and was glad to hear the sound of her footsteps receding into the distance. "I don't want any prophets," I thought.

But at ten o'clock that night I was at the place she had appointed, on the castle hill. It was a small, flat stretch of ground to the east of the broad tower rising above the valley. I went along a narrow pathway, brushing overhanging shrubs aside, and stood suddenly confronting Hanna and her prophet.

I was struck by the face that turned towards mine in the moonlight. It was big and white, with eyes like those of an ancient owl, their gaze penetrating and then suddenly dreamy. The man was in the act of speaking and he did not stop on my account.

"I want to collect the embittered ones," he said.

His gestures were those of a tired actor. He had the Jewish countenance, on which the fate of that persecuted race is imprinted like the traces of a secret malady.

"The embittered ones are the real sacrificial victims. They always fall into the wrong hands, and generally into the hands of those who are responsible for their bitterness. But there must be no class-distinction. The idea of dividing people up according to their bank-balance or the kind of work they do is too mechanical altogether. I want to help *people*, not to spit at the rich or soft-soap the poor."

He was growing more agitated as he spoke.

"These are the times when new wars are born. If I believed in the devil I would say, 'Now he's hard at work!' He lets the men of action withdraw in bitterness; he tells them they're right, that the whole business is no longer worth anything and never was worth anything. And he says the same thing to the people who can't live without a faith and an ideal of some kind. As for the rest, he rubs their noses in the blunders of the new authorities, and before long he has them believing that those are the people, not the Kaiser, who were and still are responsible for everything. Bitterness and pharisaism!"

I thought suddenly that I caught a sound of rustling in the bushes, and I signed to the man to be silent. I went a little way along the narrow path, but without seeing anything.

"I'm not afraid of anyone," said the pale-faced man as I came back.

"You should be afraid of them," said Hanna.

"I've been threatened all my life," the man said, "but now the people are with me."

I bent my head towards Hanna.

"Who is he, that he talks like this?"

There was a look of pride on her face as she answered:

"He's Toller—Ernst Toller."

She had scarcely spoken the name when the storm descended on our peaceful meeting. There were sounds as though a pack of wild animals was converging upon us through the undergrowth. "There's the swine!" yelled a shrill, almost feminine voice. "Beat him up!" shouted another.

A large party of students wearing club caps appeared and confronted us, shutting off our clearing from the rest of the world. They stood leaning on their sticks, grinning as they gazed at the three of us.

Hanna seemed to be struck motionless. I swung round and went towards them, to be greeted by a cry of astonishment—"What are *you* doing here?"

I found myself face to face with the young man who had presided over Oncken's meeting, and I felt something like a blush of shame sweep over me. Why was Hanna always right?

"You want to deal with him yourself, do you?" the young man said.

He winked at me, took the monocle out of his eye for an instant, screwed it in again, clicked his tongue and then over his shoulder gave the order to withdraw. A murmur of protest arose from the youths' ranks, but the leader had no intention of allowing his authority to be disputed. "That's an order," he said, and the human barricade slowly receded and presently vanished, moving uphill through the silvery night.

The moonlight flooded softly down over the shrubs and trees.
After a little while I followed the students, without taking leave of the others.

The next day I went again to hear Oncken. I wanted to compare him with Toller. But I mistook the time and found myself being addressed by the liberal economist, Alfred Weber.

I sat down on a bench and listened with growing interest.

"We now have a republic," Alfred Weber said. "We mustn't let it be stifled. It's very young. They're all assailing it. Let me warn you against three German diseases—disunity, disputatiousness, worship of foreigners. The Republic is weak. Its new ideas have not yet been thought out. It arose spontaneously, but is that a reason why the young should hate it? I never saw any younger generation so quickly embittered as our own. Why aren't we proud that we can at last be civilians? In Berlin the battle has broken out—Social Democrats versus Spartacists, the Republic versus the Mob. The Spartacists! Fools who don't understand that the time has come to establish our own *res publica*. Some talk as they do because nothing will satisfy them, others because they can never forget that the Kaiser locked them up—but is the Republic the Kaiser? Yet they would sooner go to the barricades with the scum of Berlin. And there are not enough young men to sweep them away! I was asked today what I think of my colleague Oncken . . ."

I felt that Weber was looking towards me as he spoke. It was pure chance, but his words seemed to be addressed directly to me.

"Oncken has been robbed of his symbols," Weber went on. "He can no longer press his Tsar's picture to his lips. His Tsar is a bad commander, a fugitive from his own land. Why should you young men have any part in this slow burial? Let the dead bury their dead, and see to it that your youth, your future and your present are not buried with them! Those officers in the cellar are like moths beating their heads against the window-panes. Perhaps it is madness that we should be seated here at our desks. Of course it's madness! We should all go to Berlin. The lecture is concluded."

Alfred Weber bowed and went out.

I went straight to Hanna.
"I'm going to Berlin," I said.
"You look changed," she said.
"Thank you."
"I didn't mean that unkindly."
"It doesn't matter how you meant it. I've got to go."
"Of course you must go."

We stood gazing at one another in silence. Now I must really go, I thought, as she handed me the money for my fare.

From Frankfurt I wrote to Professor Weber:

Dear Professor, I am doing as you advised. It isn't a question of who is right. But there must be no more war, that is the first thing, and that is what the Republic means to me. And the second thing is that the young must again begin to believe in something.

This brief and honourable message was written on a picture-postcard of the Goethe House.

I journeyed through the conquered Germany in 1918. Did rivers of tears run beside the railway-lines? Did the voices of orphaned children call out of the mist? Why had Gabens died? Were flares still soaring over the Chemin des Dames? Brill might now have gone to Tibet and got well again.

I thought of the fisherman who had called upon the flood to abate, and then of the bailiff's man who had so often had us in pawn—now his colleagues were scattered throughout the land, sticking their labels on every German house.

I raised my head and stared through the window at the clouds hanging low over the countryside. The night was dark as calamity.

As I stood looking about me in the booking-hall of the Berlin railway-station I was accosted by a young man wearing a steel helmet. "You should sign up to help us fight the Reds," he said. I put down my bundle and examined this recruiting-agent, who was about four years younger than I.

"The dirty swine!" he said. "Stabbing our glorious army in the back!"

I had not heard this charge before, and suddenly I seemed to catch an echo of Schomburg's voice. I said sharply:

"Who are you? And who are the 'we' you're talking about?"

"*Jung-Deutschland*—German Youth," the boy said arrogantly, and he did indeed look very young.

"I don't understand," I said.

"Does that mean you're one of them?" he demanded, and pressed the helmet lower over his childish face.

"I'm one of the ones that don't fall for fairy-tales any more."

"I'll bust your nose for you—that'll teach you whether I'm something out of a fairy-tale," he said. "I've shot ten of them already in the Tiergarten."

"I came to fight for the Republic."

"Then you come along with me," he said jovially. "I'll take you to the Reichstag. They sign up anyone there."

After which scarcely flattering pronouncement I followed him on my first political adventure.

I stood shivering with cold in a corridor of the Reichstag, waiting until it was my turn to be hired as a soldier in the Reichstag contingent of the Social Democratic Party. I counted the men in front of me: there were more than two hundred.

Many were obviously destitute. The man in front of me had neither hat nor coat. It was an army of hunger-marchers that was to be enlisted. My turn came after two hours. The party-official looked at my clothes and asked me why I had come.

"To defend the Republic," I replied dramatically.

"Who paid your fare?"

"A girl."

"Funny, eh?" said the clerk, but he signed me on.

Next day I listened to the defenders of the Republic as they talked among themselves. They talked of pay and food, and they hoped it would not be long before they got some action. "A chance of loot," one of them said drily, and no one contradicted him.

"It can last two years for all I care," another said.

"I want to have a weapon in my hand again," a third said. "Without a rifle a man isn't a man at all. That's why I joined, if you want to know."

I spent the whole morning talking to this man. He was a muscular giant. He didn't want the war to be over; he considered that soldiering was the only decent way of life. To him the return to civil life was like being sent into exile. "But if we go about it the right way," he said with a crafty grin, "the war can go on for ever."

He came from Silesia, but he wasn't going to let them send him back there.

"It's as quiet as a grave there," he said. "Don't I know it! I couldn't stand all that quietness."

I listened and thought of the hospital—of Brill, and the red-haired pacifist and Dr Schomburg. All of them had wanted to end the war. This one wanted it to go on for ever. Who was sane and who was mad?

I saw the man again two evenings later, when our company was transferred to a barracks somewhere in the Moabit district. "Now we're going to start!" he cried in a voice that trembled with excitement—no more danger of a pause in the eternal war.

But then the lieutenant came and announced that the company was to be marched back. "Fall in!" he commanded, and added in quite unmilitary terms: "We're going home."

"Home" meant the Reichstag, where we slept, ate and idled. The company made ready to return.

But suddenly the Silesian uttered a cry. He tossed his rifle in the air, caught it and fired it. "There they are!" he shouted. The bullet shattered one of the barrack-windows. Everyone sprang back as the man pursued his private war. He emptied his magazine, and when he had no bullets left he stood as though in a dream sniffing the fumes of cordite that came out of the barrel. He shouted "Hurra!" and then again "Hurra!" in a voice that was almost a croak, and with rifle and bayonet at the charge he dashed out into the night, through the high gateway of the barracks, to encounter an imaginary foe.

The lieutenant raised his pistol but did not shoot. "Poor devil!" he said in a tone of deep understanding.

I met Kuttner, the newspaper editor, who was acting as Inspector to our formation.

"I'll be perfectly frank with you," he said. "We haven't signed your lot up to do any fighting. We're letting the 'Balts' take care of that, they're used to the sight of blood and they know their business. In a few days' time we shall be using them to recapture the newspaper *Vorwärts*, which the bandits have taken away from us. This company of yours is a bluff, but a necessary one, because otherwise we're in danger of being swamped by the Whites. Do you understand? You look as though you were capable of understanding. Politics is nothing but a bloody pantomime. We have to do a bit of sabre-rattling too; and you, meaning your company, are our sabre."

He dug me in the ribs with a chuckle, offered me a cigarette and went away.

On the third night I noticed the portrait of Bismarck in the hall where we slept, the famous one, painted by Lenbach. I had arranged three of the red-upholstered chairs against the wall so that their backs formed a shelter between me and the coming and going in the hall. I stretched out under my army blanket and found the eyes of the Iron Chancellor upon me. How much terror really resides in this sort of commonplace portraiture I do not know, but I was shaken by it. Father had revered the man. I thought of Oncken's hard words on the day of the Kaiser's flight. I sat up, seized with the tragi-comedy of the situation. By that time I had heard the Armistice terms. Bismarck's Reich had been dealt its heaviest blow, not least owing to the inadequacy of those who had summarily dismissed him from office. The Reich that had been proclaimed at Versailles had been brought to ignominy in the eyes of the whole world at Compiègne. The Fleet was to be delivered into the hands of the enemy with guns unloaded and flags at half-mast.

Memel was lost, Alsace restored to France, the Saar put in bond. *Sic transit
gloria mundi* . . . I would have been ashamed to speak the banal words aloud
in that roomful of snoring soldiers; but then a man lying near me said:

"Who's that old baldhead you're staring at?"

I sprang to my feet. I wanted to save the picture. We might be attacked
from outside at any time.

I found the Reichstag major-domo in his quarters.

"You haven't lost anything here!" he shouted hoarsely at me.

"I'm not looking for anything," I said. "All I want is for you to put that
portrait of Bismarck somewhere where it will be safe."

I saw that he didn't choose to understand me.

"I don't talk to your sort," he said, and swung round on his revolving
chair so that his back was again turned towards me. "I'm an official of
Imperial Germany, understand?—and that goes for you like everyone
else!"

I went out and made a tour of the building, feeling that I had made a fool
of myself. Our company existed for reasons of prestige, as had already been
explained to me. But did the bluff have to be carried so far that an official of
the Monarchy had to spit in my eye? The enemy was the past—but what
were we defending here? It seemed to me that no one saw the situation
clearly; we were carrying the past around with us like a malignant growth.
Why should I be worrying about a portrait of Bismarck? Why didn't I cut
loose and demand to know how Germany was to find her way out of her
present chaos? We had been forbidden to attend political meetings, but why
did I take any notice of the order? To whom did I owe obedience?

The next afternoon Kuttner appeared in company with a little man carrying a cash-box. We were to receive our week's pay.

"This isn't enough!" bellowed one man.

The little man clutched his box in terror, glanced at Kuttner, who nodded
quickly, and handed over another packet of money.

"I didn't make the revolution," said Kuttner, as though in apology, and
we all signed carefully inscribed receipts for the extra money extorted by
blackmail. There was, it seemed, a certain order in the revolution.

I stood at a window of the Council Chamber wondering what we were
being paid for. Berlin lay about us like a city under a spell. The victory
columns towered like a mocking gesture of history over the Ahnenallee,
which the fugitive Kaiser had created to the glory of his ancestors. Someone
behind me was talking about the Spartacist leader, Karl Liebknecht, and how
he seemed to be extending his hold over every part of the town. He occupied
the office building of the Social-Democrat newspaper, where he was in-
dulging in wild orgies with his mistress, Rosa Luxemburg.

If that is true, I thought, it makes us look ludicrous. Then the door opened and the "official of Imperial Germany" appeared. He saw me and shouted in a voice of disdain:

"We've had news that the Reichstag is to be attacked today. You'd better either clear out or else do something about it."

I should explain that I had now been put in charge of a platoon with the nominal rank of sergeant. I clicked my heels, saying, "*Zu Befehl*", and then laughed at this automatic display of discipline. However, I set about putting the building in a state of readiness, and in doing so discovered the doorway which was destined, fourteen years later on the occasion of the Reichstag fire, to play such a fateful part in history.

I went down into the cellars with a party of my men, and amid the tangle of pipes lining the walls and ceiling I came upon a passageway running under the street to the dwelling of the President of the Reichstag. I went along it until I came to a locked door which did not open at my knock. I mistrusted this door, suddenly recalling the officers Oncken had talked about, the ones who had defended the Kaiser's Reich in a cellar. What had become of them? I called to some of my men, and they wedged the door with iron bars and heaped coal in front of it.

When we came upstairs again we encountered the "official of Imperial Germany." He wagged his head rather triumphantly and said that we had been in occupation of his house longer than anyone else—the first outfit had now been paid off. By this he meant the Spartacists. He vouchsafed no further explanation, but soon the building was full of rumours. I listened to the talk during our evening meal and tried to form a picture of what had happened; a strange reluctance restrained me from asking questions.

"So they gave her a bath in the Landwehr Canal!"

"Now he knows what bullets sound like!"

"An escaped gaol-bird . . ."

". . . while we were starving in the trenches . . ."

". . . stabbed the Army in the back! . . ."

"I read a poem in *Vorwärts*—'Ten thousand dead lie in a row, But Karl and Rosa are lying low . . .' But now they really are lying low!"

I overcame my reluctance:

"What are you talking about?"

The lieutenant, who had hitherto kept silent, answered me in precise terms; he did not want to be associated with the others. The Spartacist leaders, Karl Liebknecht and Rosa Luxemburg, had been caught and shot. Frau Luxemburg's dead body had been fished out of the canal, and Deputy Liebknecht had been found in a bush with several bullets in his head. The *Vorwärts* building had been stormed and recaptured by the "Balts" (this was the name given to certain formations of the returned Regular Army).

As he finished speaking, the Reichstag bell sounded the alarm. We sprang to arms and formed up facing the windows, and after a short interval the door opened and Kuttner appeared. He looked us over and said in a false-friendly tone:

"We're going to the *Vorwärts* building so that you can have a sight of a few corpses."

He gave the order, "Left turn," and we marched out behind him.

As we learnt later, the newspaper building (*Vorwärts* was the official organ of the Social Democrats) had been occupied by several groups of the Spartacists—incidentally, against Karl Liebknecht's advice—more by way of a gesture than for any practical reason. The younger revolutionaries, no doubt in good faith, had wanted to make of it an act of protest, proclaiming their view that the Republican revolution had not gone far enough. What they had in fact achieved, by this rather childish manoeuvre, was to let the troops assembled by the Government know where they were to be found. Artillery had been used before the building had been stormed, and there was a great hole in the front like a black wound.

We marched through the main entrance into the yard. Huge rolls of unused newsprint lay about, and around them the bodies of the "enemy."

"We're going to mount guard here," Kuttner said. He seemed not to like the corpses and stayed in the doorway. The place stank of rotting flesh and excrement.

"Are we to bury them?" I asked.

"Yes, but not here!" exclaimed Kuttner, throwing up his hands in horror.

"And what if we find any wounded?"

He looked sharply at me. "There aren't any," he said, and turned to go into the building.

I walked round the yard as though in a hideous dream. I looked at all the faces; I forced myself to look at all the faces. War-memories returned to me and I thrust them out of my mind. I wished I could talk to one of the dead, and was conscious of the utter finality of their end.

The men tramped through the building in search of loot. Behind a pile of paper a dead youth lay huddled. He had two sheets of paper in his hand, one folded and one outspread. I hesitated and then took them from him. The open sheet bore the following message:

"For Karl. Get away somewhere safe, we need you!"

Had it been intended for Karl Liebknecht? At least the boy had been spared the news of his death.

The second sheet was carefully folded. Blood had seeped in, but I found when I opened it that the writing showed through.

"Martha—they've wounded me, but there are still a lot of us and we aren't giving in. Some of us were weak, and this morning we sent out men with a flag of truce, but they shot them at once, we could hear it from here. I can see steel helmets over there in the mist—they're back again, as though they hadn't hounded the nation to disaster! Won't anything ever change?"

I sat down, gazing at the white face. Someone spoke to me—"Found some gold roubles?" It was Heinz, a man from my platoon. "I found a few gold teeth," he said, grinning. "What's this one got?" I sprang up shouting, "Don't you touch him!" and he shrugged his shoulders. "I'm not trying to pinch him off you," he said and slouched away.

I stood not knowing what to do. This was my punishment, my merited punishment! I was here because someone had sent me here, a grey-haired professor who perhaps believed the things he said—but how much did he understand about this world? He had uttered an indictment and I had listened unquestioning, without knowing who was on the other side. What did that word "side" mean, anyway? Had it needed this blood-stained testimony of a dead boy to teach me? I read the letter again and again, poring over it as though it were an examination text. My head was aching badly. I sat down once more, then got up and went to look for Kuttner.

The room where I found him stank of human dung.

"Look at it!" he said to me. "They were like animals!"

"I want to be discharged," I said.

Kuttner sprang up from his seat, but he did not seem surprised.

"I never trusted you! If the men in your platoon are of the same mind I shall have you shot."

I went out to round up my men, and Kuttner appeared when they had fallen in.

"If any man has any complaints, let him take one pace forward," he said.

A man stepped forward and Kuttner knitted his eyebrows, expecting to hear my treachery confirmed.

"The fish was too salt yesterday," the man said.

"And not enough of it," said another, plucking up courage.

Then they all began talking at once, but the tone was obsequious. Kuttner had never addressed them before, and they evidently thought they had better make the most of the opportunity.

The smiling newspaper man who stood facing us seemed to be reviving as though after a sleepless night. He shook himself with an almost sensual pleasure and embarked on a speech to the cluster of half-uniformed prae-torians, who broke ranks and gathered round him, infected by his joviality.

"Things are only just beginning, my lads. Everything's going to be fine from now on. Everything will be taken care of, even down to old-age pensions. . . . Now that we've cleaned things up. . . ."

I could not look at him any more, but as I turned away my head I saw the corpses at the end of the yard lying limp as only the dead can lie. One of the "Balts" had told me as we were going through the house that three hundred rebels had surrendered and had at once been liquidated.

Kuttner came up to me. He took my arm and turned me away from the contemplation of the dead.

"Well," he said, "you don't seem to have done much harm, after all. Go along to the office and collect your pay and your discharge paper and your commendation—yes, we've had one printed for you. And then where do you intend to go? To Munich? Well, it's probably the best place for you—there's a mass of hotheads like you down there."

In the train to Munich I read that the Free Corps under the command of the Social Democrat, Noske, had cleaned up the Soldiers' Councils in Bremen, Bremerhaven, Cuxhaven and Brunswick. The Brumaire of this revolution was speedily collapsing! All the reports gave the impression of political amateurishness and plain, emotional revenge. I read a new speech by Alfred Weber, but it had a hollow sound. Did he know what had really been happening in Berlin?

In Halle I bought another paper containing the order which had enabled Noske to triumph so easily: anyone resisting arrest was to be instantly shot.

The train was held up in a station owing to a breakdown, and a discharged soldier invited me to have a glass of beer with him. As we walked through the streets of the town he told me how he had deserted from the front. It was an adventurous tale. A supply-dump in Belgium had gone up in flames, and he had been one of the party detailed to put it out. There had been cases of champagne and boxes of chocolates lying about. Halfway through the job the men had mutinied, and some had seized supply-lorries and loaded them up with stuff that they had rescued from the flames. The nature of the supplies had been a revelation—so that was how the Staff had lived! My man had got away with a load of high-quality boots and shoes which he had exchanged in Aachen for a consignment of wine. His partner in the enterprise had then made him exchange the wine for fur coats. They had clashed with the military police and there had been shooting. The partner had been badly wounded, and had died, lying on a fur coat, just before they got to Cologne. My man had traded all the fur coats for a piece of real gold which was offered him in Neuwied. He had had to leave the lorry, with the dead man in it, by the roadside. He had managed to get to Berlin, but here he had been arrested by a military patrol. They had not found the gold; but when they proposed to shoot him, with a number of others, he had begged to be allowed to speak privately to the lieutenant in charge. So he had forfeited his gold and saved his life. All he now had left was a packet of women's stockings. What these had been doing in an officers' supply-dump he did not know, but the dump had been full of unexpected things—and anyway, here we were, and there was beer to be had.

The place was in fact a brothel. The girls sat in alcoves. Suddenly a special constable wearing a red armband came in and dragged out a man who was drunk and threatening to beat one of them up. "Revolutionary discipline!" said my new friend in a mocking tone, but the madame told us that three days before a raving soldier had cut one of the girls' throats. They really did not have an easy time of it, although they were all working-class.

I wanted to ask him whether the soldiers who arrested him had been some of Noske's boys, but he emptied his glass and said he was going to have one of the girls, and would I like a pair of stockings, because that was quite enough to give them. I thanked him but said I did not want to waste them, and anyway I wasn't in the mood. So he wished me well in Munich, where he said things were getting on nicely. "How far have they got?" I asked; but he had already picked up his well-lined greatcoat and was moving towards a girl in dark-red underwear who stood waiting for him on the stairs leading to the upper rooms.

5. The Tears of Niobe

I HAD my first sight of a Bavarian newspaper when I reached Hof. In a small news-paragraph I read that a patrol of Noske's troops had come upon a few sailors peacefully gathered together in an inn on the outskirts of Berlin. The officer in charge of the patrol had at once had them arrested, and, when they protested, had declared that they were resisting arrest and had them shot on the spot. I felt that in leaving Berlin I had escaped certain death. For the first time it dawned on me that this was not a matter of civil war but simply of post-war chaos. Was Munich any better? The paper carried a leading article advocating the dispossession of the Wittelsbachs and all the nobility.

In Nuremberg a young man scattered leaflets through the train. They contained Biblical quotations and called upon the public to follow Gustav Landauer, who wanted to found a co-operative State.

In Augsburg there were posters announcing a speech by Léviné. "All power to the Councils!" the posters demanded. Léviné was an independent. He was going to bring with him political prisoners who had been imprisoned for months without trial, so that the people of Augsburg might recognise their true martyrs.

I was noting down the names of the speakers when a voice behind me said cautiously, "Don't believe anything those foreigners say."

I can still feel the shudder of that strange moment. I swung round to find myself confronting a priest. He had thin lips and kindly blue eyes, and his voice sank lower still as he explained why he had spoken to me. No Bavarian wanted this revolution; the revolutionaries were all foreigners. "Look at their names!" he said. Bavaria should become an independent State; it should join with Austria, and then the majority of the people would be Catholic. Was I a Catholic? This was the way to a far better peace, the chance to break free from Prussia, and it was the last moment. He spoke as softly as in the confessional, but it was his own confession.

The conductor came along the platform, announcing that the train would soon be leaving. "Here is an address," whispered the priest, and scribbled rapidly on a scrap of paper. I took it with a nod and put it in my pocket, but later I lost it and I have never known where he wanted to send me.

I arrived in Munich with scanty luggage and little money, confused but with the feeling of having reached a new and better land. As always when I

F   81

find myself in a strange town, I made straight for its centre, the crowded Rathausplatz. I added myself to one of the groups of people engaged in lively discussion. A man was saying that the Armistice terms were an outrage. Another said that on the contrary they were a blessing, since at last Bavaria would be freed from Prussian militarism. There had to be an army, the first man said, but he found no supporters. Several of them said that Bavaria should remain neutral, that was the only way. Everything must be quietly considered, a woman said; and a man in an army greatcoat said that what was needed was drastic action, and that a few heads would have to roll. The group gradually dissolved. "I want to hear Eisner," a man said. "He's holding a meeting near here." He took two others along with him, and I followed.

The meeting was in the Deutsches Theater, and the place was filled to overflowing when we arrived. I stood pressed into a corner, but the density of the crowd gave me a feeling of companionship such as I had not known for a long time. A murmur like the surging of the sea rolled over the expectant heads, but it died down when the voice of the speaker rose above it, penetrating and clear.

"Wars invariably end in the defeat of us all. There is more hatred in peace treaties than in declarations of war. Revenge is the most stupid form of hatred. Enforced retribution merely engenders new bitterness and new war. They all talk as though they knew who was responsible for the war, but to discover the truth we need to inspect the archives of a great many Foreign Ministries. Well, let us open up our archives. Someone has to begin! We are all guilty—and I say this to you as one who was imprisoned because he would no longer endure this war."

"Now he's going to let them have it," a woman in front of me said; but the speaker continued quite peaceably.

"I accuse no one," he went on. "This is a time for reconciliation, a time for goodness. I have come from the Swiss town of Berne. The workers have held a meeting there for the first time since the war, the workers of Europe. I went there, not as one of the defeated but as one who had never wanted the war, and they knew it. They listened to me. I had no need to underline anything. There were no uniforms in that assembly, no generals or sergeant-majors, no Prussians and no shorn sheep. But there was one tremendous moment when they rose and shouted to me, 'Long live the German people!' This was when I proposed that we German workers should offer ourselves voluntarily to France to rebuild the cities that the guns of our generals have destroyed. It was a true cry of rejoicing, the true spirit! From now on we must do nothing but build!" The voice rose as the speaker repeated above the plaudits of the crowd, "Nothing but build!"

The men around me were shouting, and some were weeping.

Then the wall of humanity was breached and a pathway was formed along which the speaker came. I had the feeling that he was coming straight towards me, and I blushed, thinking of Liebknecht.

The applause was now a tempest, and the man walked smiling through it; it was a Red Sea that he himself had caused to part.

Suddenly a man sprang at him. The onlookers, fearing an assault, flung themselves upon this stranger, but the speaker stood protectively over him as he fell to the floor. "No one is to touch him!" I heard him say. "He can only be misguided." He bent down, raised the man to his feet and walked out with him arm in arm.

It was a very convincing gesture. Perhaps everything is different here in the south, I thought; and so took the first step along a new and fateful path. Perhaps only in certain climates were the true prophets born.

The next day I saw on a hoarding a poster of the meeting I had been to. The speaker had been Kurt Eisner, the Prime Minister of Bavaria! He had no bodyguard; he meant to change Germany by kindness. Perhaps he would indeed change Germany. Why should I not be hopeful?

"Special edition!" shouted a voice across the street. "Special edition!" People were hurrying towards the newsboy. The towers of the Frauenkirche rose into a blue and sunny sky; the town was bathed in an almost Italian light. "Special edition!" shouted another voice, close to me. "I don't want any special edition," I said serenely to the morning. I was at last feeling a little lighter of heart.

But then the boy thrust a copy of the paper under my nose.

I read that Prime Minister Kurt Eisner had been shot by some Count or other on his way to the Parliament building.

That afternoon I visited the scene of the murder. Eisner had died on the pavement; the bullet had gone through his brain. There were signs that sawdust had been scattered over the blood, but the spot was now marked by a shabby office-chair, presumably brought out of the Ministry building, on which stood a photograph of the dead man, and some flowers.

I stood looking at the bearded face, and footsteps drew near to me. A voice said:

"So now another stupid hero-cult is going to start."

I turned to see a young man in spectacles gazing mockingly at me.

"Are you bitten too?" he asked.

"Why shouldn't I be?"

"Because the individual doesn't count any more," the young man said.

"He wasn't just an individual," I said. "He was more. We haven't many of his sort."

"There'll be hundreds of them, if we stay tough."

I went on staring at the photograph while I wondered what there was in this voice that attracted me, and why I wanted the young man to go on talking.

He seemed to guess that he had made an impression.

"Come with me and I'll show you another weakling," he said.

We went to a big *Bierhalle* in the suburbs. I recognised the speaker directly I entered. It was Ernst Toller, the prophet I had met at Heidelberg. I looked about me, and my companion murmured an excuse and went into another room. But Toller was there and he was speaking, and I was happy to have found him again. I went and sat in the front row.

The hall was not very full. I thought of Toller's words on the moonlit night of our meeting; I could hear them still. "I want to bring together those who are embittered . . . no class distinctions . . . I want to help *people* . . ."

What now came from the rostrum had a very different sound:

"Only the Dictatorship of the Proletariat can save us! The future belongs to the Councils!"

I saw a messenger go up to Toller and pass him a slip of paper. He read it and sent the man away. Then he leaned forward and shouted into the hall:

"I have just been informed that an attempt has been made on the life of Comrade Gustav Landauer. That is filthy murder. Our side must not use those methods. That sort of thing has got to stop. We won't answer them in that way. The revolution must be cleanly fought. But we must close our ranks more tightly than ever. We must establish the Red Army. We must start the formation of the Red Army today. . . ."

It was astonishing how loud a response this evoked from the small gathering. Toller had expressed their dearest wish. For a time they would not let him go on, but at length he managed to make himself heard:

"And maintain discipline, all of you! No murder of innocents! It is unworthy of us! . . ."

Someone tugged at my arm, and I found the young man who had brought me there at my side.

"What can you do with a chap like that?" he said. "He wants to dish out weapons and then he says they aren't to be used. If he ever comes to have any authority I shall have him done in."

"What happened to Landauer?" I asked.

"Nothing. I sent that note myself. I hope you see why. Come along to Zillibiller's at ten tonight. That's where the Revolutionary Students' Council meets."

That night I sat in a capacious armchair in a house by the River Isar, listening to the Students' Council discuss the plan for bloody revolution. There were silver ashtrays on the table, and over the fireplace hung a portrait of the last King of Bavaria. The thick pile carpet absorbed the foot-steps of the conspirators, who now and then jumped up from their chairs as though propelled by springs, to move restlessly about the room.

"Who does this place belong to?" I asked my neighbour.

"A putrescent bourgeois of the declining West," he said. He was a massive, fair-haired young man with the face of a child.

"And how do you come to be meeting here?"

"Because it's my father's house," he answered and grinned. "But now you'd better listen to G.W."

I apologised in some confusion and gazed at the speaker whom they called "G.W."—the same bespectacled young man who had taken me to Toller's meeting and, with a false report, had provoked Toller to his im-passioned plea for civilised methods.

"We must clean up social democracy once and for all," G.W. said. "They have the majority because they pander to the instinct for comfort. They'll always tell you that this is what the people want. To hell with what the people want! The people have first got to understand. And the same goes for this university. What the majority of the students want doesn't matter a hoot to us. *We're* the ones who will decide who is to be chucked out and who is to be shot. If we started consulting everyone we should find ourselves landed with a list of favourites—all the fashionable professors. We should probably be let in for amicable discussions about God with the theologians, and about the Wittelsbachs with the reactionaries."

He was interrupted by applause. A small female figure with a Saxon accent stood up and began to sing out of tune, "Drench the guillotine, drench the guillotine in tyrants' blood! . . ."

G.W. let her sing and lit another cigarette. He had with him a copy of the book of the hour, Spengler's *Decline of the West*. He sat riffling through the pages as though he were consulting a dictionary. Then he abruptly closed the meeting and announced that the members of the communist section would meet here again in half an hour.

"Why shouldn't we simply stay here?" a tall, tubercular-looking young man asked.

G.W. merely glanced scornfully at him, not deigning to reply that if they did so the identity of the members of this secret cell would be disclosed.

I went out with the others; but before the door closed behind me I heard G.W. say to Zillibiller, our host:

"We shall have to do some more screening. They aren't all a-hundred-per-cent reliable."

At the next meeting I attended I had an impulse to cross swords with G.W. I wanted to shake that air of self-satisfied assurance. Perhaps I was also irritated by the undisguised disdain with which he treated all the people around him.

"What do you call a-hundred-per-cent reliable?" I asked. "I mean, how would you define it?"

G.W. clapped the copy of Spengler to, deliberately lit a cigarette and sat weighing the silence that followed my question. Then he answered, not looking at anyone:

"To be a-hundred-per-cent reliable is to have the guts to set fire to the whole of Munich if necessary, without first consulting one's conscience, as your friend Toller would probably do."

Later on, when the town was attacked by White troops, Toller did in fact hesitate to sacrifice the lives of the river guards posted on Dachau moor. Had he done so he might have enabled the forces collected in Munich to withdraw. He was subsequently charged with having caused the death of thousands of workers. The forty Dachau men, of course, also lost their lives.

"A man is a-hundred-per-cent reliable," G.W. went on, "if he can see the blood of a thousand enemies flow without his own blood flowing any faster. For example, Genghis Khan was a-hundred-per-cent reliable."

This far-fetched historical example was taken straight from Spengler.

"Or again, it is to be like that admirable Tsar who had his own son beheaded without shedding any private tears." G.W. glanced sideways at me. "With us there are no kings who weep like your Don Carlos."

"It is to no man's discredit if he can weep for his crimes," I said.

"The error lies in the use of the word crime," said G.W. calmly. "We're surgeons. A surgeon has no qualms about cutting off a leg to arrest gangrene. If he had he would be a criminal."

His face, with its feverish pallor, betrayed a hint of almost physical suffering. I did not believe in his cold-bloodedness.

He turned abruptly to me and said:

"I have a report saying where you were last."

"I wrote it myself," I answered sharply.

"Yes," said G.W., "and in a tone of penitence that cries to Heaven. It can be very agreeable to take the road to Canossa, but it doesn't prove anything."

"What's wrong with my statement?" I demanded. "I admitted I made a mistake in Berlin. Am I supposed to crawl on my stomach? I did my best to be honest—what's so suspicious about that?"

"The moral argument, all the talk about right and wrong. One may change sides on practical grounds, but not from a feeling of guilt. In the matter of guilt the decision rests with—the Cell."

He had hesitated slightly over the word "cell," and then he was silent, noting the astonishment of the gathering at the principle he had laid down. I was hearing the word for the first time. It had about it something of the

secrecy of the cloisters, and of the back rooms where the Russian conspirators had met.

"How can the Cell decide when I don't belong to it?" I asked.

G.W. stood up, thrust his book under his arm, and said, "Nevertheless!"
It was as though he had tossed away a cigarette-end and trodden on it. Disposed of! An order!

That was where it began! Those were the early years after the Russian
Revolution. The Party had become a Church, with a materialistic priesthood
driving the sense of guilt into the heart of every believer and using it as a
weapon. One sinned easily, for one was human, that is to say, weak. But
unlike the Church of Rome this Church knew no mercy. Its bishops had
powers of life and death. Death followed condemnation; the bullet in the
head followed confession; physical dissolution followed moral destruction.

I suffered under this dispensation; but then came the revolution, and all
our honest if immature arguments appeared trivial in face of the blood-
stained event.

The revolution was upon us overnight. It was March 1919. The leading
orators (not much more than talking was done) were Léviné, Landauer and
Toller.

It is hard to say how these three differed from one another. They were
all opposed to any rapid stabilising of affairs, since everything that had
existed in the past was suspect. They had a mysterious faith in the *Räte*—
that is to say, the Councils or soviets—since to them these implied direct
action, daily consultation with the masses, the approach to the roots of the
community: a hazy conception of the ideals which drew the apostles to Jesus,
and an uncritical enthusiasm for the Russian experiment.

The official Government withdrew to Bamberg when a degree of opposition to its plans became manifest at public meetings. It looked like flight, but
was in fact more a deliberate provocation and a precaution.

Léviné proclaimed the *Räterepublik*, the German Soviet Republic, in
Munich. A few thousand workers declared themselves in favour of the
experiment.

The whole thing was a repetition of the Berlin tragedy. Seldom have men
drawn so near to the problems of the century while remaining so remote from
the masses whom they wished to help.

In obedience to a secret order I set out for the university. A sailor was
addressing a gathering from the steps of the Feldherrnhalle. I was told that
he was a People's Deputy. He spoke with the utmost conviction, assuring
his hearers that "the big-heads would lose their collars," which sounded
strange, but this and other flights of fancy were greeted with enthusiastic
applause.

I reached the university just in time to be let in.

We went from room to room, our sense of power growing as we drew nearer the Rector's study. It was empty, like all the other rooms. We left the papers on the tables untouched, saying to one another that reports, examination-papers and above all manuscripts were sacrosanct. Nor did we attempt to break open the bursar's safe. (Our respect for legality is well illustrated by a true story of that spring. After the collapse of the revolt the innocent sister of our lady-cashier was sent to return the keys of the university to the authorities. She appeared trembling before the newly re-instated Rector and confessed that on the way she had been overcome by panic and had thrown them into the Kleinhesselohe lake.)

At about ten the telephone began to ring. The professors wanted to know what was happening. Were the buildings in flames, were all the windows smashed? We replied indignantly that all that was taking place was an internal reorganisation. We were not robbers or bandits. The university was to become a school for the people. Nothing would be damaged. Henceforth it was the people's property. What was the Herr Professor thinking of!

Such was the tone until about midday, when "G.W." appeared—G.W. Klein, to give him his full name. He had been visiting a factory where he had summoned the workers to attack the nearest barracks so as to provide themselves with arms. He had also demanded that hostages should be taken from among the wealthy classes. Toughness must be the watchword. This was the hour of the Red Army.

He had been told that Toller had already settled everything, and that he was near Dachau, outside the town, with his soldiers. This news had caused G.W. to explode. "He'll make a bloody Salvation Army of them!" he yelled, and left the factory.

I was again at the telephone when he entered, seeking to reassure another anxious inquirer. He snatched the receiver from my hand.

"Who are you talking to?"

I stared at him in astonishment; it was so unusual for G.W. to lose his self-control. He said over the telephone:

"If you imagine we shall ever again let you come here and talk tripe, you're very much mistaken."

Then he hung up and started giving orders.

All the professors' files were removed and stacked away in a room in the cellar. The safe was attacked with bullets, but it resisted. G.W. did not waste any more time on it, but set about ringing up the professors himself, one after another. He scribbled on a sheet of paper, as he talked to them, noting down the fate he had decreed for them. I saw that he was dividing them into three categories. It seemed that he proposed to shoot the majority. A small number were classified as "Usable," and the rest came under the heading "Let them starve." Someone ventured to put in a word for one of the professors to whom he had just been speaking. *"I'm* the boss here," said G. W. Klein. I ran out of the room, knowing perfectly well that in another minute I should be at his throat.

I paced up and down by the iron gates, and Strasser, who was the cultural adviser of our students' union, walked with me.

"I don't like it," he said. "It's a bad look-out."

An old man was making signs to us from the other side of the bars, but we took no notice.

"I shouldn't have come here," said Strasser. "There was plenty to do in the theatre. We might have put something on this evening—Schiller's *Räuber*, for instance, or a piece by Georg Kaiser—opened the doors and charged no entrance money—then you'd have seen how much they like the revolution!"

"Panem et circenses," I said softly but without mockery.

"Right," said Strasser. "That's why dictatorships always last longer than republics."

The old man outside the gate was still beckoning to us. I went over and asked him what he wanted.

"My experiment," the old man gasped. "I've been taking measurements for the last seven weeks. If I'm not allowed in the whole thing will be ruined."

"We'd better let him in," said Strasser, laughing.

We opened the gate a very little way. The old man squeezed through without standing much on his dignity. It did indeed seem that he was concerned only for his experiment.

I took him to G. W. Klein and explained what he wanted.

"All your experiments are false," said G.W. "You don't even question the laws of gravity, do you? If you could, you'd have Planck burnt at the stake, wouldn't you?"

The professor stood gazing at him in amazement.

"I am only concerned with experiments," he said. "As to what may come of them, I can only tell this when they are completed."

G.W. nodded in scorn, then abruptly asked:

"And what's your attitude to the revolution?"

It was like a punch on the jaw. The old man literally swayed and then answered:

"I am quite unpolitical. All this will pass. I have nothing to do with it."

"That's not good enough!" bellowed G.W. "Put him on the list," he said, turning to the little Saxon girl whom he had appointed to be his secretary.

I looked quickly at the list. There was a black cross at the top, and she was now writing the name of the physics professor at the foot of the column.

"You can go," said G.W.

I took the old man outside, and my feeling of oppression vanished as I reached a sudden decision.

"Where is your laboratory?" I asked.

"In the west wing," he answered humbly.

"You'd better go there," I said.

The old man bowed far lower than politeness required, and then ran along the corridor. I thought I had seen tears start in his eyes.

I was still musing on this episode when I heard the sound of a wild outcry coming from the gateway at the eastern end of the building. I dashed in that direction and found Strasser engaged in a Homeric exchange of abuse with a crowd of students outside, who were shaking the iron bars with their hands.

"They're Whites," he said. "You see how damned insolent they are and what they think of us!"

Stones came hurtling between the bars. Strasser raised his pistol and shot into the ceiling, and the report set up a series of echoes that resounded through the building. The "White" students scattered, cursing, and withdrew.

"We shall come back with weapons of our own!" they shouted.

"Why don't you try to get word to Landauer?" Strasser said. "We need rifles, otherwise we shan't be able to hold out here for long."

"I'll go myself," I said. "I've got the key to the west door."

I found Landauer in the empty palace of the Wittelsbachs. He listened to me, but said that he could not give us any weapons. Had we no other means of persuading our fellow-students? I ran back to the university building. The gates were still closed, but as I was in the act of thrusting my key in the lock a number of students in caps appeared on the other side. I stared at them in consternation. The "Whites"—the nationalist groups—had driven us out. As I discovered later, the old physics professor had opened the door to them!

The next day saw the beginning of the hysteria of a town that was in process of being "liberated."

Many towns have been liberated since then, but few from so inconsiderable an enemy, and one, moreover, of the same race. The newspapers called it "cleaning up the Red Scum." The soldiers from Württemberg who carried out the operation talked in Biblical terms. "An eye for an eye and a tooth for a tooth," their placards read.

The majority of the populace would perhaps have allowed the handful of Reds to establish themselves in power. If the Reds had won, the people would have accepted the situation. But then the others came, the troops from outside, and that settled the revolution. The thousand or so workers who had followed Toller and Landauer, and who, instead of defending their own headquarters with their rifles, had simply occupied a few public buildings, just as had happened in Berlin, found themselves marooned on separate islands while the storm surged round them. Any who sought to escape had to reckon with the likelihood that he would be seized and trampled to death by the crowd. A week previously there had been no passion in the town; but the newspapers had done their work well.

I was arrested in the Königinstrasse. It was humiliating because it was so stupid. The soldiers did not even bother to search me: I had long hair, and that was sufficient evidence. From the public park near by—the English Garden, as it was called—we could hear the volleys of the firing-squad.

Prodded by rifle-butts I stumbled round a corner and to my astonishment found a whole crowd of prisoners huddled together with four soldiers guarding them. "Here's another," said one of my captors, and I was shoved into the group.

We stood there rather miserably for about a quarter of an hour, and then something remarkable happened. One of the prisoners must have been a member of the Red Government. I heard someone whisper, "Turme!" a man's name. Then he said urgently: "Get ready! I'm going to fling myself between the rifles." Then a car came roaring at high speed round the corner.

Everything happened very quickly. The car behaved as though its driver were drunk. It careered on to the pavement, knocking down one of our guards, and then swung back into the roadway, catching two others. The fourth guard fled, dropping his rifle in his panic.

We all scattered. I scrambled over the low wall into the English Garden and came to a deep, narrow stream. I waded across and climbed the mossy bank on the far side.

Then for a moment I stayed motionless in amazement. It was the spring— oh, God, it was the spring! Daffodil and forget-me-not, and a green mist of leaf-buds on the trees, stirring in the light wind.

A man appeared from behind a bush. He was in civilian clothes, but he had a white band on his arm and a pistol hung from his belt. "This is where they're being shot," he said amiably to me. "You can't come any farther."

I looked past him towards the small Greek temple standing on a grassy hillock. Men were being stood up against it. It was very quickly over. I heard the volley and saw the smoke of cordite. I could not see the men who shot, but I saw the men with their backs to the temple fall down like toy soldiers beneath its Greek columns.

The detonations were brief and sharp, like the back-firing of a car. There were seven of them.

The man with the armband said: "Here's a new lot coming."

I moved aside and looked round. They came slowly past, walking in the same half-orderly manner, a procession of twenty hatless and collarless civilians led by two Württemberg soldiers in steel helmets. One of them was a chimney-sweep.

I advanced a few paces over the grass. For a moment I had it in mind to surrender and add myself to the column. But then I saw Strasser among them, the lecturer on the drama and literary counsellor of our students' society: Strasser, who had wanted to take over the Staatstheater "to revolutionise it from top to bottom," with Hamlet in a dinner-jacket and the ghost in Prussian uniform; Strasser who said, "It's all theatre, but that doesn't mean it has to be corny." And now, there he went, and the whole thing was a piece of bloody, provincial corn. Because he had wanted to open the doors of the university to the sons of the workers he was now to be shot to ribbons by those same workers—worse still, by the very sons.

I looked at the faces of the escort as they passed by—bricklayer's son, carpenter's son, miner's son.

I forced myself to look at Strasser. I wanted to suffer all the bitterness and reproach that must surely be in his face, my friend's face. But Strasser dumbfounded me with the most moving gesture he could have made. His eyes met mine for an instant, then he looked quickly away, putting a finger to his lips. Watch out, beware of the enemy—that was what it meant. Watch out, don't betray anything! Whom might I betray? What might I betray? It was folly; it was paradox; and yet it was sublime, Roman, saintly in its nobility.

I at once put on a bored expression, to let him know that I had understood. He should have his "good exit"—wasn't that what they said in the theatre? I even went so far as to yawn and cover my mouth with my hand. Then I turned and went slowly back towards the town.

I walked with ears strained, waiting for the sound of the volley that would end Strasser's life. But whether because the wind was the other way, or on account of some delay in the progress of the execution, I heard no other volley. I walked and walked, but there was only the sound of bird-song in the air. It was spring.

Later I sat in the beer-house known as *Donisl*, a long, narrow place that stayed open all night, where the people of Munich were wont to conclude their festivities in the small hours of the morning. It smelt of urine and beer. "Only the blood is lacking," I said to myself. I was thinking of Strasser.

"For Brutus is an honourable man," I muttered into my tankard. A girl slid along the bench towards me and asked for a cigarette. I stared at her. "I come to bury Caesar, not to praise him," I said. I meant by the quotation

to do honour to my dead friend. But was he dead? "In any case, I have no
bier," I said. The girl recoiled from me, wrinkling her forehead. I paid and
left. By the doorway I came upon my waiter in the act of tapping another cask.

"Which way to the cemetery, the Ostfriedhof?"

"Are you in such a hurry to get there?" he asked, grinning.

"I've got to find Strasser," I said, and was suddenly sober again.

They had cleared out the greenhouses in the cemetery to make room for
the dead, which continued to be brought there in lorries. Men were busy
loading the corpses into packing-cases, some of which were already filled;
trickles of red seeped through the cracks. A man with a brown beard was
breaking the joints of the bodies that could not otherwise be made to fit in. It
was a sharp sound at first, then a pulpy one.

Seeing me, he wiped the sweat off his forehead with the back of his blood-
stained hand and said in a high-pitched, amiable voice, like that of an indulgent aunt:

"If you're looking for someone, try over there on the left."

I did as he directed. They were lying in long rows. Most lay crumpled on
their backs, with bared breasts offered to the gaze of the beholder. Solemnly
arrayed in the background were the clusters of laurel which served as a
decoration at normal burials. Looking along the rows, I saw a grey army
forage-jacket such as Strasser had worn. I walked until I came opposite the
man in the jacket, and a great and bitter pain welled up in my heart. I raised
a hand in greeting, as though it were a gesture of apology, and then bent
down to look into Strasser's face.

Strasser no longer had a face. His shattered head seemed to make a
mockery of any name by which one might call him. I remembered that he
had lost two fingers of his right hand in the war. I bent down and raised the
right arm of the forage-jacket, to see if this was the man I was looking for.

But the arm also mocked me. It no longer had a hand.

I knelt staring at the stump that protruded from the sleeve, feeling dumb
and helpless, like an animal that has been beaten too much. It was utterly
devilish. I felt that too much was being asked of me.

From somewhere behind me the aunt-like voice said:

"They're both Reds and Whites. We've thrown them all in together. It
makes no odds now."

The next day I left Munich. I remembered hearing from a friend about a
woman who had founded a sort of settlement in the Isar valley. There were
only two writers in her woodland dwelling—Jean-Jacques Rousseau and
Tolstoy. She lived in their shadow.

I climbed the slopes of the valley and stopped at a village to ask the way.

There was a notice outside the village constable's house offering a reward of 5000 marks for the capture of Ernst Toller.

Half an hour later I reached my destination, a two-storied house in a rough clearing.

A dog rushed out at me, baring its teeth, but quietened down when I tossed it the crust of bread I had been chewing as I walked.

A thin, dark-haired girl appeared in the doorway of the house wearing a dress of olive-green velvet which came down to her ankles.

I greeted her with the word "*Heil*," as my friend had advised. It was the greeting used by the German *Wandervögel*.

"My name is Lily," she said, and stood aside for me to enter.

The gesture was heart-warming to one in trouble. I went up the steps, and as I did so the lady presiding over the establishment appeared in the doorway. She was a slender woman in her forties, with greying hair and a pale face, wearing a blue-grey smock tied with a brown cord. She gazed at me with that well-meaning missionary expression of which the first message is, "You see how different I am!"

I bowed my head. "I'm on the run," I said, making my voice as humble as I could.

"My name is Thierbach," the grey-haired woman said.

"Supper's ready," said Lily from behind me.

I was going to give my name, but Frau Thierbach raised a hand to stop me. "You're the nameless guest," she said.

"There are beans and honey," she went on. "We found a bees' nest in the wood." She turned and walked solemnly back into the house.

I wanted Lily to go ahead of me, but she looked at me with a cold expression.

"You belong to the Red Republic," she said sternly. "Admit it!"

"Are you a police officer?" I asked wearily.

"I'm a dancer," said Lily, surprised by my indifference.

"Well, then," I said, and went into the house.

I was just in time to see the dog jump down from the table, having licked clean the dish of beans and honey.

Frau Thierbach said reproachfully, "Naughty Pips!" and then turned to Lily and said: "The poor fellow! He must have been hungry."

I saw an expression of extreme bitterness pass over Lily's face, a wave of positive hatred. Then she said in a false voice as soft as her velvet gown:

"Well, let us meditate instead. Modern man eats far too much."

I gazed at the empty dish with two brown beans sticking to its rim.

I seemed to have landed in the very heart of falsity, but I wouldn't admit it. My thoughts were still in Munich. I had wanted to turn it into a Garden of Eden, but all that had come of our efforts was the English Garden and the execution squads.

To the north of the house was a dense wood. The next day I plunged into its depths and remained in it until evening. So long as I was there I felt hidden, perhaps because of the knotted tangle of roots rising up out of the earth and covering so much ground. Fugitives love trees, they are the symbol of permanency.

I walked slowly, touching the tree-trunks, and presently the wood thinned out and I heard the sound of bells. A white church was calling to me from the meadow-lands—and suddenly I heard the *voices* all round me.

I heard the voices of the men whom I had seen fall helplessly, like trees— "We too were baptised to the sound of bells, but there were no bells ringing when we died. Does that prove anything? Yes, it proves something. What does it prove? It proves that we deserved this end. But why did we deserve it?"

I ran back into the wood. "You did *not* deserve it!" I shouted. My cry sank down through the tree-trunks into emptiness, like water running through a sieve.

"Toller still hasn't been caught," said Lily when I got back. I nodded gratefully to her. She was kinder than I thought.

She pushed away the dog, which was trying to steal her piece of bread. Then she said softly:

"Léviné was shot today. He shouted into the muzzles of the rifles, 'Long live the Red Republic!' I wonder when someone will shout, 'It was all meaningless—not worth dying for.' "

She sipped her soup.

"That would be so much braver," she said grimly.

"What news is there of Landauer?" I asked the next morning, but Lily only shrugged her shoulders.

I groped in my memory, recalling what I could of Landauer's book on Shakespeare. It seemed to me that I might thus safeguard what was imperishable in him, by cherishing his wisdom, by going with him through the woods of the *Midsummer Night's Dream*. And indeed I truly believed that Landauer walked with me that day, a tall figure touching the leaves on the trees with loving fingers.

When I returned that evening, feeling somewhat calmer, I found Lily seated on the veranda steps playing a guitar. She started at the sight of me, as though she had been suddenly brought back to earth, and laid the guitar on the grass at her feet, doing so with great care.

"It's a living thing," she said.

I stood gazing at the instrument, feeling that I wanted to shake her.

"I met Landauer in the wood," I said at length.

"It must have been his ghost," she said with a mocking twist of her lips. "They caught him yesterday."

I had to lean against the wall to prevent myself from falling. It was a too brutal awakening from the daydream I had been so sedulously pursuing. But Lily showed me no mercy.

"I don't suppose he even noticed it at first," she said. "That midsummer night's dreamer!"

I stared towards the wood. The light of the setting sun lay about us. Lily went on:

"And now you stand there looking thunderstruck! You chose to wear the ass's head of Utopia. Landauer was wearing it too, when they chased him round the prison-yard at Stadelheim. He couldn't get it off—it had grown on him. But they got it off him, all right. They pulled his beard off, do you hear me?" She was shouting now. "I heard it from a soldier who was there. He was talking about it in the market-place in Pupplinghausen. He knew how to tell a story. Do you want to hear more?" Her face was blazing with fury. "They pulled his trousers down and shoved a rifle up his back passage and emptied it into his body—some of the bullets came out through his head!"

"Stop it!" I shouted, but the cry only infuriated her more than ever.

"Three thousand workers were shot with him. They should have said they'd been led up the garden. They should have shouted at the top of their voices that they never wanted the things he wanted. Landauer should have been made to realise it. One mustn't dream at other men's expense. Who wants freedom, anyway? All they wanted was peace and quiet, and their pay and their beer and enough to eat. And they wanted to keep their land. But these great men of yours sitting round the café tables want quite other things—they're men of culture. I'm not saying they're all Jews—or were. I'm a Jewess myself, but not one of the ones that dream at the expense of others!" She bent down and picked up the guitar again. "This country is as near to me, and as far away, as the North Pole. I have my books on India; they've taught me not to get mixed up in politics. Anyway, that is a part of the Jewish inheritance. Politics is an everyday affair, and we're too old for it. You tell Toller that, if you ever see him again."

I broke in on her.

"Has he too been——?"

"Not yet," she said, and went slowly into the house.

I went for the last time into my wood. It was one of those nights that have no end, since suddenly I became conscious of the hideous nature of *time*.

Time was a weight like lead on the hearts of those who could not forget themselves. Time was the well into which the owl's cry fell like a black drop of blood. Time was the rustle of last year's leaves, which rotting bear new life. Time was the footsteps of the other self, the footsteps of all dead friends, the laughter of the enemy, the crumbling earth in the walls of the dug-out, the unravelling of one's own self.

I walked for many hours. The crickets sang and sawed me into little pieces; what was left now of the young man running through the wood of his despair?

Towards morning I sank to the ground exhausted, knowing only that a thicket closed its friendly arms about me.

I was awakened by sounds which turned out to be those of a machine-gun being set up not far from where I lay. I peered through the leafage of my hiding-place and saw Frau Thierbach's house. I had walked in a circle! A party of soldiers were standing with their backs to me in the early morning mist. One of them was checking the machine-gun on its tripod. He swept the barrel across the house, but without firing it.

This must be meant for me. I saw myself in fancy emerging on to the steps and being mowed down.

"You flatter me!" I said aloud, but none of the soldiers heard. Did they really think I was so important? The idea seemed grotesque. I stood up, and it was as though a hand had helped me to my feet. I began to walk towards the house.

I heard one of the soldiers say:

"Do you think we ought to shoot him down here, on the spot?"

The man next to him laughed, and his reply caused me to stop short in astonishment.

"For Christ's sake, how much time do you think we're going to waste on the Jewish swine?"

I needed a pause for thought, and I took refuge behind a tree. It was Berlin all over again, my own talk with the mercenaries of the Republic, the gloating triumph at the death of Rosa Luxemburg. Had nothing changed? Well, one thing, certainly—I was now on the other side. But otherwise nothing had changed except my own painful realisation that it would always be like this; that they would always talk about "Jewish swine" without knowing anything about their opponents. But then, how had *we* talked in Munich? How had G. W. Klein talked? What should we have done to them if we had won? Who was "we"? Who was I? I felt that I must turn about and never again come out of the wood.

I did in fact turn, but as I did so a soldier caught sight of me and gave a shout. The whole party swung round in an instant, and twenty rifles were

G

pointed at me. I made a weary gesture. "All right," I said, and went towards them. They let me pass through into the house.

Frau Thierbach uttered a cry of terror as I entered. She was standing by the table in the dining-room, behind which a youthful officer and a gendarme were seated. A police-warrant lay on the table.

The officer questioned me concerning my name, my religion, what I was doing here with the two women, what I had done in Munich, why I wasn't a Jew and as to whether I knew the man whose name was on the warrant.

It was the last question that woke me up. I looked at the warrant and saw Toller's picture, and once again I read the price that had been put on his head —the thirty pieces of silver. I handed it back.

"Never seen the man in my life," I said, looking bored.

The officer seemed to have expected no other answer.

"Have you any identity papers?" he demanded in a hostile tone. "We've no time to waste. We don't do much beating about the bush with doubtful cases. Anyone who hasn't got a name can be easily crossed off the list, so to speak."

He seemed to think this an excellent joke. He laughed, and the gendarme laughed obsequiously with him.

At this moment a soldier came in bringing a small, black brief-case which I instantly recognised. I glanced at Frau Thierbach. Now I shall have a name, all right, I thought.

I stood watching while the officer explored its contents. Good God, what a lot of papers I had kept! I would burn the lot this evening. I felt terribly tired and swayed on my feet.

Then something amazing happened. The officer passed a scrap of paper which he had just read to the gendarme. Then he rose to his feet, put his hand to his cap and said to me with a little bow:

"Comrade, you must forgive me. We were quite mistaken about you. I'm delighted to meet a patriot who realised months ago what a rabble those Reds are. My warmest regards, comrade."

I took his extended hand, utterly at sea. Frau Thierbach rolled her eyes heavenwards in her relief, and Lily, the dancer, stood as though paralysed in the corner of the room, staring at the floor.

The officer bowed again and withdrew. I heard the barking of orders, the click of heels, the rattle of rifles and presently the tramp of feet as the men were marched away. The scrap of paper which had brought about this miraculous change in the situation still lay on the table.

I picked it up and felt a wave of shame sweep over my face. It was the discharge paper which I had been given two months previously in Berlin:

"Platoon-leader Regler has loyally served the Republic against the Bolshevik hordes from December 1918 to January 1919. Kuttner."

Lily came behind me, took the paper from my hand and read it.

"Whose side are you really on?" she asked.

I wanted to hit her, but I stood motionless seeing nothing but Landauer's
face, and then his exposed body with the rifle thrust into it.

As I had suspected, Toller was hidden in the crowded jungle of Munich.
A painter had taken him in. He spent the days in a wardrobe, coming out
only at night to eat, after the serving-girl had gone home. After three days of
this he said that he could stand it no longer and that he must go out into the
town. The painter at first refused to allow him to do so, but gave way after
Toller had an acute attack of claustrophobia. He dyed his hair red and pulled
out some of his bushy eyebrows before letting him go; and then the dictator
was able to walk round a few blocks of houses. The world had grown small.
Toller walked erect, looking in the faces of the people he encountered, so he
said; but he turned his eyes away from his own likeness, staring at him from
posters on the walls, afraid that that sombre-seeming man would shout and
betray him.

The painter thinned his eyebrows out still more.

"You must hold out until their first fury has died down," he said. "At
this moment they'd beat you to death, and no one would care. But in a
couple of weeks the animal will have fallen asleep again. Then perhaps you
will have merciful judges."

"The people are my only judge," said Toller. But the words rang hollow,
for in those days he himself doubted.

Meanwhile I sat under an oak-tree in the Isar valley and said to Lily:

"They won't catch Toller! He will suddenly emerge again like the idea
itself, and this time his light will shine so brightly that it will sweep away all
darkness. I believe it because I want to believe, and so long as faith resides in
a single man, then truly, truly there is faith in all the world!"

Lily called to me up in the attic—"They've caught him!"

I did not catch the words but only the sound of her voice, which seemed
changed. I got up from my couch and came slowly down the stairs.

She was standing at the foot of the stairs crying. The tears ran sound-
lessly down her cheeks. I did not understand.

"They have no right to shoot him," she said, staring out into the evening.
"His little finger's worth more than all of them put together."

I now realised what she was saying and was so shaken that I grasped her
shoulder for support, but she shook me off.

"Not one of you is worth us," she said. "We should turn our backs on your country for good and all."

The evening light fell on her face, making the tears sparkle. I saw the drops falling—why did I think of Niobe? Whom did she mean by "us"? What terrible distinction did she make? The water rose slowly in her eyes. Why did I have to look back? I looked at the tears and thought—us? "Us" was Gabens, Schomberg, Brill with his dream of Tibet, the dead boy by the roll of newsprint; it was Rosa Luxemburg, Landauer and the chimney-sweep they had shot in error—why did she shut me out?

Frau Thierbach came out of the house.

"There's a very important letter from your father," she said.

I had a last impulse of revolt.

"How do you know it's important?"

"I feel that it is," she said gently. "You're going to begin a new phase in your life."

Lily stood wiping her eyes with the hem of her dress.

"The letter's in the dining-room," Frau Thierbach said.

Father had written:

"Your testimonial to Tolstoy and your scorn for the victorious party in Munich sound like a letter of excuses written to a headmaster. I'm not your teacher, but I hope sometimes to be able to advise you. So a word about Tolstoy. What has the failure of your Munich experiment to do with that Russian who one night broke away and wandered over the steppes. He knew that he was famous and that the world would take notice. He wanted to arouse people, and for a night he was successful. He became a symbol. His protest was a cry that echoed, precisely because he fled from a castle to that wretched railway-station, and because the Tsar and all the men of power were assailed by it. Indeed, perhaps even one greater than they. You do not like to hear this sort of thing, but it seems to me that Tolstoy was challenging God himself when he left it to a poorly-clad station-master to announce the hour of his death. It was a tragic departure.

"But your friends died in the yard of a Munich barracks. Those who die in this way are doubly robbed. The flames in which Huss died, and Giordano Bruno and Joan of Arc, live in men's memories. Those who die out of sight of the world wear the aspect of criminals. The more squalid the death, the more squalid the deed.

"This should in no way lessen your respect for their end. A defeat affords no indication of the value of the cause. But do not prolong your rebellion until it becomes a chronic malady! Don't live with the dead! Go to some town where there is life. Go back to Heidelberg and wipe out yesterday.

"When you went to the front I wrote to you in soldiers' language—

avoid the back of a horse and the front of a woman. Let me now offer you a word in better taste—lose yourself! The under-tow of politics will one day pluck you back into the open sea. In the meantime, learn what it is to be light-hearted. Without women you will never learn."

I left Frau Thierbach's settlement, still touching in its poverty, and went back to Heidelberg. Like a hesitant roulette-player I dabbled in all the faculties except the theological. I sampled the honeycomb so to speak, but only for a little while; then post-war depression again overcame me and I could see no sense in any kind of study. A series of unimportant love-affairs brought this phase to a mildly humorous end.

One summer's day a student in the Literary Faculty invited me to join him on an outing in the Neckar valley. We came upon a party of students making music in an inn near a monastery. They invited us to join them and we listened to a few short pieces by Haydn and Mozart. I found it pleasant to watch the absorbed faces of the four young men, like a mediaeval painting, and I was particularly attracted by a violinist who was introduced to me as Harry. His face while he played took on a transparency which vanished when he spoke. I thanked him for the concert and his face lit up like that of a small boy. "Concert!" he exclaimed. "Do you call all that scraping a concert?"

"You've no need to talk like a fallen angel," I said amicably; and he looked hard at me and said:

"You're all right."

Thus began a friendship that was to lead to many vicissitudes, but which in the first instance rescued me from the leaden feeling of depression of which not even the magic of Heidelberg had been able to rid me.

"What you need," said Harry at our second meeting, "is fresh air. You take the University too seriously, and yourself too." He grinned, a rapid grin for which his clear blue eyes at once apologised. "To start with, you've got to forget this lunatic idea that the human animal is good. Man's nature is evil, if you want to know, and no Utopia can absolve him from this legacy. Besides which, he doesn't want freedom."

This was to dispose of Socialism in a decidedly summary fashion, but I let it pass. I wanted to know more about this man who looked like a dreaming Siegfried and talked with so much assurance of weighty matters.

I learned that he came from an industrial town in Western Germany and that his father was one of the steel magnates in the Ruhr. He said of him:

"He's a Caesar. You can see skulls like his in any museum of Roman remains. In fact, he has set up in business as a Maecenas. He buys pictures, has his portrait painted by Fiori, subsidises artists, enjoys his holidays and loves wine. The spirit of capitalism? I suppose you mean Max Weber's theory. I don't know, but all that seems to me to be changed. All that concerns him and his sort is the feeling of having come by their money honestly. What happens to the steel, whether it's made into kitchen-knives or bayonets, is no business of theirs."

"They can only justify themselves by not knowing," I said; but Harry protested:

"Are you trying to stuff me with paradoxes?" He seemed bored. We were walking high above Heidelberg, along the pathway known as the Philosopher's Walk.

I replied that one could only learn from contradictions.

"Yes," he agreed, "but not from other people's contradictions."

"From other people's suffering."

"Suffering is purely incidental. One must not try to account for it."

This was said with the utmost conviction. He will harden you, I thought to myself; and then I repeated the word. Harden? Why should I be hardened?

I quoted a poem by Hermann Claudius—"And let us quietly slumber, and our sick neighbours too"—and he grasped its ironic significance.

"But that was in other days," he said. "Now the wolves are howling everywhere."

Then the argument began.

"So you choose the one with the sharpest teeth and let him lord it over you?" I said.

"It never did anyone any harm to give way."

"But rebellion——"

He interrupted me: "No good ever came of rebellion. Read your history books!"

"So you would have thrown Brutus as well off the Tarpeian cliff?"

Harry laughed in scorn.

"Of course! That dreary mean-hearted petty lawyer, that hanger-on who murdered a great man and wanted to substitute his dingy republic for the concept of world empire!"

"The republic existed before the Ides of March," I said, pinning him down to facts. But this did not deter him.

"It's nice of you to tell me," he said. "The republic was in process of turning itself into something better."

I came back to the present. "The republic that Eisner, Toller and Luxemburg tried to found in 1919 was to replace a putrescent empire. Even Max Weber called Wilhelm II a crowned amateur."

Harry found nothing inconsistent in this. "Max Weber would certainly not have approved if a citizen had thrown a bomb at the royal coach."

"His Majesty made a dash for Holland before any of us could do anything so sensible."

"You call that sensible? Who can have the temerity to destroy a symbol and determine what is good for everyone?"

"In other words, these people whom you call symbols are to be allowed to commit any crime without being punished?"

Harry seemed to be growing weary.

"There can be no greater crime than the attempt to overthrow authority."

"In that case," I said, "how is the world ever to change?"

Harry was now thoroughly tired of the subject. He said in an exhausted voice, "It doesn't change. It simply goes through cycles."

And here I thought I had him.

"In fact, even the killing of a tyrant can change nothing?"

He answered, "Form is important, the degree and the extent," and this astonished me. It was the old conservative doctrine, uttered on a note of sacerdotal gravity.

"Where did you get that from?" I asked.

"From Stefan George. You should try him. Perhaps he can give you what you want."

This was the moment of change in that sombre period of my life which had begun with the first World War, extending to embrace the amateurish civil wars, and the end of which I had not been able to foresee. Now suddenly the end was at hand. It was the year of 1921.

Suddenly the Philosophical Faculty of Heidelberg seemed to awaken out of a hundred years' sleep. The dry neutrality of that forcing-house of doctorates was transformed into a feverish advocacy of something that had no practical purpose.

The fame of the lectures of a certain youthful Professor Gundolf spread abroad overnight. He was, it seemed, the disciple of an even greater figure, the poet, Stefan George.

Gundolf held his lectures in the afternoon, and Harry said, wrinkling his forehead and quoting Hegel:

"The owl of Minerva spreads its wings only with the falling of dusk."

Wondering how much wisdom might be expected of a poet, I went to find out. The benches were crowded. It was the sort of audience one sees only in times of crisis—sloppily or romantically clad artists, ex-officers in their old army tunics without shoulder-straps, elegant youthful Mirabeaus proclaiming with tense faces their readiness to abandon their own class, women in search of salvation, girls in spreading skirts with their hair in buns, and members of the students' clubs looking for trouble.

Harry pointed to a group of long-haired and unwashed youths, rather feminine in aspect, and said that these were the Master's own circle. He uttered the word Master in a tone of irony, adopting this frivolous note throughout; nevertheless, that evening he was prompted to quote one of Hölderlin's later poems as we strolled in the sunset along the bank of the Neckar.

But we were not looking for any exalted lyricism, only for a new scale of values. Gundolf's lectures were on a lofty esoteric plane, too much implied, too much premised, and we never really caught up with them. He was like a host, his appetite already satisfied, who had invited us to a lavish meal which we did not venture to touch. George was more positive. His contemporary poems were offered as though they were a book of law. They treated the history of the western lands as a unified process embracing all Utopias. I was struck by the originality of his selection. He addressed Nietzsche as though he were a living comrade, exhorting him to follow the way of love and not freeze upon the lonely heights. He invoked the memory of forgotten monarchs, such as the Hohenstaufens, praising their breadth and power of vision. A new dream arose in Heidelberg, and the great hope of unifying East and West seemed not impossible.

These metamorphoses had the quality of opium-dreams; but the dreams were infectious. For a time we forgot our endlessly threatened republic, and I forgot Father and his anxieties as one prefers to forget the prophets of ill-omen; until one day it all collapsed like a house built on sand.

I went to work for a modest wage in a home for sick and mentally deficient children on the right bank of the Neckar. I washed them, fed the ones that could not feed themselves, kept the elder ones from quarrelling, supervised the Sunday visits of the guilt-ridden parents, and on behalf of the medical superintendant kept a record of the behaviour of the small inmates who were threatened by so many perils.

One evening one of the children overturned his bowl of porridge and then fell on the floor in convulsions. I tried to calm him and he bit my hand. I ran to fetch the matron, and within a few minutes she had got the attack under control.

I had a volume of George's poems lying on my table. I picked it up to distract my mind and came upon the poem he addresses to the mass of his fellow-countrymen:

> *Death reaches for you all,*
> *your very number is abomination . . .*

There was nothing logical in this contempt, but on that evening it filled me with fury. The old rage flamed up in me. My dirty, dribbling, squinting, hydrocephalic children were the fruits of hereditary aberration, the third and fourth generation upon whom the sins of the fathers had been visited, God knew why—or did God know? They were the blind products of gono-cocci of which some stupid man had been afraid to tell his wife. They were due to mysterious combinations of genes, according to the latest fantasies of the biologists; and the psychiatrist and the professor of pathology could say no more about them than could I, the ward-attendant. These waifs, tormented outcroppings of disorder, were subject to no priestly law. Any reasonable man could do nothing, as he contemplated them, but shudder at the chances of life, and, if he must go further, be guided by the instinct of compassion. I looked at them as they crawled about in the play-pen. "Death reaches for you all," I murmured. That was the day on which I parted company from Stefan George.

That same day I had a letter from Father, and I never forgot the coincidence. It was as though two separate hands, that of an enemy and that of a good friend, had conspired together to drag me from the saddle.

Father wrote that he did not want to disturb me in my paradise but that it would do me no harm to be reminded of the ugly outside world. The republic had been robbed of a wise man by the pistol-shots of foolish youths. He was speaking of Rathenau. The misguided young men had bravely defended themselves in a fortress and finally blown their brains out; but those who had led them astray were still alive to agitate and pervert others.

An idiot by the name of Kapp had attempted a rising in Berlin, but the people had at once stopped work and driven him off the Wilhelmstrasse by means of a general strike. But no one had learnt anything from the episode. The official Government, paralysed by its feeling of having usurped power, was weaker than ever; the industrialists were steering the ship, and a miracle-man named Stinnes had appeared upon the scene and was buying up independent concerns and bankrupting others so that he had become a myth. All this was of no advantage to Germany, for although a great deal was exported, thanks to low wages, the "patriots," meaning the industrialists, kept their foreign currency abroad, while within Germany, in preparation for the coming showdown, they adopted measures to finance an army whose first task would be to clean up the country and privately rid them of awkward oppositions. The *Feme* murders were increasing, and Justice was on the side of illegality. There had been 354 attacks on human life during the past few months and all had gone unpunished. "Forgive me," Father's letter ended. "You want to write a doctoral thesis on the irony of Goethe. I am collecting material for a thesis on the tragi-comedy of all republics. If it goes on like this I may perhaps soon have to urge you to man the barricades again."

6. *Lotte and the Flight to Paris*

INSTEAD of manning the barricades I fell in love with a sales-assistant in Lehmkuhl's bookshop, in München-Schwabing. She had a soft, hesitating voice and a profile whose severity reminded me of the dancing girls on the later Greek vases. On Saturdays we made excursions into the mountains. A healthy innkeeper's wife in Tolz positively refused to allow "two young people like you to have separate rooms," so we blushed and took the double room. We blushed whenever this happened, and it happened very often. I read aloud to her from my thesis on Goethe, also Aristophanes; and when we had drunk a little wine I ventured upon Hölderlin's *Hyperion*. I would read her to sleep and then go out and stand by the weir, staring down at the foaming water till the moon rose over the peaks.

The papers had suddenly begun to talk about a strike against Chancellor Cuno, who everybody considered had prolonged the evil of inflation long enough, and who was destined to be almost literally swept out of office.

There was also talk of a new statesman, Gustav Stresemann, and of the entry of the Communists into the governments of Thuringen and Saxony. It all sounded like the repetition of things which I no longer wanted to remember. I listened to Vossler discoursing on the *Chanson de Roland* and talked to him about Molière and Henri de Regnier when the lecture was over.

One day in November my landlady told me that the great General Ludendorff had got involved with a *Schlawiner*, by which she meant a foreigner, and had narrowly escaped being shot near the Feldherrnhalle.

"Who cares?" I said.

The name of the foreigner was Hitler, and she thought he was probably a practitioner of black magic, but they had now locked him up. The episode had nearly prevented her from visiting her aunt; the old lady was particularly fond of *guglhupf*, a round sort of sponge-cake, and would I care to step into the kitchen and try a slice, and perhaps one day bring my fiancée. "Not my fiancée," I said—I had to get my doctorate first. But I thanked her for the *guglhupf*. As for this Hitler, I had never heard of him, and Ludendorff was nothing to me, a performing ape; but I was glad that the trains were running again, because we were going to Pupplinghausen, where I had not been since March 1919, and in those days . . .

She interrupted me:

"In those days the town was full of foreigners and they almost made a revolution!"

"Yes, almost," I said, and went into the kitchen to taste the *guglhupf.*

By sundown Lotte and I had arrived at Frau Thierbach's house in the woods. We had gone without much enthusiasm, but it was on this evening that circumstances put an end to our state of suspense.

We sat together on the couch of hay which Frau Thierbach had spread for us in the barn. The sound of hammering came from a nearby shed, where a bearded man was making copper brooches such as the ancient Germani had worn. I had seen one on the bosom of his wife, who wore a fluttering robe as she fed the animals, calling them by their names. She was now singing while her husband hammered—"As Mary through the thickets strayed—*Kyrie Eleison* . . ." Lotte sat plucking the petals from a flower and then picked up a stem of oats and tickled the nose of a cat that had strayed in.

The man in the shed stopped his hammering and began to accompany his wife on a guitar. They sang together: "The night grows dark on the heath and we must start for home." They must be dreaming of a better home than they actually possessed, since they lived in that shed. "Songs don't have to make sense," said Lotte, while the cat rubbed itself against her.

Presently the coppersmith turned to piety, as may be expected of people who go about in sandals. It was cloudy outside; a storm had passed over us and the sky was still overcast. There was a smell of farm animals in the barn. The couple next door sang a song by Hermann Claudius: "The moon has risen and the golden stars are gleaming . . ."

Memory stirred in me. I had reminded Harry of this song when he talked about human goodness being out-of-date. They sang it now as though it were a prayer: "Spare us, Lord, from tribulation, and let us quietly slumber, and our sick neighbours too . . ."

"They're both singing out of tune," I said irritably. I did not want to think about Harry and the time in Heidelberg. "Apart from which, there aren't any neighbours."

"They're singing for us," said Lotte. "Perhaps they think we need something." At this point the cat got up and walked away.

"They don't think at all," I said. "People who go round dressed like ancient Teutons shouldn't sing songs dating from 1790. They have no sense of period."

"But they seem to be enjoying themselves."

"No one can escape his own time," I said portentously. It was a thoroughly dishonest remark, because I had been trying to do nothing else for weeks.

"Escape is all that matters," Lotte said. "Why are you sitting so far away from me?"

"The better to look at you," I answered, and moved nearer. "Besides, I'm remembering things. I was very unhappy when I was here before."

"Were you here with another girl?" she asked, with her head a little on one side.

She has lynx-eyes, I thought, and her eyebrows ought to meet in the middle. The grey eyes were shining—a lynx in the farmyard!—everything seemed rather unreal. . . . And I thought of Lily as she cried out her hatred of Germany. She too had worn a fluttering garment. Lotte was wearing a low-cut summer blouse and her bare knees shone against the hay as though on a cushion. Could one lose the past in an embrace? The couple next door had retired to bed with their sick neighbours. What had Lotte asked? Why should I not answer honestly?

"I've never had a real girl," I said. "And why did you say 'another'? Or have I misunderstood?"

She bent her face to mine.

"You understand perfectly," she said and kissed me.

The shades of the past vanished into the woods over which the moon was now rising, still threatened by clouds.

It was May 1924, but I should scarcely have known the year if anyone had asked me. The blue heads of gentians were raised above the grass through which we walked next morning, resolved to hear nothing of the world except the singing of the birds. Nothing else existed. It was a trial of strength, but it seemed to us as weightless as the pebbles which we sent skimming over the waters of the Isar.

We passed the house of the writer, Richard von Wolzogen.

"He married his housekeeper to the bailiff," Lotte said. "They say he did it in the old German fashion, with a hammer and anvil."

"Why don't we go to him?"

"He's ill in bed. A cow kicked him when he was milking her."

"It must have been one of those old Teutonic cows."

I saw a placard in the village and thought at once of Toller's face looking at me from the hoardings. But it was only an election poster. The innkeeper where we had breakfast told us that the Socialists had lost 71 of their 171 seats and that the Communists had increased theirs from 17 to 62. He waited to hear what we thought of this, but Lotte only asked him why there was so little lilac growing in the valley. He didn't know.

On our homeward walk, as we were skirting the wood by Frau Thierbach's house, I was visited by another ghost, that of Gustav Landauer. Lotte saw my expression.

"I must tell you something," she said. "I've had your horoscope cast."

"Oh! And what do the stars say?"

"That it's time I started calling you *du*."

"Quite right. I was wondering about that. But was that all they said?"

She took my hand and drew me into the woods, clasping me the more tightly as she felt my momentary reluctance.

"They also said that you were to be held captive for four years by an impossible woman, that you would never so much as look at a newspaper, that you would be rich and then poor again, that you would write a lot of poems and tear them all up, that you would turn traitor to yourself and be betrayed by others, and that finally you would break out of captivity—and all because of the impossible woman."

"Do I know the lady?"

"I'm afraid you do."

Thus began my first marriage, a voyage on unchartered seas, sometimes with fair winds and sometimes with foul; with moonlit nights drowning all landfalls in forgetfulness, with dawns heavy with foreboding—a voyage that ended with a shattered rudder and sails ripped to shreds. But it is the lynx-eyes that I remember, and the smiling face from a Greek vase. Our son born of that marriage was swallowed up in the second World War—but I must begin at the beginning.

On the day after I sat for my examination Lotte suddenly decided that we should visit her parents in Leipzig. It was slightly surprising to me to learn that she had parents. She was like a creature in a tale by Hoffmann—the golden snake who caused one to forget the pampered and well brought-up town councillor's daughter.

We travelled north, and by the time we reached Regensburg I saw that she was looking anxious. At last she began to talk about her parents, and I surmised from what she said that they were poor, perhaps even poorer than my own. So then I told her about my father, how he had carved figures out of the red-brown bark of trees for Christmas presents, how he would never let anyone wait on him but even sewed on his own buttons, and how he had told us about the Greek hero who as a youth had had to wait behind the stove while his only shirt was drying.

"Shirts . . ." she said, smiling a little uncomfortably. "He has enough of those."

She seemed to want cheering up, so I told her how perilous wealth could be, and how it could rob quite decent men of all taste and judgment. I did not go so far as to talk in the pure accents of Socialism and say that poverty was ennobling, and that I would not have known how to live with her if she had been rich. It was on the tip of my tongue, but I felt that I must not refer too pointedly to what I thought I had guessed; so I just went on running

down the rich, adducing all kinds of arguments which, however, seemed only
to make her more depressed. When we stopped at the next station, which
was Hof, she got her bag down from the rack. There were tears in her eyes. I
put the bag back and took her in my arms. I seemed to have been flounder-
ing about like a bull in a china-shop, and I felt that I could only save myself
by coming right out into the open.

"I only had one new shirt when I went to Heidelberg. But you didn't fall
in love with me for my money, did you?"

I thought she was sobbing as she lay against my breast, but she was
laughing convulsively, and she clung to me as though for protection against
an onset of uncontrollable mirth.

When finally we reached our destination a lady came towards the doorway
of our compartment. I had been expecting something like a concierge's wife,
but this was an elegant figure whose clothes and general aspect made me
think of Queen Victoria. She waved to Lotte with a hand glittering with
diamonds. A uniformed chauffeur sprang forward to take charge of our
luggage and we passed him our two hand-bags. I was conducted to a handsome car, and we all got in and drove to the Grand Hotel, where a suite had
been reserved for me. While I was washing my hands in a state of some confusion, Lotte put her head round the door and apologised, explaining that her
father was the owner of the biggest department store in the town—and did I
still love her? I said, yes, but that I was a little taken aback, and if she would
find a cheaper room for me I would sleep with her again; and perhaps we could
meet on a bench in the Stadtpark, and she could bring a few rolls with her—
no, no ham, just to feed the swans—and we would set up a publishing business together, but first I must get myself apprenticed to Liebig's theological
antiquarian bookshop so as to learn the business.

"Why theology?" she asked.

I think perhaps it was as a counterblast to Stinnes, whom I had just seen in
the lobby of the hotel.

Five weeks later her father said to me that publishing was nonsense. Mere
words printed on paper! There was much more money to be made out of
materials with patterns printed on them. "Who cares what you sell—the
profit's all that matters." He assured me, speaking with the utmost eloquence, that textiles were always in demand, coming next in importance to
food itself. But the demand for books depended on the degree of education,
and education was a very tricky matter!

It was a kindly ultimatum. He told me, moreover, that he would be very
glad if I went into his business because this would make it more difficult for
his son to over-rule his two daughters, who were also shareholders. He was
very conscious of his son's ambitions, which sprang, he said, from his in-

feriority complex. He respected him for his lack of scruple but at the same time feared where this might lead.

So I became an apprentice in the textile trade. I served behind the counter, beginning with towelling, then moved on to the cottons, the printed ones, which for me were to take the place of books, and also the unprinted ones, whose quality I learned to assess by feeling them with my fingers; and so progressed to silks, to ready-made suits, to furs and shirts. . . .

I learned about salesmanship, how to smile and how to lie, to calculate and to measure, to deal tactfully or forthrightly, to study the changes in fashion and staff-psychology, salesmen's jokes and trade-union demands, government regulations and methods of tax-evasion.

I underwent this process in the security of my status as Crown Prince, subject to no one but the old Wolf, my father-in-law, who harshly corrected my mistakes and humiliated me in public, and then would invite me to lunch. He had an astonishing faculty for keeping business and private relationships separate.

The old Wolf! Why do I refer in these terms to a man who never did me any harm and whose very humiliations served to make a Christian of me? Because his hard eyes and thin lips taught me more about the nature of the employer than all the lectures by Jaspers, Gundolf and Max Weber put together, and because he really was a wolf, as his business required him to be.

His model was Stinnes, the originator of the vertical trust. His object, too, was to breed his own sheep, to spin the wool himself, to weave the thread, to control the distribution, while at the same time he built up a mass-producing organisation of which the output would be sold to the public through his own retail shops.

He reckoned to make a profit at every stage, as well as gaining by a large turnover at reduced prices. Small concerns driven into bankruptcy were to be swallowed up. He wanted to dictate prices. He boosted sales with relentless and noisy advertising. The inflation and the craving for articles of concrete value brought the customers in masses to his doors.

He was always on the alert, ready to buy instantly whenever there was a lull in the devaluation of the currency, and he constantly dinned into his subordinates the lesson that even the largest turnover was worthless if the stock was not instantly replaced.

The surging crowds in the main building at the corner of the Geschäftsstrasse, where he would stand on the steps in an elegant grey suit, watching the women pour in obsessed with the desire to buy, made the place sometimes look like the selling-up of a bankrupt business; but in fact he was conducting a lightning campaign against devaluation. Even when the money earned between opening and lunch-time lost its value by the afternoon, that masterly gambler still emerged victorious. He would have covered himself by buying new stock during the morning, using credit which the bank across the road from his seething establishment never failed to grant him. The bank manager had only to look out of his window to see the crowd of purchasers which afforded the best security.

I was carried away with enthusiasm for all this feverish activity. As to who lost by it, I did not ask. All profits were instantly sunk in new goods or new premises, which sprang up out of the earth like mushrooms. Presently I was given the job of managing the newly established Berlin concerns. Some of these had been opened under my name, while others were limited companies controlled by the Wolf.

He had entered the firm as a director on a percentage basis and had put his profits into new undertakings, which were his own property; however, they remained affiliated concerns, benefiting by bulk-buying and a central administration which saved them something in overheads. The Head Office, working in close personal touch with all these subsidiaries, continued to help them in various ways after they were securely established.

The books were so involved and there was so much cooking of the accounts that Theseus himself would have been at a loss to disentangle that Ariadne's web, let alone the taxation authorities. Costs of transport, for example, figured not only in the overall statement but recurred as separate items, as between factory and factory and in deliveries from the central warehouse to the branches which I nominally controlled. Here again Stinnes was no doubt the model. The law of the jungle operated everywhere. In October 1923 the Ruhr industrialists had set about transforming their so-called patriotic strike against the French occupation into a far-reaching private bargain with the French General Degoutte. It was a blatant betrayal of their own country, but who cared? Certainly not Stinnes, who claimed 100 million goldmarks indemnification for "occupation losses" and received them. The Wolf revered him for his nerve, his audacity and his contempt for the people; and he was resolved to follow his example, at least in his treatment of the workers.

Exactly why he should have entrusted me with the conduct of his "purge" was something that I never discovered. Perhaps he reckoned that he could count on my discretion: I was, after all, a member of the family. I did not fail him.

The shirt-makers went on strike whenever they saw a favourable opportunity. These were normal trade-union tactics, but the Wolf chose to regard them as the barest scoundrelism and ingratitude, besides being unpatriotic. After a first paroxysm of fury he proceeded to counter-attack. At that time the dismissal of workers was forbidden by law if there was work to keep them employed. I had to arrange for our representatives to send in two sets of order-forms, one giving the real figure and the other a much lower one for the benefit of the authorities.

I went with these forgeries to the Ministry of Labour to secure permission to work short-time in view of our dwindling turnover. This was granted and was presently followed by permission to lay off a given number of workers. So out went the "agitators," as the Wolf called them. Only "reliable workers" were reinstated.

Looking back, I simply do not know how I could have lent myself to these manoeuvres.

When finally the mark was stabilised the regulations forbidding the dismissal of workers and the closing of factories ceased to be put into effect. By December 1923 the official figure of unemployment stood at 1,800,000. The unions were powerless. Wages were stabilised on a gold basis. The rate had been 51·5 pfennigs an hour; the industrialists offered 20 pfennigs. Both were starvation-rates. Did I think of this as I sat in my director's chair? Did it ever occur to me to visit one of my workers in his home in Neukölln?

There are always defences to be found against a threat to our peace of mind. I often worked long after office hours. How could I be expected to find time to worry about the workers? After all, they had their unions, but what had I got? This was the fraudulent logic of class morality, and it paved the way for even more specious arguments. Without employers there would be no employment. I was the one who was responsible for my workpeople, and it was I who passed sleepless nights, not they. I was then twenty-five, my memories of 1919 blotted out by this hypocrisy, to which was added a feeling of loyalty to the clan and the overwhelming personality of the Wolf. I belonged to the pack, exactly in Kipling's sense. It had its own laws and its own blinkers, and sometimes its moments of surprising tenderness, like those flowers which blossom overnight on the spiky leaves of a cactus.

Thus it came about that in August 1925 I paced up and down the corridor of a private nursing home, a prey to the half-comical agitation that afflicts all men whose wives are in labour, just after a violent dispute with the Wolf on the subject of one of our managers' treatment of his assistants. I took the old-fashioned view that in dealing with subordinates one did not remind them of their state of dependence when other people, such as customers, were present. The Wolf, however, was against all sentimentality, as he called it. The tone in which he had spoken to me had not been deliberately humiliating but was so informed with the coarseness of his mind that one felt humiliated in the name of all humanity. An echo of those forebodings which in 1918 had driven me to the barricades in Berlin, and then to the shambles of Munich, sounded through these quarrels and contributed its own measure of shame.

H

But now, as I stood there frantic in my concern for my wife, and cursing the Wolf, who had not spared me even on this day, he suddenly appeared in the lobby of the clinic with a box of orchids, led me into the nurses' kitchen and presented me with a bottle of champagne. Everything would be all right, he said. He knew just what I was feeling, he had been through it three times himself. "It's just that one feels so helpless," he said. He had already loosened the cork and produced the glasses with a gesture of such genuine kindness that I could only gaze at him in astonishment.

By a pleasant chance the sister entered at this moment and told us, smiling, that it was a boy. The cork flew to the ceiling. "That isn't really allowed here," said the sister and hastily withdrew to salve her conscience.

"Now there is one more of us," said the Wolf, and this time he was truly talking about the "pack"—the closed group prowling through the jungle of the century, sleeping in the same lairs, in the security bought with its money, and spreading the warning among its members when an enemy approached. None left the preserve without notifying the others, and generally went protected, by the motor car, by the barriers of social life. There was the reserved box at the opera where Furtwängler conducted. A limbo of enchantment! One talked about the building of villas and the buying of pictures. (Industrialists of the Stinnes school prided themselves, while they carefully salted away their capital abroad, on being patrons of the arts. They commissioned their busts by Fiori and they bought Van Goghs, many of which, however, were later found to be spurious. The Wolf was a collector of rugs from Smyrna and Afghanistan. One walked softly in his lair, treading a carpet of solid investments.)

All this sounds as though wealth had had an overwhelming and narrowing effect upon me; but it was far more the fear of letting my love for Lotte grow cold in the harsh wind of social problems. I drew further and further away from the people, to whom I had spontaneously dedicated myself five years before, and further away from myself. I was a victim of the nervous disease which was to become known as the "managerial sickness." The office became my place of refuge.

My countless daily activities drained me dry of the energy which might have been devoted to better things. I spun my wheel, mindless as a mouse in a cage, and over feast-days and holidays there brooded a dangerous calm. I must have feared that at such times the other side of me might rise in revolt, and so I made a point of working on Sundays and devoted my holidays to health-giving pursuits under the instructions of my doctor. However, one holiday lasted too long and I wrote a short story about Van Gogh, his blazing suns and skies and the boats pulled up invitingly on that beach at Les Saintes-Maries-de-la-Mer. It was a good story and I read it to Lotte.

"You should give up your job and go back to that sort of thing," she said.

We were walking along the mole of the little harbour where we were holiday-making, with the evening breeze blowing in our faces, and I pulled the manuscript out of my pocket and tore it to shreds and let it scatter where it would.

And the Wolf continued to vary his stock-in-trade as though he were nothing but a harbour exchanging gifts between unknown empires. Did he ever suspect that on a fine day in autumn, thanks to the double-dealing of his principal associate, the whole thing would founder like a ship running into an iceberg?

Unlike the boy in the old fairy-tale, who bartered his useful ass and bartered again and again until he was left with nothing but a useless whet-stone, the Wolf had gone the other way. He had made himself rich by barter until he was like the woman in another fairy-tale, who grew big of a mira-culous fish. He hungered for ever greater and more splendid palaces, and seemed indeed on the point of believing that he was no less than God when the storm broke and he had to go back to the beginning and start again in a hovel, to continue the fairy-tale parallel. But it may be added that the hovel was a very handsome house which he had generously bought for Lotte and me and converted into flats.

It occurred to me later that the *hubris* which brought about his downfall might have been influenced by that dubious fable of the talents in St Matthew. Like the puritans, the Wolf believed that to accumulate money was to do God's will and he "received mine own with usury," as the Bible puts it with such startling frankness. And when his lavish gains, brought him by his servants at the expense of the customers, were piled up mountain-high, he believed that all this had been earned by his own toil and sweat. He said as much, with great indignation; but the protest had no value in law, although I think he may have continued to believe in it when, bitterly lamenting, he retired in solitude to his St Helena in the last house that remained to him.

While he was still at the height of his success the Wolf was accustomed to visit me in Berlin every Sunday, and we would inspect the factories and shops together. He never relaxed until evening, and then generally in a box in one of the operetta theatres; but even here he would talk to me in the intervals of his worries over the Dawes Plan and foreign credits, about the new labour laws, which he thought far too lenient (although they envisaged the gradual destruction of the trade unions), and above all about the indirect taxation, which he regarded as a cancer in the body politic. When the curtain rose again on the Czardas Princess and her ladies and lovers, he would fall silent and sit listening like a child.

I did not share his anxieties; I was not myself. One of the symptoms of the managerial sickness is the divided consciousness which does not permit any close study of reality. Shock-treatment was needed to bring the two halves of me together again.

One morning when I was in one of my shops, showing a saleswoman how to drape a length of material over the customer's shoulders so that she might see how elegant her new dress would look, someone clapped me on the shoulder and a voice cried in astonishment:

"Well, bless my soul—it's really you!"

It was Harry, my friend of Heidelberg days. There he stood with his long face and the shock of fair hair, his blue eyes wide with astonishment. I was suddenly homesick for Heidelberg; I wanted to ask after Gundolf but he said, "All for the love of a lady, I suppose?" I nodded, handed back the material to the sales-girl and invited him into my office.

He waved this aside. "It's the lady I want to see. She must be a honey!"

I invited him to my home. I can still see Lotte seated by the fireside in a blue silk dress, deliberately ignoring Harry. But by midnight she had accepted his invitation to go for a drive into Brandenburg.

After this they went out in his car nearly every day, while I went to my shirt-factory. Arriving home late one night I found a note from Lotte saying that she was too tired to wait up for me. Early next morning—I was always first at the factory—she appeared at the breakfast-table in a new wrap, her eyes shining with an unwonted brilliance. I remarked upon this and her face clouded over.

At the week-end she refused to come on an excursion I proposed because she said the child bothered her. I found the *Chartreuse de Parme* on her writing-desk. She complained of feeling depressed.

Then she began to show an excessive solicitude for the child, wanted to know all about my business activities, and proposed that I should take some extra leave and that we should go to Italy. Once again we would make the journey by coach from Sils Maria to Como, and I would recite Nietzsche's poems to her, and we would forget that we must ever go home.

Two days later she begged me to give up the business. Harry came at midday to take her out for a drive. I saw that she had dressed with especial care, and she pinned the rose he had brought her to her bosom. I wished them a pleasant afternoon and returned to the factory.

That evening she told me that she was in love with Harry. We sat together by the fire in our big corner room in the Hohenzollern Strasse and talked about free love. We agreed that one must not be narrow-minded in these matters, and presently Lotte took leave of me and went out.

The workshops suddenly became strange to me. I was still the first to arrive every morning, but I felt that something had changed.

One day I surprised myself by falling into conversation with one of the workmen, although I knew that he was a trade-union official. I would have liked to tell him of what had happened in Munich, but he answered so disdainfully that I gave up the attempt and went instead to the Kronprinzen Palais to see Franz Marc's paintings. That evening Lotte and I went to a fancy-dress dance, such as were popular in Berlin at that time. I met a fairhaired girl called Magda, who danced with great abandon and, having once danced with me, refused all other partners. I took her home.

The next morning we had another discussion about free love and how simple all these problems were if one cast off the old bonds and discarded the notion of possessiveness in love. Marcel Frischmann, the *Simplizissimus* artist, was present. He wrinkled his forehead. "All this fits you like a ready-made suit," he said, by which he intended to imply that I had now gone over to the methods of mass production in my love-affairs. He was teased for being old-fashioned, as much by Lotte as by Magda.

The two young women became friends. At week-end parties at our house, to which the young expressionists came, and actors and actresses from the Scala Theatre and the painter Kurt Werth, they first danced together before consenting to dance with Harry and me, "to get back to normal again." Everyone wanted to appear more emancipated than the rest. We were all the victims of a kind of blackmail which found its expression in the words, "being modern."

I returned from lunching at Werder where Magda and I had sat for hours drinking wine under a blazing sun, to find Lotte in the house alone. After drinking a bottle of the wine I had brought with me, we made love, but without thinking of it as a return. We laughed and said that we were being unfaithful to Harry and Magda. This seemed to us quite fascinatingly modern.

But the real betrayal was much more simple and more dangerous. We lied and lost the power of really loving. Instead of looking for all the manifold possibilities in a single being, we sought variety in a feverish promiscuity.

The lesbian, homosexual and hermaphrodite night-clubs in the Luther Strasse and elsewhere, with their reek of cheap scent, provided the fulfilment of days whose only warrant seemed to be the love-encounters of the night.

Magda despised the queers, Harry defended them, Lotte had a pitying smile for the youths clad in women's garments and I was conscious of many things—the lawlessness of prevailing custom and clothing, the impress of eroticism on all our doings, the mockery of my daily labours, the ever-present threat of surprise and the possibility of scandal, Magda's sturdy defiance of the abnormal, which she held to be an insult to her sex, and my own highly personal discovery that all these things had existed while I was manning the barricades, not to become fully known to me until the present time, and still scarcely deserving the name of vice: for was it not more truly vicious to fritter away one's life behind shop-counters, to own motor cars in which one did not explore the world, to buy pictures which one did not trouble to look at and to earn money for the sake of a marriage which this same money was driving on the rocks?

I resolved to relax my daily routine, and naïvely indulged in deep-buried dreams of fast living. Quaintly enough I was first tempted by enjoyments such as might have appealed to my parents' generation. I supped with Magda in a private room in a restaurant in the Friedrich Strasse, betted on horses, gambled on the stock exchange with money taken out of the business and opened an account for my mistress in my most expensive branch, of which she at once availed herself with the thoroughness of a Renaissance courtesan. These man-about-town goings-on were far removed from the reality of life in Berlin, into which I hoped to enter by these means, and I sometimes caught a smile of mockery on the faces of Lotte and her painter-friends when I took leave of them in the evening to pursue my sophisticated career.

Harry was the only one with the honesty to warn me that I was deceiving myself and that Magda was no longer sufficient to console me for my distress at having lost Lotte. Perhaps he suspected that he himself had got too deeply involved and that his love-affair was foredoomed, or perhaps it was an instinct of male solidarity that caused him, after the first exuberance, to rally to the side of an old friend.

I saved his life one night, in one of the homosexual dancing-places, when in an excess of high spirits he leaned out of our box and emptied a bottle of wine over a herculean lady with a beard. She could have disposed of him easily, even without the aid of the revolver she produced, and she looked like doing so, for, spoilt and arrogant as he was, he refused to apologise. I thrust myself between Harry and the revolver and explained that he was merely startled because he could not make out whether the lady's beard or her bosom was false, and whether she was a boxer or an actress in disguise. She laughed at my agitation, put away the gun, offered me her hand to kiss (she had fingers like those of a dock labourer), declared that Harry was of no account and went off with a gesture worthy of Walpurgis night.

In 1925 a presidential election was held in Germany. The right-wing parties got 10,700,000 votes, the Social Democrats got 7,800,000. A second vote was necessary. Incapable of self-confidence and in a state of morbid apprehension, the Socialists withdrew their candidate and advised their supporters to vote for the clerical candidate, Dr Wilhelm Marx. They referred to him as the "lesser evil." It was an extraordinarily silly slogan, not aggressive but merely suicidal. They lost this battle as they had lost those of Kapp and Cuno.

I missed my father's letters; he no longer wrote to me now that I had become an industrialist. What was he thinking about this election of a defeated Field-Marshal to the presidency of the republic? I could guess, but I did not try to revive our interrupted correspondence—it was a part of the morality of that anarchic time that family links were to be brushed aside as mere old-fashioned sentimentality. And events were crowding in on all sides to bring about the enforced solution of my problems. It was Father himself who later beckoned to me.

A trifling event brought down the whole house of cards. A woman-friend persuaded me to go to Lotte, who was taking a cure in Bad Nauheim, and tell her frankly that I was sick of playing the fool and loved no one but her. I arrived early in the morning, found the sanatorium still asleep, told one of the sisters that I was the husband of Frau Regler, and followed close behind her to a door from which Lotte emerged, radiant, looking like a bride, and cried out: "Harry!"

I turned on my heel, caught the next train, rang up my lawyer in Berlin and gave back my business to the Wolf, with full possession, full powers and stockrooms worth a million gold marks.

My two secretaries were in tears. I closed my private bank-account, drawing my last month's salary, stuffed the money in my pocket, and after a few words over the telephone with one or two of the directors left the building in the Potsdamer Strasse and strolled into a café.

It was like the removal of a too-thick overcoat, like the loosing of bonds, like an earthquake. There are a thousand possible metaphors, but none that fully expresses the almost sensuous relief that I experienced at this upheaval in my life.

I opened my hands and let a world slip through my fingers—workshops, sales-counters, customers and accounts, together with all the trappings, the pictures, the box at the opera, the private supper in the private room, of a comfortable and cushioned life. I shrugged away a world to which in my heart I had never belonged.

I sat in the café in all the blessed insecurity of the suddenly poor and saw a van belonging to the business drive past. Tomorrow or the next day Lotte, too, would drive past in search of me, but from a sense of guilt, not love; and the nurse would go past pushing my son in his pram, and even then I would not show myself; and my share-holdings would drift here and there in the ebb and flow of the market; and Magda, the little sense-drunk, dance-crazy creature, would find her account closed and would have to look for another benefactor.

It was the most thorough-going renunciation, and the Wolf was at a loss to understand why I asked nothing for my share in the business. No doubt in discussing the matter with his amazed fellow-directors he put this forward as evidence that I had never been a businessman.

So there I was, empty-handed amid the bubbling, laughing, weeping, laborious and still entrancing tumult of Berlin.

I sought to pick up the threads, such as they were, of my former existence. I went to the *Vorwärts* building and saw the renovated façade and the rolls of newsprint being carted in on which the fruitless leaders would be printed, comments on the Dawes Plan, undertakers' advertisements. Kuttner would be sitting in his office, seeking, as ever, to bridge the gap between left and right and top and bottom, being all things to all men. There was no thread for me there.

I walked along the Wilhelmstrasse, where in 1919 I had voted for Scheidemann with a rifle in my hand. The victor of Tannenberg was now installed there as President, the man who had lost the 1918 offensive: a jest against all reason, spinning threads that certainly were not mine.

Perhaps it was foolish to go in search of anything, better to let chance decide. And presently I fell in with a student friend of my Munich days. We sat and talked and he said:

"I can see it all—Lotte, Harry, Magda, the night-spots, the delusions, your mad quartet spinning in the whirlpool of this chaotic town. You'll never get well so long as you stay here. One can only get one's balance in the parts of Germany which have a feeling of Italy, but never in this place, where one is so close to Russia—so close, in fact, that at this moment you look like something out of Dostoevsky!"

I accepted his invitation and a week later arrived in Nuremberg, which was as German as its own Dürer and, below the surface, as forbidding as its own Streicher, although this was something which at the time I did not see. There were many Jews living there, Jews of the unassuming, humorous, cultivated kind, who were later to be blotted out from the German scene.

But in that year of 1926 they still lived in security, humane judges, eloquent barristers, manufacturers of toys. They held musical evenings, went to first nights at the "little theatre" where pacifist plays were given, supported Coudenhove-Kalergi's plan for a United Europe and laughed at Streicher's gutter-sheet, *Der Stürmer*, which accused them of celebrating Black Mass with white girls. They spent their holidays in Florence and Assisi, were warmly hospitable and the best customers of the booksellers. In short, they were as strong and as weak, as honourable and as corruptible, as other decent citizens, and in all respects the opposite of the sub-human monsters which the drunken, unspeakable Streicher was already beginning to depict in his paper.

I got a job on the staff of their local newspaper. I went there one morning and applied for it. The Aryan editor, Robert Gall, talked to me for an hour and then took me on as an editorial assistant. To supplement the very small salary which was all he could afford to pay me, he offered me a room in his own home and his wife's cooking, to which that charming lady at once agreed. A month later he put me in charge of the Sunday edition.

I filled my front page with brief comments on events all over the world—anything that seemed to me of interest. Robert Gall and I became friends. We constantly exchanged ideas, worked at each other's desks, broke up whole pages on the stone when they seemed to us too innocuous, and wrote as though the whole of Europe were hanging on our words; but we really owed our freedom to the eight thousand Jews who were our regular readers and who did indeed represent all that was best in Europe.

I came to know many of them through the articles I wrote, and perhaps it was their encouragement, the praise of the beautiful Jewesses of Nuremberg and the advice of their wise, humanitarian menfolk, which finally made me resolve, after so many false starts, to become a writer.

I met Luppe, the Mayor. He had a face like an El Greco painting, with contemplative, almost melancholy eyes, and a natural dignity that never became theatrical, even when he performed the ceremonies of his office. He was absorbed in his work without letting himself become too immersed in details. He was meticulous to the point of pedantry in dealing impartially with the rival political parties, but he could be a Solomon in his judgments.

Streicher launched an attack on him in his paper, accusing him of having acquired an overcoat out of public-assistance funds, an utterly grotesque charge to bring against a man in his position. Gall and I warned him that the schoolmaster, meaning Streicher, intended to pursue this smear campaign. Luppe merely smiled. We insisted that he must hit back, and finally he agreed to institute proceedings for libel, but I think he was slightly scornful of our obstinacy in the matter. He had no thought of what was coming, but we could smell the brimstone.

Streicher was receiving large sums from the Franconian industrialists. His campaign of subversion gradually gained ground, basing itself on the resentments of the impoverished *petite bourgeoisie* and smothering its political objectives in a reek of sexual sensationalism. Even schoolchildren read his paper.

The Jews remained inactive, perhaps from a sense of dignity but perhaps also from the secret fear which they had inherited from their forefathers. But Gall and I stood firm. We looked for witnesses, seeking them out at the meetings which Streicher held with increasing frequency. We instituted proceedings and finally brought him into court.

Streicher was condemned to six months' imprisonment and I had the satisfaction of hearing his deputy bellow in protest on a public platform at this
"mockery of justice." But it made my blood run cold when he compared the
imprisoned man with Jesus and bade the audience rise to honour the martyr
with two minutes' silence.

My articles pleased Luppe, and one day he said to me that I was capable
of better things than helping Gall to edit that "parish magazine." He had put
my name forward for the post of secretary of the Democratic Party in Hesse,
the president of which province was due to arrive by air from Darmstadt in a
few days.

I passed those days in a state of feverish uncertainty, but I took the precaution of procuring a press air-travel warrant, just in case.

On the morning of the day of decision our news-editor proposed that
I should take his place at a double execution in the prison. He seemed to
think he was doing me a favour. As I sat talking to him (he had a packet of
unopened sandwiches on his desk; he found that lunch gave him indigestion
when he was more than usually busy) I had a sudden vision of what my new
job would be. I should be an official, a speaker at public meetings, an oracle
for the masses, a whipper-up of votes. I should spend hours in an office,
wearing a salesman's smile as I had done in the Berlin shop, while I sought
with prudence to reconcile conflicting business interests. No doubt there
would be battles to be fought against other Streichers, and this was an attraction. But the office routine, the boredom of dictating meaningless letters, the
secret conflict between the smooth necessities of an official career and the
thoughts in my own head—suddenly I knew that I should never be able to
endure it!

I went to the airport to meet the visitor from Darmstadt. A single-
engine plane came gliding in and I said to Baron Lochner, the airport
manager:

"Is this it?"

"No, this one comes from Prague. It's on its way to Paris."

"Can I go in it? You promised me a warrant."

"Yes, if there's a place. You'd better let me get you something to eat.
But what am I to tell Luppe?"

"Just say the job doesn't suit me."

An hour later I was flying over Strasbourg Cathedral.

I do not know which Paris I was looking for. Later I found quite other
ones, and tomorrow will bring me new surprises. There are a hundred
different Parises, and those who come to her with faith bring a thousand
more. She patiently endures their spoiling and misunderstanding, the use

they make of her and the fulsome praises they bestow. But through all misuse, the exaggerations, the tawdry misconceptions, she inspires a love that is constant, taking a thousand forms—a sense of belonging that ends only with death.

It was the first time I had sought to escape from Germany. I came to Paris as the pilgrim and the suppliant that I have been ever since. No other city in the world makes solitude so endurable, or so readily becomes a conquest, without even a struggle.

I knew no one. I had brought nothing with me except a notebook in which I had started to write the story of the exodus of the Jews from Egypt. If only because my mind was so occupied with that ancient, fateful tale, I could not fail to come under the spell of the entranced light and the lightness of that city, so steeped in history, which more than any other conveys the sense of having triumphed over its past. What was the miracle of the Red Sea compared with the graceful dance of the bridges over the Seine! And that dark-avised Moses who with thunder and lightning had set the yoke of God upon his people's shoulders, how could I seek to recall his harsh, relentless speech amid these people who read and lived Marcel Proust?

Flight from a party-machine had brought me here, but when I considered what I should do, Paris returned no answer, neither approving nor disapproving but greeting me with a cool indifference which caused me after two days to reach for my notebook again. I went on with my Bible story, and then it seemed to me that Paris took note of my presence, becoming attentive and sympathetic. I came by a copy of Gide's *Retour De L'Enfant Prodigue*. I read it in the Café du Dome. This was the sort of language I was striving for! Not to be afraid of tales so often heard. To re-write simple things in a simple way! How often had I tried to escape from the habit of reading the Bible! The figure on the cross no longer meant anything to me, not even the one by Grünewald, though truly it depicted a new depth of suffering. The Raphael Madonnas had long since offended my sense of the mystery of motherhood. And from force of habit the very words of the Lord's Prayer had become no more than a perfunctory murmur over the soup-plates.

But here was this Protestant Frenchman, this cultivated ironist, adorning one of the most familiar of all Bible stories with new words, that is to say, investing it with new life. To me it was a revelation. I was enthralled by the dialogue in the farmyard, timeless as a picture by Giorgione. Why should I not do as much for that ancient shepherd of the Jews?

I wanted in the first place to write for myself, the restless soul for whom the pages of the Bible, when I turned to them for solace, seem to echo with the murmur of a Sunday congregation. Did one return to the Bible at the end of every revolution? The Prodigal Son must surely have dreamed of his return home.

I found a café near the church of St Severin where an atmosphere of accepted poverty prevailed. I began to write without thinking much about eating. The saucers with the prices of the drinks I consumed were crowded round my writing-pad, like so many beggars' bowls. The waiter Jean counted them in the evening. By the third day he had become friendly, because now I was a regular customer, an established figure of whom a picture could be made. He watched me use up one writing-pad after another, but he never asked questions.

I wrote of the slave labour and the terrible wall which the Jews were forced to build round the city of the dead; and so real was this growing wall that I sought to make every reader feel that it was still there, a wall running through all our cities and all our lives, only in rare moments to be breached. I have only now realised that it was this same wall which so oppressed me on the Chemin des Dames.

My loneliness in the heart of Paris helped me to portray that state of infinite imprisonment in which every living creature is enclosed. Rilke had dared to describe this solitude in his *Malte*, and Gide had done so again in his *Enfant Prodigue*, and in the tender discourse between the two brothers had even shown how the fear of the breaching of the wall may sometimes be overcome—by a love that asks nothing in return. And this was what I too sought to achieve amid the stridency of Paris, with lovers on the *banquette* opposite me silent in each other's arms. I wrote of how Moses in the high solitude of the mountains acquired the gift of hearing and breached the wall, in communion with God Himself.

It looks to me now as though I was very young to be wrestling with these weighty matters, but perhaps they are such as one can attempt only in an apprentice work.

In three weeks I had reached my Sinai. The battle was over. I had seen nothing of Paris except the great edifice of Notre Dame, the green angels endlessly in the act of descending into the Seine, and Jean, who congratulated me when I told him that I had finished. He brought me a glass of *marc* with the compliments of the *patron*.

That night I had misgivings but they made me bold. I wrote to Thomas Mann, who was at that time in travail with his own story of Joseph, to ask him if he would look at my Moses, which was called *The March of the Shepherds*. He replied, with the courtesy that was characteristic of him, that he always avoided reading books having any bearing on the work he had in hand. I translated my dialogue between Aaron and Moses into French and sent it to Gide, telling him how much I owed him. He answered no less promptly, saying that he was gratified to have inspired such excellent work.

Encouraged by this, I sent my manuscript to a publisher in northern Germany who was on the look-out for young, unknown writers. A telegram of enthusiastic acceptance summoned me to Lübeck.

The reviews of my book might well have caused the young author, who had honourably striven with God, rapidly to turn away from God. They were highly flattering. I am now thankful that they terrified me and thus saved me from the sin of pride.

7. *Marie Louise*

A FRESH love-affair preserved me from the ever-tempting embarrassments of premature fame. At the house of my publisher in Lübeck I met a painter of many parts. He came from the North German plain, loved women and drink, acted, played the concertina and wrote about the aged decaying people of his birthplace. It was all enveloped in the fumes of alcohol, as he was himself, but it also had a scent of the spring fields into which he beguiled his fair-haired wenches. He invited me to a party in Worpswede, a village not far from Bremerhaven, which artists had made their own, he said, and where there was no distinction between peasants, visitors and painters.

I found there a marquee crowded with fair-haired girls and peasants rolling in good-humoured drunkenness. There were waving fields where poppies shone amid the thistles and a wide sky with shafts of light thrusting like spears through the rolling clouds. There were cottages with thatched roofs drawn protectively down over their windows, serious merriment everywhere and a light of maidenly expectation in every girl's eyes.

For three days and nights I drank with my artist, who presided over the festivities into the small hours of the morning like a Renaissance buffoon, then slept for twenty-four hours in an empty house in the place called the Devil's Moor; and the next evening I met Marie Louise.

She was the girl I dared not let myself believe in.

"It was a vision conjured up by that Court Jester," I thought two days later, when I was seated again outside the hut on the moor. "She said she would come today, but now I'm sure that she was nothing but a dream."

The elderly peasant, my host, sat beside me making himself a pair of straw shoes. We did not hear Marie Louise coming, so softly did her footsteps fall. She had an oval face and dove-grey eyes keen enough to search out every four-leafed clover in its hiding-place. When she raised her small breasts it was as though all the pears and apricots in the garden trembled on the bough, and she was one with them. She came towards us with an armful of broom and bell-heather which she had picked as she came, greeted the old man and turned to me, holding the bunch high in the air.

"It's time for the wedding," she said.

MARIE LOUISE

It was a Breughel wedding. The company ate at long tables, and the meat was carried round on huge trays. The guests as they arrived all pressed money into the hand of the bride's mother—it was a communal wedding. It smelt of hay and of roast meat, and cows from the meadow came and rubbed themselves against the fence. Two brass instruments were blaring. We drank corn liquor and beer, and the girls wore black silk coifs with ribbons of lace framing their rosy cheeks. There was not much conversation. When the bride danced for the first time we all clapped our hands. Someone cried out as a stork with outstretched legs flew somewhat too symbolically over the dancing couple; and the corn waved all about us and the water in the dykes gleamed beneath the sun.

"We will always come back here," said Marie Louise.

"Where are we going?" I asked.

"You said 'we,' " she said. "Did you notice?"

"You started it," I said.

"Well then we've both done it," she said, and picked a blade of grass and, stretching it between her thumbs, blew a plaintive note.

"Does that mean we're engaged?" I asked.

She blew another note and nodded, and her eyes smiled.

"And where do you suggest we should go from here?"

She dropped the blade of grass and sat gazing for a moment at the girls in their silk coifs, the garlands and the trumpets, the birch-trees and the dykes, all that long-tended countryside. "Paris!" she said.

When we arrived at the Gard du Nord she had 105 marks and I had 85. We squandered a fifth of the entire sum on an epoch-making meal and then took a tiny room in a hotel in the Rue de la Goutte d'Or which was used as a place of resort by the ladies of the town.

In the evenings I visited the shooting-booths on the Boulevard Rochechouart and won boxes of sweets as prizes, which I then exchanged for fried potatoes and fillets of herring in a *bistro*. We drank tap-water, and sometimes Marie Louise recalled that peasant wedding while I remembered dinner-parties in my house in the Hohenzollern Strasse in Berlin. Then we would laugh and go on foot to the Louvre. We argued endlessly.

"Why don't you want to buy the Botticelli frescoes for the hall of our villa?"

"They look too fragile, I think, if we're going to have all that Greek statuary in the garden. Besides, I shall have to save some money for a Watteau—for the bedroom, you remember."

"But Watteau's much too shadowy."

"And Boucher is too pink."

"And the Fragonards are not all quite proper."

"Well, that leaves us with Uccello. He's not so well known, so we ought to get him cheaper."

"I don't think I'd be able to sleep with all those spears about," said Marie Louise.

"Well, then, let's not decide today, and go and eat our herrings."

One can still live on the Louvre and go short of nothing. It was our church and our history-book, our theatre and our refuge. It taught us to study mankind and ourselves, filled us with love of the antique and scorn for Byzantinism; it taught us that this must be loved and that may be passed over, but that nothing must be hated. We drank it in, feeling that we must hoard it up within ourselves, since this time could not last for ever.

But all Paris was something to be lived on, a garden of living beauty in which one might store up substance for the lean years—the Tuileries gardens and the Luxembourg, the bridges over the Seine linking the garment of the sleeping city, the glowing windows of the Sainte Chapelle speaking a truer word for the union of Church and Monarchy than any poet ever wrote; and the homeliness of the cafés where the white-aproned figures of the waiters seemed to proclaim that only between one flourish of a dish-cloth and the next are we permitted to sit at the tables of this world.

"And then, they speak French," Marie Louise would add, but with a soberness in her grey eyes which showed that for her this was no joke.

Our money ran out and there was nothing for it but to return to Germany. We made a last pilgrimage, watching the sun rise from the Sacré Cœur and making our way slowly down through the crumbling houses of Montmartre to the boulevards, then we walked to the Luxembourg, passing the little Helvetia Hotel, where five years later we were to stay as political exiles. But it had no message for us then, and the poet Joseph Roth was not yet to be seen peering out through the windows of Foyot's. And who could conceive of political perils in the sunny tranquillity of the Luxembourg, amid the cries of children, with the toy boats sailing on the pond?

A week later we were in Berlin.

Berlin was no less tumultuous than Paris. That drugging apathy had not yet fallen over the city, through which nothing was to be heard but the tramp of marching feet, the menacing approach of the New Men. But there was a difference. The sense of form was lacking, the measure and the taste of Paris. Everything was exaggerated. Yet in that hectic climate it grew rich flowers of its own.

It had the best theatre in the world, with producers such as Reinhardt. The capital was creating little Berlins in all the larger provincial towns. *Hamlet* was played in modern dress, new truths were discovered in a whole series of modernised classics. Germany made no bones about cutting loose from tradition. Berlin campaigned against the Army. Max Pallenberg as the Good Soldier Schweik strutted across the stage at the Nollendorfplatz Theatre, mocking his sergeant-major. Broad-mindedness was in the air. It was a great time for satirists. The impressionists were more honoured than in any other European country, and Derain, Chirico and Leger were on show at Flechtheim's.

Translations of *Ulysses* and Dos Passos's *Manhattan Trans er* were published. A Dürer copper-engraving went for 42,000 marks at one of the crowded art-sales. Tolerance and earnestness of purpose were everywhere, and there was still no feeling of fear abroad: the cheap edition of Lenin's writings was as readily subscribed as the poems of Gottfried Benn.

Here, too, the café was a club where all worlds mingled—but the political know-alls were still shunned. A love of diversity characterised those circles which controlled the Berlin Press, its theatre and its publishing houses. There was a genial humanity in the literary cafés where the little street-wench waiting for custom might be sent the price of a drink, tactfully enclosed in a matchbox. One heard of people's ups and downs and did not dwell upon the major disasters, but something might be done to procure drugs for those who sorely needed them.

Never, in short, had Berlin been more human. All this was made possible by the momentary wealth procured by the Dawes Plan; but without that Attic salt which was in the blood of the Jews, and of Berlin, this wealth would never have been transformed into first-rate newspapers, a vital theatre and the humorous good-nature that was characteristic of the city at that time.

We arrived there in the autumn of 1929. We saw the star on the steeple of the Gedächtniskirche, the Ufa Palace and the famous Romanische Café, and we promised ourselves that we would make this our Paris. "And you'll promise faithfully, no politics?" said Marie Louise.

"What do I care for politics?" I said. "The autumn tints are all that I can see."

"And shoe-blacks and café-terraces and millions of girls!"

"In exchange for them you have all the literary types sitting in the cafés."

"I only want one—he wrote a book on Moses."

"And how many people in Berlin have read it? Here I shall have to write about orgies in cellars, and 'coke' addicts and broken marriages."

"No," she said. "Not the past but the present. Listen to what that man's singing."

A hunchback was standing in a doorway beside a pile of newspapers. He had a drum slung round his neck and beat it as he sang. I wanted to pass on,

I

but Marie Louise was intrigued by the peal of laughter, shrill as a trumpet-call, with which the man concluded each verse of his song. So I stood and listened.

> *A Communist, the silly tyke,*
> *Didn't know what Hitler's boys were like.*
> *In a Brown House he showed his head,*
> *And now the bastard's good and dead!*
> *Ha ha ha!*

It was a brutal welcome. I could not conceive of a news vendor like that in Paris. I looked to see what paper he was selling and saw that it was the one edited by Dr Goebbels, *Der Angriff*.

"Murder in broad daylight," I said.

Marie Louise turned furiously away.

"And he's a hunchback," she exclaimed.

But we were very soon sucked into the whirlpool of Berlin and German politics.

We went to the Romanische Café seeking only for distraction among its eccentric clientèle, many of whom were known to us; and the first person I saw was Gumbel, a fellow-writer, several of whose articles on German justice I had published in Nuremberg. He had a copy of a book with him, his own, entitled *Four Years of Political Murder*. Nothing could restrain me from examining it.

I turned the pages under his direction. There were certain things which I was curious to know about. Within a few minutes I was immersed in the book. I read that the murderer of Karl Liebknecht had suffered two years' imprisonment and that his accomplice had got off with a small fine. As for Rosa Luxemburg's murderers, one had been allowed to get away and the other had done two years. The officer responsible for the shooting of twenty-eight sailors had been imprisoned for three months in a fortress!

Gumbel was now talking to Marie Louise.

"If you're Heinrich Vogeler's daughter," he said, "then you must know plenty about it. Your village is full of the orphans of workers who were shot."

"There is no escape," said Marie Louise decidedly. "We must go and see Father."

She had not seen her father for some years owing to a domestic upheaval. We visited him the next day. He had remained a Communist. We had, indeed, intended to stay away from him. He lived in Britz, in one of the new blocks of flats, where space was wonderfully economised. You could not get a coffin in or out. "So we're forced to die on the barricades," he said.

Humour is the best way of breaking the ice. He and I soon became friends, and Marie Louise told me his story. In 1917 he had been an official war-artist attached to one of the general staffs, and while in this position had written a prophetic letter which had actually reached Ludendorff and the Kaiser. The letter described how Christ had appeared on the Potsdamer Platz preaching peace, and the commander of the Berlin garrison had had him arrested and secretly shot in the Moabit prison.

Vogeler had been put in a mental home, but had been released after the revolution. He had thrown open his big farmhouse to political agitators and idealists of all kinds, and his daughters had cooked for them; but after a time his wife had left him and had gone to live by herself in a cottage on the moor. Vogeler had then handed over his establishment to the *Rote Hilfe*, the Communist charitable organisation, and had gone to Berlin, where he was now living surrounded by "comrades" who always addressed one another as such. Among them was a young man named Bill Moll who also had a tale to tell.

At the end of the war, a vain and callow youth, Bill Moll had become a member of a gang of criminals. He had been posted to keep watch while other members of the gang had carried out a planned assault and robbery. The victim, a wealthy man, had died of heart-failure while they were tying him up, and the gang had bolted without troubling to tell their look-out man. He was still keeping watch when the police arrived and found both him and the dead body.

He was condemned to death for murder, but at the last moment the sentence was commuted to one of life imprisonment, and after he had served nine years a deathbed confession by one of the real murderers had led to his release. His first thought had been to go to Mexico, where there was a religious sect, worshippers of the Madonna, who lived a communal life. He had found something of the kind with Erich Mühsam, the father and protector of all prisoners of the republic. That is to say he had found a daily free meal, gladly offered. But he wanted more than this, and he was hoping that Vogeler would help him. Vogeler had to help a great many people.

We thought of ourselves as positive interlopers, since we had come asking for nothing. But then we discovered that we lacked a great deal, at least in the view of Vogeler and the comrades. For them, all people were parasites who played no active part in the movement of history; this was an unwritten law, a growing pressure which finally became moral blackmail.

To visit Paris, to write books or to paint flowers as Marie Louise did— these, in the eyes of the comrades, were positively shameful activities, and I made little impression by telling of my Berlin and Munich experiences. Millions were voting Communist—in May 1928 three and a half millions. I too must learn to change my views and make a fresh start—or did I consider that I had some special claim to be an onlooker?

Marie Louise warned me against all this. I never heeded her warnings, and all the great misfortunes in my life were due to this obstinacy.

"I saw it all happen in 1919," Marie Louise said, "when they sat round arguing in our farmhouse while we three girls did the work. They were too busy putting the world to rights to think of washing. They turned our garden, where Petri had given concerts, where Carl Hauptmann had rehearsed his plays and where Rilke had written some of his early poems, into a vegetable plot. I'm all in favour of a good vegetable garden for a house full of people, but still, men don't live only on vegetables. The hedges weren't trimmed any more, the carrots rotted in the rain and the lettuce went to seed. And we girls did nothing but work. There was a big walnut-tree which they wanted to cut down, and I asked them to spare it as a birthday present to me. But when I woke in the morning I heard the comrades sawing away! They aren't good or kind. Father has forgotten all that."

I took her to the May Day demonstration. What a year 1929 was! The winter had been a severe one, with the unemployed freezing to death in the back streets and on the steps of the underground. Industry had been "rationalised," and the coming of the conveyor-belt, and the upheavals attendant upon the relentless march of industrial progress, had filled the shelters for the homeless. A settlement proposed by the Wages Tribunal had been accepted by the unions but rejected by the employers, and 200,000 steelworkers were out in the streets, supported by miners whose working-hours had been cut down. The Tribunal had accordingly solved the problem by issuing revised terms, very much to the disadvantage of the workers. The president of the Tribunal was Severing, the Minister of Labour, himself a former steelworker.

Hatred grew, nourished by the Communists. In February 1929 there were 3,000,000 unemployed, and although many of these received state assistance it was a very beggarly dole. The Communists organised hunger marches and sought to bring about unofficial strikes, without success because the employers had got rid of the agitators in the factories and the unions were opposed to them. A new term came into use in the Vogeler circle—"Socialist-Fascists." By this they meant the Social Democrats, whom they accused of having betrayed the class-struggle. They had shown themselves incapable of turning such victories as the 1918 revolution, the Kapp *putsch* in 1920 and the defeat of the Cuno Government in 1923 to the advantage of the working-class. They were the victims of their own terrors and of the pressures brought to bear on Germany, some from outside the Reich. They had possessed neither the foresight nor the imagination to create new sources of employment. I personally suspected that they had no belief in their own principles and were not seriously attempting to use their power for the benefit of those who had elected them.

A hint of corruption always pervades the seats of power, to which the newly promoted are more susceptible than the members of a traditional ruling class. So it is understandable that in April 1929 a Berlin Chief-of-Police named Zörrgiebel, looking down into the street from his office-window, should have been visited by the dark thought that the masses might be overloud in clamouring for their rights on that First of May, which since Bismarck's time had been the accepted festival of the workers. No higher motive can be attributed to his decision to put an end to these demonstrations, in which the masses so commonly fall foul of the tribunes of the people, making unreason of democracy, as Coriolanus said. Certainly, when his pictures appeared in the newspapers after the tragedy, the coarse, bibulous face beneath a round, bald head, it was impossible to credit him with any particular subtlety of calculation or delicacy of scruple. Nor, probably, did he even want to upset anyone. He just wanted to be undisturbed and he wanted the thing that comes so easily to German minds—obedience!

The philosophic-minded may be disposed to argue that he wanted form as opposed to chaos, but it was really much simpler than that. Form is the Parthenon, the ultimate balance of weights and stresses. The simple-minded Zörrgiebel was nothing but a master telling his dog to lie down.

In short, an official edict went forth forbidding the traditional May Day demonstration. The Communists at once urged the workers to defy it. The historians are perfectly right who see this clash between the two left-wing parties as the beginning of Germany's drift into a fundamental disunity which Hitler was to resolve. We heard the words: "Lie down!" and were outraged.

Marie Louise and I left our attic-dwelling that morning and walked along the streets where we were accustomed to buy our household provisions.

"We won't think about the past," I said. "We'll just stick to everyday reality. We're in Berlin, and this is a street made for people to walk along. We aren't armed and we don't want to break any windows. In a hundred years we shall all be dead, but at this moment the people in the street want to march and feel that they are not alone and that their solidarity——"

"I hate that word," said Marie Louise. "It's too new. And I don't mind telling you I'd much sooner be walking along the Boulevard Rochechouart!"

I wanted to kiss her for those disarming words, but then the smile vanished from her face. She was looking over my shoulder at something hideous which changed everything and left no more room for jesting. I turned quickly and saw the police come storming down the street.

They looked like giants clad in blue-black. Perhaps it was sheer terror which caused them to appear in our eyes even larger than they were as they towered over the screaming, shabby crowd which ebbed away in a pitiful tide beneath the rise and fall of their truncheons. We heard no words amid the clamour around us; we only knew one thing, that they were wrong. And even today, now that I have cut loose from all party affiliations and political commitments, as I look back over my numerous errors and my short-sightedness, seeking for a truth that takes no account of my most deeply held desires, even now I know that it was no accident that, on that day, I was swept back into politics for a tumultuous decade.

Perhaps it was the horror in Marie Louise's eyes, the same horror that was to distort the faces of Jewish girls not many years later when they were dragged off to the gas-chambers. The horror of uniforms and executioners. The loneliness of the persecuted abandoned by God. There are a thousand things that might be said, but it makes no difference whether the executioner is German or Spanish, whether he wears Russian uniform or the trappings of the Church. Revolt against the misuse of force springs from God.

"I'm making myself a pepper-pistol," said Marie Louise with a quiver in her voice two days later.

She was hollowing out two sticks of bamboo in the manner of the youths of Bali, who shoot birds with them. There was nothing of violence in her voice or in her fragile-seeming face with its new, tense expression; neverthe-less, she had encountered violence, and with all the sturdiness of her peasant nature she was making ready to defy it. She did so throughout her life, which was overfilled with harsh experience, until she came to engage upon the last battle with death. The pepper-pistol was placed in her coffin.

By the third of May "peace and order" had been restored, or so the announcement ran: a typical piece of officialese, for only the twenty-five dead were at peace, and the bullets of the police had provoked feelings of profound disorder among the workers. Thirty seriously wounded people lay in hospital.

Police headquarters in the Alexanderplatz, which had been responsible for the lamentable order to shoot, was crowded with men and youths charged with having provoked the police by attacking them. Smashed rifles were the only exhibits produced in evidence—there were no dead policemen.

"The demonstrators seem to have been remarkable shots," said the Press sardonically; "all they managed to do was to blow off the butts of their own rifles." But no amount of jesting could obscure the memory of that fateful First of May. Claims for compensation for injury received were officially re-jected as "political agitation."

And the workers were divided into the rival factions of embittered Communists and hesitant Social Democrats. The Swastika was the real victor.

The Swastika was gaining steadily in strength, but we did not know it. Our eyes were dazzled with visions of a miracle, the victory of the underdog. Russia had a hypnotising effect upon us. There were films from Moscow showing the transformation of criminals into useful citizens, not by punishment but by arousing their civic conscience. The staff of Moses smote the rock and the water flowed.

I wanted to know more, above all about mankind in the state of uttermost abjection, those whose days and nights were passed in prison-cells. I went to Britz in search of Bill Moll, the young man who had been recently discharged from prison, and invited him to visit us.

He came and talked, and as I listened to him our attic in the Detmolder Strasse seemed to become a prison cell, so that I was quite startled when Marie Louise crept quietly in and put food on the table. Bill ate as though he were half-starved, and suddenly he jumped up and went out and did not return for several hours. He had walked for miles, simply for the sake of feeling that he was no longer in prison. Were there any stars? No, he had seen no stars, and anyway they meant nothing. You could see stars between the bars of a prison-cell, but they were a mockery, and to hell with them.

He jeered at all such conventional fancies and I was infected by his passion of feeling. I remember how one evening he brought me a copy of the printed regulations issued to prisoners. I think this was when my prison novel was born. The preamble read as follows:

> You are now a prisoner. The iron bars over the windows of your cell, the locked door and the colour of your clothes all serve to remind you that you have been deprived of your freedom. *God* could no longer suffer you to misuse your liberty with sin and evil deeds. So He has said to you, "So far and no farther! . . ."

I looked at Bill, his youthful, somewhat distorted face that bore the imprint of the death-sentence. God had spoken falsely; Bill had been innocent. No one could have put that head back, once it had fallen. Would they all, executioners, judges and gaolers—and God!—go on their knees before the dripping blood and confess that it was not so simple? That chaos prevailed and injustice, confused cases and muddled decisions? That only One was right, He who had torn the judge's robes off them—"He that is without sin among you, let him cast the first stone!"—would they admit it?

I allowed God to rise again, I bent and helped Him; I needed Him if I was not to be overwhelmed by the melancholy that assailed me as I thought about these matters. But I resolved to try to show that the root of the evil was contained in those words printed in the prison regulations. This was the cancer in the body politic, this arrogance and effrontery, this moralising in the name of God, when the true attitude towards crime and punishment must be one of humility and the desire to understand.

Marie Louise said to me:

"Bill still has the taint of the prison-cell. Are you so attracted by the smell of suffering?"

She said it without reproach but with a hint of warning in her voice, as though she foresaw whither it would lead me.

For me it was an act of self-liberation. I shed the symbol which I had acquired from Rilke during the war-years. The wall was no longer an allegory of God and Death, of human despair and the barricades. It became something precise and concrete, the walls of all the prisons in which countless men were separated from mankind, the thoughtless product of a dubious morality, the easy way out. And the prisons stank of sweat and urine, of whitewash and rotting food, of brutality and loneliness, and overbearing judges and nights in the condemned cell.

I was not prone to Utopian ideas; I did not look for easy panaceas or for judges Solomonic in their wisdom. But if, as I came to realise from my visits to the criminal courts, it was hard to find the humane and merciful judges called for by the sickness of our time, at least the individual might be put on his guard against that complacency which is at the root of arrogance. This was the message I wished to impart. The reader must be made to stop and think whenever he encountered the words, "They deserved it." I wanted to bring about a pause before the condemnation—that salutary moment in which men recollect their own shortcomings. Nothing sensational, but a small shocked pause; not comfortable humility but a striving after truth and the renunciation of self-righteousnesss.

"I hadn't done a thing," Bill would say to me when he told some story of prison intrigues and punishments.

I came to realise more and more that men were shaped by their background. The only solution was to create a better environment. But before this could be done the lies and the hypocrisy must be disposed of. That was the first task.

I set about it in a loosely constructed novel which I called *Water, Bread and Bullets*. What was important in it was not the account of a suppressed mutiny in a modern prison. We have had more dramatic accounts of that sort of thing, particularly in films—the length of piping used as a weapon, the warders made hostage, and in the end the white flag. But in my story the flag of surrender was red, not white. Every line of it was a protest.

After passing many evenings with Bill Moll I had come to share both his bitterness and his recalcitrance. The book was not written at the instance of any political party. I did not greatly like it. I was tricked into an excessive dogmatism, carried away by my desire to get to the heart of the matter like one of those tiny human figures on Notre Dame in process of being swallowed up by monsters. But in my own mind I was a crusader. I stormed white-faced out of the prison-cell uttering my cry of protest, and herein perhaps lay my state of dangerous blindness. A short passage will serve to show what I mean. The book included a savage analysis of the Christmas story. One of the prisoners carves a model of the holy crib and stands smiling at it. Whereupon he is addressed by the scowling and heavy-handed author as follows:

"There is nothing for you to smile at. Who smiles at the sight of a half-frozen child? Who does not know that straw is no bedding for a newly born infant? Can anyone grin when a helpless human creature is born into a world of cold and dirt?

"Does any prisoner smile at the political implications of this fable, or rejoice in the spectacle of the three old men with crowns, lying on their stomachs?

"There are lies that are wonderfully long-lived. How long is it since kings made obeisance before the children of the poor, bringing gold and precious stones? What is the reality?"

My friend Attikah Wertheimer, a leading art-historian at the Prinz-Albert Museum, read the first draft of the book. He liked it as a whole, but this passage caused him to wrinkle his high forehead.

Wertheimer opened a book of mediaeval madonnas that he had brought with him. He turned over the pages while I listened to the voice of a newsboy shouting in the street, "The Sklarek brothers loot Berlin!" The Sklareks were Jewish profiteers.

Marie Louise was seated behind a screen by the window painting a miniature which she would not let anyone see. Wertheimer turned over the pages until he came to Jan van Eyck's Rolin Madonna.

For a moment I weakened. I was filled with a longing to lose myself in the enchanted river-landscape of the painting and forget all else—the dark cell and the executioner's block, the abortion laws and the unemployed men's suicide, the procession of the homeless, the red flag, the helpless Ministers, the bawling Nazis and the heedless priests, and even the half-starved children of Neukölln and Barmbeck.

But it would have been desertion. Knowing that behind the screen Marie Louise was painting one of her small miracles, I repeated with a greater emphasis what I had said in my book:

"That sort of thing is treacherous. Even if it was once true, it's a lie in these days. It distracts one's thoughts from the things that have to be done. It's immoral because its very piety corrupts and smoothes the edges of the class-war. No one must fold his hands, hands that can be used."

Marie Louise coughed slightly behind the screen. Was I talking too loud? Did she think that I was drowning a nobler voice?

Not until evening did she emerge from her hiding-place, and then she left the room without a word. I found a sheet of paper on her table bearing a line from St Matthew, "Man shall not live by bread alone, but by every word that proceedeth out of the mouth of God."

Beside it lay a copper plate on which a madonna was engraved, smiling against a background of flowers beneath a crescent moon.

The next day I apologised.

"I know you didn't really mean it," said Marie Louise consolingly, "and your book ends wonderfully."

She began to quote and I was astounded that she should know so much by heart:

"Who will rid us of this state of mind and the world it belongs to, which condemns instead of helping, sacrificing the thousands to its doctrine of expiation, and safeguarding nothing but the property of the over-fed? . . . Who will tear down the prison-house and for ever renounce the scorning of the weak?"

She was standing by the window of our single room staring into the thick fog outside—a fog in which hungry figures prowled, some to become thieves by morning. Why did I inflict all this misery on Marie Louise? I ought to be earning money to take her to the south, where a blue tide would wash the sea-weed round her feet and there would be the scent of oleanders in the morning. Why compose jeremiads which no one wanted to print? (We had been waiting for weeks to hear from Kiepenheuer, the publisher.)

"After all," she said—and not for the first time she had a surprise in store which was to lead to a new phase in our lives—"it's all in the Bible already. That's why I find you odd. But I love your book because you suffered as you wrote it. You did truly feel yourself one of the prisoners."

"I still do," I said.

"It will make people see a lot of things—the stupidity of capital punishment, the arrogance of judges, the——"

"It'll probably end up in the wastepaper basket," I said bitterly.

"But now you've served your sentence," Marie Louise went on, "we'll go to the south and stay a long time—somewhere where they eat *bouillabaisse*."

I kissed her hand, pierced by the gallantry with which she made light of our penniless state. There were tears of frustration in my eyes.

And then she said:

"Kiepenheuer rang up a little while ago. He wants to publish the book, and he'll pay an advance. Aix-en-Provence was the place I had in mind."

A last breathing-space was granted us. Madame Vieille-Tessier let us have the cottage in the park of the Château Noir where Cézanne had housed his canvases while he returned to his eminently respectable home in Aix in the evenings. The air was heavy with the scent of resin and lavender. The song of the crickets would sometimes cease abruptly in a strange and sudden pause that was like the onset of eternity, and in the silence one could hear the tapping of a woodpecker or the screech of a jay.

The carpet of pine-needles drowned the sound of every footfall, including that of worn boots dragging over the pavements of Berlin.

Marie Louise painted. She portrayed in miniature landscapes of moss, like Dürer's *Rasenstück*, the secret stir and growth of the grasses, the thrusting of the buds and intertwining of the roots; pictures pervaded with the sense of the timelessness of spring which made it easy for me to forget that I had brought her to this golden world by means of a novel about prisons.

"This is a place where life is tidied up," she said, "and I have a surprise for you that will prove it."

She led me through a pinewood named Paradou to a place where the trees opened out and the green expanse of a pool lay before us. The keeper of the dykes was a man of neat appeararance, although everything about him proclaimed the true peasant. He caught a carp for us, cooked a rabbit in lavender and rosemary, and gave us slices of golden melon. Then Marie Louise nodded to him and he said without preliminaries:

"I was wounded twice, once at Verdun and then on the Chemin des Dames."

The words gave me a slight shock.

"A German blew up the blockhouse at the point of the salient, but we used gas and finished him off, and half-an-hour later I got another wound in the chest. I didn't wait to be discharged from hospital, I went out over the wall and came down here and hid among the ridges of Mont Saint-Victoire." A note of affection crept into his voice and he glanced towards a sturdy, dark-haired peasant-woman who was cleaning a drawn fowl at the spring. "She brought me food and kept me going for two years. The gendarmes were looking for me and once they followed her up into the hills, but she led them such a dance that in the end they got stuck in a place where they couldn't get down and she had to fetch help to rescue them. After that they left us alone. Goodness always works in the end, but sometimes you have to ram it down people's throats the way you fatten a goose for Christmas."

I couldn't say anything then, but later I told him about the wall and that it was I who had blown up the pill-box. A light shone in his eyes, and presently he went into the house and came out with a volume of Mistral's poems in which he had written, "*A mon frère qu'ils ont poussé à me tuer—Amitié toujours.*"

Marie Louise gave him a water-colour beneath which she had written, "*Il n'y a plus de mur.*"

The three of us embraced one another, but the dark-haired woman, his wife, was too shy to join in the kissing. She gave Marie Louise a bunch of garlic and a jar of green olives.

Following this episode we lived for another six months in our Provençal paradise.

It was 1931. We visited Avignon, and Marie Louise made copies of the Gobelins in the papal bedchamber while I became absorbed in the ancient history of the Palace of the Popes and the schism in the Catholic Church.

I stood one evening near a church overlooking the famous bridge and watched a girl coming up the hill towards me. As she approached me she drew back her low-cut blouse, offering a bare breast, and said, "*Viens, cheri, tu souffriras quelque chose de très bon.*" I was fascinated by her use of the verb *souffrir*, but before I could make any reply a priest came out of the church, saw us both and chased her away with a peremptory gesture. She paused in her retreat and turned to say vindictively that she knew what he was after, but it wouldn't be any use his looking for her in the town.

I was profoundly shocked by this hint of a secret understanding, and without looking at the priest I walked down the hill. An oppressive heat lay over the town, rendered more intolerable by the gusty blowing of the mistral. Everything seemed fluid, eyes stung by wind and dust saw strange distortions, and there was a sort of whimpering in the air, like that of animals, which vanished when one wiped away the sweat to see.

An old woman lit a red lamp and hung it on an iron bracket. I was thinking of the lordly gesture with which the priest had waved the girl away, and suddenly I stumbled over an empty tin which a gust of wind had sent rolling along the narrow side-street. At the same moment a sheet of newspaper blew against my face. I took hold of it and was about to throw it away when I noticed a cartoon of a priest, furtive but with a grin on his face, creeping into a house adorned with just such a lantern as the one that was now swinging wildly in the wind only a few yards away from me.

I looked round for a café, but finding none, went on towards the mediaeval ramparts separating the town from the river-valley, still with the sheet of newspaper in my hand. I went out under the nearest archway and sat down amid the waving grass near the broken bridge, and here, with the rush of the river in my ears and by the light of a hanging lamp, I read the tale of an unhappy priest who on his way to Lourdes had deserted his flock in Paris to visit a brothel, where he had suddenly dropped dead of heart-failure. It was a true story, tragi-comical and painful. Why did I not throw the paper away?

"This is something you must write!" an inner voice said to me. Then I heard the sound of a cough. A Senegalese with a smooth, proud face was standing beside me. The girl had sent him, he said, in case he should be what I was looking for rather than herself. I did not laugh, but I jumped hastily to my feet before he started to take his clothes off.

The wind was growing stronger. I clung to the soldier's arm and drew him back into the town. At the open window of the first dust-enveloped house we came to, a woman stood naked in the lamplight, combing her hair. At the far end of the street there appeared the figure of a priest (or did I dream it?) gazing cautiously about him to vanish like a nervous animal.

What had come over me? There was a flash of lightning, and I saw the white teeth of my Senegalese gleaming in a smile. I gave him some money and turned in the direction of the Palace of the Popes.

I started writing that same night. The story was to be of Pan's assault upon the guardians of morals, uncomplicated by religious problems. Or so I thought; but then I put myself in the place of Pan under the name of Leon, the doubting pupil of an abbot, confused, before he leaves the monastery, by the clash of Heaven and earth. He goes to the colonies, sides with the natives in a breach of the law and pays for it by being sent to Devil's Island. Finally, he returns to Avignon, to be reunited with a friend of his youth, Anatole, who in the meantime has become secretary to the Bishop, on the same evening that he finds a dead priest in a brothel. He uses the startling discovery to provoke a state of turmoil in the town, setting churchgoers against free-thinkers and bringing about a quarrel between the Bishop and Anatole; and finally he stages a mock-miracle, supposedly the resurrection of the dead.

The thing was a satire, the most vigorous I ever wrote, a mordant fantasy on the theme of religion and morality. I was proud of it and grateful to Avignon for having inspired it. When it was finished I went with the free-thinkers on a propaganda tour of France, in particular to advocate the cause of Franco-German friendship. I wrote a comedy about a church with a fraudulent reputation for miracles which was accepted by one of the small theatres controlled by the Berlin Staatstheater. I felt a sort of tight-lipped pleasure in thus assailing the Church of my childhood—was it the pride of Lucifer? But it may be said that my novel was not wholly destructive. It contained a foreshadowing of the "worker-priests" who were to startle the French about 1950.

"Those who share the sufferings of the people," said my Leon, "have no need to wear skirts. Any kind of uniform destroys the spirit."

I returned from my propaganda tour to rejoin Marie Louise in the cottage in the park, which looked more overgrown with creepers than ever. I wanted to send off the manuscript of my book and asked her, quite casually and taking her approval for granted, what she finally thought of it.

She shook her head and said: "Wouldn't you rather burn it?"

I leapt to my feet, and she ran to me and kissed me—"I didn't really mean that."

"What do you honestly think?" I asked.

She began to pace up and down the little room and there ensued one of those debates which I like to call "telegraph-wire conversations." One watches the telegraph-wires from the train, the way they seem to be forever on the point of coming together but never do, except for a fleeting instant when they are united by another telegraph-post.

She said: "The book has turned into a public confession."

I said: "It will turn into a best-seller."

She: "Will anyone be any the better for it?"

I: "We shall be able to live better."

She: "There's a great deal of vanity in Rousseau's *Confessions*."

I: "But I've written objectively. I had St Augustine in mind."

She: "The best-seller of the moment is a book called *Mein Kampf*."

That was a telegraph-post. Suddenly, there was Germany, which we wanted to avoid.

I said: "We can go back."

She said: "I'm afraid we must go back."

I: "One loses one's sense of reality abroad."

She: "This isn't abroad for us. Cézanne loved this cottage."

I: "He was the son of a well-to-do family in Aix."

She: "He was an artist just as you are."

I: "If it's a best-seller I'll buy you this cottage."

She: "And I'll paint a picture for you every month."

I: "John XXII said, 'How can a man rest happy in paradise . . .' "

She: ". . . while in Berlin thousands of people are putting their heads in gas-ovens and there are six million unemployed."

Another telegraph-post. I looked at the manuscript and asked, suddenly very uncertain: "Shall we send it?"

She said: "Of course. It would be a crime to do nothing with it."

"Besides we only have enough money for another month."

She sighed. "And even in paradise tomatoes have to be paid for."

"Do you think we shall still like Berlin?"

"We can both go on the dole."

The third telegraph-post. We went together to the post office to send off the manuscript. And in a Marseilles newspaper we read that Hitler, the Austrian, had got himself appointed to the traditional office of "Gendarm" of the small town of Hildburghausen, and had thus become a German citizen. He was going to present himself as a candidate for the Chancellorship of the Reich.

A few weeks later we had a letter from Berlin to say that the book was accepted. There were one or two points regarding its final revision to be discussed. Another letter contained a cheque and also my publisher's proposal that I should become his reader. The sales of the prison novel had passed the ten-thousand mark, and one of the book societies had chosen it. Fortune had descended upon us overnight.

"Shall we buy the cottage?" asked Marie Louise.

"But of course."

She looked at me and said, "Thank you. *Tu es charmant*." Then she went into the next room and began to pack. Three days later we arrived in Berlin.

The city was in a state of fever. Battered and bloodstained corpses were deposited nightly at the doors of the police stations, sometimes bearing the insignia of the Reichsbanner, the Republican private army, sometimes the star of the Communists, sometimes the Swastika, sometimes simply a policeman's number. But there were even more dead bodies that bore no bloodstains and wore no insignia but only the imprint of despair, that pale-green shade which gas imparts to the skins of those who die by it.

We lived in a block of flats which had been built with the aid of a State subsidy and was reserved for the use of artists and writers. It was cheap, but scarcely one of the occupants was able to pay his rent; neither salaries nor the earnings of the so-called free professions were adequate. Many of the apartments contained no furniture other than a mattress on the floor. People ate their meals off packing-cases covered with newspaper. But none starved; each man helped his fellow, and those in need went from one door to the next, knowing by instinct where someone had found work and there was a little bacon or cheese to be had.

There were still publishers in those days who, if they believed in an author, were prepared to take the risk of paying him a monthly allowance so that he might work in security. I was lucky enough to have secured such an allowance in addition to my reader's salary, and the first royalties on my prison novel would soon be coming. But to live surrounded by universal poverty and hardship was to become readily receptive to a revolutionary creed. There is no need for any involved, ideological explanations of my reasons for joining the Communist Party. It can all be summed up in a sentence—"Things can't go on like this!"

The open-handedness of the artists, however traditional it may appear, had really very little to do with the *vie de Bohème*; it was more like the unwritten law of bondsmen living in the expectation of war. Private life and privilege were dishonourable at a time when tens of thousands were on the verge of starvation. That the Berlin artists and intellectuals were among the first to realise this was not merely because they were themselves affected, but because they possessed the imagination to do so.

The National Assistance Board announced that 7,000,000 Germans were receiving assistance from the winter-aid fund, the *Winterhilfe*. The State was doing something, but its means were scanty, and in the hungry nights the dream of a saviour was growing in men's mind. Since the Churches had nothing to offer, eyes were turned to those who most loudly proclaimed the way of salvation, the Communists and the supporters of Hitler. Although they differed only in the amount of money they disposed of for propaganda, both talked in a high moral tone; and so both attracted idealists who were rapidly transformed into partisans filled with hatred for the other creed. There could be no understanding between them, and none was ever sought.

The Communist cell established in our block of flats—the *Zelle Künstler-block*, as it was designated—knew where its equivalent Nazi group held its meetings in the Schöneberg quarter, which streets it controlled, and when it might be expected to make trouble at Communist meetings. The things that went on during those months did nothing to relieve the general misery or to affect the overall political picture; it was a matter of taking up strategic positions and preparing for the struggle that was to come. This was the purpose of both sides, and there was on both sides, among the rank-and-file Nazi storm-troopers and the Communist red-front fighters, a sacrificial belief in the justice of their own cause.

But there can be no doubt that things were a great deal easier for the storm-troopers. They were more free to use their weapons, thanks to the leniency of the judges, most of whom favoured Hitler long before he came into power. The red-front men could be sure of receiving harsh prison-sentences if an opponent was killed, while villas in wealthy quarters of the town afforded hiding-places to the storm-troopers. Like the Caesars of old, the new despots had a fatherly feeling for their bodyguards. The Communists had to console themselves with the thought that martyrdom was always a part of the ancient Christian creed from which, however distorted, their Socialist doctrine had sprung.

I was organising secretary of our artists' cell and had to see that the Party orders were carried out. I took charge of all the weapons which our members acquired, either by smuggling or as booty in street-fights. It was a Party slogan that no "individual" terror must be exercised, the use of the word implying that the Party would not be opposed to mass-terror, and even the public erection of the guillotine, when the time came. It was a childish and rather humiliating form of self-deception, but these finer points did not trouble the Party leadership. Nor were they quite honest in their condemnation of acts of violence. Their private instructions did not always correspond to the principles proclaimed in the Communist newspaper, *Die Rote Fahne*. But the official prohibition tended to discourage their troops, who were likely to find themselves abandoned for propaganda reasons if they got into trouble, and it drove many of the bolder spirits over to the side of Hitler.

I had no personal contact with the German Communist leaders and so had in the first instance no reason to mistrust them. I had heard Hitler speak at meetings, and also Goebbels, who from being the obscure disciple of Professor Gundolf had become the leading Nazi propagandist. I was not convinced by them, but I was impressed. They employed every device; they believed that the lie was justified; their methods were hysterical but shrewdly conceived, their appearances always dramatic. They struck an almost religious note and seemed to be attracting all the more dubious elements among the intellectuals. In fact, however, no writer of any standing went over to them.

They referred to us as Jews, which to us was no term of abuse, since we owed so much to the gifted minds of German Jews that Berlin without them was inconceivable.

The intellectuals wanted to go on acting, painting pictures, sitting in cafés writing articles—above all to be let alone and not told whom they might consort with.

Paradoxical as it may seem, it was this desire to be let alone which finally drove them to collective action. They hoped one day to regain the freedom to live private lives in an ordered community. But no one could remain isolated amid the thronging distress of the half-starved towns. When every town threatened to become a shanty-town the ivory towers tottered. Every suicide dragged out of a gas-filled room seemed to point a finger of accusation.

To avert one's head from the sour smell of hunger on a neighbour's breath was simply cowardice. In this Marie Louise was whole-heartedly on my side, fearless when stark need confronted her. She did not think in political terms, she was bored by my Socialist outpourings, and perhaps she secretly suspected us writers and thinkers of being partly responsible for the state of affairs. "It only fits where it touches," she would say of all our theorising.

When she saw that things were going beyond all bounds she plunged into activity. She was utterly without self-righteousness, unconcerned to argue about who was right and who was wrong. A hungry child meant simply that everyone was wrong, and then the only language that mattered was that of action. She would rise in her indignation as though rebuking God, and still

K

be as cool and steady-handed as a helmsman meeting the first gusts of a gale.

I was anything but cool-headed. With events rushing to their climax one needed to know how the attack would develop. Hitler had talked of modern literature as the scribbling of half-wits, and of modern art as garbage: "Those pre-historic stammerers like Chagall, those pitiful daubsters like Picasso, who should all be castrated." I knew there was the enemy and that I could expect no mercy from him.

I remembered a chance encounter with Julius Streicher during a visit to Nuremberg a few years before. I found his gross figure occupying the chair next to mine in a barber's shop. This was some time after he had served his prison-sentence, and I think he may never have realised that I had been concerned in that business. He was rather drunk. Growing confidential, he produced some photographs of naked girls and passed them over to me, saying that they were all girls who had slept with Jews but had come to their senses "in time" and were now his mistresses.

"What does 'in time' mean?" I had asked, and he instantly replied: "Before we twist the necks of all the Jews and bloody highbrows!" He dug me in the ribs with a leer. "You look like one yourself, but don't you worry, we'll do a bit of sorting out."

On the day when I applied for membership of the Communist Party—I was sponsored by a painter-friend of mine who said that I would have to enrol as a candidate because the Party needed to be convinced of the suitability of bourgeois members—I found myself thinking of Streicher. There would no longer be any question of sorting out where I was concerned. I was now definitely on the list of those destined for the long knives. I thought of that tubby figure, the repellent, leering face with the little pig's eyes, and was thankful that I was no longer neutral.

We stuck posters on the walls in the Berlin suburbs. We organised protest-meetings of penniless workers evicted from their tenements, and fed as many as we could in our small apartments to give them the feeling, if only for an afternoon, that someone cared what happened to them. We filled backyards and back-alleys on Sundays with the sound of our singing and with our inflammatory speeches. We helped the Red Front youths who came within our jurisdiction to sell their newspapers and to deal with the Nazi patrols who tried to drive them off the streets.

The scales were trembling and no one knew as yet on which side they would come down. The weary and aged Hindenburg was still President of the Reich. The Chancellor was a General who understood the gravity of the situation and realised the necessity for social reform. We regarded Schleicher as simply another "lackey of capitalism," as the current formula had it, but at least he left us in peace to prepare the revolution which alone could rescue the unemployed from the streets and put them back to work. We made ready for battle and came in the end to rejoice in our state of preparedness. It induced a feverish excitement in which everyday considerations were swept away.

We worked day and night, exposing scandals, putting forward demands, provoking newspaper attacks, agitating for the release of the imprisoned. Our lights burned into the small hours.

There was a rumour that our block of apartments had been converted into a fortress. In fact, a non-commissioned officer and four men could have cleaned the whole place up.

We held a cell-meeting on the 18th of January 1933, at which Hielscher, the nationalist, was the guest-speaker. We talked about Hindenburg. The decision whether Hitler or another man was to become Chancellor of the Reich rested with the old Field-Marshal. Many of us were sinking into a state of numbed indifference; the tension was very hard to bear. "Hielscher will explain everything," said the branch-secretary. Hielscher was standing by the bookshelves looking at the titles. He said abruptly: "The old man will *not* send for him. You don't realise how unshakeable a Prussian Field-Marshal can be. Besides, he pledged himself to abide by the constitution, and he has always done so."

The political leader of the cell was a tall and weedy aristocrat who was particularly strongly opposed to any dealings with the aristocracy. He stood up, holding a sheet of paper in his hand.

"I should like to read you something which throws light on Hindenburg," he said, and read as follows. " 'Germany has suffered grievous misfortunes. The splendid days of the Kaiser and his heroes are past. But the children who in this place sing *Deutschland über Alles*, these children will restore the ancient glories of the Reich. They will overcome the dread evil of revolution and live to see again that golden time of great, victorious wars.

" 'And you, the schoolmasters, have the task of educating the youth of the nation in this sense. I shall not live to see it. I shall be with God. But I shall look down from Heaven and rejoice and bless your deeds.' "

Hielscher had listened impatiently. He took a step forward and demanded: "Where did you get that rubbish? What's it all about?"

"It's part of a speech delivered by Hindenburg in Hanover in 1925, shortly before he became President," said our youthful political secretary. He went on in a voice of biting irony: "Does anyone here believe that the old man has changed since then? He'll turn out to be right—we shall go to war again. But that we should trust that blood-stained old war-horse for a single instant is sheer imbecility! When are you going to get rid of your idols? A Field-Marshal is a stuffed shirt, not a human being. And the man

who told us all these things in 1925, Professor Theodor Lessing, was driven
out of Hanover like a mad dog—just as we shall very soon be driven out of
Berlin! But you'll stay here, Hielscher, and be killed in the war, and the
old man will look down from Heaven and bless you, and God save the
Kaiser, Amen!"

During the following days we heard about a new scandal, that of the
"*Osthilfe.*" The State subsidies intended to help the hard-pressed landowners of East Prussia to put their estates in order had been squandered without any government supervision. Hindenburg's son had been among the
beneficiaries. The Nazis had suddenly unearthed the story.

How much would anyone dare to tell the old man? Would he relax his
principles to save his son and the family honour?

None of us intellectuals foresaw that this was the explosive charge that was
going to breach the ramparts. We merely distributed leaflets giving the
Communist version of the affair. But Hitler, more skilled in the arts of blackmail, moved into the Kaiserhof Hotel, near the Chancellery, so as to be on
the spot. General Schleicher was still at the Wilhelmstrasse—the great alter-
native. The convocation of the Reichstag was postponed till the 31st of
January.

Rumours poured into the editorial offices. No one knew what was really
going on. We expected to be suddenly called out into the street, and this
time the ministerial doors would go down as though they were made of cardboard.

The people in our action groups whom I encountered were all delirious
with excitement. Only those writers who had not joined in the daily battle
were alarmed and fully conscious of the danger. Kiepenheuer, the publisher,
told me that he had sent the proofs of my Avignon novel to an associated
publishing house in Holland. For the first time I heard the word "exile"
spoken. I thought them all disgusting cowards and hurried back to my
artists' colony, where at least we felt ourselves to be one with the hungry
millions whose hour had struck.

"They're talking about going into exile!" I cried to Marie Louise, who was
busy with her washing. She needed no further explanation.

"Paris is never exile," she said. "Shall I start packing?"

The news reached us that afternoon that Röhm, the leader of the Brownshirts, intended to hold a demonstration outside Communist Party headquarters. It was a deliberate provocation and any self-respecting Government would have taken steps to prevent it, if only for the sake of its own
prestige. This Government, however, was in the last stages of dissolution.
All that remained was to turn the equivocal Schleicher out of the Chancellery

and bring pressure to bear on the Old Man, two trifling hindrances, and then the mounting tide could engulf everything. But possibly the sound of 15,000 marching boots would move the enemy to take up the challenge: he would set up his machine-guns in the windows of the Karl Liebknecht House and mow down a few hundred, and the rest would advance over the corpses to destroy him, and so it would be a good, old-fashioned revolution just like the ones in the history-books.

I am sure that this was the kind of thing Ernst Röhm had in mind. Brutes of his type need the smell of danger to stimulate their glands. I saw him that afternoon in the Bülow Platz, standing on his rostrum gazing with quivering nostrils at the tightly breeched bottoms of his marching troops (he only looked at them after they had gone past) and then looking across the square at the blank windows of the Communist building, behind which nothing stirred.

The Party leadership had vacated the premises. Having failed to rally the workers and surround the house with a protective wall, and being secretly persuaded of their own defeat, Thälmann and the members of the Central Committee had shut up shop and gone home. Indeed, some had already gone into hiding.

The Party leaflets which were circulated on the following day talked about "the lamentable failure of the Nazi provocation," and once again summoned the people to revolt, while at the same time they condemned all "acts of terrorism." Never in a time of extreme social upheaval was a great popular movement afflicted with such ineffective leaders.

A secret order had in fact been sent out summoning the "people" to converge on the Karl Liebknecht House. If enough had turned up, a hundred thousand or so, the police cordon could have been brushed aside and we could have filled our square and forced Röhm to withdraw.

But those of us who obeyed the order amounted to perhaps five hundred, drawn from fifty different Communist cells, reinforced by a few hundred unemployed workers who were drifting about the streets, embittered and half-starved, and ready to try anything against the well-fed Brownshirts. At the first police charge, which drove us out of one of the side-streets, I received a heavy blow from a rubber truncheon on the shoulder. I still believe that it was sent by providence to open my eyes. I staggered into a nearby house, shut the door behind me and stood for a long time with my shoulder throbbing, feeling that once again I had been betrayed, but on a far bigger scale than in the days of Liebknecht's death and Munich.

After twenty minutes or so I left the house. There were police about, but they let me pass; I was alone and therefore of no importance. I passed by the Volksbühne Theatre, where my play was due to have been produced at about that time.

I went on to the Wilhelmstrasse, where my publishers' offices were, but they were closed. I wandered on down to the river embankment and gazed at the Trade Union Building, which was also the headquarters of the Free Thinkers Association, on behalf of which I had once toured France. The Association had three million members. How many members did the trade-union movement possess? It had triumphed in the past over Ludendorff, over Kapp and over Cuno. I read the legend on a placard: *Alle Räder stehen still, wenn dein starker Arm es will*—"Every wheel will cease to turn if your strong arm wills it so." But where was the strong arm? The place was as empty as though it were a public holiday. I visited one of the officials. "We'll let him come into power," he said, meaning Hitler. "In six months he'll have cooked his own goose."

The 28th of January marked the end of that grotesque period. I went to see friends and found among them Dewald, an out-of-work actor. He had been to the "Green Week," a yearly agricultural exhibition, and as I had also received an invitation I asked him to tell me about it. He blew out his cheeks, rounded his stomach and screwed his monocle into his eye. "Splendid show!" he said, posturing. "Most distinguished gathering. Minister of Food and everyone. Doubtless his last public appearance. 'The smaller domestic breeds are gaining ground,' he said. True enough. True everywhere. Thanks to the Socialists. But we'll soon be changing all that. We shan't put up with General Jellybelly much longer. The Right Honourable Gentleman also spoke of the great longing of the masses to return to Nature. Meaning allotments. We need a million more of them. Splendid if it gives people something else to think about. Trouble is, they will sit about among the cabbages reading the *Rote Fahne*. They get above themselves. Grow too many vegetables and don't eat enough bread—bad for the millers. However, everything will soon be different. Good, I thought, now he's going to tell us about the *Osthilfe*; but instead we had the national anthem and the tour of inspection. Reporters everywhere, including a disgusting lot of Jews. They should have had the sense to clear out by now. Fourteen years of Marxism, and now it's over."

Dewald then stopped imitating a Prussian Junker and adopted another style. He pulled a lock of hair down over his forehead.

"My patience is exhausted!" he screamed. "I shall be the first Chancellor in history with a beetle under his nose! My kiss-curl will mesmerise the German people. The pouches under my eyes will become the new ideal of manly beauty. My lumpy chin will be a symbol of the will-power with which I shall change the face of Europe and the world. I shall brush aside the insignificant general who dares to stand in my path! The Socialists will creep back into their holes while the Communists distribute protest-leaflets from house to house. I tolerate no opposition!" screamed Dewald in the monotonous but hysterical tone of the Führer. "There is no proletariat, I have sent it to Moscow. There are only the German people, and they will follow me into the blackest pit, for they are true and recognise their master and like having their bottoms kicked. This Schleicher has already been nearly two months at the helm, in the place where I should be standing. What does he think he's playing at? Perhaps he'd like to do a deal with the Communists! But I'll wring his flabby neck and before a week is past there'll be one general the fewer and a great leader in the Wilhelmstrasse, I swear it by my kiss-curl and my beetle!"

The telephone rang. Dewald picked up the receiver and listened. He nodded once or twice and hung up. He looked suddenly older and said:

"Schleicher has resigned. Hitler's the new Chancellor."

He hurriedly brushed the lock off his forehead. He gave us an apprehensive glance, as though he expected us to strike him dead.

The weather forecast stated: "The shrinkage of the high-pressure area over Central Europe continues. The temperature in East Prussia has risen several degrees."

"It sounds plausible," grinned Dewald. "Central Europe is shrinking and the Prussian Junkers are thawing out."

The leading article in the *Berliner Tageblatt*, the Ullstein paper, said sombrely:

"Never was the very existence of the Reich so threatened as it is today."

At seven that evening I stood with a young Communist woman-journalist among the dense crowd outside the Chancellery. I had a small automatic in the pocket of my winter overcoat. As I stared up at the balcony a dangerous thought came to me—"In Paris I shot for prizes to exchange for food. What could I get here by shooting? Death and a place in history!" I shifted the automatic for greater safety to my hip-pocket.

Goering's paunchy figure appeared at an open window, and from a tree above us a man yelled, "Long live the Chief of the Luftwaffe!" The torchlight-procession of storm-troopers and Stahlhelm formations went marching past.

The young journalist and I exchanged glances from time to time as we stood hemmed in by the crowd. Marianne had been editress of a highly successful weekly for working women, and hundreds of thousands of readers had enjoyed her counsel, her understanding and her humanity. But if at this moment someone were to strike her to the ground, no more than a ripple would pass through the ranks of her countless readers. "As bad as that, is it?" they would say, hastily throw her last number into the dustbin and meekly go with the tide.

The shouting became a roar. Adolf Hitler had appeared at another window. He raised his hand in the Nazi salute and bowed several times in a hurried, perfunctory way. Around us all arms were raised except our own, and someone shouted: "Look, the Communists are here too!" But no one attacked us. They were flushed with victory, ready to be indulgent to two insignificant people who had come to witness the dawning of a golden age. Hitler withdrew into the brightly lighted house. "And where might *our* leaders be?" Marianne murmured in my ear. There was a look of unutterable despair in her eyes, despite the sardonic twist of her mouth.

BOOK THREE

8. The Bread of Exile

OVER the radio I heard the news of the Reichstag fire—the Reichstag where in 1919 I had defended the republic of Ebert and Scheidemann against the Spartacists. It had been our barracks in those days—in time of revolution you make use of any building that stands empty. Down in the cellar I had discovered a door to a disused passage communicating with the official residence of the President of the Reichstag. I had barricaded it against an eventuality that never arose. It had remained blocked, its existence forgotten, until . . . Until yesterday, perhaps, now that Goering, the new President of the Reichstag, occupied the official residence. This was certainly a way by which the incendiaries could have entered.

I wondered; and I wondered who would print this interesting speculation. At all events, I had to see the burning building.

I stood with a cluster of people near the Peace-Columns, staring at the Reichstag cupola, from which smoke was still rising. A man began to read aloud from a newspaper. According to the official account, a Bulgarian had set fire to the building, a Dutchman had been caught and a German deputy had been arrested. Or perhaps a carrier-pigeon had dropped a lighted torch on the roof, or a bat, or a Jewish buzzard! I walked sadly away.

In the afternoon I visited my friend Herbert Korth. He let me stay, and on the following afternoon we were visited by a certain Dr Pagel, whose wife made inconceivably fragile figurines of Oriental princesses out of wax.

Pagel had announced the moment he entered that the Communists were responsible for everything. He was rather drunk. Suddenly he pulled off his leather belt and, using it as a noose, tried to strangle me with it. Hitherto we had been on the friendliest terms. He could even quote some of my poems by heart. But he had never liked it when, in obedience to Party orders, I joined in street demonstrations. "You let yourself be dictated to by people you know nothing about—they may not even exist!" And now he thought that events had proved him right. Where was the left-wing Führer? The leaders had not shown themselves, and I had been driven into hiding in the studio of a milk-drinking poet with a cough. Was it this that had goaded him to a sudden frenzy? The question occurred to me during the instants in which I was turning blue in the face. Then the poet came to my rescue, shouting in a voice of thunder that no one had ever heard him use before.

Pagel recoiled in terror and I was able to get free. I snatched the belt and flung it out of the window, and then found myself praying that no SA man was passing below. They were already constantly on my mind.

"He's *my* guest," said Korth to Pagel, "not yours!"

"I forgot," said Pagel, and then told us what had happened to him. We understood everything by the time he had spoken a dozen words.

"Some of the Nazi boys fetched me down into a cellar last night. There was a half-naked man lying on the floor, a 'red swine,' so they said. They had been beating him up and he was bleeding. His heart was weak. I've never seen such wounds. I said that if they only wanted me to bring him round so that they could start hammering him again I wouldn't touch him, but they laughed and said I could take him away with me if I liked. I gave him an injection and hoisted him over my shoulder. When I got him up the stairs I found that they all had their motor-cycle engines running outside. 'Are you going after others?' I asked. It doesn't do to ask too many questions. 'We've got the next-door cellar jammed full,' one of them answered. 'The engines cover their idiotic screams.'"

Pagel looked at me. "That's what things have come to, thanks to your lot!" he said. It was scarcely logical, but I felt it deeply.

I went out and wandered again through the town, looking for the Berlin I had known—it could not all have vanished overnight. Now that I was homeless I had an especial need of it, for Berlin, too, had always been in a sense homeless, adrift like a ship with a dragging anchor. It never stayed long in one place and it played at all the things it did. It made theatre of its theatre; it played at elections and revolutions, at fetishism and fantasy, at Freud and Reinhardt and charitable works and the aberrations of justice— and now it was playing at National Socialism.

I passed the Scala music-hall, where six months before I had watched in astonishment while Rastelli, that acrobat of genius, did his morning work-out. Across the street a porter in a resplendent uniform was sweeping the doorway of the Eldorado. This was where the chaotic polyglot world had forgathered to drink and dance and pursue its affairs of the heart, with the moustached sexologist, Magnus Hirschfeld, encouraging his patrons to go arrayed in whatever clothing best suited their disposition. Men had worn silver stars in their hair, women had worn beards; and as to what they wore in their hearts, this their raiment might disclose. They were as complex as they were primitive, making festivity of the misfortune that sundered them from the normal world. They had been tolerant of all things and peaceably disposed. Were they still? Cars belonging to SS leaders stood outside the door. Was the establishment being cleaned out and cleaned up? I saw a drunken man come out and it was the Chief of the Berlin police; behind him tripped Hanussen, the clairvoyant. I should not read so many newspapers, I reflected; then I might never have seen their photographs and could have mistaken them for common homosexuals.

A sort of orgy, certainly not notable for humour, was going on in official circles, a stampede of functionaries of all denominations, as eager to place their incompetence at the service of the new dispensation as any trollop to sell her flesh on the Tauentzienstrasse. It was like a panic-scramble for the boats aboard a sinking ship, riddled with intrigues as lethal as cyanide, denunciations as effective as a knife in the back. Men of worth and experience were cuffed out of posts in which they had honourably served to make way for the time-servers; the scientific work of years was abandoned at the pleasure of laboratory-assistants ready to lick the boots of the new masters, and able to point to a successful denunciation, or even a corpse, as evidence of their zeal. It was a time of ambushes and cloak-and-dagger stratagems, and hordes of novices and amateurs rose to the surface of Berlin life. I watched it happen until the day when I met Erich Franzen.

I had gone out that day meaning to visit the Romanisches Café, to see if any acquaintance of mine was there; not merely from curiosity, but more from a desire to make a last, decisive test. Would W—— still be there, slipping out to the lavatory from time to time to give himself a shot of morphia? Would Orlik still be making his lightning sketches of new arrivals? Would Flechtheim, the art-dealer, come over to my table to show me the latest—the last!—number of his witty review *Querschnitt*? Perhaps Donath would be there, who did tricks with a boomerang; and Ilona, to whom I might send fifty pfennigs in a matchbox, so that she could sit for another hour or two over a cup of coffee.

I was within a few yards of the entrance when someone grabbed me from behind and swung me round. For a terrified moment I thought it was the police, but then I saw that it was Erich Franzen, the writer. He spluttered at me in a sort of fury, "You aren't going in there, are you? They comb the place three times a day!"

I said that this must surely be an exaggeration. He glared at me and then apologised for doing so. Leading me down the Tauentzienstrasse, he told me in a toneless, monotonous voice that the block of flats in the Fehrbelliner Platz, where my apartment was, had that morning been methodically surrounded and besieged by the new police in a text-book military manoeuvre. Dozens of our friends had been arrested and taken to Police Headquarters in the Alexanderplatz. My own apartment had been looted, with others.

"My books!" I exclaimed, more shaken by this than by anything else.

"It's war," said Franzen, "and the military have won—or the gangsters. Look at the Reichstag fire. It takes a gangster mind to conceive the notion that the other side can be utterly discredited by a single act of incendiarism."

"We had nothing to do with that fire," I said.

"That isn't the point. You could have done it, or better, you *should* have done it; then they would have believed in your revolution and they wouldn't have got on top with a rush at the last minute. The people now naturally think you're capable of anything. Tomorrow they'll be lynching you. But I don't know why I keep talking about 'you,' as though I were different. We're all sheep with these wolves around."

We were strolling past the window-displays in that west-end quarter of the town, and a street-girl in high-heeled shoes gave us a quick glance in passing. I do not know what instinct told her of our especial circumstances. As she came back she said in a low voice, without looking at us, "If you want a hide-out you can have my key." Franzen understood at once. "Thanks, but not yet," he said, and got out his case and offered her a cigarette. Then he said to me, "Probably by now they've found out where you're lodging. The attic at my place is unlocked. Come before dark and leave early in the morning. I shall soon be in the same boat myself."

Berlin contained hundreds of thousands of workers who yesterday had been my comrades. Now that the time had come there were only Korth and Franzen, two equally threatened writers, and a street-girl, to offer me help against being struck down. With a lump in my throat I saw Franzen go off in one direction and the girl in the other. Then I felt ashamed. I thought of Karl and Emil and the whole devoted group of Red Front fighters who for months had agitated with us and remained faithful. They had run the same risks as we had, they had listened to us, they had gone to these lengths because they believed in us. Who had the right to reproach them? I had two people, they had no one. I could take to flight, but poverty kept them tied to their homes; they would be hunted like hares out of their forms. In any case, I was not going to run away! I would not let Berlin be taken from me!

Half an hour later I went to the station, where my trunk had been deposited in the cloakroom, got it out and took a ticket to the north. In Marie Louise's village I would be able to think everything over.

I had known the Worpswede peasants since 1918. They were as silent as their own dykes. Their humour, when it reached their lips, was like a well-aimed skittle-ball. The painters of the artists' colony loved, drank and painted. Politics was regarded as an intruder.

When I got out at the small station I gave my modest luggage to a carrier, who took it to my mother-in-law's house, and here the grotesque farce of my exile began. The young, quite beautiful wife of the local pastor had once told me, that she had an overwhelming preference for poets "and exceptional people of that kind."

And now, in March 1933, this woman sealed my fate. I do not reproach her, she is exonerated from all blame by the universally unhealthy state of the times. In addition to which, she was pregnant, and therefore liable to extravagant notions. In short, instead of eating pickles, as pregnant women commonly do, she denounced me to the local police.

She discovered my harmless trunk on the carrier's cart, and, with the sharp-sightedness of an alert citizen, conceived the idea that it must contain incendiary bombs.

The trio of gendarmes who burst into Vogeler's house found, together with my underpants and two water-colours, a book by Kafka and a volume of Goethe's lyrics. But I knew that they had discovered more in Berlin and I also knew that Herr Streicher, now triumphant, would never forgive me for having got him into gaol. I fled through a back door over the heather to Frau von Garvens, a woman beyond suspicion who offered me a bed for the night. The next morning I made my way to Bremen and took the last train westwards.

On this day Germany elected its Führer. I heard the news in Cologne, where I changed trains. I wanted to go to the Saar, to tell my father of my new defeat. I did not know what I would ask him. I was confused.

I went to a cinema to fill in the time between trains. Scarcely had I taken my seat than the latest news appeared on the screen—the electoral results of the threatened Republic!

Here were the last Germans whom I had an opportunity of observing. I looked at the terrifying figures on the screen. The crude handwriting in which they had been scrawled on a smeared glass plate was horribly appropriate to the ugly event. The cinema was a shabby one. Cigarette-ends lay smoking on the floor, and a smell of lysol streamed through the constantly opening door of the lavatory. The teen-agers around me chewed pop-corn, and an old man spat noisily on the floor. Were circumstances trying to make my departure from Germany as easy as possible?

I reached my home-town, Merzig, in the middle of the night. At that time it was separated from the Reich, like the whole of the Saar. I climbed the garden fence at the back of the house and saw from the light in Father's room that he was still at work. When I knocked he rose quietly and came and opened the door without asking who was there. He seemed not at all surprised to see me, and there was something wonderfully heartening in his calmness. He sat down at his desk again. "I have another ten minutes' work to do," he said and looked steadfastly at me. I mustn't seem frightened, I thought, and I stared at the familiar objects on his table to steady myself. He pointed to a key lying beside the metal ink-pot. "Go and fetch a bottle or two, and put them to cool."

As we raised our glasses for the first time he said:

"You'll survive him."

"Thank you," I said, and emptied my glass and he filled it again. The clock struck, and I thought how this would irritate me if I were working. How could he manage to write in a place like this?

"Still the same clock," he said. "I thought of you last time I wound it."

"Thank you," I said again. Then there was silence. We did not seem to be able to find anything to talk about.

He searched through the compartments of a brief-case that opened like a fan. It contained a great many hand-written sheets. He took a few out, looked them over and then put them back again. He glanced at me sidelong with his dark, kindly eyes and said:

"They were written to you, but I didn't send them. I didn't want to depress you."

I loved him very deeply at that moment.

"I'm not depressed," I said. "There is just one question I want to ask you."

He stood up, his face looking old.

"Ask me tomorrow. I'm tired, and so must you be. Don't wake your mother. Take my bed and I'll sleep on the couch."

The next day I told him what I had in mind and asked:

"Should I go on with it?"

"Of course," he said at once. "You want to try and prove that they're the ones who set fire to the Reichstag. It may sound stupid and pointless. But nothing is pointless that helps to expose great liars and deceivers. We must never give up, even if we're no more than a finger plugging a single hole in the dam."

"So I should go to Strasbourg?"

"Certainly, if that's where you can find the plans of the Reichstag to support your theory."

"But it will mean going into exile," I said.

My father smiled.

"I'm fifty-five years old. I've been living in exile all my life."

I arrived in Strasbourg next day, but when I went to the National Library I was told that although they had excellent drawings of all the public buildings of the Wilhelm II period, these were not available to the public. It seemed that everything connected with Wilhelm II was kept locked in the poison-cupboard. The blue-prints of the Reichstag were inaccessible.

I had to use devious methods. I got the library photographer to make reproductions of architectural drawings which had nothing to do with what I was really after, starting with the Stefansdom in Vienna and working gradually through the nineteenth century. Finally, being persuaded that I was a genuine research-worker, and having been promised a handsome *douceur*, he agreed to let me have photographs of the Wilhelm II buildings, which were clearly so essential to the book I was preparing. But then I found that I had run through my money. A woman-journalist came to my rescue. She let me use her own telephone to get through to Paris, and she found Willi Münzenberg's number for me.

I told him what I was doing and he at once understood its significance. No, he said; he had by no means given up publishing, but was starting a new business outside Germany. They were planning to issue a *Brown Book*, an exposure of the Nazis, and I might consider myself engaged forthwith as a contributor. "Don't worry about money. Bring me those photographs!"

A money-order arrived next day and I paid the photographer. "I hope you will point out in your book that Wilhelm II was utterly lacking in taste," that worthy man said.

I did not examine the photographs until I was on the train and locked in the lavatory. They were exactly what we wanted. The ground-plan of the Reichstag cellars showed the passage running to the presidential residence, where Goering was now installed. The secret entrance used by the incendiaries had been found!

L

9. *The Brown Book and the Pamphlets*

WE had our headquarters in an apartment in the Rue du Faubourg Saint-Honoré.

Our commander was Willi Münzenberg, publisher, Reichstag deputy, organiser of international strike action, aged forty-two, slight of figure, with brown eyes, thick hair and a longish face. There was a warrant out for his arrest, issued by Dr Frick, the Nazi Minister of the Interior.

The second-in-command was Otto Katz, a Czech journalist and considerable linguist, aged forty-three, with a thin-lipped, hard-bitten face, lined with suffering, that had hitherto been known only to the higher agents of the Comintern, and a tendency to lean his head over on his right shoulder. He was always very neatly dressed.

There was Babette Gross, a full-figured woman with an engaging expression and clear, shrewd eyes, warm-hearted but a good hater, much given to explosions, her clear-headedness not unswayed by emotion.

There was Kroenen, the official Party-controller, who smelt of tobacco, and Abush, the assistant-controller, a half-educated journalist and persevering disher-up of predigested materials, uncertain in his judgment on tactical matters.

There was Max Schroeder, a former art-historian who had joined the Party largely because of his disdain for Berlin's Bohemia. He was an elegant writer and a witty observer through half-closed eyes, an excellent archivist, but in constant need of prodding, alcohol and tobacco.

The book we were compiling was to be another *J'Accuse*, a full-blooded, documented attack on the Nazi regime, dealing with the atrocities committed by the storm-troopers, the stifling of human rights, the use of terror for electoral purposes, the propaganda methods of Dr Goebbels—and also refuting the tale, broadcast throughout the world, that the Reichstag fire was the work of a Dutch vagabond named Van der Lubbe, instigated by the Communist Dimitrov. The work of preparation was conducted with as much secrecy as possible; but the book's appearance was intended to produce a major explosion.

Münzenberg was accustomed to pay brief, daily visits to the scene of our labours and grin at the sight of our weary faces (he never seemed to realise how much he asked of us until someone collapsed). He read manuscripts, often tossing them aside after a perfunctory glance, and dictated telegrams, manifestos and lengthy reports of political meetings. He was as foul-mouthed as a cab-driver and as variable in his moods as only genius can be, at one moment exultant and at the next filled with wrath and melancholy, ex-aggerating all things, seeing enemies everywhere, and no end to our defeat.

But *The Brown Book* grew. Newspapers from all over the world were scrutinised for items of German news. Emissaries who could go without risk were sent into Germany, and every new fugitive we could lay hands on was invited to visit us and tell us his experiences. There were ex-Ministers among them, journalists, adventurers, working men, former secret agents attached to the republican War Office, friends of the luckless Lubbe who had been in contact with a certain official at Police Headquarters in Berlin. Our offices were like an island where the shipwrecked struggled ashore, somebodies, nobodies and Quixotes, the broken and embittered victims of the new over-lords—all were contributors to *The Brown Book*.

Münzenberg received them without any precaution, quite untroubled by the terrors that caused the Party officialdom to subject every newcomer to a rigorous if inept examination. All he cared about was the book, which was to be a document of historic importance—and what did it matter if we ran the risk of getting shot?

There was no end to his activities. Among other things, he organised the London "counter-trial" to coincide with the trial at Leipzig, which began in September that year, of Lubbe, Dimitrov, Torgler and the others accused by the Nazis of being implicated in the Reichstag fire. He invited God and all the world to join him in what to him was nothing less than a Crusade. "I'm amazed that you haven't sewn a cross on your jacket," someone said.

Liberal Peers came to visit us from England: the Duchess of Atholl promised her collaboration. Labour Lord Morley wrote a preface. The red-headed eloquent Labour M.P., Ellen Wilkinson, toured Alsace and Lorraine with me to talk about the book. The sister of the Swedish Prime Minister came. Edouard Herriot and the leaders of the French Bar placed their services at our disposal. For a little while it seemed as though a single persecuted *emigré* might succeed in uniting the citizens of the world, all those who hated injustice and looked on all that Hitler stood for as a personal affront. It was like a gigantic league for the defence of decency.

Until the very last moment Münzenberg was dissatisfied with our work. I remember him flinging a whole sheaf of corrected proofs at the feet of Katz, who was admittedly a bungler, and stamping out of the office where we had laboured so strenuously for months in compiling this record of human baseness.

The Brown Book appeared, to be at once translated into ten languages.

Münzenberg was constantly turning up in triumph with a new edition. Moscow helped. The Soviet Government regarded the arrest of Dimitrov as a direct challenge, and was not sparing with its funds. The English edition reached Australia before the Leipzig trial had even begun; but it was the "counter-trial" which shook the American Left out of its isolationism.

I had been entrusted with the chapter on the Nazi torture-chambers. Münzenberg read it in draft. I had exaggerated nothing. It was the only time I ever saw tears in the eyes of that generally unsentimental and tough-minded man.

He gave me a copy of the special light-weight edition of the book, printed on flimsy paper for clandestine distribution. "One of them has reached Dimitrov in his prison-cell," he said proudly.

Marie Louise had come to Paris to join me. With *The Brown Book* completed I wrote a short story called *Death in St Michael's Church*.

It arose out of an exciting piece of news that reached us from Germany. Cardinal Faulhaber, the resident cardinal of Munich and Bavaria, had delivered a series of sermons to a growing congregation, attacking the cheap paganism of the new Government. His courage and dignity inspired me with a singular hope. Thus had Pope Leo I defied Attila. It often seemed to me that the Church of Rome had outlived its time, but there were still some among its princes who knew how to live and die greatly.

My tale was about a Communist prisoner of the Nazis who escapes and takes refuge in the church where Faulhaber preached. Fatally injured by his persecutors he dies in sanctuary, seated in a confessional. He sits listening to the service, comparing, with the pitiless lucidity of the dying, his own new faith with that ancient creed, and sparing neither. He dies to the sound of singing voices, rising to the lofty ceiling in a swelling tide of hope.

This work was awarded the Heinrich Mann prize in Holland for the best "anti-Fascist short story." It was a distinction such as seldom comes the way of an *emigré* writer.

On the evening of the day when the news reached us, Marie Louise and I went to dinner with Clara and André Malraux. Malraux read us some passages from his *Temps du Mépris*, also the story of a prisoner in Germany. Fascinated by the theme of death, the dark threshold, as he always was, he had evoked the political climate of those feverish months with a sureness that I think no other French writer could have equalled—many of them, enclosed within their own long-matured way of life, maintained an attitude of reserve that was often painful to us. Marie Louise, whose French was limited, asked me to tell him how much she liked the ending, when the prisoner's wife lulls their child to sleep with a tale of fishes who wear fur coats to protect them against the cold. The little scene spun a web of tenderness. "Tell him that that is what we have to get back to," said Marie Louise. "—to unpolitical things!" I was struck by the vehemence with which she said it, as though she were fighting to escape from the strands of a more sinister web. I translated her words faithfully, without comment.

But in the *Métro* she suddenly said to me, "I must go home." She spoke this time without any vehemence but I was utterly shattered. The walls of the tunnel sped past us, then the train slowed and for the hundredth time I read the words—"*du bon-dubon-Dubonnet . . .*" The train stopped and people got in, strangers who knew nothing of us, so wonderful is the anonymity of great cities. The doors rattled, we started again and I stared at my shadowy reflection in the window, thinking that once again here it was—the wall that sunders us, even the nearest and dearest—the weeks of silence, and suddenly there is a separate person at one's side—at the very moment, poor fool, when I was feeling sure of myself!

When we came to our station Marie Louise said she would like to go on. "Right to the end," she said, and it must have felt to her like the end of the world, for it would not be easy for her to say what she had to say. I nodded.

We got out at the Porte d'Orléans. I asked her if she wanted to take a bus back, but she shook her head. "I'd like to walk all night," she said. We walked round the fringe of Paris, the "zone."

The shanties where the very poor lived were plunged in silence, unburied coffins. It was hard to conceive that children lay asleep beneath those roofs of corrugated iron. A yellow moon rode through restless, dark clouds.

She's back on the moor, I thought, seeing the barges on the canals, think-of the new studio we shall never share because of the new masters, smelling the scent of pines, remembering the armful of wild-flowers that once she brought me.

Empty buses were driving into the depots for the night. Now and then I glanced sidelong at Marie Louise, her thick, fair hair, her clear, grey eyes, thinking how German she was: the Germany whose enchantment no tyranny could destroy, fresh as summer rain, orderly as the cornfields, dreaming as the pine-woods, those guardians of silence, light as the flight of butterflies.

What right had I to drag her with me into the hazards and uncertainties of this life of exile? Every day she spent in Paris made her more an *emigrée*, and perhaps before long the way of return would be finally closed. Should I tell her that it would be better for her if we separated, or would that be another blunder, even worse in its consequences than the months of blind self-assurance which was now collapsing about my ears?

We walked for hours, and she talked about the colour of the sky and the boats on the Seine and the silhouette of the Eiffel Tower that was with us wherever we went; but she said not a word about her decision. By the time we reached the Étoile she was tired and asked for a taxi.

She left Paris the next evening.

As a matter of precaution I did not go with her to the station. We arranged that she should write to me by way of a friend.

For a long time I had no news of her. Münzenberg kept us all hard at it during the day, but in the evenings I wandered by the Seine, wondering and worrying. Had they taken her as a hostage? Should I get word saying that she would not be released unless I returned? The towers of Notre Dame, tranquil and aloof, were bathed in the western light. Who in this city worried about the troubles of a hundred thousand *emigrés*?

I gazed at the green angels on the cathedral, which looked as though they were in the act of getting ready to come down and bathe in the Seine. One was like Marie Louise, the same faint smile and steadfast eyes. I had a sudden vision of her in the grip of those brown-clad figures, the chains ready. . . . I ran back to my hotel. There was no letter, and the woman-friend through whom she had promised to correspond had also heard nothing. . . . The days seemed endless. I waited in the expectation of a letter written under compulsion, a trap; or official threats; or the report of her death.

I cursed myself for having let her go. Passing the German Embassy one day, I suddenly made up my mind to walk in and demand news of her; and then stopped at the doorway, realising how absurd this was.

The next morning I started to write a pamphlet, but then broke off and went to the Louvre. Passing the winged Victory in the entrance, I thought suddenly of a picture that Marie Louise had often visited, Raphael's fair-haired Woman of Aragon.

She sat against a background of purple velvet, her fragile figure invested by the painter with an extravagant dignity, the oval of her face smiling across at the Mona Lisa. Beside her hung Baldassare Castiglione, the noble humanist, and beyond him François Premier, the royal faun who played the lute, spoke Latin, Spanish and Italian, engaged in jousting and founded the Collège de France.

For the first time I understood why Marie Louise had so loved this corner; it was because the people in the pictures were so comfortingly removed from our own raw and graceless epoch. Why was I devoting my life to the fight against those gangsters in Berlin? To clear them out and pave the way for others—and lose my love?

In this frame of mind I went to Münzenberg's office, meaning to feed myself with the latest news—there were new sensations every day—and fortify myself in my new-found resolution to be done with it all, to throw the whole business overboard.

Münzenberg invited me into his own room, where there was a man who had just escaped from Germany. He brought news of Carl von Ossietsky, the imprisoned editor of the liberal review *Weltbühne*: They had tortured him. He had to stand to attention whenever a Nazi guard passed him. They forced him to kneel in the mud, they beat him and trampled on him, calling him "Polish swine."

There was also news of Mühsam, the anarchist, who for years had played no part in politics but had devoted himself to helping people whom he considered had been unjustly imprisoned under the Republic. Generosity was his only crime, and perhaps an excess of sentimentality. He had been secretly hanged from a latrine-door.

I had been thinking that I would send Marie Louise a message to say that I would promise to give up politics for ever if she would come back to Paris. But now I dismissed the thought. These things were larger than ourselves and our private lives. No one had the right to give up.

I went on with my work, and as I still heard nothing from her my terrors grew. One morning I went to Notre Dame and lit a candle. I did not pray, but I bowed to the High Altar and the stained-glass windows before going out again.

And next day the miracle happened. The door of our small hotel-bedroom opened, and Marie Louise was there!

"There's no miracle about it," she said almost sternly. "I got a new passport without any trouble. They're very sure of themselves—absolutely sure. It's all quite different from what you imagine, and Malraux is a romantic."

"That's simply a cliché," I said.

"One of mine in exchange for a hundred of yours," said Marie Louise with a little, remote smile.

We talked and talked, and at the end my head was spinning. She had come from a land of bubbling enthusiasm and released desires. The evil and oppression with which we were concerned affected only a relatively small, defeated section of the people. The great majority believed in the new order and were transformed. She had brought newspapers and reviews, in one of which I found a passage from the poet Gottfried Benn, asnwered by Klaus Mann. I remember it well, because the date of the reply was my birthday. Gottfried Benn assured us exiles that if we had stayed the German people would not have treated us "too badly." I said bitterly, "Not too badly! Not too many broken bones. Only one eye gouged out, not both. Only one kidney smashed. They would have burnt our flesh only with cigarettes—not cigars!"

I felt chilled and the most hateful suspicions arose in my mind. Her new passport lay on the table, the photograph embossed with a swastika. What if they had let her come back simply as a spy, telling her that her family would be held accountable for her behaviour? Such things were by no means unknown. I looked at her neat, braided hair, her smooth white neck, the blouse of hand-woven material, everything about her that appeared flawless and unsullied, like a room with white Easter curtains opening its windows to the spring. Was she capable of betrayal?

Perhaps tomorrow she would go home again. . . . I turned away my head, but the passport was still there, and she seemed to have become a stranger, herself stamped with the swastika.

I watched as she stood a photograph of her mother on the table, and beside it one of herself which, as I learnt later, had been taken by a Propaganda Ministry photographer as an example of "typically German beauty." She had worn a Friesian costume, with the lace cap framing the oval of her face so that she looked like a bride. Her eyes were lowered and she had used no lipstick. This was the new German fashion, as opposed to that of "decadent" Paris, but they need not have made her appear so lifeless and simpering. I stared ashamedly at the photograph, tormented by all the demons of mistrust, and then she ferreted in the bottom of her case and brought out the "pepper pistol" which she had made years before to protect herself against the Berlin police.

"In case they should come here," she said, and looked at me with her grey, steadfast eyes. I took her in my arms and kissed her.

Thenceforward I reverted to the habit of forming my own opinion of events.

The sentence may have a strange ring; but it must be remembered that I belonged to a political party resembling a religious order, in which acceptance and obedience, not speculation, were the first and last requirement. The intellectuals in particular were made to understand that only their talents were required of them, not their thoughts. We were all under the spell of the Russian code, which, discarding the substance of religion, the more rigorously applied its forms. Superficial judges have called this the "Jewish inheritance in Socialism," but I think that they can have no practical knowledge of the way in which the Jews by laughter and tolerance ease the bonds of their own philosophy. The Talmudists played with the Word as they uttered it, making doubt the accepted brother of faith. To the Bolsheviks the Word was harshly indivisible: it was the minds of their intellectual adherents that they split in two, allowing no questions and treating laughter as a crime. This I discovered as the walls of that false monastery closed more tightly about me.

Most Party-members adapted themselves with resignation to the changing slogans. Others lived a double life, doing what was required, paying lip-service to the pedantic utterances that were supposed to spare us the necessity of thought and keeping our own counsel. We exploded now and then, when an attempt was made to throw too much dust in our eyes. But in general we acquiesced, quick to deceive ourselves with new hopes.

The famous "night of the long knives" in 1934, when Generals Schleicher and Von Bredow, and Klausner, the Catholic leader, and Röhm and Gregor Strasser and countless other leaders of the SA, were murdered on Hitler's orders, caused tremendous rejoicing among the German *emigrés*. There were prophecies of an early collapse of the régime. The fact was simply that a palace-revolution, partly planned and partly invented by Himmler, had been savagely suppressed before it had even begun: but to the hopeful spirits outside Germany it appeared like a *Götterdämmerung*, a trumpet-call, the herald of a new dawn. There were as many false reports as there were false interpretations of the event. Hitler himself contributed in his fanciful way to the confusion. I remember his reference to the murder of Röhm—"I further ordered that the ulcer poisoning the wells of our national life was to be burnt out of the raw flesh!"

We laughed heartily at this mixture of metaphors, overlooking the fact that the surgeon who had burnt out those watery ulcers had in the event achieved a notable victory. Discarding every legal consideration, he had left his followers free for a week to settle all outstanding accounts, public or private, warranted or otherwise. All that he now lacked was absolute command of the Army, and this he secured when Hindenburg died. A decree was issued on the 2nd of August 1934, confirming him in the joint offices of President and Chancellor.

I heard the news at the printers, while I was engaged in correcting the proof of an article foretelling the early downfall of the new Reich!

And on the same day I listened to a speech over the radio.

"We can only pray to Almighty God that our work and our struggle may be for the good of the German people; that He will give us strength to safeguard the freedom and honour of the German people in all eventualities; and above all that we may follow the right road, and enjoy the blessings of peace and preserve the German people from the tragedy of war, as the illustrious dead desired with his whole heart."

The voice was Hitler's, and the "illustrious dead" was Hindenburg.

The Frenchmen I talked to during those days all advised me to try to subdue my "*emigré* psychosis," and when I shouted at them in a fury that all this was no more than a smoke-screen, mere crocodile's tears, they shrugged their shoulders—"*On verra!*"

And in Germany around the frames of a million photographs of Hindenburg was draped the conventional black crèpe. More often than not it was the famous "Potsdam photograph" of the meeting between Hindenburg and Hitler at the beginning of 1933—the old Marshal in full uniform and Hitler in a neat black suit, bowing low before him. To a hundred thousand or a million white-collar workers that photograph had become a talisman—the leader of the New Men making obeisance to the aged victor of Tannenberg. No one will ever know how many doubting hearts were won over by that bow!

This obituary address, eighteen months later, with its shrewd mixture of noble emotion and political cunning, was equally effective. The name of God came glibly to the lips of a speaker for whom it was nothing more than a figure of rhetoric; but this was something that the ingenuous citizens of Germany were not within a hundred miles of suspecting, as Hitler well knew. The "illustrious dead," over whose coffin it was thundered, had always believed in God. Hitler took advantage of the fact. The devout seemed to succeed the devout; and at the same time the man of peace assumed the mantle of the old soldier who had said that he would look down from Heaven and bless the victories of Germany revived.

It was useless for us to mock the "corporal" who could now create field-marshals and declare war as he saw fit. The newly joined recruit in the German barracks was required to repeat as follows:

> I swear by God this sacred oath, that I will render absolute obedience to the Leader of the German Reich and People, Adolf Hitler, the Supreme Commander of the armed forces, and that I will at all times be ready, as befits a brave soldier, to fulfil this oath at the cost of my life.

Among the leading *emigrés* Willi Münzenberg was the only one who saw clearly where this oath would lead the world, and who did not deceive himself with fruitless dreams of revolution and the barricades. A prophet in the wilderness, he now passed his days in a small room at the back of a house on the Boulevard Montparnasse, seated at a desk piled high with papers. He had still not learnt French, and he hated dictating letters. The telephone was scarcely more than a token of his isolation. When it rang his secretary would dash in and answer it, while Münzenberg waited impatiently and finally solved the problem with a single sentence. He had the calm and intensity of a chess-master walking from board to board, playing twenty games at once. He had given up all thought of under-cover work in Germany, although this is not to say that he had given up the struggle. He had simply decided upon other means. He knew that Hitler intended war. The objectives were all laid down in *Mein Kampf*—the Saar, the Sudetenland, the Polish Corridor, the Westmark—that is to say, Alsace-Lorraine—and Austria.

This liquidation of the Treaty of Versailles would be followed by the conquest of Europe. Münzenberg, a man who also had a touch of the Napoleonic, had no illusions as to the ambitions of this other corporal. He saw that Germany was being made into a fortress. Men such as Ulbricht, Merker and

Dahlem, directing the German underground from abroad, might shoot their flaming arrows at the walls of concrete, like boys playing at redskins, but he for his part was beating his drum through the forests of Europe, warning the tribes against the day when the garrison of the fortress would break out. He was not over-particular in the things he said; he believed that cynical lying must be fought with an equal cynicism. His books were hastily thrown together, and where material was lacking he filled in the gaps from his own profound knowledge of the enemy.

They appeared at very short intervals. His *White Book* on the shootings of the 30th June so infuriated the Nazis that, at the height of their victories, in 1940, they arrested an entirely innocent member of his packing-room staff, who surrendered to them, and condemned him to eight years' imprisonment and the loss of civil rights.

Another of his books, entitled *Nazi Leaders, Look at Yourselves*, consisted of a series of thirty-three biographical sketches of the new masters of Germany. Shrewd and sure in its judgments, written without pharisaical moralising and mercifully free from Communist Party cant, it was like a light piercing through the deceptively comforting darkness to illumine a putrescent, maggoty place; it rang with the cry, "They are unclean!"

That this was treason against Hitler's Reich was undeniable; but those who saw it as treason against Germany were confusing the police with the criminal, the doctor with the disease. And what was at stake was not merely Germany but all Europe, destined for the holocaust when a few more years had passed. Münzenberg never doubted that war must come and was tormented by the vision, although he very rarely spoke of it. In our Paris of 1934 he was like the prisoner on Elba, awaiting his hundred days, steeling himself for the trial which he knew could not be avoided. In his heart he hated war, and he was still under the influence of Lenin, who during the first World War had proposed that he should become leader of the League of Anti-Militarist Youth.

He sent Otto Katz, his principal assistant, to Spain, which was then on the threshold of civil war. In the course of what was described as a "private attack" a safe was hurled out of the window of one of the German consulates. The documents it had contained found their way to Paris, and Münzenberg's publishing house issued a book giving the names of all the German agents in foreign countries. "They are preparing your downfall! Cry Havoc! Cry Havoc!" He shouted it to the entire world. And he did so in very precise terms. He published a book entitled *Hitler Means War*, containing photostats of documents relating to the expansion of German heavy industry and the speed of her rearmament.

This, of course, was another act of treason to Hitler's Reich. We feared for his life, but he would allow none of us to serve him as a bodyguard. His secretary saw to it, however, that he never went anywhere alone, and during his meetings in cafés a former chauffeur sat at an adjacent table, half-hidden behind a newspaper but with a pistol ready in his pocket.

Münzenberg was the only one who had learnt to question the accepted tenets of Communism. To him the German workers were no longer an exploited army of serfs but tragic accomplices in the catastrophe that was being prepared. He understood well enough how easily men deceive themselves, but he could never forgive them for the part they played in enabling Schacht's prodigious gamble on the proceeds of a future war to be made to appear like the economic miracle of the age. He was constantly in trouble with the official guardians of the Party ideology, but he bribed his way out of it by finding jobs for them in his very successful Paris business. And with the instinct of a thoroughbred he did not let himself be trapped into a visit to Moscow, which would have been the end of him. "I belong to the hunt," he once said, "not to the Court and safety by the fireside and the samovar."

Perceiving my restlessness in the summer of 1934, he sent me to the Saar to collect materials for a book designed to play a part in the plebiscite, to be held under the auspices of the League of Nations in January 1935, whereby the Saarlanders were to decide whether they wished to be reunited to Germany.

It was here that I first saw the leaflets which the Party was circulating in Germany. It was a happy event. I was sick and tired of the line taken by the official Party newspapers, the dope that filled them, the unreal talk about "rapidly approaching victory" and Hitler's early collapse. I remember one particularly depressing example which, for its sheer silliness, deserves to rank as an historic document. After the massacre of June 30th Hitler had convoked a meeting of the Nazi leaders at which he had extolled his "act of purification." It was the triumphant howling of the wolf who has finally destroyed his rivals for the leadership of the pack; the murders were in the truest sense of word a salutary blood-letting from the point of view of the régime. However, the Communist *Rundschau*, which we were expected to treat as gospel, commented as follows:

The Nuremberg Party Meeting, 1934.

Just as children in the dark cry louder as they grow more frightened, so do Hitler's bellowings grow louder as he sees his end approaching . . . The fanfares and the beating of drums, and all the resounding phrases . . . could not hide the fear and uncertainty that the Führer's words revealed . . . The Führer fears his own bodyguard, and the bodyguard fears its Führer . . . Thus did the bloodstained tyrant speak, trembling before the growing anger of the betrayed, exploited and brutally oppressed masses.

(*Rundschau* 1934. No. 50)

A piece of asinine wishful thinking! It was shameful to have to acquiesce in this sort of thing, this tawdry, hired optimism. For the most part we shrugged our shoulders and kept our opinions to ourselves.

I see the small group before me. Anna Seghers, the novelist, acquiesced despite her not inconsiderable intelligence. Ludwig Renn, the ex-officer, continued to observe military discipline. Kurt Stern maintained a disdainful silence. Koestler seldom appeared, and always had somehow the aspect of a stranger who feels that he has been allowed in on sufferance. Manès Sperber disposed of doubt by raising the discussion to a loftier plane, thus check-mating the official mouthpieces. I myself did not think of protesting. It was my Catholic upbringing that made this questionable obedience easy for me: I had less difficulty in accepting the hierarchy. If one felt bound to re-pudiate the Pope, to become a heretic, then one must proclaim one's heresy not in any back room but openly, like Luther, regardless of blazing Papal bulls, or like Thomas Münzer, from a fortress with a musket in one's hand— such was my father's axiom. It is to this day a source of satisfaction to me that I never gave any of these petty functionaries the chance to reprimand me or administer any spiritual admonition. Malraux helped me. The talks in his apartment in the Rue du Bac were the best antidote to the official formulae. Malraux was sharply critical of any "Roman" who came to spy out the land, but friendly to the "Athenians" who brought news of the outside world—a poem by Guillèn, a hitherto undiscovered Paul Klee, an idol from Teotihua-can, a Peruvian mask, or a rare *bon mot* on the part of one of the even rarer statesmen of Europe. Surprises were always welcome. We strove to pierce through the tangle of reality, and all were believers in tolerance. There was the incorruptible Guéhenno, the brilliantly clear-headed Chiaromonte; and there was Clara Malraux, logical, proud and rebellious, who so sanely teased me for my tendency to revert to type and become indiscriminately obedient.

I was also helped by surprises such as the sudden appearance of the clan-destine leaflets. Seated with Otto Katz, the secret agent, in the Schloss Café in Saarbrücken, I felt myself part of a fighting movement such as I should have liked to organise. This was not shooting at a giant with blank cartridges; it was mine-laying. The mines must surely be effective, for Hitler feared none but the secret enemy and over-estimated only what he could not see.

The little pamphlets were carefully printed on flimsy paper. I turned them over and over; their existence alone could promote unrest. German towns were named as the places where they had been printed. I must confess that for a long time I did not think of studying their contents. The challenge was what mattered. The pamphlets were like molehills suddenly appearing all over a field, and it seemed that all the earth must be undermined.

They were disguised in the most ingenious fashion, some being tucked away in seed-packets such as are sold in Germany. On the outside were pictures of vegetables and flowers. The colours pleased the eye, but the producers of this illegal seed were not so innocent as to suppose that Hitler's police would be deterred by this brightness from looking inside the packets. Therefore they were filled with real seeds, together with the usual instructions.

"To be sown in March or April under glass and planted out in May. Height about three feet. Blooms throughout the summer in various colours."

Further information was given, but in the middle of the text an unknown voice would speak of Hitler's evil deeds and call for the sowing of other seed.

Packets of shampoo were distributed, and amid the scented powder lurked the leaflet proclaiming that Germany reeked of blood.

The Gestapo confiscated the leaflets which suddenly appeared on the counters of post offices. In the schools teachers warned the children to keep an eye on their parents' letters from abroad.

Illicit texts were sent out disguised in the binding of German classics. The third act of Schiller's *Maid of Orleans* was replaced by the Communist Manifesto, which was still worth reading.

This book was also confiscated; a special section of the Gestapo instituted a strict control of the post offices. But they overlooked a pamphlet which, ostensibly giving instructions for the development of photographic film, was accompanied by a free sample of printing-paper. The paper came in an authentic Kodak packet, and no amateur photographer would expose it by daylight. Thus the dark-room prompted the recipients to think about the Führer.

I now saw more of the young men who came secretly from Germany to collect this material. They were a race apart, neither gay nor oppressed but with a dry, matter-of-fact manner from which all romanticism was lacking— hard when it came to an argument, but grateful for enlightenment. They thawed out somewhat at secret meetings in reliable houses, but they guarded themselves against over-close contact with the outside world; they needed all their nerve for a quite special world whose climate the rest of us could scarcely imagine. Sometimes they showed me the scars of wounds they had received in January 1933, and I thought how quick I had been to condemn the Red Front boys as deserters. Contrasting their life with my own relatively comfortable existence in the tranquillity of Paris, I was ashamed.

When once, during that visit to the Saar, I asked what effect the pamphlets were having, I received only an evasive answer. For a long time I thought that I had been tactless and had not found the right tone.

But one evening I had to make personal contact with an important Party official in Saarbrücken. I was taken up to an attic-room where a small meeting was in progress. The stiffness of the gathering, the oppressive mistrust of each man for his neighbour, was a reminder that in all this campaign nothing romantic remained, but that it was toughness against toughness. I arrived in time to hear the last words of a young man who had been reporting on conditions in Germany. When he had finished speaking he produced one of the leaflets from his pocket and tossed it with a gesture of utter disdain at the feet of the high official.

"We've been circulating that for months," he said. "We've gone with you so far, but now we're sick of it. For God's sake, who do you expect to convince? Who are you aiming at?" He pointed with his foot at the pamphlet and concluded with a devastating finality: "We aren't going to risk our lives any longer for that crap!"

He went back to Germany the same night. All those who listened to his outburst had rushed to placate him. They had even admitted that all was not as it should be and had promised better things for the future. As the meeting broke up, each of us departing singly and at intervals, according to the ritual of conspirators, I saw the high official clap the tormented but forthright boy on the shoulder, and it was a relief to feel that everyone had so much understanding for the nervous strain under which the under-cover workers lived. But a few weeks later I asked one of our contact-men how our young friend was getting on. He drew a hand across his throat. "Good God—suicide?" I exclaimed. "No," he said. "The axe!"

For a moment I seemed to feel the axe on my own neck, but I still had no inkling of the appalling secret that underlay this execution.

And here is the brief, but all the more painful, chapter entitled *Ulbricht*, whose reckless policy has for so long overshadowed our lives. (He is now the Communist viceroy of the separated and maimed eastern region of Germany.) He had a face stiff with malice that was conscious of its own ugliness and sought to relieve it with a symbolical Lenin-beard round the plump chin, a hairy appendage that did not, however, rid his faun-like mouth of any of its petty-bourgeois arrogance. His eyes, the right sharply observant and the left half-closed, were hidden behind a schoolmaster's glasses. His forehead, furrowed with the wrinkles of unfruitful thought, was rendered higher, but not more intellectual, by the retreating hair. He had the look of a lapsed priest who visits obscure houses. Everything about him told of thorough-going inadequacy and a semi-education that did not even know how to disguise itself. In short, he was a Professor Unrat of the revolution who played at history and imagined his (incidentally very effective) official intrigues to be Machiavellian statesmanship.

I no longer remember why I was admitted to that meeting. I think it was a matter of a fugitive from the Saar who had become suspect in Ulbricht's eyes, like that other boy from the Reich. Comrades from Germany were present on this occasion too. They were questioned by the Chairman of the Committee at that time. I forget his name, which is not inscribed on his tombstone—like all GPU officials, Ulbricht kept the list of his victims in his head. The chairman had a roundish face and was evidently at pains to introduce a note of respect into his voice.

The young men's reports were objective as ever, but it was clear that they were gratified by their reception. Ulbricht noted down everything they said —about strikes against Hitler's "workers' front," about sabotage, secret organisations and the growing discontent of all the workers.

Finally Ulbricht took the young men away with him, on some friendly pretext, as they told me later. He took them to a nearby café where he went over the whole proceedings again and, after uttering brief threats, got them to give him a true and authentic report on conditions in Germany. They admitted that Hitler's workers' front was as solid as a rock, that the strike action attempted by small trade-union groups was pointless and ineffective, and that the Nazis, far from immediately arresting malcontents, knew how to win them over. They promised a great deal, but conditions in the factories were much improved, and although the pressure was greater, the wages were higher. Once again Ulbricht wrote everything down, and then he praised the messengers, saying that a true Bolshevik must always honour the truth.

Then he sent them away.

For years he collected "authentic material" in this fashion. He never warned his chairman or suggested to him that he was over-optimistic. He fattened his victim, whose death would bring him his reward. He had only this object in mind, and, pedantic spy that he was, he was not troubled by scruples. He was a Saxon and possessed the penetration and love of detail which is characteristic of that industrious people. He had voted for all the decisions of the "optimistic time." When he considered that the moment had come, he struck. His *"dossier"* was devastating. His rival was exposed as a painter of over-hopeful pictures, which, to the order then prevailing in the Kremlin, was synonymous with counter-revolution—and with death.

The Lenin-bearded man smiled with satisfaction after bringing his accusations. He had nothing of Lenin but the beard, and it may be useful to draw a brief comparison between the creator of modern Russia and the Viceroy of unhappy East Germany. Lenin raised his visor when he had to do battle with his comrades; Ulbricht kept his spectacles fixed on his nose and hid behind an equivocal smile. The Russian strove for the happiness of his people; Ulbricht practised treachery for his own advantage. Lenin unmasked the enemies of the revolution; Ulbricht denounced party-rivals. Lenin fought; Ulbricht spied.

He will no doubt regard this comparison as highly unjust, for he regards every man as a potential traitor, and considers himself not only justified in playing the spy, but in duty bound to do so.

He also considered himself entitled to make use of the special position of the underground workers in Germany for the benefit of his minority campaign. The chaos of the underground movement helped and covered him.

"One of these days we'll send him to do under-cover work." This threat hung over the head of every comrade and Party-official during the period I have described. To be ordered into Germany was a punishment, similar to that practised by every army in the world. Sinners have always been sent to the front—*pour se racheter*, as the French say. But in most armies the procedure is governed by a code of behaviour that is not lacking in chivalry. Ulbricht and his staff possessed neither the education nor the experience to be aware of any such laws. The men were always sent secretly, with the punitive nature of the order underlined, for it was an almost unforgivable error to have doubted or uttered a word of opposition.

But once he was in the Reich, as I was told later by numerous young men who escaped their cruel fate, the suspect candidate was followed by what I might call the "Uriah letter," if this reference to King David's misdeed were not sacrilegious (for David acted under the influence of overwhelming passion and was later deeply penitent, whereas the Party officials remained utterly cold, and based—as they do to the present day—their right to commit these crimes on "historical laws" of which they were the executives).

Sometimes, after the departure of the candidate, a hint would be given to the underground, sometimes it would be conveyed directly to the Gestapo. A hint was all that was needed. The amount of treachery and informing had washed out all nuances. The comrades murdered in self-defence, the Gestapo from force of habit.

We who lived abroad ascribed the losses to the cunning of Himmler, and no doubt the majority were the victims of his skilfully devised system of persuasion and threats. We wrote obituaries for the fallen heroes, and heroes they all were, including those who in despair had fallen into the net and were physically unable to withstand tortures.

Occasionally one appeared who belonged to both the under-cover and the external "apparatuses"—what a significantly cold-blooded word that is for an institution that was concerned not only with the unmasking of informers but also with the welfare of the fighters! He would come to us for protection or comfort, or perhaps simply for a night's rest.

I took them in; Marie Louise gave them food and prepared a bath for them. As a rule they had vanished the next day.

We looked at one another when we found nothing left behind but a pair of dirty socks—not even a note of leave-taking.

M

"Why don't they scrap the whole thing?" said Marie Louise. "That one certainly wasn't an informer."

"It's none of our business. It's for the safety of the ones who are working over there."

"And who then get murdered by your own people without anyone knowing about it!"

"I know. It's a dilemma."

"It's a crime!"

This concluded our discussion, which was often repeated.

10. *The White Nights of Leningrad*

A LITTLE, bespectacled man with a faintly ironical grin appeared in our bed-sitting-room in the Rue de Tournon, in that narrow-fronted hotel near the French Senate where Johannes R. Becher, later commissar of education in East Germany, wrote poems about the cathedral of Bamberg and where for a time Koestler lived and worked. Marie Louise was next door, engaged in what a French police-inspector who called upon us had described as the only work worthy of a woman—cooking a meal.

The visitor, who spoke broken German, was a Russian journalist named Koltsov, a member of the editorial staff of *Pravda*. He wanted to hear what I could tell him about the Saar. I told him the plain truth, which was that in all probability the forthcoming plebiscite would result in an overwhelming victory for Nazi Germany; and when he expressed surprise that I should want to have any part in that hopeless struggle I flew into a rage and said that his own countrymen had not been afraid to wage civil war with invading armies pressing in on them from all sides.

He smiled, but then his manner changed and he asked me abruptly how much I knew about Russia. I answered that I knew something of Russian history and the history of the Russian Church, but that as to recent developments I knew very little more than was to be read in the papers.

"I think it would be a good thing for you to go and see for yourself," he said.

He called again two days later to say that he had secured an invitation for me to visit Moscow. He had even got the tickets, but I myself would have to procure some sort of travel-pass. Once I reached the frontier at Negoroloye there would be no further difficulty, since I would be the guest of the Russian Government.

Three days after this Marie Louise and I were in Copenhagen. We might have gone on to Sweden the same day, but I met an old friend in the street and suggested to Marie Louise that we should break the journey; I knew my friend had important news for us both.

"I don't suppose Father will run away," she said, teasing me. "He's too busy with his Five Year Plan."

My friend was Marcel Frischman, the best of the former *Simplizissimus* artists. He was a short, squarely-built man in his early thirties, with the muscles of an athlete and the mind of a Chaplin. He came of a Polish family, had grown up under the threat of pogroms and had a wide knowledge of Russian literature. Familiarly acquainted with the shy, strange characters of Gogol, he loved all those who live on the fringe of society, beggars and gaolbirds, harbour-trollops and homeless sailors; but close as he was to the raw underside of life, he had the ability to look along a dingy street and turn it into poetry on paper with a few strokes of his pencil. He had loved the old, vibrant Berlin and the Germany in which Max Ernst had conjured up his magic woods and Paul Klee illuminated the background of a world of dreams.

I knew at once that he would tell me about the state of art in Germany and that it would be no happy tale.

"*Zieh Leine, Junge*," he said, speaking the Berlin jargon which he used when he was excited. "Make up your mind to it, boy. I'm no Cassandra, and anyway she didn't know the half. But there's nothing more for us in that country."

He bought some of the delicious *smorgesbrod* that is on sale in the streets of Copenhagen and took us to the hotel where he and his wife had found a lodging. There was a touching loneliness about those two which at first I did not altogether understand. Unlike the exiled writer, who loses his public when he is cut off from the land of his native tongue, the artist can do his work anywhere and hope to find understanding patrons. But they seemed far more like *emigrés* than we did.

We sat on the beds eating the *smorgesbrod* and drinking good, strong coffee made over a spirit-stove, and we did not talk much until the meal was over.

Then Marcel told us about Germany. The *Bauhaus*, the centre of contemporary art, had been closed down. Painters and architects had fled, and a horde of booted young men had ransacked the studios. All modern paintings had been removed from the art-galleries, and Goebbels and Goering were proposing to make a sort of Chamber of Horrors of them, a public exhibition of decadence. The review *Querschnitt* had "gone blonde" and so had *Jugend*. Marcel paused and laughed, and said:

"*Simplizissimus* had been brought into line too."

It was unimaginable—the paper that for three good decades had fought militarism, overweening clericalism and every form of extremism, assailing all the follies of the age with its rapier of devastating satire! Thomas Mann and Hamsun had been among its contributors, and Marcel had done over five hundred cartoons for it. Now it was to serve the purpose of the Nazis.

"What are they doing with it?" I asked.

"Propaganda," he said dryly. "There's us—and there's them." He looked at me. "And where are you heading for? I mean, what's the next stop?"

I said that we were on our way to Russia, and his face clouded, so that I felt bound to offer excuses.

"They're looking for something," I said. "The Nazis simply give orders. There's no anti-Semitism in Russia—there are Jews in the highest places. I don't know what's happening about art, I'll write and tell you. But certainly they wouldn't turn a man like Klee out, and this summer there's to be a Congress of Writers. They collect Cézanne and Van Gogh, they're opening up the galleries, they protect church pictures although they're atheists. They respect the life of the artist . . ."

I was talking with some uncertainty, and he smiled at me and said:

"Well, let's hope it's all right. I wonder when we shall meet again . . ."

After we left them, Marie Louise and I walked down to the harbour, where the graceful bronze figure of the water-nymph rises against a background of sails. There was a ship from Germany, marked with the swastika. The evening was filled with light and the soft ripple of water. The shade of Hans Andersen seemed to hover about us, offering the consolation of one of his tales; and we needed consoling.

"They sat on their beds," I said, "as though that was the way they had always lived."

Marie Louise's lips were sadly smiling, seeming still to bear the imprint of the kiss that Marcel's wife had given her at their leave-taking.

"The worst of it is that they love Berlin so much, and that they belong there." She looked towards the Nazi ship and said in a hard voice: "Much more than *they* do!"

The next day we resumed our journey, by way of Stockholm, Abo and Helsinki to the Russian frontier.

Leningrad was still the window to the West, so the writers assured me who had invited me to their club. Within the first hour I underwent a transformation. We had travelled there skirting Germany as though I were pursued by the police, not frightened but resentful of my fate; and I had been received by total strangers as though I were the envoy of a foreign power.

They plied me with questions about our fellow-exiles in the west. I liked the energy with which they demanded how such a writer as Gottfried Benn could rhapsodise over the new régime, but I did not know how to answer them. And what had I thought of Heidegger's rectorial address? I was astonished at how much they knew, and I had plenty to say about Hitler's philosophers. But then a question was fired at me that checked me in mid-stride. Did I think that Malraux would remain loyal to the Revolution?

I answered vigorously, conscious of the mistrust that Malraux's enemies had spread abroad. The question in itself was simple enough. Malraux had never joined the Communist Party, but had since 1933 given it all the support his principles allowed. To talk of loyalty or disloyalty was nonsense, I said rather sharply; the Party should be thankful for sympathisers of his stature, who were worth a dozen Aragons. But then they said that this was not what they meant. They were afraid that the fastidious author of *La Condition Humaine* would be repelled by the crudity of the Party leaders in Paris. I laughed and said:

"I don't suppose the lion in the zoo worries very much because there are ordinary wild-cats in the next cage."

This brought even louder laughter.

"But what if they're in the same cage?"

They meant the Party, of course, and no one knew better than I how burdensome it could be, the embarrassment that accompanied the weekly attendance at the meeting of the cell, the compromises one had to make with oneself if one was not to be openly derisive of the inadequacy of the presiding officials. It was wonderful to discover how different everything was in Russia.

"Malraux will never go into the same cage," I said. "And those of us who are in it have plenty of ways of avoiding the incompetents. It's simply a matter of tactics. And after all, we're in France, we aren't known. But we can see how things are boiling up in France, and how they're coming over to our side."

This brought a chorus of questions. I seemed indeed to have become an ambassador, rather than a mere visitor. I told them about the bankruptcy and closing down of one of the biggest factories, the rapid growth of unemployment, the armed fascist bands, the corruption of the police, the Chiappe scandal. I said that it all had the smell of Germany in 1932—political murders, inflation, share-swindles, the clamour for a "strong man."

"So you think they're heading for revolution?" my enthralled listeners asked, and I assured them that I had no doubt of it.

One of the circle was a man with a short beard. It was he who had asked the question about Malraux. He now suddenly asked:

"You aren't afraid of saying these things here?"

I shook my head.

"In Paris I had to be careful of the things I said. But why should I be afraid here?"

I gazed round at them, and they seemed suddenly to have become withdrawn from me. I had an uncomfortable feeling that they thought I was talking simply to flatter them. I seemed to read a hint of disdain in the cool eyes and tightened lips. I said:

"I met Ilya Ehrenburg in Paris and he told me the joke about the two men walking across the Red Square. One of them suddenly says, 'Watch out! Be careful!' The other says, 'But why? There's no one anywhere near us.'

The other murmurs, 'One of us is bound to be a member of the GPU!' . . .
I didn't think it funny. It's a story rooted in fear. I used to be called a
Catholic. So far as it's true it's because from my childhood I have been keeping a watch on myself. A watch inspired by fear—fear of the dark, fear of
uniforms, of priests, of the past. But this fear has vanished now that I know
who is master of Germany. I'm not afraid of dictators. They grow out of
weakness, they're symptoms of disease. And police-forces are no better for
the fact that you find them necessary here."

The man with the beard stood up and said:

"In fact, you really are the rebel of your prison novel?"

To my astonishment he held out a copy of the Russian edition of my
Water, Bread and Bullets. I had had no notion that it had been translated
and published in Russia.

I told him so and he laughed.

"You'd better take proceedings against the State Publishing Trust for
pirating it," he said.

But I was delighted.

"The difference is," I said, "that here you publish me. In Germany they
burnt me!"

I asked him his name and he said:

"It's Lebedev. You won't have heard it."

"But of course I've heard it!" I cried. "You wrote *One Week*—a wonderful
book—a masterpiece! You're Lebedev! The Kleist of Russia!"

It was his turn to be delighted. They all were. They were not politicians
but writers, and Lebedev himself was a poet. They were not afraid to show
their feelings. And perhaps it had something to do with the light rising
from the Neva—were we not in the town of those wonderful white nights
described by Dostoevsky?

We embraced one another, and Lebedev offered to show me round the
town. "This is where everything began," he said as we went down the steps.
There was a note of pride in his voice which I took to be that of a touching
local patriotism. But it was really far more, as I came to understand two
years later, when I heard of the brutal end of that little group of writers.

We picked up Marie Louise at our hotel.

"I'm glad you came," she said, looking at Lebedev.

She seemed to like him, and as we emerged into the street he said:

"I will give you all Leningrad, which is also blonde!"

We came to a canal with small houses on either side and a tang of the sea
in the air.

"It's like Holland!" exclaimed Marie Louise, and there was the moor in
her eyes, and the clear light of the skyline.

"What do you want me to tell you?" asked Lebedev.

"How it began," said Marie Louise. "This town that was once St Petersburg."

So Lebedev talked of Pyotr Alexeivich Romanov, who was Peter the Great. To acquire a mastery of maritime matters he had gone to work for a Dutch shipbuilder in Zaandam. He had visited England. He had studied Latin, French, English and Dutch; and he had returned to Russia resolved to westernise his peasant people.

"All this was nothing but a swamp," said Lebedev, flinging out his arm. "The steppes were too narrow for that huge man. He wanted an outlet to every sea. He tore down whole woods on the islands of the Neva estuary, he drained the swampy waterways and he built his Petersburg. A madman! He slept in a little house among his slaves, loved alcoves and needed to tie himself down, so it seems, because he feared his own bursting passions. His travels had rid him of his Russian mistrustfulness. It became the tradition for Russians to visit the west. Lenin himself gained greatly by doing so."

"That is something to be said for the west," remarked Marie Louise.

"There's more than one way of looking at it," said Lebedev. "I take care not to let myself be cramped by our present official version of history. That is why I praised Peter. But I could say plenty against him."

He went on to recall how Peter, after capturing the rebellious sharpshooters, had himself beheaded them on the steps of the Church of St Basilius in Moscow.

"He even invited the foreign ambassadors to witness the performance," I put in.

"Which meant at least that the victims were able to proclaim their names to the world," retorted Lebedev, "instead of dying anonymously in a cellar."

"We're getting rather blood-thirsty," said Marie Louise. "Was there not a Tsarina who tried to save her country with the help of a monk?"

"Rasputin? Well, there are conflicting stories about him, too—on the one hand that he was a lecherous witch-doctor and a political adventurer, and on the other hand that he was a true patriot seeking to preserve the dynasty."

"And which do you believe?" asked Marie Louise. "What do they teach you in schools?"

Lebedev did not answer but pointed to a big building which I recognised as the Winter Palace.

"Catherine the Great?" said Marie Louise.

"We don't call her 'the Great,' " said Lebedev.

"Do you disapprove of her because of her love-affairs?"

"We don't discuss them."

"Perhaps it's a pity you don't," said Marie Louise so sharply that Lebedev was somewhat taken aback.

"Do you think we're terrible puritans?"

"I only know the men from whom Gustav receives instructions in Paris. I wouldn't want to have anything to do with any of them—not in my private life. They're all men who have either a badly-concealed contempt for women, or else the badly-concealed opposite."

"Go on," said Lebedev.

"I haven't come here to study statistics," said Marie Louise, "but to find out what your attitude is to women. The comrades in the west are if anything worse than the capitalists. The secretary has to be a mistress if she wants to keep her job. The job is simply the bait, and they all get caught up in the machine; they spend their lives intriguing, and they make no attempt to spur their men on to special efforts."

"When should they make these special efforts?" asked Lebedev.

"In their free time, when a man can show what he really is. But they no longer have any free time. They're all bogged down in party routine— sacrificial rabbits, masochists who want to make us submit to their crude ideas."

I laughed and said:

"Why do you have to come out with all this here?"

"Because this is the place to say it," snapped Marie Louise. "The *emigré* world is like a sick-room—a place where you mustn't mention sickness. But no Party interferes with you here, no Party-law. You're making a new beginning and everything is possible." She looked up at the Winter Palace. "Will you think me mad if I say that Catherine was truly a great woman? She chose her own lovers and brushed aside the old, lying traditions."

Lebedev gazed at her in astonishment.

"Those men were nothing but gigolos, professional swindlers, murderers of a Tsar."

"Murderers of a Tsar?" Marie Louise repeated. "That can scarcely be a term of reproach in Bolshevik Russia. And when you talk about professional swindlers, I suppose you're thinking of Potemkin. Well, I agree with the Austrian Emperor for whom Potemkin built those cardboard villages. He said, 'The semblance has just as much reality as the show of courtly brilliance.' "

It was the first I had heard of Marie Louise's admiration for Catherine the Great.

"Her reign started with two murders," I said. "She flogged peasants as brutally as any of her predecessors."

"Agreed," said Marie Louise. "But she made this country great. She fostered its growth as though it were the child in her own body. Don't you Russians ever talk of her now? Is she nothing to you but an enthroned maenad? How much do you think about love?"

I made a murmur of protest, but Lebedev did not seem to be put out by the question.

"We went through our wild phase," he said. "We took love as you take a glass of water. All that is past. As to whether we should follow the example of her Imperial Majesty . . ."

He made an indescribably delicate gesture with his hands and shoulders that instantly appeased Marie Louise's surprising storm of wrath.

"You should follow your hearts," she said in a level voice; and he accepted the words at once as a challenge, and took her hand and kissed it.

"I'm afraid that if I now show you round, as though Your Majesty had asked for another voyage on the Volga, you'll accuse me tomorrow of being another Potemkin!"

"Of course not," said Marie Louise. "How could I misunderstand? But I hate generalisations and sometimes I'm afraid for all of you. That's why I wanted to come. The problem of women has never been sensibly managed since the days of Eve. I'm afraid that even here you have got no further than to acknowledge the formal equality of the sexes. That was why I got worked up. You must forgive me, Comrade Lebedev."

It was the first time in the six years we had been together that she had used the word "comrade."

"Shall we go to the Hermitage," said Lebedev, "and see the Titians and Rembrandts? It was your Catherine who built the Hermitage."

"Thank you," said Marie Louise and blushed.

The gallery had not yet been arranged on Marxist lines, but the guides escorting the groups of people whom we saw going round all talked like members of the Central Committee of the Party. Marie Louise asked to be allowed to go alone to look at her favourite pictures. She had prepared for this visit in Paris, and had brought a book on Rembrandt with her. She was in a fever of excitement and seemed to have forgotten all about Lebedev. I asked him to translate some of the guides' remarks for my benefit. He did so hesitatingly at first, but then was infected by the comically one-sided nature of the fragments he retailed to me. We exchanged smiles, both wishing we could initiate Marie Louise into the official approach to the history of art.

But she went from room to room refusing to listen.

"I'm looking at pictures," she said haughtily, when I tried to talk to her. "There's really nothing you can tell me about them."

"She's wrong," said Lebedev and went on to give me an account of "art policy" as it had been pursued in his country during the past ten years.

A tribunal, composed of a number of sub-committees, determined the correct line. The dividing-line was the moment of the Tsar's abdication. Previous to this there had been art of every school—impressionist, classical, baroque, Byzantine, Gothic and folk-art. Now, however, only two schools were acceptable—naturalism and symbolism. Naturalist portrayals of the leaders and events of the revolution. Symbolical representations of the new or the desired world: apotheoses of liberation, optimism in bronze and marble, Lenin in the form of a lighthouse, collectivisation as a yard-long fresco, water-colours of utopian dawns, simple allegories of triumph.

Everything had to be made intelligible to the most primitive Soviet citizen. Lebedev sought to find the right words, seeing that I was not disposed to laugh but was seriously considering this development. The Soviet citizen, he explained, had to be preserved from losing himself in dreams, from being trapped into ineffectiveness; above all, he must not be allowed to stray into the wilderness of the abstract. This was regarded as the greatest danger. A Paul Klee served only to confuse the world of order with metaphysical unreason; a Kandinsky was a debauch in a chaos of colour. Picasso introduced a new dimension and with it constant disturbance.

Did they want tranquillity? I wondered as we walked through the rooms that Catherine had built. Did they want peace at last?

It seemed to run counter to all their dialectic, to the free flow of ideas, to flexibility. But Lebedev assured me that this was how they wanted it. They disposed of the moderns with the most convenient of guillotines—they called them decadent. The class that was rising must hold itself remote from that which was sinking. It was healthy; it lived in the light of day and no longer in half-darkness. It wished to see its own life portrayed in art, and all art commissioned by the State must conform to this desire.

"There is the dilemma," said Lebedev. "Art does not easily conform to a planned economy. At least it cannot be produced to order."

We saw Marie Louise in flight from a German-speaking group in the Rembrandt room.

"But how do you solve it?" I asked.

Lebedev's eyes were upon Marie Louise; he seemed to be regretting that all his wisdom should be wasted on me. He made another gesture with his graceful hands, like a sceptical student of the Talmud, and was on the verge of uttering some witticism when Marie Louise beckoned to us. He was the first to reach her. She seemed excited, and as I drew near them I heard her mocking the German-speaking guide—"From the Marxist standpoint this— from the Marxist standpoint that! It's all he can say about any of the pictures!"

Lebedev was smiling at the indignant flush on her cheeks. He egged her on by pointing to Rembrandt's *Danae*—the naked woman rising up from her cushions in ecstatic, ravished welcome of an invisible Jupiter.

"You see? For us Jupiter does not take the form of a shower of gold or we shouldn't have hung the picture. We don't permit loose morals."

Marie Louise did not rise to this. She stood gazing dreamily at the flawless body, that seemed both to absorb light and to dispense it.

"An offering like that is beyond price," she murmured.

Lebedev persisted:

"I said loose morals. Why don't you take up the gauntlet?"

"The gauntlet?" said Marie Louise, suddenly aroused. "That is a wholly feudal concept!"

"*Touché*" said Lebedev.

"And that's feudal too!" cried Marie Louise.

She was now in a rococo mood, but Lebedev did not lay down his arms.

"Why shouldn't we cross foils?" he said. "We accept what was good in the past."

"Then why don't you accept Catherine's loose morals?"

"*Quod licet Jovi, non licet bovi,*" said Lebedev. "What is permitted to Jupiter is not permitted to the common herd."

"Now you've turned monarchist!" cried Marie Louise in triumph.

They continued in this vein, strolling from one room to another. I followed rather unwillingly; I was dying to see more of Leningrad. But they went on talking light-heartedly about everything under the sun, from Repin to Pasternak. And in the end everything was mixed up—ironical comment on the Soviet approach to art, criticism of the pictures themselves, admiration for the good taste shown by the imperial collectors, and then back to a frivolous and friendly rejection of the official attitude. By that time we were again in the Rembrandt room. Marie Louise had opened her book and was studying the reproduction of one of his later pictures. Lebedev peered over her shoulder.

"What are you looking at? The blinding of Samson. A woman's assault upon a leader of the people! And what do you think a Party official would say about that?"

"Insufficient class-awareness on the part of Samson," said Marie Louise.

"Excessive sexuality," said Lebedev.

"Look at that wonderful bed," said Marie Louise.

"And where did the gold bracelets come from?" asked Lebedev and took Marie Louise by the arm.

"That's enough," I said unhappily. "You may be enjoying yourselves, but I need air."

They stopped at once. We went out into the street and I let them walk ahead of me. Lebedev suddenly turned and said:

"Are you cross? It was only foolery."

Marie Louise took my arm and laughed.

"He was jealous," she said, "and I can't blame him. I've been monopolising you, and he's been wanting you to talk to him about history. That's his hobby-horse. What can you tell us about the Marxist interpretation of history?"

We were again passing the Winter Palace. Lebedev leaned against the railings, seeming relieved.

"Let me think. Have you heard of Father Gapon, who led a procession of demonstrators to this palace in 1905?"

"He was an *agent provocateur*," I said. "The police allowed him to organise the demonstration."

"Quite right. And do you know where our mistrust comes from?"

"Tell us more about it," said Marie Louise. "I've felt that mistrust ever since I've been here."

"It is incidents of that sort which sometimes make one despair of everything," said Lebedev. "The hidden evil. I don't particularly mean the priest, Gapon. He was just a small police spy such as existed under even the earliest Tsars. They listened to the women chattering at the wells. But I mean the conclusion we draw in these days. Because spies and informers exist, anyone and everyone may be a spy and an informer. So everyone must be on his guard, and nothing and no one is safe. How can that possibly be healthy? Only confidence and mutual trust can be really fruitful. This state of incessant watchfulness and mistrust is like a disease."

"Of course!" I cried, delighted. "Your attitude is the one I was sure I should find here."

He made a gesture, brushing the remark aside, and I apologised for interrupting.

"What difference would it have made," he went on, "if Gapon had not been a police agitator? He would have been hanged, that is all. The procession itself is all that matters. The peasants came as true believers, singing hymns and carrying pictures of the Tsar and banners bearing the names of the saints. They had come to present a most touching petition, drafted by the priest himself. But the Cossacks rode them down and tore the banners and the pictures to shreds. It was something that had to happen. This was when it was made manifest that the Tsar, the Little Father, was no true father, and that obedience was more important than religion. The blood on the banners of the saints was more eloquent than all the sufferings of the atheists who were hanged for throwing bombs at the Tsar's sledge in the name of the same ideals. And twelve years later this palace was attacked in good earnest. . . . But I have no need to tell you about that."

"Tell us about the revolutions that failed," said Marie Louise.

"Do you find them more interesting than the one that succeeded?"

"No," I said, "but we need to know about them. And tell us more about the attitude of the Church. To me that is vitally important."

"I'm not sure that from your point of view it is really so important,"

Lebedev said thoughtfully. "The Church in the West has never been, as it was here, a mere adjunct of Caesarism. Here the real guilt always lies with the rulers of the State. The Church was simply an instrument, an array of functionaries, never a counterpoise to the temporal power. There was no rivalry between them. Religion as such scarcely needed intermediaries in this country. The people had invented their own legends, they had created their own saints. But from the time of Peter the Great the priests were bound to submit to the throne."

We had reached the heart of the matter and I felt that our journey was truly beginning.

"I can't accept that," I said. "A Church can come under the knout, but it can never surrender without being guilty of an act of gross betrayal. Are you saying that there was no conflict between the spiritual precept and the imperial decree—that they were absolutely identical?"

We had been walking as we talked, and now we sat down on the broad flagstones at the edge of the Neva. Marie Louise huddled in her coat.

"What position were the priests to take?" asked Lebedev. "What position is possible when the head of the State wears the aspect of God and is all-powerful?"

"A thousand opportunities were open to them," I said. "When a government outrages the principles which priests profess, and for which they are held in reverence, it is their duty to proclaim the fact. But instead of this your priests tolerated the *synodiki*."

Marie Louise asked the meaning of the word, and Lebedev explained it.

"Ivan the Terrible, the perfect specimen of a bored Tsar, used to amuse himself by torturing his prisoners. He flung them into pits filled with iron spikes, he roasted and burned them, in fact he did everything that the Inquisition did in the West. And then he compiled the *synodiki*, which were lists of names of the victims. He sent the lists to the monasteries, accompanied by a sum of money, asking them to hold Masses for the souls of the dead and to pray for himself."

"What outrageous cynicism!" exclaimed Marie Louise.

"The monks were even worse," I said. "This was the moment for them to raise their voices, to refuse absolution without repentance and to tell the Tsar that his money smelt of blood."

"It smelt more of money," said Lebedev, getting up, "and so they said nothing. Come, and I'll show you something."

We walked back into the town and presently came to a church with onion-towers, rising before us in a tranquillity untroubled by all the turmoil of revolution.

"That was the centre," said Lebedev. "Beneath that roof dwelt God and

Tsar and Pope, in one person. There was no other centre. We were all satellites encircling that sun. Let's go in."

The church was empty. From the middle of the central dome hung a pendulum on a long cord, which just grazed the floor as it swung. It was similar to the one which Léon Foucault had set up in the Pantheon, in Paris, in 1852. Foucault knew that a pendulum keeps on the same course, although the earth turns. By strewing the floor with sand, so that the pendulum left a trace as it swung, he was able to afford ocular demonstration of the fact that the earth revolves upon its axis.

But why was such a pendulum hanging here? Beneath the high dome the ikons stood untouched in a glimmer of gold.

"It's beautiful," murmured Marie Louise, gazing upwards. She had understood at once.

The marks traced by the pendulum in the sand were the hieroglyphs of a power, vast beyond man's conception, that needed no ikons. It was a reminder that served to put man in his place, that encouraged him to explore the marvels of the universe and warned him against the danger of gods made in his own image. It was a simple, precise refutation of that conjunction of Caesarism and Papacy that had for centuries preoccupied the Russian mind.

Marie Louise pointed to the ikons.

"I have never liked those saints," she said. "They all have dark circles under their eyes. They look as though they'd had a night out."

Lebedev smiled, happy that the day should have ended so well.

"Not that the pendulum solves our economic problems," he said. "But it fills our lungs with a fresher air; it blows away a lot of musty thinking. It humbles us, too, and rids us of the illusion that we are of such world-shattering importance. Perhaps it may also bring us back to poetry."

I looked for poetry and found it.

I found it in a public garden, a so-called culture-park, surrounded by the canals which Peter the Great had built to drain the swamp.

I pictured the nameless thousands of serfs who had lived and died upon that sodden soil, with hopelessness in their eyes and the whistle of the knout in their ears, from which there was no release except through death. From the hovels in which they lived they had been able to see the lights of Peter's house, which was not very big, for the gigantic Romanov had liked alcoves and low ceilings, but was the more extravagant in its debauches, at which vodka was drunk by the barrelful, and peasant girls ravished and whipped and meat devoured as though at a perpetual wedding; while all around the most patient people in the world ate their thin soup and went in perpetual fear of a corrupt bureaucracy and a spying police.

Now there were the gaily painted roundabouts of the pleasure-garden, from which grown-ups as well as children smiled at me, and boats for lovers on the canals. It was true that such things were no monopoly of Soviet Russia, but I could understand why Lebedev walked with his hat on the side of his head and a lightness in his stride as though he had been drinking champagne. It was a new Russia, no longer the land of the "Insulted and Injured," no longer huddled in wretchedness through the long, white nights. The stream of a new-found freedom flowed broad as the Neva itself, with laughter riding upon it like the coloured boats; and every day was somebody's Sunday, and there was no looming figure of a sombre Tsar to cast a shadow upon those bright afternoons. The people no longer peered through the branches at the pleasures of their masters; their joys were no longer the crumbs that fell from the rich man's table. Those who came to the garden could rejoice in what was their own; although perhaps it was only the older generation, returned from exile in Siberia, who could be fully aware of the contrast between the present and the past.

It was the voices of the older people that were most loudly raised in the public discussion groups. These groups were to be seen everywhere, always with a lecturer or "explainer" who was generally a young man, alert-eyed and neatly clad in an embroidered smock. He would sit hatless, with a stick in his hand, discoursing upon topics of everyday interest, sometimes basing his lecture on a political text, and the voices would be raised in eager questioning and debate.

We came upon a number; but there was one "explainer" who must have disapproved of us, for as he glanced towards us, standing at the edge of his group, Lebedev said abruptly to Marie Louise:

"I'd like to take you on a roundabout."

I watched her climb on to a giraffe, while Lebedev mounted a black horse in front of her. I don't know whether he had bribed the man in charge, but the roundabout seemed to go on spinning for ever. Lebedev had turned in his saddle and was leaning towards Marie Louise, talking earnestly, as though he were reciting poetry, while a flush rose on her cheeks. Suddenly he stopped, blew kisses to her and to me, jumped off the machine while it was still going and vanished into the crowd. A minute later the roundabout began to slow down, and I hurried to help Marie Louise down from her giraffe.

We made our way to the gates of the park as though we were under orders to do so. Marie Louise was silent. Not until we were back in the town did she say:

"That is the way one should always say good-bye."

"He'll come and see us tomorrow," I said.

"No. He's got us tickets and everything for Moscow—for tomorrow."

"Oh."

"He's very wise."

"I wish all revolutionaries had his gift for suddenly jumping on a rocking-horse."

"It wasn't a rocking-horse."

"I'm sorry—an Arab steed."

"And now he's on his way to Turkmen."

"He'll bring back carpets for you, and a cap of kingfisher's feathers."

"He'll bring back poems for me."

"And they'll be read aloud at the Congress of Writers."

And so we went to Moscow, the other Rome, feared by the West; the cynosure of the East, the seat of the World Communist Party, the residence of Stalin.

We arrived at the northern railway-station and found the booking-hall crowded with families in peasant clothes, seated on their bundles in a state of placid tranquillity markedly at variance with the modern, mechanised thunder of the railway.

Marie Louise's father, and his son, Jan, her half-brother, had come to meet us. Vogeler pointed to these people and said, "They love travelling. It's an urge. There's nothing one can do about it." There was something apologetic in his manner which left me silent. I saw nothing to apologise for in the spectacle. People who travel and move and sleep the night in railway-stations are at least living and not broken, even if they are flying from a catastrophe. In that case the evil can be seen, it is not hidden away in back-alleys, and it cries out for a remedy. To me those groups of people seated on their household belongings were a hopeful portent, but I did not know how to say this to Vogeler, who seemed to want to show us a fully matured new order of society.

I was more tempted to answer his ten-year-old son, who tugged at his father's sleeve and said, "Tell them that they're *kulaki*"—it was the disdainful term used for peasants who had formerly been rich.

The boy conveyed an impression of ready-made politics and current slogans, seeming fixed in his thinking before he had had a chance to learn to think. He seemed to be rebuking his father for telling lies. But how can a ten-year-old judge when a grown-up is lying? There was something aggressive in his self-assurance, and from the first I felt ill at ease with him. I hoped he was an exception.

But Vogeler seemed happy at being able to dwell in obscurity, aided by a State which suppressed half his personality and made of the rest a fragment of the whole. As we walked to his home in one of the State buildings, skirting the secret, forbidding bulk of the Kremlin, I remembered how he had once illustrated Oscar Wilde's fairy-tales, those charming, fragile fantasies of

N

a vanished age which he had understood so well. In those days he had believed with the old Bishop that the world's burden is too great for any man to bear alone, and it was in this spirit that he had painted, like a melancholy prince who bows to destiny.

The pictures he now showed us were very different—bright splashes of colour shaped in rhombs and triangles and fitted together like a jigsaw puzzle. But they were not purely abstract designs; there was always an underlying motif—a hint of the Soviet star, the hammer and sickle, or a fist. This smuggling-in of Party symbols was distressing to me.

"What do you think of them?" asked Jan, looking at us with searching eyes.

Marie Louise did not let herself be drawn.

"What do your friends think?" she asked her father.

"You mean the Party," said Jan, correcting her. "Well, Durus said that sometimes he's on the right lines, but generally there's still too much petty-bourgeois formalism."

At this Marie Louise laughed, rescued by this jargon from her momentary embarrassment.

"We had great fun at the Hermitage, Father. We examined all the pictures in the true Marxist spirit. We didn't leave much of Rembrandt!"

Vogeler laughed too, and the boy Jan, suddenly disconcerted, withdrew with a disapproving expression to the corner where his work-table was.

We then looked at the pictures which Vogeler regarded as his best. They were like posters, painted in strident colours—crude blues, poisonous yellows, glaring reds. I praised the portrait of his new wife, Sonya, which was hanging on the wall; but it was clear that this encouragement only disturbed him, like the notes of the pied piper's flute. The time of portrait-painting was past, he said. It was mere unproductive vanity.

"Does that mean you're supposed to paint like a robot, without any individuality?"

"No, but we have to learn from the masses."

"The masses! What on earth does that word mean? How can people who are only just learning the alphabet dictate to you about art?"

"Haven't you ever looked at children's paintings?"

"But surely that is an entirely different thing. Children's art is interesting because they live half in a world of fantasy. Their colouring is not in half-shades. They dream and play and paint without inhibitions, and the object they paint is not subject to utilitarian laws. They remind us of things we have forgotten; they wake up sleeping minds. But what have the 'masses' got to say? Who are these masses? Your son simply calls them 'the Party,' and he's probably right. You're a first-rate portrait-painter, but you don't want to admit it because you are being made to conform to a new concept of art."

We went on disputing until late into the night. Vogeler was very friendly, and happy, I think, at being made to recall other and better days. I never discovered how much he admitted to himself.

In his youth everything was offered him, but in 1918, dazzled by the promise of Utopia, he abandoned it all—the tales of his childhood, the quietness of sunsets, the peasants on the moor, the timeless riches of Ceylon which he had portrayed with so much love, but which, to conform with Communist precepts, he had now to depict merely as examples of colonial exploitation.

He travelled abroad and recovered something of his former quality. There was always a shadow, an undertone of tragedy, a hint of the Party countenance, in the sketches he brought back; but the timeless faces of human kind— woodcutters, herdsmen, dancers, women working in the vineyards—were none the less drawn with a spare lucidity, the midnight sun fell tenderly upon the landscape of the icy sea, the woods flourished in meticulous, unpolitical profusion.

But when in his small room in Moscow Vogeler set about transforming these sketches into oil-paintings, he did so strictly in accordance with the official, ideological line. He was the most innocent of Tolstoyans in the grip of a cold bureaucracy. It never occurred to him to adopt a sceptical attitude to the new ruling class. He believed that he had no right to criticise. He conformed to the point of unreason. When in 1940 Stalin ordered all German-born citizens out of threatened Moscow, Vogeler obeyed without question, though as a faithful Soviet citizen he was beyond suspicion. All the German-born party-bureaucrats secured exemption. Vogeler's son, already in a high position, was asked to intervene on behalf of his father. He refused. Vogeler was deported to Turkmen; after an exhausting journey he died in a shepherd's hut. His last postcard, which reached me after the war, is a pathetic indictment of a régime which never knew pity. In 1955 Ulbricht had the cynicism, in an attempt to cover the truth and court the German West, to send an agent to Worpswede, Vogeler's home town, there to organise an exhibition of his works, praising Vogeler's allegiance to the U.S.S.R.

I went for a walk with Sonya in the Moscow culture-park, and we passed a flower-bed arranged in the form of a picture of Stalin. I do not know what it was that made one so instantly aware of the difference between Moscow and Leningrad. Perhaps it was Sonya's unbending character, perhaps the mistrust of which one became conscious directly there was any mention of the West.

Sonya Karski-Vogeler was the daughter of a Polish Bolshevik. He was dead, but his wife was still living, and in the Kremlin; it was said that even Stalin was afraid of her Marxist rigour. Sonya hated her, as Mitya Karamazov had hated his father. She believed she could see through the old lady, whom she held to be a gossip and mischief-maker on a transcendental scale and a profiteer at the expense of the system. In those days ration-cards for the use of people in government circles were graded in twenty-six different classes.

Sonya hated the official jargon but defended her country, with true Russian distrust, against all foreign critics. Only in one matter did she refrain from criticising me—she wanted to know all about Münzenberg's work and *The Brown Book*.

Her constant interest in that hidden doorway through which Goering's incendiaries had passed aroused in me a suspicion which was confirmed one evening when she took me for a walk round the Kremlin. It was a moonless night and the street-lighting was very dim. We passed by a doorway in which a man was standing, visible only as a shadow. Sonya fell abruptly silent. Not until we had come to the river did she whisper, tremulous as a girl in love, "Did you see who it was? It was him!" She meant Dimitrov. To her he was the only one who stood beyond good and evil. He was the revolution which must burst forth anew; for only from outside Russia could the revival come, the new blood. Russia itself was a bureaucratised deception, mere rumbling entrails.

And now she walked with me in the culture-park and talked Marxist jargon. The culture-park was no Garden of Eden, or fairy-tale land, she said, but an intrinsic part of the Five Year Plan. People did not come here to relax but to concentrate their energies; not to forget themselves but to discover their unity with the whole. The animals were not merely a distraction but designed to serve the cause of scientific education. Games were designed for the formation of character and to stimulate healthy rivalries which would then be employed in the service of the State. Abruptly she broke off to tell me a story.

"When I was a girl I once went to the Kremlin to see Dzherdzhinsky, the head of the GPU. I was amazed to find a man of such importance in a bare room furnished simply with a table, a chair and a camp-bed. He knew I had come to ask about all the shootings that were taking place. 'It's a hateful necessity,' he said, 'but someone has to clean out the latrines.' I did not like the sound of this, and he saw what I was thinking and without a word handed me a wire-puzzle. I looked at it without doing anything with it, and that pleased him. Then I started trying to separate the bits of wire, but lost patience and tossed the puzzle on to his table. 'So you aren't ready yet,' he said, and dismissed me. He had wanted to find out if I had the nerve for under-cover work."

Sonya turned back towards the games-booths.

"Now we give everyone those puzzles," she said. "Everyone can find out for himself what's the matter with him." And she concluded in a louder voice which instantly sounded suspect: "Self-knowledge, the highest degree of self-knowledge—that is the objective. That will solve everything."

I had been feeling for days that she was on the verge of exploding. Now she did so, and I shall never forget that moment in which it became clear to me that no amount of rationalism would ever rid this Russian people of its habit of self-destructive introspection, its Dostoevsky inheritance.

We had passed by a wall on which there was a placard setting forth the targets of the current Five Year Plan. "This will be done. . . . Production will be stepped up to this extent. . . . This figure will be achieved. . . ."

"The biggest bluff of the century!" she cried suddenly. "Always 'will'—never 'must' or 'should'!" She was silent for a moment and then went on: "Hope is the opium of the people. We did not make sacrifices under the Tsars. They took everything from us. Now we give of our own free will. Now we sacrifice ourselves. From one plan to the next. And it's all for *us*. We're even told why—for us, for us, for us! Say it three times and it's true!"

I did not interrupt but listened in silence, taking care not to look at her as we walked.

"We're becoming an industrial State," she said. "Agriculture needs machines, so light industry is allowed to go down; we eat less and we wear holes in our shoes. The peasant comes to the town and becomes a factory-worker, and betrays his own livelihood. So then light industry is boosted again, but then we haven't any guns to defend us against our enemies. So what are we to do about that?—go without jam, without underclothes, without blankets. Sacrifice, sacrifice, sacrifice—three times over! And perhaps somebody complains that without shoes we can't go to the culture-park, or writes an article about the queues outside the bakers' shops. Well, but can't they see that these things have to be, that all this is historical necessity?"

We turned down a side-path, and she went on, looking straight in front of her:

"Perhaps they're all moaning everywhere, all with their own ideas—perhaps even the peasant is beginning to think he knows better. The rats will soon be gnawing at the Kremlin walls, and a Pugachev crops up in every Novgorod—there was a snake there with a hundred heads, better to cut them all off before they become a thousand. . . ." She broke suddenly into a parody of Stalin. "Everyone whose head reaches higher than mine must lose that head. Everyone has a traitor inside him. Tomorrow I will cut them down. Let the people sleep and ride on the roundabouts and dance folk-dances until the sword, hanging by a thread, sweeps down upon the neck of one of those in high places, nearest to me. It must be no insignificant mocker, but one close to me; then no man will sleep easy in his bed and we shall be saved. . . ."

She stood still abruptly and looked at me with fiery eyes. She was shorter than I, and I felt that I ought to lift her up to say that I felt no desire to laugh at her.

"Now you think I'm a Trotzkyite," she said, "and you can report me to the police if you like." Her voice sank.

I was very much shaken. Children ran past us, playing with brightly coloured balls. I watched a boy in top-boots sink slowly down to earth from the parachute-tower. There was a sound of clapping from a crowd of dancers, and I had a glimpse of a girl in a white blouse spinning like a top round a man who stood stamping his foot.

I said as quietly as I could:

"In my circle we don't betray anyone to the police."

"You Germans are all so noble, aren't you?" she said scornfully. "All high breeding and Nibelungen-loyalty!"

I had to try to break down this morbid distrust. I said carefully: "That's why I left Germany," and after a pause I added—"That's why I'm here."

She did something that was certainly unusual for a former student of the Marx–Lenin Institute. She bent suddenly, and seized my hand and kissed it. Then she turned away and vanished among the crowd of dancers without once looking round.

I paid a visit to the sanatorium near Moscow where Dimitrov was convalescing. There were few people about, and I was told that I would find him on the second floor. I went along gloomy corridors containing pieces of old furniture, the windows half-hidden by looped-back curtains. The great-aunt in *The Idiot* might have lived in that house. I felt that the Chinese vase must be standing somewhere on its wooden pedestal, still unbroken. There was a smell of dust, then suddenly of scent. I followed it until I found myself looking in at the half-open door of a rather sombre room. I drew back, startled. A man was standing at the other end of the room who, fortunately, had not heard me approach. He was occupied with his toilet.

The man put down the hairbrush and picked up a scent-spray, studying himself in the glass while he sprayed himself. I now had a better view of his face, which was roundish. His penetrating eyes lighted up somewhat. He put down the spray, smoothed his wavy hair. I realised now who he was, and would gladly have withdrawn to spare us both embarrassment, but he called out in the broken German which he had learnt in a German prison:

"Come in. I'm just ready."

I felt slightly ashamed of my own behaviour. It had been sheer journalist's instinct, the instinct that makes no man a hero to his valet. What did these trifles matter? This was the man who had defied Goering single-handed. I remembered the picture of his hand thrust out in condemnation of those Leipzig judges. The hand I now saw still bore the traces of handcuffs. Dimitrov had known very well that the scaffold had been set up for him in the prison courtyard, but he had spoken out with a courage that the whole world recognised, and he had asked no quarter.

I went in and silently offered him a copy of the flimsy-paper edition of *The Brown Book* which we had smuggled into Germany, taking pride in the fact that I was among its contributors. He recognised it at once and smiled and said:

"That was a great help to me."

This was my first encounter with the head of the Comintern, that world-wide conspiratorial organisation for the fostering of revolution which was as much feared as it was grossly over-rated.

Dimitrov showed me the array of gifts that had reached him in a single day—food, wine, flowers, clothing and numerous other articles, a child-like tribute but without sycophancy. Many were accompanied by nothing more than a word of greeting, unsigned.

Was it a sense of shame that caused me to feel chilled? Perhaps it was only the monstrous contradiction in the evaluation of a single man. Here was a half-starved people bestowing the best they had to offer on a man whom all Germany shunned as an incendiary, some preferring to hear nothing about him while others accepted every tale of his villainy recounted by the Goebbels radio. The great disturbance of all values had begun. It was no longer a matter of truth-seeking or understanding, or of forgiveness. One had to take one side or the other. "Who is not for me is against me."

Contemplating those gifts, in that old-Russian villa, I took my own stand, although the subsequent twenty years were to show me that one must not do so, but must always keep a foot in the doorway—and for my part, head and shoulders as well—so as to have a view of the other side, so that comparison is possible, and change and doubt can work their salutary shocks upon the mind.

Dimitrov thought it "terribly funny" when I told him of the circumstances in which I had discovered that underground door beneath the Reichstag. "In 1919 I fought against the Spartacists," I said. "Now I'm on the side of the Spartacist Dimitrov." He frowned, not liking this. Then he shrugged away the thought and led me to another room which was almost entirely filled with a high, carefully-made bed.

"This was a real Spartacist," he said, and told me that it was the bed in which Clara Zetkin had died. He was still contemplating it, lost in thought, when we heard the sound of two men coming along the corridor. We went out to meet them. They were Wilhelm Pieck and Walter Ulbricht, the German Communist leaders.

Together we drafted the text of an appeal to the people of the Saar. I remember Pieck reading out one of my sentences in a tone of mockery. "Fascism and freedom are as much a contradiction as fire and water, or Heaven and Hell." He looked at Dimitrov. "Nonsense, don't you think? Since when have we believed in Heaven and Hell?"

I said sharply:

"The people in the Saar believe in them, and those are the people I'm writing for."

"Quite right," said Dimitrov.

I never saw so disconcerted an expression as that of Pieck, or so swift a change of front as that of the hypocritically smiling Ulbricht.

"It's the popular form of speech," he said. "Just what we want."

It was then that I obtained permission to make a film which the film-producer Ivens, a Dutchman, had suggested to me. It was to be used in the Saar plebiscite. We would give a picture of the daily life of the Russian people, showing what they ate and drank, how they moved about the streets, how they spoke to the police, how they lived—not in slums, as Goebbels asserted, not under the knout or in a state of terrified oppression.

A week later I heard from Koltsov that he had obtained an invitation for me to attend the Writers' Congress. On the same day Ivens, the Dutchman, told me with a broad smile on his youthful face that the budget for the film had been approved. I received a cheque in payment for an interview I had given to a Leningrad newspaper. When I rang up to ask about this, thinking there had been some mistake, I was told that an interview was work, like anything else, and that in the Soviet Union nothing went unpaid-for. Commissions were offered me, journeys were proposed. Dimitrov warned me that the film was my most important task, but my nerves were fluttering in a slightly dizzy astonishment.

Marie Louise suggested that we should give a party. She knew the shops where foreigners could buy things.

We got vodka, camembert, butter, pumpernickel and preserves, and conveyed these treasures to Vogeler's apartment.

"Caviar!" he exclaimed and shrugged his shoulders. "It reminds me of 1910 when I did a book-plate for Crown-Prince Wilhelm."

Jan sniffed at the butter.

"If it comes from the black market it shouldn't be put on this table! I'm a pioneer!"

Sonya saw that I had something more up my sleeve. She looked at me and said, "Well?"

Marie Louise laughed:

"Father, have you forgotten the parties at Worpswede, with concerts by Petri and Rilke's poems and dancing in the open-air theatre? Those were real parties. This is just a tiny affair. Do you mean to say it isn't allowed?"

Sonya burst out: "We're allowed to do anything, but we don't want to. We want to rise with the rest of the people, and for the present we want to suffer with them."

"What do you mean by suffering?" Jan demanded. "We have everything we want. We've no use for the things capitalists have. Everything in the Soviet State is much better."

"All this fuss over a little caviar," I said, "and you still don't know where the money came from. It's the money I've had from the State publishers for my book, *Water, Bread and Bullets*." I paused for effect and then said casually, "I daresay there'll be more caviar. I've just had an invitation to attend the Writers' Congress."

It was rather much, but they bore it. Vogeler, the shy North German, sniffed in embarrassment, and Sonya sprang up and embraced me. Jan came and took my hand.

"Will you make a speech in Russian? I'll help you."

"Jan!" exclaimed Sonya; but everyone was happy.

Vogeler accompanied us back to our hotel and said with a touching diffidence:

"Perhaps you'll both have time to come to me and sit for your portraits."

"Gladly!" we said together.

We began work on the film the next day. I had to get it finished before the Writers' Congress, which meant working at record speed, because apart from the actual shooting, thousands of yards of film from the archives had to be examined, to select and match old material with the new. But the sense of urgency was universal in Moscow, and besides, I was no longer an exile but among friends.

We tried to make everything look as natural as possible. I stood in the Red Square with a copy of Goebbels's *Völkischer Beobachter* displaying a cartoon of a monstrous woman, a Red commissar, beating Russian peasants to death, while Ivens stood by in concealment with a film-camera. Another member of the team came up and tried to snatch the paper away from me, protesting against the open display of Nazi propaganda. What followed was entirely spontaneous. A little crowd collected, at first merely curious but growing indignant when they realised what the dispute was about. There were black looks, raised fists, talk of "provocation" and other attempts to snatch the newspaper, all of which Ivens filmed with great delight.

Finally, a policeman appeared. One of our assistants produced our permit and explained what we were doing. Ivens had to intervene to convince him, which took some trouble.

When it was over, and we were walking towards the Lenin Museum, Ivens said in triumph:

"You see how the capitalists lie about us? We might quite well have been arrested for trying to stir up a public demonstration—the film might have been nothing but a pretext. There's no getting away from the fact that you were flourishing a Nazi cartoon. You heard that man talk about provocation. Provocation to what? Provocation to attack and abuse the Government. But even if it had been genuine nothing would have happened. Everybody criticises all the time. The whole country is alive, and I think it's wonderful. Even if we'd been taken to GPU headquarters it wouldn't have mattered. You'd have told them who you were and pointed to your record, and I might have talked about my Zuider Zee film, which was just a forecast of the things that are happening here. But here everything is done on a big scale and everyone benefits. They respect a man for his past; there are things by which you can profit for the rest of your life. The old Bolsheviks, who took part in the revolution, have places reserved for them on the trams, for instance; you don't see them clustered in the doorway like bunches of grapes! I find everything so organic, grown from real roots, so true to nature, as we say in Holland."

His enthusiasm was infectious. We made a film which was a fairy-tale—soothing-syrup for the doubters and caviar for the mockers. (By a grotesque chance it never reached the public.)

Half-way through I became conscious of its lack of logic. The sight of angry faces might convince an audience of the genuineness of the scenes I provoked, but they had no means of knowing what the lips were saying—it was a silent film. Ivens protested vehemently:

"Anyone who worries about the finer shades is a bad propagandist. Simplicity is what counts. The Nazis tell lies and the Russians tell the truth. That is what the message has got to be."

"But how are you going to convince people of this?"

"Are you convinced?"

"Yes."

"Then you have only got to act as though you were."

I let myself be persuaded, for whenever doubts assailed me Ivens would answer them with fresh Nazi newspapers secured from the office of the Hungarian, Bela Kun.

After five weeks, Ivens took me along to the studio, where the cutter had nearly finished putting the film together. He asked for a run-through, and to me it was a revelation.

It started with a panorama of Moscow. Then my head appeared against the walls of the Kremlin, and the church of St Basil looked down on the excited group studying the copy of the *Völkischer Beobachter*. It switched abruptly to a view of the empty and desolate steppes. A mirage appeared, of a farm with modern equipment, and was transformed into reality. Pictures of poverty and misery were succeeded by pictures of groups of laughing men and women. Everything was designed to underline the contrast between the present and the past. But the cumulative effect, the sharp cutting, the sweep and flow and profusion of images, the variety of the faces, depicting the mingling of a hundred different races in a two-thousand-year-old history—all this possessed such vigour and reality that it seemed to me that the very quality of the photography and *montage* would justify the propaganda. The ending was a sort of symbolical coda. Workers and peasants came together like tributaries flowing into a mighty stream, villages became towns, the flood swelled and poured over the Red Square as though the tide had broken down the dams of life itself—gymnasts and runners, wrestlers and athletes—could there be so much health in a half-starving nation?— singing girls, dancing children, rowers, skiers, gliders. The camera swung away from them and was turned upon Lenin's mausoleum, and the round face of Dimitrov appeared. He raised his arms, embracing youth and faith and victory. . . .

The film ended and the lights came on. I put my arms about Ivens and embraced him. He grinned happily.

"Faith moves mountains," he said. "In return you can try and get me a card of admission to the Writers' Congress."

Outside the Bolshoi Theatre, where the formal meetings were held, huge banners had been hung with pictures of Lenin, Stalin (the man who was never seen, except on ceremonial occasons) and Maxim Gorky. Gorky gazed somewhat ominously down at the street, his features unmarked by age, his hair cut short, looking rather like a fox-terrier liable at any moment to run between someone's legs. But the papers praised his kindness and all that he had done for Russia. It was also known that he suffered from tuberculosis and had lived for years in Capri for the sake of the climate. A photograph of him playing chess there with Lenin was much on view.

For days, so we were told, Gorky had been closeted in his cottage near Moscow, preparing his inaugural address. No one had been allowed near him. It was to be the speech of his life.

Great hopes were entertained of it by the many foreign writers who had arrived, among them Louis Aragon, vain to the point of comedy, anxious for everyone to know about his friendship with Mayakovsky, the "trumpet of the Revolution," and of his acquaintance with Yagoda, the head of the Secret Police. "We shall be given directives for a century!" he boomed.

Klaus Mann was there, the sensitive ugly duckling who was not told nearly often enough that he was a swan, sometimes betraying a hint of that melancholia which in 1949 was to overwhelm him, to Europe's loss.

Oskar Maria Graf was there, the anarchist from Bavaria. He brought with him the best of reputations. When he had learned, at the time of the burning of the books, that his own name was not on Goebbels's proscribed list, he had exploded in fury, "I do not know what I have done to deserve this insult. For God's sake, burn me!" He came to the Congress wearing the *Lederhosen* of his native Bavaria, delighted as a child at the prospect of meeting Gorky. "He wrote *The Mother*," he said, "and that is enough to justify a lifetime!"

Ernst Toller was there, the pacifist of Heidelberg days, the Munich revolutionary, the prisoner of Landshut, grey-haired now but with the same mournful look in his eyes, a concern that was all for the suffering of others, never for his own. His plane had been delayed, and he entered the theatre only after Gorky had begun his address. The photographers rushed at him with their magnesium flares, and he exclaimed furiously, "Can't you see who's speaking?" He hid his face and crept into a seat. . . .

Gorky was speaking. He had no voice; he was sometimes inaudible; but he had the most appreciative audience in the world.

He settled the glasses on his nose, smoothed out his manuscript under the glare of the powerful arc-lights and, constantly assailed by the flashlights of the over-zealous photographers, read a speech that lasted three hours.

What it all amounted to was the tilting of a proletarian Quixote against the windmills of bourgeois idealism. His Rosinante, although skinny, felt sure of herself; harnessed with the conventional trappings of the Communist State, she merrily kicked up her heels at everything that came her way. It was as unusual as it was radical. She got her first laugh, from the packed rows, when Gorky made her kick Immanuel Kant out of his grave and force the philosopher to admit that he would never have worried his head about "the thing in itself" if he had been a primitive man clad in skins. Primitive man, said Gorky, was a materialist.

He smiled at the thunder of applause and went on to demolish the myths in which, up to the present day, poets and historians have sought to veil the materialist thinking of our earliest ancestors.

I looked along the frantically applauding rows; they were listening as though to an oracle. An interpreter was seated between André Malraux and myself, a full-bosomed, perfumed lady by the name of Ballabova. She was doing her best, turning to right and to left, to give us in French a summary of what Gorky was saying. When Malraux helped her out with a word she looked gratefully at him with handsome, dark eyes. She knew Icarus and

ANDRÉ MALRAUX

Daedalus, whom Gorky mentioned, but not Phaethon. However, it did not matter, because Gorky was methodically sacrificing all the figures of legend on the altar of dialectical materialism, stripping away their mythological garments and revealing them as *udarniki* who had sought to increase the productivity of the workers in the caves of the primitive world.

Poor Icarus! He twice had his tail-feathers pulled out. He was not the symbol of man's *hubris*, since no such thing existed in the Promethean State of Russia. He was merely the technical progenitor of the Russian rocket. And Tantalus was not condemned for having aspired too high and angered the gods; he was simply "primitive man in the midst of phenomena which he did not understand." The myths, in short, were all born of the sweat of fear. As for the Christian God, Gorky flew against him like a jet fighter, confident that all those assembled in that baroque auditorium in the year 1934 would be amazed at the way he burst through clouds into emptiness, because there was no God! I quote: "He was an artificial summing-up of the products of labour."

"*Quoi?*" asked Malraux.

"*Généralisation des resultats du travail,*" said our interpreter.

I felt absurdly responsible for the speaker, and looked past Malraux to see what the others were thinking. Klaus Mann was drawing on a scrap of paper (it is true: he had drawn a bearded man against a background of sandbags, and soldiers with fixed bayonets—was it a picture of God?) Plivier was asleep. Oskar Maria Graf was nodding contentedly, while Aragon looked up after every sentence and smiled at other members of the audience. I thought of Nietzsche's madman who had run about the market-place with a lantern in broad daylight, repeatedly proclaiming, "I am looking for God," and then said that men had killed Him. I had never forgotten his tremendous cry— "How shall we drink the sea dry? What were we doing when we broke this earth away from its sun?"

It was hard to accept a vision such as this. Nor could any man easily outbid Dostoevsky's Grand Inquisitor. But Gorky had no thought of going beyond him. He merely offered a formula, that of a self-satisfied atheism which brushed aside all the problems of nihilism as mere perversity.

"He's very strict," Koltsov had said to me. "He hates mystical writing. He regards Dostoevsky as our greatest danger."

I had leaned back in my seat, but our interpreter warned me to pay more attention to what she was whispering. Malraux laughed and said, "*Ils le font travailler.*" He meant God. I whispered back, "*Je préfère Nietzsche.*" Malraux saw that I was suffering, and with that serenity which had done so much to ease my exile he said, "*Monsieur est un peu en retard.*" This time he meant Gorky.

Gorky was by now becoming rather hoarse. In a reedy voice he set about destroying the West. He left not one stone on another. The role of the *bourgeoisie* in the sphere of cultural productivity had been depicted in exaggerated terms. Particularly where painting was concerned they had forced everything to submit to their own laws.

I was growing angry. "Not such bad laws either," I grunted, thinking of Titian's *Earthly and Heavenly Love*, the Sistine frescoes and Gozzoli's *Procession of the Kings*.

But in this, of course, lay the reason for Gorky's scorn. The feudal lords were rich, therefore criminals, their brocade cloaks stained with the blood of the people. And the poets were toadies and flatterers. Not one had told the story of Stenka Razin or of Pugachev. They were talentless and characterless.

I looked at the white-haired man with his deep-set eyes. Gorky was then sixty-six. No doubt he had reached the peak of his career; he had come to his Mount Nebo and before him lay the Promised Land. The picture was complete in itself, but Gorky pressed the analogy too far. Moses's forty years in the wilderness became four thousand years, and everything good in them stood condemned before his implacable seat of judgment.

He became grotesque. It was in ancient Egypt, he said, that we must look for the origins of the corrupting bourgeois literature; but not, as we might think, in the deeply-moving laments of Amenemhet I, or in Amenophis's hymn of praise to the sun-god, or the rhythmical working-songs of the fellaheen—no, bourgeois literature began with the Egyptian fables about thieves.

The harsh sentences in all their limitless banality exercised a kind of spell. At first my wits were benumbed by the sheer spate of words, and it took me a little time to realise that there were things that had to be defended. Had Sophocles and Aeschylus written mere tales of thieves? Dante and Shakespeare? Goethe—Rabelais—Voltaire? . . . I sat muttering to myself, in the fog of my disquiet, while the great figures of European literature, authors and heroes, passed in a procession through my mind.

Malraux glanced towards me. "*Qu'est-ce que dit Regler?*" he asked the interpreter. "*Je crois qu'il gronde,*" she said with a professional smile. "*Il y a de quoi,*" said Malraux.

I did not look at him, but his sympathy brought order to my thoughts. Perhaps we should excuse Gorky on the score of age and ill-health; perhaps he really did take this over-simplified view of history; perhaps he was only saying what his public wanted to hear. But it was noteworthy that he evaded the main problem—what kind of literature was possible if all the human cares and perplexities of mankind were to be eliminated?

There was an interval and we went outside to cool off. I told Malraux of the Indian custom, when they have relieved a donkey of a heavy load, of putting a stone in its place, so that the donkey's back does not ache.

"Gorky doesn't seem to think that the Russian back is so sensitive," I said.

"Perhaps," said Malraux, "he doesn't think it will be so easy to remove the burden."

Our interpreter came up to us, beaming with delight, to say that we had been invited to visit a home for neglected children at Bolshevo.

"I could do with a little air," said Malraux in a tone which left no doubt as to his meaning.

"*Oui, il fait frais aujourd'hui,*" said our helpful interpreter.

The home was somewhere to the north of Moscow. I was surprised to learn that it had been built by the police.

"You'll see," our interpreter said, and went on to give us a long account of the children we should find there.

There were some who had witnessed the shooting of their parents. They had seen people transformed into animals by the famine of 1921 and had become animals themselves. They had no conception of property or the value of human life; they could neither read nor write. They became outlaws, with a gangster's morality, allied only against the police. They appeared at railway-stations, creeping in from the grey steppes like creatures of another world, rootless, purposeless, hopeless, watching the trains with hungry, dispossessed eyes, obscene in their gestures, those who had reached the age of puberty—in every respect the opposite of the orderly, docile citizen, filled with the spirit of self-sacrifice, which the régime was striving to create.

"But we shall make good *komsomols* of every one of them," said our interpreter rather sweepingly. "And here we are."

The cars (we were a fairly large party) stopped at the side of the road. A young man was awaiting us wearing a blue cap and a moustache like that of Trotzky, whom he somewhat resembled.

The interpreter whispered as we got out, "He committed robbery and murder. Now he's in charge of everything!" She pointed with pride to the array of tidy buildings.

The young man said with a polite bow that he would like us to divide into separate groups and go where we pleased, without guidance. The whole place was open to us. It was a holiday, which was why we heard no sound of tractors. The boys were occupied with their hobbies. They had been told of our visit, but they did not wish to be paraded as exhibits. We should see them exactly as they were.

We were delighted. At last we were to see something that was not put on for show.

We went into a small room where a dozen art-students were making life-studies of a model standing on a platform. I looked at the drawings. All were the work of beginners, some hopeless, others in the uncertain middle stage between primitive and effective representational art. I should not mention this episode at all had there not been a real artist among them—he was the only one who was working at an easel and allowed to use oils.

The supervisor had come in behind me, and something prompted him to whisper that they had been unable to find a female model and had to make do with a male. But I was looking at the boy's picture. The figure was drawn with considerable skill and precision of line, meticulous in its anatomy, with a quite unusual colour-scheme of green and violet tints that shed a fluctuating light reflected from limb to limb. But the picture was like a hymn of praise. It was the painter's happiness in his subject, a sort of humble rejoicing, that so delighted me.

I wanted to tell him so and stumbled against the stool on which he was seated; and then, perceiving the crutches leaning against his thigh and the wasted calves beneath his trouser-legs, I suddenly realised that he had suffered from polio. His disease had created a masterpiece!

We returned to Moscow in the mood of those who have received an unexpected present. The Congress seemed more hopeful. Delegations arrived asking to be told about the life of Russia, the true life. A woman asked for more love-stories. The old writer Olescha made a public confession and sounded like Simeon in the Bible with the Christ child on his hands. After him Boris Pasternak, then totally unknown to me, a handsome, shy poet, recited some verses which reminded me of the mystical aloofness of Rainer Maria Rilke. Bukharin spoke and was listened to with nearly as much respect as Gorky; and his speech was gold in comparison with Gorky's dross.

He attacked what he described as the "Wagnerians" among the poets, recommended the use of fewer brass instruments and less high-flown language, and in particular he mentioned the poet known to everyone as Bezymenski, a second-rate writer of dithyrambs.

The younger people in the audience applauded wildly.

I met Bukharin again at the banquet held by the Government at Gorky's country house. A horseshoe-table, overloaded with cold dishes and decorated with flowers, had been arranged in a long reception-room whose windows afforded a view of birches and box-trees.

The master of the house sat at the turn of the table, often rising to his feet but seeming rather helpless, particularly as the drink circulated. Gorky was quite without arrogance or pretentiousness. When he replied briefly and shyly to those who rose to drink his health one could almost forgive him for his speech at the Congress.

Next to him sat Molotov, stiff, eating little, occasionally adjusting his pince-nez. Gorky's daughter-in-law was on Molotov's other side, then came Ehrenburg, then Bukharin, and then, by the special grace of Koltsov, Marie Louise and myself.

I complimented Bukharin on his speech, and especially on the fact that he had urged the young not to be afraid of depicting the modern world with all its contradictions.

"Otherwise art is degraded to mere pamphleteering," he said. He left all the dishes untouched and his little red beard twitched contemptuously whenever his eyes happened to fall on Voroshilov, at that time Commander-in-Chief of the Red Army, who was steadily getting drunk.

I wanted to go on talking to him. "All this is truly Oriental lavishness," I said, pointing to the loaded table. "Where else in the world would writers be treated with so much honour?"

"Less would have been better," he said dryly.

"Are you thinking of Lenin's bag of sugar?" I asked.

He did not know the story and asked to hear it. It had been told me in Paris by Hugo Eberlein, a member of the Comintern, whom in 1935 we were to meet again in the Saar, and who later mysteriously vanished.

In 1918 Eberlein and Léviné, the German revolutionary, had crossed over from the eastern front. Léviné had been caught by the field-police in Lithuania, but had escaped and gone to Munich, where in 1919 he was shot. Eberlein had got to Moscow and gone to the Kremlin, where, he told me in a voice warm with enthusiasm, the guards standing round a wood-fire had embraced him when he said that he was German. He had been taken without ceremony to Lenin, who had received him in one of the big rooms, passionately interested to hear the latest news of the German revolution. Tea was served while they sat talking about the Workers' and Soldiers' Councils. Lenin sipped his tea, and finding that there was no sugar in it jumped up and left the room. He was away some time and finally came back with a little piece of paper torn from the pages of *Pravda*. He had gone from room to room looking for sugar, and finally had got a little from Kamenev. He gave it all to his guest.

I had been very touched by this story, which revealed a humanity, a feeling for the everyday things of life, that was totally lacking in the Party men I had encountered, with the exception of Willi Münzenberg. When I had finished telling it there was a momentary silence in our group. From across the table came the rumble of Voroshilov, who was drinking a toast with Kaganovich. I thought I heard Malraux's voice in the distance, and there was a burst of unrestrained laughter from Oskar Maria Graf.

I pointed again to the table, feeling the need to say something polite.

"You've gone from sugar to caviar. The country has made progress."

Bukharin smiled with a faint irony.

o

"Too materialist," he said, "but forgivable at table."

Koltsov, who was acting as Master of Ceremonies, came to tell us that Oskar Maria Graf was going to speak.

Marie Louise clapped her hands, and Gorky gazed benevolently at her. We had grown very fond of Graf during those days. He detested cheap emotion and could be shattering in his bluntness. The son of a Bavarian baker and a frequenter of the Munich cafés, he had become known through his soberly recounted autobiography, *We Are Prisoners*, and had made himself popular in Moscow by his stormy challenge to the Nazis—"For God's sake, burn me!"

Children followed him about the park, gazing in astonishment at the leather shorts which he continued to wear throughout his visit to Moscow as a protest against pomposity. He feared neither misunderstanding nor suspicion, and referred to the Austrian Social Democrats as "*the* Party," as though their presence as an opposition party in Moscow would be highly desirable.

He had refused to pay a visit to "Snow White," by which he meant Lenin in his glass coffin, and he considered that the discussions that went on were far too solemn—"almost like Prussians," he said.

He said this in the speech he now made, and he went on to say that in his view the October celebrations should not take the form of a military parade (at this point he looked towards Voroshilov, who was, however, no longer in a condition to hear) but should consist of dancing and singing, and that the festival should be held earlier in the year, because of the weather and for the sake of "the wenches," so that it could all take place in the open air and there would be a chance for the young folks to get away into the bushes.

I chuckled over this, having been prepared for something of the kind. Graf had startled everyone in Koltsov's publishing office by signing a contract for a book and immediately asking for his money. It had looked like pure greed, but he had turned to me with a wink and said, "Let's see how long it takes the bureaucracy to cough it up." He was genuinely interested in testing the working of one of the State-controlled concerns, about whose sluggishness many tales were told.

Koltsov had been resourceful enough to produce the money immediately, but back in our hotel Graf had behaved even more strangely. Always mindful of his humble origins, he took exception to the lordly style of our accommodation. He climbed the hotel stairway, loudly singing a peasant song, and then showered roubles down on the staring rabble, that is to say the hotel guests, below—a mixture of Villon and Pantagruel. With the money that remained to him he proceeded the next day to buy fur-coats, and when he was told that he would not be allowed to take them out of the country, since they were women's coats, he called for a pair of scissors and started to cut them to shreds, saying that he could do what he liked with his own. Koltsov intervened, laughing, and promised to get him a permit.

But he was enjoying this party, which was honestly sybaritic and un-marred by the windy talk that went on at the Congress. He was drinking vodka out of a tumbler, and he had a full glass in his hand as he made his brief speech, warning the company against too many military parades and then going on to thank Bukharin for having reminded us of our heritage from the past.

Suddenly he raised his glass and said: "Try to remain good Socialists."

The Russian interpreters whom I could see sitting with the leading political figures seemed to stammer over this and were perhaps relieved when, directly Graf had emptied his glass and sat down, another figure rose up in the background and came slowly up the middle of the room between the wings of the horseshoe table.

The thick cloud of tobacco smoke gave him a spectral aspect, and I was suddenly overtaken by the strange thought that this occasion might have an historical parallel. Yet it could not be said that it resembled Macbeth's ban-quet! Gorky was no Macbeth, but rather, in his diffidence, a vagabond peep-ing into the kingdom of the rich and wishing that it might vanish.

The spectre had drawn closer through the mists of smoke, and was al-ready speaking. It was Karl Radek.

Bukharin, at my side, was gazing stonily at him. Only now do I realise that this banquet was the last of its kind to be held in Russia. For the last time there was an unrestricted meeting of minds between East and West, both being accorded an All-Fools-Day freedom to say what they pleased. Radek took advantage of it. Perhaps the warmth of vodka and the sight of so many foreign faces had robbed him of his judgment, so that he believed we could see what was taking shape beneath the surface, and would presently come to his aid, and that of Bukharin and Koltsov and all the others who were threatened.

But as he confronted us in that late hour of the night, pacing up and down between the drunk and the sober, the writers and the Cossacks, the heads of the State and Gorky, the honoured one-time vagabond; as he turned from one side to the other, alarming his friends and appealing to the foreigners, I do not think it occurred to any of us that he was placing his life in jeopardy. Not until he opened his shirt and beat his bare breast did I realise how serious it really was. Bukharin bowed his head. He seemed to be painfully shocked by this exhibitionism, although he and Radek were close friends.

Radek spoke first in Russian. Since he spoke several languages fluently I suspected that his words were intended more for his own Government than for ourselves. I asked Koltsov to interpret, which he did.

It was a Dostoevsky speech, an act of ecstatic confession and self-flagellation. "We must look more deeply into our hearts and scatter the eggshells of our self-deception!" he cried. "We must seek our own private peace of mind."

Radek lived in a big apartment in one of the buildings reserved for high Government officials. He had an enormous library. Everything classified as "enemy literature" passed through his hands. He was the only one to know all the arguments of the opposition.

How he protected himself against a cleavage in his own mind is something I have never understood.

And now he walked amid this feasting company of writers from all over the world and accused himself. He told us of his errors, and that the collective system could never be too highly prized. He said that we must put aside personal ambition, never cling self-righteously to our own opinions, but always listen to the voice of the people, follow the lines laid down for us by the Party, acquiesce in what the dialectic ordained.

He spread his shirt wider apart. There was now no stopping him. I found him terrifying, with his gleaming eyes and the little, ugly fringe of beard on his chin that served only to emphasise the thinness of his lips. He was certainly drunk, but this had loosened his tongue without impairing his wits. "He's talking too much!" Koltsov whispered to me, and glanced anxiously towards the Government people. I noted Molotov's tense mouth and Gorky's wrinkled forehead. "He's in a mood to throw everything overboard," said Koltsov, and craned his neck to see whom Radek was now facing. But what was there for Radek to throw overboard? All sound in the room had died down.

"We are still far from our objective," said Radek in his high-pitched voice. "We thought the child had come of age, and we have invited the whole world to admire it. But it is self-knowledge, not admiration, that we need. The Revolution is no safari, a source of agreeable thrills. Heroism is of no worth in itself. Executions must be evaluated, not made mysteries of. We are all still petty bourgeois!"

Koltsov gripped my arm as though he knew what was coming next. He reached for a glass of vodka and poured the fiery stuff down his throat. He alone understood, as I realised later, that Radek with this many-sided speech was taking a step nearer to the limbo that was destined to engulf him. It was his last big public appearance. With his shirt hanging over his belt he paced up and down amid the cigarette-smoke and the clinking glasses, but always keeping at a certain distance from Molotov, and suddenly he directed his attack at the Germans. He upbraided them, talking of his bitter disappointment at their swift betrayal of the Revolution, the way the workers had adapted themselves to Hitler, and the ease with which the literary calling had been *gleichgeschaltet,* brought into line. It must be said that not many had fallen upon fruitful ground!

He was now speaking in German, but not from courtesy. His purpose was to insult and offend. He had been well known in Germany for a long time. In the summer of 1923, at the time of the Ruhr occupation, he had made a remarkable speech about the youth, Schlageter, a member of one of the extreme right-wing fighting groups, who had shot at some half-starved Ruhr workers in the belief that in doing so he "stood for Germany," to recall the phrase used by the Nationalists. The French, foolishly behaving as though the war were still on, had summarily executed him. But Radek, instead of condemning the boy, had cited him as an instance of how good faith is exploited by the so-called "great," who always find it so easy to agree among themselves. He had talked of Schlageter as a "courageous soldier of the counter-revolution," a "martyr in the cause of German nationalism" and, referring to his state of self-deception, a "wanderer in nothingness." His speech had been unsentimental but filled with an understanding for which I had given him credit since that day.

But now he stopped before Malraux, rubbing his grotesque fringe of beard.

"Why," he demanded, "did Malraux ask the *komsomols* what they thought about death? Why does he adopt this unfruitful attitude in a century in which the individual has at last been given the chance to fulfil himself in community with others?" And suddenly he cried: "Comrade Malraux, too, is still a petty bourgeois!"

I do not know how many people at the crowded table realised the implications of this charge. It seemed to apply equally to the Government which exalted such a writer: for Malraux, by his status alone, was the most honoured guest at the Congress.

It was a cheap triumph for Radek, since Malraux, with his innate sense of good manners, would certainly not attempt to reply in the circumstances. But it was a sensational climax to this concourse of people from different worlds over which the omens swayed, the spark of mistrust, the gloss of a transparent diplomacy.

Radek kept on coming back to Malraux's speech to the Congress, which he so misquoted as to make it clear that his intention was to provoke him.

Malraux had suggested, far too delicately, that it was not enough for the writer merely to depict the surface appearance of noble or desirable qualities, sacrifice, heroism, tenacity; he must invent, he must go deeper. "Your classic writers give a richer, fuller picture of the inner life than is to be found in the Soviet novels. . . . Every man tries to think out his own personal life, whether he wishes to do so or not. If you eliminate psychology it simply means that those who have seen most deeply withhold their experience from others."

Like an evangelist Radek strode up and down between the pots of caviar and the remains of roast chicken.

"Petty bourgeois!"

Gradually I came to understand the reason for his fury. The Press chief, the arranger of life, the day-to-day tactician with a poison-cupboard in his ivory tower, the agitator and fabricator of slogans, was irritated by Malraux the poet, the questioner, the psychologist, the rebel. "Art is not an act of submission but of conquest," Malraux had said in this town where every publication was censored. None of the Russian speakers had dared to say it.

"Petty bourgeois!" Radek thundered, repeating the words with a drunken obstinacy as though he were stumbling over them. Then, beneath the basilisk gaze of Molotov, he returned to self-accusation, and in the end his discourse became a mere mumbling, the firework display petered out amid the hubbub of talk and the general indifference which finally he seemed to share. He picked up glasses as he passed, perhaps finding comedy in his own pathos. I will not venture to say that he foresaw that tragic hour when he was destined to stand alone before his judges.

Finally, he faded away through the tobacco-smoke and vanished like a ghost into some other part of the house, and I heard Koltsov breathe a sigh of relief.

"The party's over," he said in an exhausted voice.

I saw Bukharin get to his feet, and then Molotov; they stood gazing over the tables as though at a field in the aftermath of battle. Koltsov took my arm and led me towards Molotov, saying that he would introduce me. He told Molotov who I was, and talked about my film and about the Saar.

"You must make Thälmann your banner there as well," Molotov said drily.

We moved on, and Kaganovich, who was then Mayor of Moscow, said, "We will welcome you in Moscow after the victory." I remembered this promise five months later, when for the second time I fled to France.

Voroshilov was briefer. He cursed the Nazis. "May the devil rape their grandmothers!" he said to me and the others standing round.

Gorky held my hand for some moments and said, "Take care of yourself." There was a slight tremor in his voice, and the words were both a warning and a blessing. He was again the man of his early writings, who understood how much all human creatures need compassion; perhaps Radek's outburst had recalled them to his mind. Then Oskar Maria Graf burst in between us, holding a bottle in one hand, while another was sticking out of the pocket of his shorts.

"Comrade Gorky," he said, "must take something with me—very thirsty —need to do a lot of drinking. . . ."

Gorky nodded in scarcely veiled surprise and Graf thanked him and vanished towards the garden, where the engines of numerous cars were beginning to roar. I looked round for Bukharin and Radek, but they had vanished without taking leave of anyone.

Stalin had cried off at the last moment. To the Congress he had contributed the remarkable thought, "Writers are the engineers of the soul."

The phrase appeared in all the papers, and one asked oneself, what is wrong with it?—why does it sound wrong? Was the soul in need of technicians, or were the technicians looking for a soul? Was it not a sort of kowtowing to the robot? All kinds of thoughts occurred to me when I first heard the words. I may say that I did not hear them with any sympathy. From the first moment (and not twenty years later, after his death) Stalin appeared to me the prototype of the vain second-rater, building himself up by the use of propaganda into a myth for the gullible, and with the aid of a diabolical police-force keeping a mistrustful eye on all those who were superior to himself. That he was presently to set about methodically destroying them was something that not even the most alert suspicion could foresee in the year 1934. At the time I found him merely intimidating and at the same time grotesque. That he should allow himself to be called the "engine-driver of the revolution" by the railwaymen, the "admiral of the Volga fishermen" and (by the coastguards) the "lighthouse of the century" rendered his tame adulators more ridiculous than it did him. He called writers the engineers of the soul—and kept away from them. What could he have had to say to Malraux's speech? *"L'art est la conquête des sentiments et des moyens de les exprimer; la conquête sur l'inconscient (presque toujours), sur le logique (très souvent)."* Was it his sub-conscious that had restrained the leader of the Party from contributing anything more than a bad impression to the Congress?

I asked Sonya about his absence from the banquet and she exploded, "He despises the whole lot of you and he wanted to show it!" She was in the same furious mood as she had been that day in the park. "He's not a Russian, he's a savage. He comes from the tribes that still sacrifice animals and pursue vendettas. He's bound to hate a man like Malraux."

"That was a reason for coming," I said. "It has never hurt a tyrant to listen to poets. Alexander or his father stepped out of the light for Diogenes, and Dion, the tyrant of Syracuse, received Plato as a guest."

"Shall I tell you the real reason why he didn't attend the banquet?" said Sonya. "It's because you foreigners couldn't be searched for weapons. He's frightened, just like Ivan the Terrible. Besides, you might have laughed at his official food-taster."

"You're letting sheer hatred get the better of you," I said, genuinely distressed. "Some day you'll suffer for it."

She laughed harshly.

"They want to send me to do under-cover work in Germany. That way at least I'll die an honourable death."

Every propagandist is a schizophrenic. He lives a double life in the maze of his own creating, with no thread of Ariadne to show him the way out, and no Daedalus-wings either.

I believed in my film, which I was to take with me to the Saar.

But a difficulty arose. The completed film had to be approved by the Comintern. I asked Bela Kun to see it for this purpose and he flatly turned it down, saying that the whole thing was much too crude and over-simplified. I pointed out that the Saar miner was not subtle in his thinking and that Goebbels was likely to win with his campaign of abuse, threats and lies. Kun was not impressed.

"The picture of our workers living in better houses doesn't prove anything," he said coldly. "Anyone can fake up a bigger and better birthday in a film-studio. As for sports parades"—we had included a sequence of Dimitrov at Lenin's mausoleum welcoming a procession of athletes—"they are the most stupid and unimaginative kind of display that was ever invented."

Thus spoke the one-time Communist dictator of Hungary, who had come to hate the sight of uniforms, and the frequenter of cafés to whom a good joke was more important than the whole of Marx. He now had the power to pronounce the death-sentence on our well-intended piece of propaganda. (Three years later he was shot in a purge.)

I spent the day going the rounds of Moscow, wondering why I had not foreseen this.

It seemed like the reward of virtue when that same evening, and by pure chance, I achieved my aim. Kun came into the Hotel Moskva with a blonde actress who was still wearing her make-up and the Paris gown in which she had been appearing on the stage. There was no need to ask what part she had been playing. She was a picture of everything that the words vice and depravity meant to Moscow. Accompanying them was a plump actor, wearing a dinner-jacket and a monocle, who also still had his make-up on. He was the cartoon-capitalist, as the left-wing theatre had been depicting him for years—a bloated monster of greed and rapacity.

I looked at the two of them, and then raised my glass to Bela Kun, saying, "Here's to crudity and over-simplification!"

He was enough of a Hungarian to see the point. He laughed and said:

"All right! Come round tomorrow and I'll put our stamp on that rubbish of yours. And may God be with you in the Saar!"

Two days later I left Russia to travel, by way of Warsaw, Prague, Vienna and Switzerland, to the boiling cauldron of the Saar.

In Vienna I remembered suddenly that I had written to my father from Leningrad, asking him to address his reply to Vienna in October. Would it be an echo of my own raptures upon my first glimpse of the Garden of Eden?

He wrote:

> I have delayed answering as you suggested. Let me plunge straight *in medias res.*
>
> You talk about the art-galleries, and how simple people are encouraged to look at pictures and learn how difficult painting is. Splendid! You talk about the pendulum in the church, and about the children's playgrounds and the culture-park and the instructors, all of which are free. Splendid again! But then you tell me about the public humiliation of a drunkard by exhibiting a *papier mâché* model of him with his name underneath. That may be trifling in itself, but it is none the less a gross assault upon the most sacred human rights. What you call the *chistka* is even worse, the public scrutiny of private lives. All that, my dear, is highly suspect. I am speaking mildly. There is a flavour about your letter for which I cannot find suitable words. What is the point of this display of dirty linen in public, this socialist Inquisition? I am tempted to paraphrase Anatole France—"Are the poor of Moscow no longer allowed to die under the bridges?" Can the beggar in Moscow never drink champagne? Can no one have his private thoughts? You have always insisted that everyone has a right to his own privacy. I remember your once saying that God Himself desired this privacy for men, and that when any man in an access of despair sought to bare his soul before Him, He would turn His head away and contemplate His squirrels. I prefer to look at the squirrels, my dear; and that applies to all your recent experiences. You must beware of your own impulses. We want no more collective masochism, we have had enough of that in recent centuries. I care nothing for the "criticism of the masses"; it is a contradiction in terms.
>
> And now a word about our Saar plebiscite. I know you want to have a hand in it, and I know you will be disappointed in the outcome. We are Germans: it is a sentimental fixation which has not altered by a hair's breadth. Moreover we are a frontier people, which never has a good effect on the character. And finally, we are utterly provincial: how can we be expected to think in terms of Europe as a whole? However, you should not be deterred, in spite of everything, from telling the Saarlanders a few truths. They are a much troubled people, racked with doubts, and you may be able to sow a few seeds. But don't expect victory! I drink to your sanguine spirit! . . . Your affectionate Father.

I sat in a taxi, on my way to the Vienna Westbahnhof, a prey to conflicting emotions. They seemed to be reaching out their hands to one another—

Lebedev in Leningrad, Sonya in Moscow, Father in the Saar. . . Was I really the victim of my own wishful thinking? . . .

Twenty-four hours later, on a sunny October day, I arrived in Saarbrücken. On the platform were men carrying posters depicting a full-bosomed, homely matron with open arms, into which a ten-year-old girl was running. The text, in the Saarland dialect, ran *"Nix wie hemm!"*—no place like home. Dear little Saar was hurrying to a smiling big-hearted Germany. Goebbels understood the importance of that symbol. He had learnt it from the Jewish writer Freud—the return to the womb is the most deep-seated wish of all.

BOOK FOUR

11. Dear Little Saar

FROM the start there were not many of us. We thought of ourselves as the David who would overthrow the National Socialist Goliath. There are wishful dreams that defy reason. The little no-man's-land between the Third Reich and France, its area 1910 square kilometres and its population in those days three-quarters of a million, gave us the illusion that we could continue to maintain the independence which for eighteen years had been guaranteed by the League of Nations.

It was a quite childish belief, induced perhaps by the extraordinary density of the population. The area was inhabited by 402 people to the square kilometre as opposed to 133 in the Reich—ten times as many as in Spain and more than twice as many as in the British Isles. We possessed a considerable feeling of solidarity, we of the Saar. We might have formed a phalanx, as the Roman legionaries had done in moments of danger. But in 1933 that new voice was heard over the radio, breaking harshly into the tranquil, light-hearted music by which the Saarlanders lived—the voice of the "Führer," implacable, urgent, over-heated. "Prussian," they called it, and to the people of that region the word meant much the same as the word *Boche* means to the French.

I came from Russia resolved to do battle with that voice. By chance I had been born in the Saar, and therefore had a right to mix in its affairs.

Since 1933 I had struggled with agonising doubts, and my first visit to the Saar during that year had left me with a sense of profound depression. It was a pilgrimage that had taken me there. The Bishop of Trier had summoned the faithful to visit the holy relic belonging to his cathedral, the Sacred Kirtle. It would be difficult to say why he had chosen that particular year. There were evil tongues which whispered that he had done so to oblige the Nazis. The pilgrim-trains ran daily through the Saar valley and crossed into Germany without worrying about the frontier. During the few months of my exile I had learnt to identify the Third Reich with terror, force and persecution. No *emigré* could return without risking his life. I wondered whether the pilgrims were conscious of the change of air when they passed from the liberal atmosphere of the Saar to that of the Nazi State, and to find out I joined one of the parties under an assumed name.

Directly the train started everyone began to pray. When presently I looked out of the window, to see where we had got to, I found that we were passing my native town. It was still within the boundary of the Saar, but the ominous frontier was very near. A priest intoned prayers and we repeated his words; and as we did so I took leave of the place which from the start of my exile I had tried to avoid so as not to endanger my parents. I saw the chapel where the procession of the Feast of the Assumption had always paused, and then I looked up towards my brother's vineyard— how remote it all seemed! We crossed the stream of the Seffer, where as a boy I had stood with Father watching the floods; and on the Galgenberg, Gallows Hill, I saw the mental asylum which since March 1933 had housed a dozen patients calling themselves Adolf Hitler. We passed the church at Besseringen where we had sometimes gone to confession when our sins seemed to us too heavy to be entrusted to our own parish priest. The frontier was drawing nearer—would I soon be forced to take leave of all this for ever? I saw the St Gangolf valley, where I had sweated out the injuries inflicted by war; and there was the Mettlach tunnel, beyond which were the ponds belonging to the castle of the Von Boch family, where I had skated in winter and waited hours in vain for Maria, the bailiff's daughter. It was a landscape that had always welcomed me with loving arms, and that seemed as far removed from politics as the litany we continued to repeat with a childlike devotion.

The pilgrims as they prayed glanced through the windows to right and left, reckoning the value of the crops in the fields we passed. When the priest paused in his prayers and general talk broke out, it was about nothing but the Sacred Kirtle.

"Do you know that He wore the tunic as a child and that it grew as He grew? It grew with Him for thirty-three years, until the last moment, when they tore it off. It is crocheted in a shell-stitch."

Another voice said almost dreamily:

"No, you're wrong. It's knitted, and in a chain-stitch. He stood naked in the sun. It was at about this hour."

"He cried out for water."

"And they offered Him vinegar."

"When one sees all the vineyards on the hills . . ."

"Our poor Lord Jesus!"

I went into the next compartment. I was touched but at the same time terrified. What had they offered Mühsam when they struck him down? Was Mühsam different? His travail had not been private, nor was that of Ossietzky. Did no one here seek to compare one thing with another? Was it pointless to remember these things? Should not a new wave of sympathy go out from this pilgrimage to all those who suffered in the Third Reich?

I thought of the charges with which for months past the National Socialists had been bombarding the Catholic Church. They reviled it for its riches, contrasting these with the poverty of the industrial workers; they hinted at vice in the darkness of the monasteries and talked of the priests as spongers and parasites.

We crossed the frontier and pulled up soon afterwards in the little wine-growing town of Serrig. The sight of SA men on the platform made my heart thump, but nevertheless I leaned out of the window. One of the police was near enough for me to touch. He saluted and asked if everything was all right in my compartment. I nodded, unable to speak for the constriction of my throat. He saluted again and walked on, and behind him came ambulance-men and nurses with first-aid equipment and stretchers. They all wore swastika armbands, and smiled and were helpful and gentle in their manner.

The poison worked exactly as it was intended to do. The SA men saluted a banner bearing the picture of the Madonna, and I heard a Gestapo man say to our priest—"May Jesus Christ be praised!"

That episode had come as a shock, but there were other things that hit me even harder. Now, upon my return from Moscow in the late autumn of 1934, when I had my first sight of young men in jack-boots strolling through the streets of Saarbrücken, and, despite the official prohibition, greeting one another with the Roman salute, anger rose in me again and I banished all doubts and misgivings from my mind. I have never engaged in any fight merely because I was sure of winning.

We toured the countryside, and the cars which we left standing outside meeting-places were often burned. I made arrangements for showing my film in all the villages, but showed it first to an audience of Party-members, feeling confident that this pre-view would be the most successful performance of all.

It took place in a beer-hall. I spoke only a few words. It seemed to me that in that Nazi-threatened region the picture of the Moscow sports-parade (with Dimitrov and all the display of high spirits) was enough in itself to make explanations unnecessary. There were young men present who had come from Germany. They came to me afterwards and shook me by the hand, asking if they might see the film again. I promised that they should. I meant to take the film to the remotest corners of the land, and to speak as well—anything was better than the Nazis.

But a second run-through was not given. The secretary-mistress of one of the leading Communists attacked me on the grounds that I had included only Dimitrov and not Stalin. I explained briefly that this was intentional and had been done so as not to make the film look like Communist propaganda. They gazed at me with the stony eyes of police officers.

In short, despite Bela Kun's official approval, the film was banned! The

Party-censors knew that it could be of help in the battle against Hitler; but they also knew that it might later prove to be a black mark in their personal dossiers. It was confiscated, and all the trouble and expense, Ivens's talent and the helpfulness of the Russian work-people, went for nothing.

I wrote a speech which I delivered in numerous variations to the miners and peasants until January 1935—the tragic, humiliating month. Its first utterance was directed at friends who had loaded me with advice. They wrote to me from Trier, where they were now priests, or from the Ruhr, where they were engineers; they wrote with the best intentions, and some wrote with hatred. Something in my attitude gave them pause, but they all used the phrase "a unified Germany," and all believed that it was a dangerous adventure to stand for the world and in doing so lose one's own country. One of them—he was later killed by the Nazis—offered to intervene with Frick on my behalf. No one, he said, could go on living in a state of pursuit and banishment; and, moreover, he was sure that my expatriation, of which he had heard, was due to a misunderstanding. He knew Frick, who was as scrupulous and correct as any judge. A passage from his letter remains in my mind. "Don't you see," he wrote, "that in a few years there will be nowhere for you to go? Every country will be either German or under our control." I sent him my speech and heard no more from him.

> From tomorrow on [I wrote], the newspapers across the Rhine will be calling me and my friends traitors because we are urging upon our fellow-countrymen throughout the length and breadth of the Saar that in this plebiscite they should vote for a postponement—a postponement, not a secession. They must not return to an enslaved country or of their own will recognise the new masters in Berlin. It seems to us that we have changed masters often enough. We have good reason for wishing to retain our independence. For centuries the storms have swept first over our land. Our houses have been the first rampart against shell-fire. We know those shells, we have made them ourselves with French iron and German coal. What is there German about coal or French about iron? Your Führer says, "Everything is German!" This means that tomorrow our own shells will be exploding in our faces. The whole thing is a bloody farce. Look the jester in the face! Is it a face at all?

While I was speaking on these lines in a mining village a woman of a somewhat woebegone and by no means pampered appearance cried out, "He is as beautiful as a young god!" It was not me she was talking about but Hitler.

The word "Separatist!" was often scrawled on the walls of our meeting-places. I never pretended to ignore it; nothing was to be gained by dodging the issue.

"Who is it who has separated us every thirty years?" I demanded. "Who has played with our land? Who would not set Belgium free in 1916; who plundered the French mines until 1918; who wanted to annex the whole of Europe? A separatist is anyone who seeks to sunder mankind with national boundaries, ramparts of cement, armoured fortresses, barbed wire and patriotic balderdash. We have been digging our own graves long enough. We don't want to use the Roman salute or the French salute; we want to raise up the poor in the ways that God intended, and not towards an earthly god who treats us all as creatures beneath contempt."

This speech was delivered with many variations.

Sometimes, when we were driving at night and there was a moon, we saw a car following us. It bore a number belonging to the Third Reich and contained a party of youths armed with pistols but wearing plain clothes. Their orders were to ram us at a curve in the road and then hasten to our aid with an ambulance which would take us to the nearest hospital in the Reich; a Nazi doctor would there attend to our injuries in such a fashion as to ensure that we ended up in the morgue. "In the homeland, in the homeland, there shall we meet again!" sang these young thugs outside the inns where we were speaking.

The Saar was not the most progressive part of Europe. Most of the miners were peasants who left their wives to look after the fields while they spent the week working to earn a little extra money in the pits at Völklingen, St Wendel or Sulzbach. Many returned to their villages only on the Sunday, weary and exhausted, with probably no thought in their heads except for the wife whom they would embrace that night. They did not much care for politics, but were swamped with the subject from the moment Hitler came into power in the Reich. How much impression our speeches made on them we learned when our votes were cast, in January 1935. We might have realised the situation earlier. Why were we so blind?

There was a youth of twenty-one who came to the Saar from the Ruhr, a Communist whom the storm-troopers had caught in March 1933. He had been unemployed and had never attempted to conceal his opinions; he stood for the Red revolution, and continued to say so even when they beat him with steel rods. They battered the teeth out of his head, filled him with castor-oil and went on beating him while his body drained itself in convulsions. He was subjected to some months of this treatment and got away finally when they made a show of releasing him and took him back to his own district, where they hoped they might find some of his friends.

He told this story to the workers of the Saar. He was one of them, with the same reek of hunger, the same look of longing that they could see in the eyes of their own children, and with lips drawn tight in hatred. They might have seen in him a brother who had suffered as they had suffered. Why

P

did they not understand that he had suffered for them? Was it the confrontation with reality that frightened them? The boy was precise enough in his utterances. He put a finger to his mouth to show the empty tooth-sockets; and once in a gesture of despair he pulled the shirt down from his shoulder to display the swastika that had been branded on his flesh with cigarette-ends. But it seemed that they could not endure these demonstrations. They blamed him for having suffered so much, and held him guilty because he was defeated. The very fact that he was one of their own kind caused them to react the more stubbornly against what he had to say. He bore the infection with him. "Not this one, let Barabbas go free!"

I was at one of the meetings at which he spoke. His dry, factual story shook me deeply, and I was sure that no one in the big hall would ever again believe Fascist propaganda, after being shown this evidence of the Fascist reality. But then a voice that I shall never forget shouted: "What are the French paying you for this swindle?"

I thought the boy's wounds would burst into flame. I thought he would rush down from the platform and strangle the heckler, and that the working men in the audience, their pores blackened with coal-dust as though it were a stigma of martyrdom, would rally to his aid. But what came up from the hall was a burst of laughter that robbed me of every illusion. The workers believed the slander. The boy had got what he deserved, his hash had been settled. In a little while the place was empty; and he stood there in an attitude of utter helplessness on the platform, holding his shirt in his hand.

I did not readily abandon self-deception. I had embraced a creed which held that one could always count on the working class, since it was the mainstay of all progress and of every religion.

Our woodland villages were filled with miners. They started in the pits when they were scarcely more than children. Boys whose beards had not yet begun to grow carried the long, heavy hoses behind the workers at the coal-face and sprayed water over the gaseous dust; they led the half-blind pit-ponies along the galleries and pushed with their shoulders against the laden trucks. It was a trade calculated to poison and embitter the mind of any man.

Since the Treaty of Versailles the Saar mines had become more dangerous. The French maintained a working only so long as it was profitable; then they removed the props and let the roof fall in. The sound of creaking was to be heard everywhere, roofs sagged above the heads of the grimy workers and the danger-curve rose steeply.

But where the overseers were concerned nothing was changed. The French had kept on the toughest foremen and brought in others equally brutal. They prowled through the galleries, reckoning up the loads on the trucks as they saw fit, accepting bribes and sometimes using the measuring-rods brutally on the men; and sometimes a man would hit back with his pick. It had all been the same in the days of Wilhelm II. There had been no change of system in the darkness of the pits, and to the miners the outside world still looked the same. But since 1933 there had been one small difference—the name of Hitler was openly spoken. It was something to hurl as a threat in the face of the overseer—and it was good to have something to threaten with. After the "night of the long knives" and the murder of Röhm, when the news reached the pits that Adolf Hitler did not spare even his closest friends, it became clear to the miners that Hitler was "their man." They did not say this aloud; indeed, to us they said the opposite. But they voted that way. They did so on the 13th of January 1935.

When I drove to my home-town to vote I found the little Protestant school, where the polling took place, surrounded by Hitler's storm-troopers in plain clothes. They at once formed a lane along which I had to pass; in their eyes it was an alley-way of shame. It had been laid down by the League of Nations Commission that any public demonstration would invalidate the result of the voting. So my former schoolmates stood glaring at me in silent hatred as I walked past them into the building. The polling-room was presided over by a League official with a representative of the right-wing parties on one side and a Socialist on the other. I saw that one of these was my godfather, an upright, admirable man, devoted to his calling. When it was my turn to vote he bent his head over the list and muttered my name in a hurried undertone, although by the regulations he should have announced it clearly. My spiritual father, under Canon Law, was ashamed of me. The poison of propaganda had worked with him too; he no longer looked to see whether the Nazis were lying. I was wrong—it said so in the papers.

I went behind the curtain and made my cross in the circle which was intended to preserve my homeland against the organisers of a new world war. I knew that in doing so I was signing my own decree of banishment and that tomorrow the Nazis would proclaim me a fugitive. They would be right. I should have turned my back on the land, since to remain in it would mean death.

As I was getting into my car my parents appeared round the corner, coming towards the school. It was the last time I saw my father. He did not notice me in the car; only Mother saw me, and cried out a hurried word of warning. Father saw nothing but the yelling youths who were celebrating my departure with jeers and cat-calls. I saw his expression, the twitching of his lips at the edge of his moustache, the light of disdain in his deep, dark eyes. I thought of his letters, his wise, ironical judgment of Stinnes and the *Feme*-murders, of the Social Democrats and of the Kaiser—how would he be able to go on living if the Führer won? He had opposed the Kaiser just as he opposed the French occupation troops; he hated force, and revenge even more. He had been a devout Catholic all his life, but he was feared by all the divines of the district, for he would allow no priest to lapse un-challenged into unchristian obscurantism. He was profoundly convinced that democracy, with all its faults, represented a far higher principle than any form of government by strong men. When I had paid him a surreptitious visit one night a few months previously I had found him as sceptical as ever. But it was he himself who on this occasion had brought a bottle of his best wine up from the cellar, to help us both to forget that his eldest son must creep under cover of darkness into his house. "Every country gets the house-painter it deserves," he said, raising his glass to me. Now his face seemed to grow frozen with contempt and pity as he contemplated the screaming youths outside the polling-station. He seemed even to stagger in his walk, as though physically afflicted by this demonstration of voting methods. Only later did he learn that his own son had been its object. And by then he knew the out-come of the voting, with which my second period of exile began.

A last ordeal lay before me. On the Sunday after the plebiscite a triumphal procession marched through the streets of Saarbrücken. The people turned out in their thousands, as a year before they had gone on pilgrimage to Trier.

We watched them from behind the curtains of a room in the Kaiserstrasse which an elderly Jewess had allowed us to use. We heard the bands already playing the Horst Wessel song, and we heard the children who accompanied them screaming for our blood. They came from the pits and the fields and the wretched hovels by the refuse-dumps and cried out for revenge upon us. They came in the triumph of "liberation," as they thought—the Society of Goat Breeders, the Society of Pigeon-fanciers, the Women of the Father-land, the Men's Choral Society and the Society of Wounded of the 1914 war. They were filled with rejoicing, and there was not one who would not have lynched us had they found us. But we were hidden behind the windows which the old woman had decorated with paper flags in flower-vases, bearing the colours of the Kaiser's Reich.

With me was a Social Democrat who shed tears as he listened to the children's cries. Hugo Eberlein was also there, the treasurer of the Com-munist International who supervised the spending of Moscow's money. He was doing sums on a writing-pad, and he showed me the figures. Although he was disappointed and dismayed by our defeat, he hid his distress behind an air of cynicism. "It's not a bad balance-sheet," he said. "We owe thou-sands of francs to the paper-suppliers. The rent for the Party-house is five months in arrears, and the printing-presses are in hock. Nothing but creditors. That is the one victory that we owe to Herr Ulbricht's inspired slogan." He waved the grisly sheet of paper before my eyes, and it looked as though it were not the first time he had cast such a balance-sheet. Down in the street the happy victors streamed past. All they saw was the full-bosomed mother-figure of the posters, while we saw the death's-head and the swastika.

Next morning, when the radio at the inn called *Der Stiefel* announced that 85 per cent of the population of the Saar had voted for the return to Germany, a young woman belonging to the inner propaganda circle collapsed over the round beer-table at which she was seated in an access of despair. "In whom can we still believe?" No one ventured to try to console her. She had fled from the Reich when her husband was arrested. She had worked day and night for the *status quo*, but she had refused to have anything to do with Ulbricht's ludicrous fourth slogan, "A Red Saar in a Soviet Germany." After many meetings—she must have conducted at least a hundred—she had been convinced that the Saar workers were going to give Hitler a tremendous punch on the jaw. She was certain of victory. She proclaimed delightedly that Hitler would never endure the defeat but would march into the Saar; and then the workers would have to man the barricades, forcing him to fight for each house in turn; not a pit must be allowed to fall into the hands of his munitions industry; and the French workers would come rushing in from Forbach with arms and supplies.

She had spoken on these lines and now was the victim of her own propaganda. Like a female David she had thought to smite Goliath with her sling. Now Goliath's laughter echoed over the radio, and tomorrow he would indeed march in, and all the flags would be waving to welcome him. We stood round the sobbing girl without saying a word. The plump innkeeper wiped his eyes with his apron and drew a large mug of beer, evidently with the idea of offering it to her; but then, no doubt perceiving that the gesture would be in vain, he drank it himself, and put the glass down on the counter with a sigh. "Eighty-five per cent!" intoned the radio.

I escaped that night by way of the Forbach woods, over the Spichern mountain into Lorraine. As I passed by the German military cemetery I remembered that my grandfather had fought here in 1870 against the French. But Father had said that the soldiers lying in those graves had died for an illusion. There were no visible frontiers to be seen, but only tombstones which taught men nothing. I thought of this too at that moment.

Approaching the frontier I remembered that Kaganovich had proposed to hold a party in Moscow to celebrate our victory. It was a cold, clear, starry night. The Great Bear hung over the Warndt, at the break in the Maginot Line. I encountered no frontier guards and no Nazis. They were all celebrating. Rockets soared upwards from the Saar valley, and on the Winterberg a bonfire glowed.

12. God in Moscow

THE year 1935 revealed to me a world of hypocrisy which left me crippled in spirit.

A Congress of Writers was held in Paris by André Malraux, Aragon, Ehrenburg, Koltsov and a large number of liberals who were opposed to all forms of tyranny and in particular hated the bloodthirsty nightmare of the Third Reich. The only Germans to attend were *emigrés*.

At this congress Gide proclaimed his allegiance to Communism. The Party had the sense not to attempt to subject him to any form of discipline; he spoke his own language. With him were Malraux and some of his personal friends, partly sceptical, partly fired with enthusiasm by his speech. Louis Aragon, flattered and filled with pride at the success of this sensational conversion, for which he took the credit, was among the admirers. Gide's declaration was everywhere regarded as an event of world-importance, so hopeful was everyone in those days, and so profoundly did we still believe in the influence of writers.

It was in an atmosphere of feverish excitement that the author of *Les Caves du Vatican* appeared on the stage in the huge, ugly Mutualité building, unfolded his manuscript and, in an almost cold voice, delivered the speech that warmed so many hearts—half an hour later the text, already printed, was to be bought on the streets. It was like a summons to another St Bartholomew's Eve, but one that in no way called for bloodshed. Gide smiled indulgently at the bourgeoisie whose end he prophesied, and who the next day were to attack him in the solidly established and immovable *Figaro*. He knew that he was outraging them, and he enjoyed doing so; but what he valued far more was the right, which he had always claimed for writers, to change his views and embark upon a new course, and to announce the change in public.

After Gide, Malraux spoke, precise as always: "*Il est dans la nature du fascisme d'être la nation et dans la notre d'être le monde.*" Later, very dignified and forestalling his *Musée Imaginaire* by ten years and his *Metamorphose des Dieux*, he was heard to say to a devoted audience:

"*Tout œuvre d'art se crée pour satisfaire un besoin, mais un besoin assez passioné pour lui donner naissance. Puis le besoin se retire de l'œuvre comme le sang d'un corps, et l'œuvre commence sa mystérieuse transfiguration. Elle*

*entre en domaine des ombres. Seul, notre besoin à nous, notre passion à nous
l'en feront sortir."*

This was the level on which we wanted to fight for a new art. But it was
difficult to maintain so high a level. The Soviet writers present did not
understand one word, though they excelled at boasting of their five year
plans. It was all most embarrassing. They were as smug as Hitlerites.

Ehrenburg, the Paris representative of Bukharin's *Izvestia*, and the "coach"
as it were of the Russian delegation, realised how much these young Marxists'
naiveté could damage the U.S.S.R.'s reputation in the West. He rushed to
the Russian embassy and cabled for more sophisticated delegates, having first
asked our advice. I proposed the witty, talented Isaak Babel, Malraux favoured Boris Pasternak; it was our contribution to the Potemkin village that
we wanted to erect for the sympathetic West.

Babel and Pasternak arrived twenty-four hours later by aeroplane.

I still remember Isaak Babel's calmness and astonishing detachment. He
walked on to the stage, drew a lamp towards him, and sat down like a story-
teller in an Eastern town. He told Jewish stories; he was most comfortably
relaxed, as though the huge auditorium of the Mutualité Theatre contained
no more than a handful of students, instead of five thousand ardent and
curious fellow-travellers. He was wildly applauded. Then Pasternak
appeared. I recognised him at once, a tall man with a horse-face, high cheekbones, and a strange, far-away look, who talked with the shyness of a
released prisoner. He recited a poem that had little to do with our day-to-day
problems. He was still the follower of Rilke who had been spared the harsh
pressure of official ideology. They had not destroyed his humanity. Malraux
took a liking to him and Ehrenburg protected him against questioners.
Pasternak stepped quickly out of the limelight; he did not believe in running
risks. He was born too late; one could see it even when we had a meal
together in a restaurant near Les Halles. Ehrenburg gave me a translation of
the poem he had recited. I still have it among my papers:

> But sometimes things tear off their masks
> let honour fall and lose their power,
> when there's a reason for a song,
> when there's a pretext for a shower.

Two days later I myself addressed the congress. My speech took shape in
an unexpected fashion. I went to Notre Dame, as I always did when I had
something serious to think about, and when I felt in my pocket for a few
francs with which to buy the traditional candle to burn before the smiling
figure of the Madonna, I found that I had with me some of the illegal leaflets
that were being circulated in Germany. I paced up and down in the light of

the rose-windows, memorising what I intended to say. I made up my mind to say something about the ineptitude of our own propaganda. But when, next day, I stood on the platform, the thought occurred to me that in doing so I might be helping the enemy.

I gazed at the thousands of heads beneath me. This was no exile. The frontiers had been abolished and the writers' international had been called into being! I looked at Gide and the old pacifist, Barbusse, seated at the committee-table, and suddenly I forgot all my carefully composed speech. I brought two of the leaflets out of my pocket, held them in the air and challenged the Gestapo agent who was certain to be seated in the audience as a spy to come up and look at them.

I talked like one of those fair-ground wrestlers who challenge the young men to come and try their strength against them.

I wanted to make them all feel the sense of insecurity that, with the coming of Hitler, was spreading among mankind, and to urge them to close their ranks. Half-way through the speech I broke off and, turning to the table, handed Gide and Barbusse each a copy of the leaflets. "They are being circulated at this moment!" I cried turning again to the audience. "And none of the spies who are seated among us has been able to prevent it! I want to say a word to that spectral figure from the secret police who follows us around as shadow follows the sun. I want to say this to him: 'You have killed Mühsam! You are holding Ossietzky! But you cannot silence our voice! You will never extinguish our love for the people, or the flame of our passion for truth!' "

Then something remarkable happened. With a strange, dry, rustling sound the whole assembly rose to its feet, as though I had waved a baton and called upon them to sing the choral passage of the Ninth Symphony. But what they sang was very different.

A figure beckoned to me urgently from the wings. It was the German poet, Johannes R. Becher. I went towards him behind the painted canvas fly, and he hissed at me:

"You must be mad!"

"Can't you hear what they're singing?" I asked in a voice that trembled with emotion.

"That's just it!" he said, having to shout now against the mighty chorus that arose. "The Internationale! You've ruined everything—you've given us away! This congress can't pretend to be neutral any longer. God almighty! You'll be turned out of the Party!"

I looked at his pale face, not knowing whether to laugh or cry. The air was quivering with the sound of a thousand voices. Gide and all the others on the platform had stood up, all realising that this was no *coup de théâtre*, nothing pre-arranged, but a spontaneous outburst. Barbusse had joined in

THE AUTHOR WITH PASTERNAK AND EHRENBURG

the singing. Paris was declaring war in its own fashion on the unknown
agent in the auditorium and his masters.

"It will be heard across the Rhine," I said, breathless.

"You're a saboteur," said Johannes R. Becher, the poet.

Four days later, at the meeting of the Communist cell, I was taken very
seriously to task. The Party-representative said:

"It is not for any individual comrade to decide when the Internationale
shall and shall not be sung, more especially when we are part of a Popular
Front and have to exercise restraint."

"They were singing from their hearts," I ventured to say.

The others smiled somewhat scornfully, and Anna Seghers, the novelist,
said:

"That's sentimental rubbish. What we're discussing here is a matter of
tactics."

I detested her assertive, mannish air. Surrounded by weak men, she had
deliberately adopted this Prussian tone.

"Well, see if *you* can provoke a spontaneous demonstration of that sort!"
I said.

The Party-representative came to her support.

"Revolutions are not required to be spontaneous," he said in the tone of a
magistrate on the bench.

I made a final retort.

"In other words, the Internationale is nothing but the last point on the
agenda—a routine way of winding up the meeting!"

"I will not tolerate sarcasm," said the Party-representative. I think his
name was Abusch, and that he later became State secretary in East Germany.
"We are at present in an under-cover phase. Whoever breaks cover is a
counter-revolutionary."

I said no more. Through the clouds of tobacco-smoke in the little back-
room I saw Anna Seghers, frowning, nod her approval of this last pronouncement. Egon Erwin Kisch, the reporter, seemed to find it somewhat
overbearing and hysterical; he shrugged his shoulders. Kurt Stern, my
neighbour in the place where I was then living, looked reassuringly at me.
All the others sat like schoolchildren who have been reminded that the cane
is always in readiness behind the blackboard. They were like dogs with their
tails tucked in. I heard the sound of the singing voices. . . .

The Party-representative concluded:

"The song is like everything else—*a means to an end.*" And he went on in
a livelier voice to disclose the matter to be discussed at the next meeting:
"How shall we turn the renewed persecution of the German Catholics to
the advantage of the Party?"

Thus I came to study the Nazi newspapers with greater care. What a year of Jesuitism 1935 was! Himmler's paper, *Das Schwarze Korps*, was suddenly filled with attacks on the Catholic clergy. Now that the 700,000 Catholics of the Saar had been safely incorporated within the Reich, Catholicism need no longer be humoured. One could go back to the old game of flinging lighted torches into the monasteries. *The song was a means to an end.* Himmler's paper stirred up all the mud at the bottom of the pond; he made use of the rivalry between Catholics and Protestants, and by his atheism gave the defeated free-thinkers of the left something to laugh at and something to hate. Hitler himself did not take up any position in the matter. The work was divided between Himmler and the envious, jealous Goebbels. They looked round for the weak spot and finally decided to follow the popular line of attacking the riches of the Church.

The whole campaign was one of utter pharisaism. It was true that the state of financial security of many churchly institutions contradicted the Church's own teaching of insecurity and humility in the face of God; but which among the new rulers of the Reich was in a position to throw stones?

Germany was dumping her industrial products abroad, forcing her creditors to accept goods of doubtful value, in breach of trade agreements. Schacht, President of the Reichsbank and arch-conjurer of finance, was building castles in the air, juggling with the exchanges, liquidating debts by decree, instituting half a dozen different orders of currency and generally dressing up the economy in garments calculated to deceive the eye. In addition to this, fortunes were being transferred abroad, not merely by the leaders, who lost no time in providing against their possible exile, but also by the business community, who were not, perhaps, wholly convinced of the permanence of the financial wizard's contrivances.

And through this fog sounded the notes of Himmler's horn, sternly proclaiming, "Monks are gambling in currency! Priests are robbing the people! Bishops are speculating!" The song was indeed a means to an end.

Prosecutions were instituted in a great blaze of publicity. I read the story of a Franciscan monk named Otto Oertel, the treasurer of his monastery near Cologne, who had learnt from Schacht how to play one exchange against another. He had taken advantage of the fluctuations of the mark against the Dutch guilder, and with the profits had bought industrial shares. He became the scapegoat on which all the fire was concentrated. The bishops hurriedly recoiled from him, but it did them little good, because Himmler declared that their very haste showed their complicity. The Public Prosecutor, in a series of fulminations, talked about the degradation of the holy vesture, the misuse of religion and the hypocrisy of the bare-footed men of God.

Otto Oertel got a ten-year prison sentence.

At times of great crisis I have always looked to see the attitude of the Christian Churches, the Protestant no less than my own Catholic Church.

During that summer the Westphalia-Anhalt Explosives Company was visited by a terrible disaster. Sixty workers were killed in an explosion. They were the first victims of the second World War. Germany was rearming with excessive haste.

I sat in the Café de la Paix turning over the pages of the newspapers I had borrowed from Münzenberg. The German Government had ordered a State funeral. Bishops of both denominations were invited to deliver funeral orations. The Catholic bishop talked in vague terms of a sombre fate and an inscrutable deity, whose grace he besought, speaking in the toneless voice of a beggar who does not look at the passer-by whose alms he solicits. Then one of the provincial Protestant bishops spoke—I think the Bishop of Westphalia. His name was Dr Peter, and he had been in residence under the Republic.

I hoped that Peter—what an appropriate name for the occasion!—would not descend to the formal, liturgical tone which his colleague had perhaps felt himself obliged to adopt. He knew, like everyone else, that these men had been destroyed by the armaments race. Had not the Bible supplied him with the words to use—"All they that take the sword shall perish by the sword"? Was this not the exact case, and should not a man of God repeat those words again and again?

I looked at the photographs of the funeral, the coffins, the black-veiled, weeping widows, wondering if the bishop would have had the courage to speak out, rising above the universal conformity. The coffins were draped with swastika flags, which was a bad sign. But the bishop's actual words were worse than anything I had feared. "Death is swallowed up in victory," said Dr Peter. "Thus we are freed from the inscrutable hostility of this event. We must pray with the Führer: 'Oh, God, let us not fail in courage!'"

Now even God had become a means to an end.

That was in 1935; and shortly afterwards a letter reached me from Moscow which was also related to the problem of that year—must the song always be a means to an end?

Koltsov wrote:

> . . . Our publishing house therefore proposes that you should write a life of Ignatius Loyola in the Marxist–Leninist–Stalinist sense. We can

offer you an advance of 900 roubles per galley-slip, plus a royalty on the sales, which, in view of the growth of cultural interests among the labouring masses of the USSR, should amount to hundreds of thousands of copies. In order that we may discuss the matter in detail, Comrade Kamenev, who is acting as general editor of this historical series, invites you to pay another visit to Moscow. A visa and railway-tickets are at your disposal at the Russian Embassy.

It seemed to me like a gift of God that I should at last be afforded time to think out the problem of political morality to its conclusion.

I put everything else aside and spent my days in the Bibliothèque Nationale, immersed in the agitated sixteenth century, the history of whose rebellious peasants, in their battle against their feudal lords, I had already pursued.

In the early summer of 1936 I had made sufficient progress to be able to accept Kamenev's invitation. His name had been mentioned in connection with the investigation into the murder of Kirov, but since Koltsov had replied to my letters in his name, I did not attach much importance to these suspicions.

When we arrived in Leningrad Marie Louise proposed that we should go at once to the Writers' Club. "To see if he has brought any Persian songs back with him?" I asked. She did not answer. It was as though she already knew something.

There were no familiar faces in the club. I asked for our friend, Lebedev. He had not been there for some time. Perhaps he was in Siberia. No one knew for certain.

In the train to Moscow Marie Louise said:

"It's terrible to hear the name of Siberia spoken here."

"Siberia is a coming land," I said. "It's being opened up. It isn't a prison any more. He'll bring you a white fox."

But I had difficulty in speaking the words, because shortly before we left Leningrad I had learned that Lebedev had been arrested as a "member of the opposition" and that no one knew where he had been taken. The modern socialist *lettre de cachet*. It was an ominous introduction to my book. Would Sonya still be at liberty, who gave herself away so often?

Koltsov welcomed us in Moscow. He said that there was no need to start work immediately, but that I should take time to look about me. I asked to see Kamenev and he came to the publisher's office. He had an air of very discreet dignity, and was a most attentive listener. I was relieved to find that the mention of his name in connection with the Kirov murder had not involved him in any serious embarrassment, and I well remember how flattered I was to be working with an intimate friend of Lenin. I told him of my plan for the book, which was discreetly to underline the parallels between the life of Loyola and that of Lenin, and also the differences in their philosophies.

"Don't make comparisons," Kamenev advised. "Give us a true picture of Loyola and leave us to draw our own conclusions."

"There are twenty different Loyolas," I said.

"Then give us a practical one," said Kamenev. "One for domestic use."

Not until a fatal August day in that same summer did I understand what he really wanted—a portrait of a tyrant.

"He wants you to make comparisons," said Koltsov when I was alone with him.

"Then why did he say the opposite?"

"Revolutionary technique. We all say the opposite."

"Is there no Danton among you?"

Koltsov produced a brochure in German and handed it to me.

"A Party inquiry," he said. "Read it. The hearings were in German."

Seated on a bench in the park I read the declarations of German workmen employed in a Moscow factory who had recently taken part in a *chistka*, a gathering for the purpose of self-criticism. I expected to find a new clarity and a tone far removed from the confessional of my childhood. I read several dozen avowals, and several dozen times I read: "I have been a very bad workman and have altogether failed to understand how much I owe to the Party. I shall strive to be a better member of Soviet society and to follow the example set by Comrade Stalin, the great leader of the World Revolution."

I had an unpleasant taste in my mouth, as though someone were making a fool of me. I called upon Schmückle, the brother-in-law of my former teacher, Gundolf, and borrowed a volume of Dostoevsky. I read till morning. Here was humility and rebellion even against the unnamed God, despair and hope, bitterness and joy in prayer, sudden storms of passion and faith as scarcely perceptible as the first small leaves of the chestnut-tree; subjection and the shouting of defiance; a man of my own flesh—even the servants with their bowed heads possessed a greater dignity than was to be found in the sycophantic utterances I had read that afternoon.

I had a frank talk with Koltsov, who did not conceal his scepticism regarding the honesty of those confessions. He had no liking for the German workers. But, he said, the former beggar-king of Central Europe, a Swabian, had recently arrived in Moscow and was concerning himself with the problem of vagrant children. An interesting man. The Nazis had shot him, with others, but he had not been mortally wounded and had managed to get away. He was now patched up and able to work again. I asked eagerly if I might meet him. A beggar-king! I had written a novel on this very subject, *Die Strolche Christi—The Vagabonds of Christ*, who had taken messages from

farm to farm and village to village in aid of the rebellious peasants of the
Reformation. What might not such a man do for the youthful victims of the
revolution! He could restore the confidence of twelve-year-olds whose faith
in life had been cruelly destroyed, make them into new Vagabonds of
Christ, listen to their tales and laugh when these were interspersed with
too many oaths. He could make them forget the nights passed in the
ditches and the woods, and bring them again to a respect for men, teaching them that all the killing and the persecution had been no more than the
sickness of a time of crisis. He could promise them Bolshevo, the institution I had visited, the paradise of the unjustly oppressed. God knows, they
had a right to curse and display their frostbites and their wounds, and to spit
through their rotting teeth at the grown-ups who had suffered them to endure such a childhood! . . .

The beggar-king, a hollow-eyed, feverish person with sour-smelling
breath, came to call upon me at our hotel, bringing with him a sheaf of
letters which I read with care. He had, he told me, written them at the
children's dictation. I found myself wondering whether he had fallen into a
doze and had gone on writing the same thing over and over again, like a de-
fective gramophone record.

> Until now I have been a useless member of society. I have had no
> class-consciousness. My parents were kulaks, that is to say, enemies.
> Now I ask society to accept me, and I promise Comrade Stalin, the
> great leader of the World Proletariat . . .

I checked to see whether there was a single letter that omitted the name
of Stalin. There was not one.

I thought of the boy Jan, Sonya's son.

"Have you no young people capable of uttering a protest?" I asked
Koltsov. "These children have grown up with hunger and rats and stinking
fish. It is the business of your revolution to make them all healthy and useful,
and not just the few dozen in Bolshevo. Instead of which I am shown a man
who was once a stormy petrel and is now a parrot, and I'm offered the stam-
merings of terrified lackeys!"

Koltsov made as though he were about to speak, but then he checked himself and asked me to go on.

"At least you can understand why I'm disappointed?"

He nodded. "Because of the seventh of April," he said to my astonishment.

I asked him what this date had to do with it. He coughed and said:

"So you don't know? Destitute children have, by official decree, ceased to
exist since April the seventh. They are either locked up or put in a camp.
Any that break out are beaten and imprisoned or . . ."

OLTSOV

KLAUS MANN,
THE AUTHOR AND
EHRENBURG

"Or what?"

"The same decree lays down that children from the age of twelve upwards may be shot."

"It's impossible!" I cried. "But what about Bolshevo, where the boys played Mozart and I found that talented young painter?"

"It was an honest attempt. It has been given up."

There was a heavy pause, and then Koltsov went on:

"Why don't you console yourself with the thought of the good that has been achieved. Or why don't you simply tell yourself that I'm exaggerating, that even if the decree exists it is not being implemented, that no Russian would dream of shooting a child . . .?" He broke off. I had never seen his face so pale. He picked up his jacket and said: "I must go to the office. Come round at about midnight and have a vodka."

I stood at the window watching him as he went along the street. He was small, like a figure out of Gogol, and there was a slight hesitation in his walk. No doubt Stalin had laughed yesterday at his satire on the inefficiency of the Moscow apothecaries. He had become a sort of Pasquino. But did he know how far mockery might venture to go? A sense of unsafety came over me. Koltsov vanished round the corner into one of the main streets. I thought suddenly of Lebedev.

The feeling of insecurity did not leave me throughout that evening; indeed, it increased. I went out and walked in some confusion through the outskirts of the town. The Government buildings in the centre had become oppressive to me; I seemed to feel their dubious emanations, the incalculable brooding over new decrees in a hundred offices. A sort of paralysis assailed my legs as I approached the Lubianka, remembering only just in time that it was better to make a wide detour to avoid the headquarters of the police. Moscow was a hostile town—why had I not noticed it in 1934? Somewhere on the far side of the Moskva I spoke to a workman. When he heard that I was a foreigner he crossed himself, gave me a glance of deep mistrust and hurried to get away from me.

The moon had risen high in a deep-blue sky when I came to a house in the basement of which lay a huddle of human bodies. All were clad in rags, with the gleam of bare flesh showing through, and the green light made them look like corpses. I drew nearer and saw that they were adolescents, former candidates for Bolshevo and now candidates for execution, by decree. My foot stumbled against a loose bit of planking which fell with a clatter down the slimy steps into the area. In an instant the recumbent bodies came to life. A boy jumped up and looked at me with startled, hate-filled eyes. Like a pack of hunted animals they all scrambled to their feet and rushed past me up the steps. In certain moments a verse of the gospel flashes into my mind. I saw

the half-naked, dirty children running towards the town where the diamonds
sparkled in the towers of the Kremlin and where Lenin lay in his glass coffin.
"Suffer ye little children to come unto Me," I said looking in the direction
of the Basilius church, "and forbid them not."

I felt that I could not yet go back to the hotel. Marie Louise would see my
face and know what I was thinking, and I would tell her everything and make
her even more unhappy than she was already.

I was still standing by the house when someone touched me softly on the
elbow. I swung round hastily to confront a fair-haired young woman with
a brightly-coloured head-scarf encircling her rather worn face. She raised her
skirt with both hands above her unstockinged knees, and stretched out one
leg in a gesture of clumsy enticement. I shook my head with an unnecessary
brusqueness and then hastily fumbled for a rouble-note and gave it to her.
I felt clumsy in my inability to say a consoling word to her. Although I
had never in my life resorted to prostitutes, I had been with friends to their
houses and at the beginning of the emigration, in Montmartre, had been perfectly ready to act as interpreter for my youthful and amorous fellow-exiles.
In doing so I had struck up a friendship with one of the girls, a negress,
which lasted for some years. In short, there was nothing unusual in the
situation. So why did I stand there like an awkward schoolboy?

It was part of the Marxist creed to regard prostitution as an outrageous
and characteristic product of capitalism, and I had accepted this view of that
most ancient of trades. Koltsov had on one occasion proclaimed that no such
commerce in human flesh could occur in the new Russia, adducing a string
of high-sounding arguments. Now this girl stood before me, far more
painful to look at than any western woman, since she had probably been
impelled by hunger and possessed neither aptitude nor technique for the
business. She was betraying a principle of the Party just as I, it seemed to
me, was betraying the *filles de joie* of the West when I thought of my far
more tolerant attitude in Paris. She took my hand and kissed it, and then
stood waiting; but I recovered from my momentary stupor, nodded to
her and went quickly away.

The demons of restlessness were riding me. I thought of a friend at whose
door I had often knocked and where I read French newspapers. I liked
his friendly, ironical attitude to the Soviet system. Despite his fragile
physique and rather delicate health, he had a considerable understanding
of the peasants, and he defended crudities on the part of the régime which
to me were beginning to look like dangerous blunders. I thought that
I might rest there for a little while before going on to keep my midnight
appointment with Koltsov.

There was no light in his room, but the concierge was still up and seated in the doorway of the house, glad that the heat of the day was over. He was a German. He stopped me as I was about to go upstairs and whispered in my ear that my friend had been arrested—because of the new regulations—I would know what he meant. . . .

I assumed I did know, and thought of André Gide instantly. He was at that moment making a much publicised, officially conducted tour of the Soviet Union. The people who had promulgated the new, harsh decrees relating to private morals were not being very logical.

The concierge was still whispering. My friend had probably "had it"—he used the Berlin expression, crooking his forefinger in a gesture which I misunderstood. He looked very obscene, and I thought he was taking an entirely mistaken view of my relations with the arrested man.

I had had enough of misunderstandings for one day, and I exploded angrily, saying that I did not understand why any act of love should be punishable, whether it was love between men or prostitution or anything else. If a man chose to make love with his goat, provided he treated the animal decently, I did not see that it was any affair of the State.

He raised his hands in supplication. I must not talk so loudly. Nobody in Russia talked loudly. In any case, the movement of his finger had been intended to convey something entirely different.

I left him and went back towards the centre of the town. I was resolved to call Koltsov to account. That was the expression I used in my thoughts. I held him responsible for this arrogant and senseless arrest.

"Everyone is guilty or else no one is," Marie Louise had said when I told her what had happened to Lebedev. What would Koltsov have to say?

The cook opened the door. Koltsov was still at his office, but the samovar was going, if I would like a cup of tea, and there was a couch for me to rest on. The old Russia, with its fevers assuaged by ready improvisation and hospitality! Old peasant custom, and also something of the life of the partisan, who must depart as hurriedly as he came—was this simplicity only to be found in these days in the home of a journalist?

I picked up a paper from the table and sat down. It was an issue of an anti-religious paper called *The Godless*. I found in it a drawing of the Holy Mother with her child. Mary was seated surrounded by gentlemen in frock-coats, apparently getting drunk on champagne. The caption said that in view of her way of living it was understandably hard to guess who the real father was.

Not a particularly witty way of belittling the founder of a religion; indeed, one might go so far as to call it a breach of taste.

I threw the paper back on the table, exclaiming aloud, "It's just as reactionary in its own way!"—and the cook came back to ask if I had called

Q

her. I said that I hadn't, but I would like to know what she thought of the picture. She picked it up and stood studying it for some moments without understanding it. When I explained what it meant she crossed herself and looked at me with mistrust. I assured her that I did not agree with it, and went on to talk about the true and deep significance of the legend of Mary. Finally I said that I could not understand why a Socialist State should not respect the mere fact of human creation, or why an illegitimate child should be despised.

I talked more than I need have done. She understood me at once. Since I knew all about it, she said, perhaps I could explain to her what homosexuality was. The question had a startling appropriateness after my experience that evening. I did my best to explain the matter to her, and she nodded gravely and said: "We once had two billy-goats who were like that. We killed them."

It was a rather summary parallel, but what was I to say against it? The cook thanked me and said that she was going to bed. She put the paper carefully back on the pile from which I had taken it, and departed.

Soon after this a young man came in without knocking. He addressed me as "comrade," and I invited him to sit down and poured him out a cup of tea. Since he did not seem disposed for conversation, I again picked up the atheist journal; but when he saw me do so he leaned forward and put a hand on my arm.

"Don't read it!" he said. "It defiles everyone!"

He spoke seemingly flawless German. I asked him how he knew the paper, and he then introduced himself.

He was a priest whose church had been closed during the last of the social "purges" (the big political purges were still to come). His vicar had been banished, but he himself had got a job in a factory with the help of a friend. "A priest must be able to do anything," he said simply. Nobody interfered with him. He said no Masses. He worked and lived quietly.

He confessed that to keep silent was hateful to him. Ought he to speak out?

I heard a faint sound of movement in the next room. Was someone spying on us? A slight shiver ran through me, but then I was angry with myself. There were no spies here: Koltsov was the most broad-minded of hosts. Or was this man an *agent provocateur*? I dismissed the thought. The priest said, "It's like the days of the catacombs, isn't it?"

To avoid answering I asked him if he had read Dostoevsky. He answered quietly that he loved Alyosha, but that in these days his heart was more with Ivan, the restless one, who spoke the truth about our own time. There were no longer any Alyoshas to be found. The young were all hard and fanatical, impudent and without pity, trampling over the corpses of their parents.

There were three million members of atheist societies. He pointed to the paper—"What filth!" he said.

There was now complete silence in the kitchen. I imagined an eaves-dropper with his ear pressed to the door.

"They jeer at all the symbols," the priest went on. "In the schools they teach them anatomy and blasphemy."

Encouraged by my readiness to listen, he became aggressive. The Church was unjustly persecuted, he said; it had never done anything but good. The people needed it. Without faith there could be no healthy growth. All evil came from atheism.

In his devout earnestness he heaped platitude on platitude, and he con-cluded, so it seemed, with the threatening prophecy that a war must come!

The old escape! "Ten thousand must be visited by the sacred madness!" The cry of the crusades. Attila as the scourge of God! The missionary on the heels of the ruthless conqueror. And no self-criticism, no thought of the beam in one's own eye. So closely did all the panaceas of force resemble one another. I forgot my worry about my gaoled friend, and my discomfort at the thought of the half-starved woman of the streets.

"How can you possibly want to see these unhappy people involved in another war?"

He answered sharply:

"Since 1922 about two thousand five hundred bishops have been shot, about three thousand five hundred priests and two thousand monks. Does that mean nothing to you?"

"Yes, it means that there must have been reasons for so much hatred. You are young. You were probably not here in 1920. I read the report of the International Red Cross Commission on the famine in this country. I did not read it here, but in the West."

"The Church was not responsible for the drought."

"We need not argue about who was responsible for it. I simply read what happened here in 1920. It was an appalling disaster. Whole towns perished. The very Soviets reeked of hunger, even the people in power. Chlorinated water was sprinkled in your churches; prayer is no protection against pestilence, but quicklime is. People did not pray any more—they cursed. Dead bodies were flung out of the windows of houses. Young boys became bandits—and they still exist, I have seen them. The commissars found parents eating their children. The Volga lands, the source of bread for millions of people, were burnt out like the city of Gomorrah; the fields did not even produce enough straw for the dying to lie on. Have you heard of all this?"

I had grown so excited that I quite forgot the eavesdropper who might be standing on the other side of the door.

"Funds and supplies were raised all over the world, but they were not enough. There was just one institution that might have brought immediate aid—but it did not give a penny. It was deaf to the cries of the children. It possessed an immense store of jewels that could have been sold abroad—gold, pictures, valuables of all kinds. . . . I have the details here in my note-book—but I have no need to tell you what that body was."

"How do you know," asked the priest, "that this was not a trial sent by God?"

"I have always marvelled that priests can talk in that fashion," I said, "and that they do not feel the hands of the dying children clutching at their throats! It is almost inconceivable that not a single one should have had the courage to admit that it was not God but the Church which refused to show mercy."

"The Church's riches are a part of its ceremonial. A sacred chalice raised above the heads of a despairing congregation is a greater comfort than a week's supply of bread. Can't you understand that?"

"I will not attempt to give an opinion, but let me tell you a little more. . . ."

In the next room a saucepan suddenly fell with a clatter to the floor, as though it were a warning. It occurred to me that earlier that evening Kolzov had shut the window. The audacity of this priest! Did he not realise that the listener in the kitchen was concerned with *him*? Was he defying the police, deliberately thrusting his head out of the catacombs? Was he sick of leading a mole-like existence, so that he no longer cared? I could be of no help to him, for this was a country with quite new conceptions of morality.

I now thought again of my friend who had been arrested, because the way in which he expressed compassion did not suit the man in the Kremlin.

I looked at the priest as he sat tightly clutching his empty tea-cup. You burned your rebels, I thought, whenever it suited you; but your cardinals preserved and pampered their acolytes as though they were precious vessels. What difference was there? "The song is a means to an end," I quoted. "Like the chalice. But it was not just a single chalice. In 1922 a search of the monasteries was instituted under President Kalinin. Do you know what was found? . . ."

I held up my little notebook like an accusing finger, and then read:

"Thirty thousand diamonds, seventy-two thousand rubies, four hundred thousand kilograms of silver and over four hundred kilograms of gold!"

"Well," said the priest, "and does that not prove that people gave gener-ously to the Church because the Church was their friend?"

"The Church was the friend of the princes, of the boyars and of the Tsars, who paid for Masses to be said for their tortured victims. You have succeeded in arousing all my old hatred of you and your kind! One never seems to get any further. Why don't we talk about your real meaning and what you ought to be? The ferment. The trustee of the people. The shield of the oppressed. God's watch-dog. Must I instead recite all the charges against you?"

He merely nodded, and once again I marvelled at his assurance. Was it due to his present life as a worker among working-people? Had he discovered that they needed something more than the promise of earthly happiness? Was it for this reason that he was not worried about the listener on the other side of the door?

With these thoughts in mind I embarked hesitatingly upon my list of charges—that the Russian Church had been opposed to the abolition of flogging, that it had endorsed serfdom, that it had treated the childish Tsar, the idiot who played with model warships in his bath, as though he were a god—this, that and the other. . . .

I talked for a long time, but I felt that these old arguments rang hollow in my mouth. Lebedev had vigorously uttered them, and where was he now? Was I to constitute myself accuser in his name? Perhaps this young man was one of those with new ways of thinking whom Lebedev had hoped for, purified by life itself, converted by the pendulum swinging from the true sky.

Once again a suspicious sound came from the kitchen. It occurred to me suddenly that I might go softly over to the door and thus indicate to the priest that he was being spied upon. I did not want to be responsible for any misfortune that might befall him. In this battle I was no longer on either side, as the events of the night had shown me.

But if one man was endangered by another I was on the side of the threatened. This young man was threatened. I resolved to make an explicit gesture. Instead of going to the door I went to the table, picked up the pile of atheist papers, opened the door of the stove and began to thrust them in one after the other. The priest stood as though struck by lightning.

"So that you may not misunderstand me," I said, ramming the papers in with the poker.

"Then you are really a believer!" he cried in an almost boyish voice, and he came and embraced me, his eyes shining in the light of my *auto-da-fé*. And then the door opened. But it was no police informer who entered but the cook, who I thought had gone to bed long ago. She brought with her a dish of cakes warm from the oven. While I released myself from the priest's embrace she set it down, and then she went on her knees before him asking for his blessing. All my notions had been wrong. It was I, not he, who had been listened to. The priest was the guest of a Christian woman. She had waited until she knew from the tone of his voice that he did not regard me as an enemy.

He made the sign of the cross above her head, and for an instant I was tempted to kneel as well. Our little group was like an island, and I seemed to hear the approach of a flood-tide against which we all needed shelter. But I did not kneel.

I passed the night in Koltsov's apartment. He got home in the early hours of the morning and slept until midday. We had breakfast together. There was an empty place on the table where the papers had been, but I did not tell him what I had done. I had gone over to the side of illegality without yet being able to realise all the implications. I talked about my homosexual friend and the street-girl.

"You're growing bitter," Koltsov said, busily eating. "You're judging too narrowly. I have a suggestion to make. You said you wanted to visit a factory. Well, go and do it—take my car."

I was not sure how far he held it against me that I should have been so outspoken in my criticisms. I drove with a slightly uncomfortable feeling to the factory, resolved to look around with more tolerant eyes.

The chief engineer at the factory was a Rumanian, the husband of the German actress, Carola Neher, a taciturn man with melancholy eyes. He let me go where I pleased. There was nothing out-of-the-way to be seen. Wheels turned, transmission-belts rattled, oxyacetylene burners roared, steel saws cut harshly through softer metal and an electric gantry picked up piles of rusty scrap and dumped them in a melting-oven.

Amid the hubbub I heard a shriller note, as though a machine were crying out in pain. An elderly workman sprang forward and disconnected his transmission. He had broken the tool of his machine. As the wheels slowed he returned to his place and stood with his head bowed. I was struck by his attitude. He seemed to have been overtaken by a sort of paralysis, as though someone had dealt him a blow on the back of the neck.

As I started to move towards him the chief engineer jerked me back and asked me to go with him to his office. I looked round as we went and saw a man in uniform approach the workman, who turned at once and allowed himself to be led away.

There was something unreal about the episode; the men bore themselves like marionettes. I glanced round again, thinking, "A robot leading off a robot!"

The chief engineer confirmed what I already suspected to be the case— the workman had been arrested. He had broken a machine-tool two months previously. On that occasion the high cost of the tool, which had to be imported from abroad, had been deducted from his pay; but since he had repeated the offence he was now guilty of sabotage.

I stood in the office, a glass box in the middle of the machine-shop, and suddenly lost control of myself.

"Won't the union do anything about it?" I demanded. "Won't they get someone to defend him? It was an accident that could happen to anyone. He was probably nervous, after the first time. And what do the other men in the shop think about it? Won't they stand by him? This can't be in the spirit of the revolution!"

"The union is the Party," the chief engineer answered bluntly. "It has already decided against this man."

"But then, everyone must work in fear and trembling!" I cried.

He gazed thoughtfully past me and said in a firm voice:

"Perhaps that's what we need."

He uttered the words with a startling emphasis, seeming to have no fear of denunciation. The post of command in which we were standing gave him courage to do so. For an instant he looked to me like a rebellious captain who, although surrounded by his men, dared in that place at least to question his orders.

I repeated the sentence—"Perhaps that's what we want?"

He gave instructions over the telephone. I stood there with my head spinning. What we need? But why? So that we may realise what we've got into? To kindle rebellion? Had I understood him?

I had an impulse to tell him that I did understand; that I realised that he was in the front line, holding the fort, and that he knew what he wanted.

I wanted to say this to him, but caution prevented me. How could I be sure that he was not a *provocateur*, trying me out? And even if he wasn't, what had all this to do with me? Was I to risk my freedom at the last moment? No one here was to be trusted. I thought how quickly the man in uniform had come to fetch the workman. The thing to do was to keep under cover, act foolish, smile, talk like everyone else.

"Yes," I said. "No doubt one has to be strict to educate workers as primitive as these."

"Of course," the engineer said; but he was plainly disappointed, and there was a quiver of scorn on his lips which for a moment made me feel ashamed. He picked up the telephone again and ordered a car for my return journey. I was being dismissed.

I understood him better a year later when I learned that he had been shot as a "spy"—that is to say, when he had died the death of all honourable opponents of the Party.

The next day Marie Louise and I went to see Vogeler.

He came home after we had arrived, soaked to the skin by a rainstorm, and smiled with a shy pleasure as Marie Louise helped him out of his wet clothes and hung them on the line to dry. He seemed to be unused to so much solicitude. Sonya was now studying how to improve the world at the Lenin School, and deliberately neglected her household duties on ideological grounds.

Marie Louise made tea, and as he drank it Vogeler told us how the heavy rainfall had flooded the foundations of an important new public building, ruining several months' work.

"Luckily no one was hurt," said Marie Louise to the youthful Jan on his return from school. He had already heard about the disaster.

Jan frowned.

"But the saboteurs will be caught and punished," he said. He drew himself upright, running a hand through his fair hair. In his other hand he had a photograph of Spanish militia-men which he had cut out of the paper. He flung back his head as though defying the world; and Marie Louise said in a clear voice:

"It was a cloudburst, Jan. You'll have to punish God."

Jan said contemptuously:

"Do you believe that rubbish? We know better. It was Trotzkyite rats!"

Marie Louise looked sternly at him. She was fond of the boy, but at that moment he must have seemed to her a complete stranger. Without irony, but also without indulgence, she closed the subject:

"Take care that God does not punish you."

Somewhat taken aback by the firm and confident tone of this warning, Jan left the room, but not before saying:

"You don't understand anything about the class-enemy."

Marie Louise said after a pause:

"Perhaps I should go after him and help him."

"It's the new demonology," I said. "They only believe in the devil and call him the class-enemy. He's the scapegoat. Thanks to him everything can be accounted for. It's Christianity in reverse. These are still Dostoevsky's people."

Indeed, the fevered doubts of Dimitri and the piercing absolutism of Ivan Karamazov were everywhere to be seen. The boy's attitude was the same as that which had led to the arrest of the unfortunate workman. Cloudburst or the breaking of a tool, both were judged in the same arbitrary fashion —sabotage. A failure of nerve, a slip in a calculation, a defect of raw material, a trick of wind and weather—it was all the same, all sabotage. Nothing was any longer to be explained in a natural way. Drinking and loving and writing and going for a walk, the drainage system and the spectacle-lenses, the premature birth and the observation of the stars, all were considered in relation to the enemy, and the enemy was everywhere. The gentle words of

Jesus, troubled in the garden of Gethsemane, and been turned into a chilly warning: "Take ye heed, watch and pray: for ye know not when the time is"—the time of arrest.

I went to the headquarters of the German writers who had fled to Moscow and had found there a sort of sinecure.

In the half-dark anteroom I found my friend Schmückle, the brother-in-law of Gundolf. He had once advised me against writing any more historical novels, which were a sign of weakness and could easily be regarded as a flight from Socialist reality. He was looking far from well, and when I asked what was the matter with him he answered with a sigh. I pressed him, and he said in a low, miserable voice that he had been asked to attend an interrogation. Certain of his articles which had appeared in *International Literature* were now held to be ideologically unsound—I fancy there had been a lapse in the direction of idealism. Johannes R. Becher, with whom he had collaborated for years, and Bredel, his probable successor on the editorial board, had been entrusted with the task of interrogating him. I protested against that word "interrogate." His head sank forward. "I'm lost," he said.

I took his hand and he looked gratefully at me.

"Plenty of people have come through here during the last hour," he said, "but not one has said a word to me."

There were tears in his eyes.

"The cowards!" I cried, and at this he begged me to go, saying that he would never forget what I had done. He raised his hands beseechingly.

"You don't know where you are!" he said.

This psychosis, the daily possibility of a lapse into sin, was fostered on the highest level. Any act of kindness was to be viewed with suspicion, and there was no such thing as mercy, so that too was ruled out.

Only our latest knowledge of man's mind can serve to explain the inexplicable. Stalin had definitely the strongest intelligence in his circle, but it worked in an amoral sense, the hands of the clock turned constantly widdershins. But the good and healing beams no longer moved his people to mutual help, but made them rigid in docile subjection.

Fear was everywhere—with Stalin himself, despite his contempt for men.

It became known at this time that he had refused to receive André Gide at the Kremlin, although Gide's visit to the Soviet Union had been regarded as a great propaganda success. It was an open admission of the fear which a man of outward power but lower level (I use the word in the sense of Indian philosophy) has for a man on a higher level. Those possessed of devils are filled with discomfort when they cannot destroy what is superior to themselves, as we know from the Bible story of the herd of swine. Stalin would not even admit Gide to the so-called "purification trials," although Gide had asked to be allowed to attend them. It was a second self-betrayal on the part of the dictator, who never understood how far he humiliated his own people, and was presumably convinced that he was doing the only right thing.

I talked that evening to Marie Louise about Jan and his teachers. The boy was exceptionally alert and intelligent. Could one ascribe his sullenness to ignorance? Marie Louise judged him otherwise:

"They're proud in their godlessness. They'll never develop."

She saw only one side. I visited the children in their pioneer-camps, read to them, listened to their talk, composed their small quarrels. They needed a "roof." Everything around them had become uncertain. The parents had suffered famine, German invasion and Tsarist prisons; peace was all they wanted. The children wanted more. The house must be made secure. Every critic was therefore a source of disquiet, and whoever came in conflict with the State was an incendiary. The critics of the collectives were the most dangerous of all, for the collective was the new safety. When the young expressed their hatred they said, "It's the best world; it deserves the best feelings."

Among those who had been instructed this hatred soon grew cold. They saw the sacrificial victims fall to right and left, to the glory of a single idol, and it did not trouble them. They were aware of nothing but the pyramid with the image of God at its apex. For the new generation the intermediate levels existed only to raise that picture still higher. There were no demigods. Sonya could still see Dimitrov; Jan saw no one but Stalin.

It was largely on account of Jan that after the first descent of the police on the writers' circle I led a double life. I never considered it a betrayal, and perhaps I was helped in this by my Catholic upbringing and my preoccupation with Jesuitism, although the relationship in itself distressed me. It was a protective measure, and a painful one, enforced upon me by the impulse to speak my mind which I often found it hard to suppress. I will not seek to justify it in loftier terms: I had no intention of betraying the godless for the sake of God. Fear had driven any such thought out of my head, the increasing, nightly dreams of persecution that left my pillow damp with sweat in the morning. (Those dreams went on for years. Time after time I landed helplessly by parachute on the Red Square and was at once taken before Stalin, to awaken as he condemned me to death. Only on one occasion, shortly before his death, did I have a kinder dream. I stood in a bare and polished room in the Kremlin and to my amazement heard Stalin say that I was right. He pointed to his colleagues and said, "What can one do with cretins like these?" I at once went too far and exhorted him to stop and consider how he would appear at the Last Judgment! A confusion of youthful concepts undoubtedly related to the cruellest "father figures" of history.)

I talked to Koltsov about Schmückle's case. He had no very high opinion of the fugitives from Germany, although one of them shared his bed. "There's news from the real front," he said. He meant Spain. The newly-born Republic was far from secure. There was a threat of military counter-revolution in Asturias, and a general strike had been proclaimed which collapsed on the 8th of July. The building-trade workers in Madrid were using bombs against the strike-breakers. A woman leader of the workers, Dolores Ibarruri, was warning the miners of Oviedo not to let themselves be overwhelmed. "It is time to get your rifles out of hiding!"

"That's where the front is now," said Koltsov, and he groaned. We came to talk more and more frequently about Spain, where the fight was against the same evil that had driven me out of Germany. I would not stand idle, I said, without being very clear what I meant by my words at the time.

He laughed at me and called me a romantic; but one evening he surprised me by producing an official invitation for me to visit the German Volga Republic, with Marie Louise and Vogeler, and the writer Plivier, and the theatrical producer Piscator.

Once again my shaken but still genuine optimism returned.

"Volga! Volga!" The river-banks where the Potemkin villages had sprung up during a night of illusion, and where still lived the descendants of the peasants sold to the Tsarina by a German prince. Those lands so often ravaged by a corrosive wind that destroyed the corn-crops. The endless horizons broken by the small church-towers of German piety. I knew about the farms where large-scale but intensive agriculture was practised. The farmhouses all had carefully tended kitchen-gardens, and there was clover for the rabbits and maize for the hens. German industriousness had left no corner untilled, fighting with a heightened ardour against the melancholy of the steppe and singing psalms on Sundays. Travellers in the time of the Tsars had brought back a brightly coloured picture of roses in the garden, geese in the meadow, pigs in the sty, the warm scent of cow-byres, the hams smoking in the chimney, the bottled fruits.

We found none of this in that summer of 1936. We found—was it really only the transition to new forms?—neglected houses and empty byres, overgrown gardens and rotting tree-stumps, hacked as though the trees had been felled by a hurricane—but it had been an ideological hurricane.

The fruitful system of intensively cultivated individual farms and small-holdings had given place to the fodder-factory—by enforced decree, and "for the good of the people" so it was said.

We saw mountains of corn by the threshers. Tractor-drawn ploughs were tearing up the harvested fields in furrows a kilometre long. We were told that the new Government had on one occasion diverted the Volga to forestall a disastrous drought at the last minute. Prometheus himself was at work!

I listened in some astonishment to the statements of the representative of the Ministry of Agriculture, a round-headed young man who never left our side. He talked a language of his own. A peasant had drawn our attention to a row of hillocks at the edge of one of the State farms, telling us that they were the graves of peasants who had opposed the new order. The next day Marie Louise asked the young man about them.

"Yes," he replied, glancing at the row of black crosses in the sunshine with the complacency of a cicerone who has the answer to every question, "that was during the period of collectivisation."

No more than this. A stage in the development of a planned economy. He was quite untroubled by any thought of the human suffering which that graveyard represented. His nerves were in good order.

We attended some kind of celebration in the Soviet building and did not return until late to the lodging that had been assigned to us. Marie Louise exploded:

"So you have to come all the way to the edge of Asia just to discover that there are men without hearts!"

She was still brooding over the young man's answer. I tried to talk to her about the new developments, but she said obstinately:

"I've been round and I've looked carefully at everything. I saw their bread. They eat it damp, so as to make it go further. They won't starve, but in a few years all their teeth will fall out."

"They fought in the war," I said.

"Yes, and their new masters want to make the war go on for ever. Why have they gone and ruined all those prosperous farms? No peasant any longer eats the things he has prepared for himself but only what comes to him from a foreign kitchen."

"It isn't a foreign kitchen."

"It's a slave-kitchen. The Nazis accuse the Soviet commissars of using whips, but that's nothing compared with the destruction of private life."

"They're dealing here with something that is at least as important."

But she would not listen to me.

"These huge, inhuman collectives are the invention of icy minds. There has never been a greater collective than the one that consisted of twelve apostles. Jesus brought the number up to thirteen. The family is the cell."

The parallel did not seem to me very appropriate, but I was not in a pedantic mood; there was something compelling in her scorn.

"The collective is a more effective family," I objected, without very much conviction.

"It's an unreal family."

"Even so," I said, "this unreal family has succeeded in harnessing Nature."

"And they've never eaten so badly in their whole history!"

I felt that I was weakening; but it was not easy to abandon my crusader's zeal, after tilting at so many windmills.

"Is food really the deciding factor?" I asked; and the peasant in Marie Louise answered promptly:

"When the people who work in the fields cannot satisfy their hunger, then something fundamental is threatened!"

"They have bread and cabbage-soup——" I began, but I was allowed to say no more. Marie Louise refused to let the conversation degenerate into the usual Party platitudes. And perhaps that is why I remember it so well, because when it was over nothing more needed to be said about our experiences on the Volga, which may also apply to other countries.

"Did only cabbages grow in the Garden of Eden?" she demanded.

"How can you tell," I said, "after only a week's visit?"

"That's quite enough for me. I know the things that matter."

She jumped out of bed and began to dress.

"Where are you going?"

"Anywhere where I don't feel shut in," she said, picking up her big handbag.

We walked out over the steppe and presently came to one of those ominous church-cemeteries with the neat rows of graves. The sun was just rising, tinting the ground-mist on the horizon a bluish-pink.

"You're all wrong," said Marie Louise decidedly. "This Socialism is a fraud, and that's why even the people here are longing for someone else."

"For whom?" I asked, shocked. "For Hitler?"

She shook her head.

"I can't tell you in front of these nameless crosses. The peasants showed me those little bits of paper." She paused and said: "They showed them to *me*, not to you."

I waited, and she opened her bag and got out the small pocket-Bible which she carried with her as though it were an amulet. I was astonished to see that the bag also contained her pepper pistol. She seemed to have noted something down while she was visiting the peasants' cottages. She opened the Bible. "Here it is," she said.

The sun was dispelling the mist. I saw a camel lurching slowly along in the distance; a tractor roared past it, as though in a demonstration of progress. The land lay about us in early-morning indifference, and the crosses at our feet seemed long forgotten. But the small, slender woman at my side was not to be impressed by the fatalism of the awakening steppe. It was as though she drew strength from the graves, whose secret she knew.

"I looked up two of those papers," she said. "Luke, chapter twelve, verse four; and Revelations, chapter nineteen, verse twenty."

I suddenly knew what she meant. Plivier had made the same discovery the day before—quotations from the Bible were included in the parcels which were still being sent from America to the Russian peasants. I had assumed that they were simply designed to stress the Christian spirit in which this harmless assistance was offered.

"By no means harmless," said Marie Louise. "I don't know what I did to make them trust me. They guard anything that has escaped the censor as though it were worth its weight in gold. Plivier didn't tell you that the people who sent them were clever enough to disguise some of the text-references as though they were place-names and dates. For instance, Lucas-ville, 12 April. Revelation town. And so on. Listen to this." She turned to the twelfth chapter of St Luke and read: "'And I say unto you my friends, Be not afraid of them that kill the body, and never can do more.'" Then she read from the Revelation, "'And the beast was taken, and with him the false prophet that wrought miracles before him, with which he deceived them that had received the mark of the beast. . . .'"

I said, intending to be sarcastic, "Man shall not live by bread alone . . ." but she misunderstood me and took this for my agreement, just as the priest had done when I burnt the papers in Koltsov's flat. She clasped my hand and pressed it to her heart.

"I think this journey has been worth while," she said in a voice that trembled slightly with emotion.

The next day the special train took us back to Moscow.

I wrote a short report for the German section of the trade-union broad-casting station in Moscow. The censor deleted everything that could be interpreted as criticism. A reference to bare pastures, as opposed to lusher fields in well-watered areas, was struck out because it must not be suggested that there were *any* bare pastures in the USSR; and a reference to a mother helping another mother to suckle her child vanished for the same reason: there was no such thing in the USSR as a woman who could not suckle her own child.

I had written: "The food was still monotonous, but machines and men had conquered the harsh winds of the waste-lands." The first words were struck out. We were in a land where only conquest might be mentioned.

The song was a means to an end.

I made no complaint. Indeed, I had given up protesting at anything, having made up my mind to drive out Satan with Beelzebub, where I per-sonally was concerned. I resumed work on my book on Loyola.

The book was to be my last test. I do not know who talked me into thinking that one could put this Russian system of government on trial; it was the desire that drove me on, the feeling of being dispossessed. And the story of the book was destined to be one of disaster.

I wrote for nights on end, depicting in broad terms the corruption of an idea that embraced the world; in a word, the tragedy of a mission. I wrote about the fatal interference of the monks in high politics, their dominating influence over weak monarchs and their unscrupulous intrigues against strong ones, their misuse of spiritual power for very earthly purposes, the terrorisation of the simple-minded and the persecution of the enlightened—crimes *ad majorem Dei gloriam*. I depicted the blazing pyres on the horizon, gave the reasons for the persecution of the Jews in Spain, the enforced baptisms, the thefts and murders—*ad majorem Dei gloriam*. I said little about the cheap charges of sybaritism levelled at certain of the monasteries; the ascetics had always seemed to me much more dangerous.

Nor did I seek to draw comparisons, but they forced themselves upon me. Sometimes they appeared favourable to the Society of Jesus, sometimes to Stalin's mock-religion, and sometimes I assailed both for their unconcealed brutality.

Before tearing up those particular pages I asked Koltsov to get Kamenev to read them, but Koltsov always found ways of postponing a meeting with Kamenev—not until a month later did I understand why. He himself liked the book, and he promised to give Kamenev a report on it. He was pleased by the prudent methods I had adopted, the hints, the double meanings; and he thought he perceived what might be termed the tactical frontier on which the book was fighting—the frontier of bloodshed. I was seeking by indirect means to convey the message that human lives should not be played with, that nothing should be done that was irreparable; I was aiming at the abolition of the death penalty and the gruesome new Russian principle whereby political offenders were held to be infinitely worse than ordinary criminals. To show what a one-sided justice was the outcome of this Jesuitical morality, I included a general survey of the motives which had prompted most of the executions in past centuries.

The parallel with Russia was often dismaying, but Koltsov liked it because Russia was never mentioned. "It needed a Catholic to do it," he said. I swallowed the doubtful flattery, perhaps because I already had a suspicion of what would happen to the book when I formally submitted it.

I lived with the *Exercitia Spiritualia*, and analysed the "holy" deeds of violence, the blood-path at Thorn and the hideous passage in the history of Vienna when the Brothers of Jesus "purged" the town of Protestants.

I was so preoccupied with this work that I might have forgotten all about the present had it not been for events in Spain, which were increasingly calling attention to themselves.

Nothing decisive had yet happened there. The workers, it seemed, had their rifles in readiness; but the opposition were raising so much clamour about the "tyranny of the Reds" as to make it apparent that they were seeking to prepare foreign opinion for a war of revenge. Conservative opinion in Europe followed the same line; the left-wing movements showed no interest. Moscow for many reasons took a hand in events abroad. Nothing was any longer spontaneous, since everything was ordered from above. But since the Russian leaders thought it desirable in this case to recall their own revolution, there was presently talk in the factories about the defence of Madrid, which was likened to a new Leningrad, and about the Russian partisans whom the miners of Asturias were seeking to emulate. There was also talk of a repetition in western Europe of the "forty days that shook the world." These things were printed in *Pravda* and repeated by factory-officials and school-teachers, so that a strange enthusiasm was kindled among the Russian masses, which had about it an over-emotional quality, as though it expressed a sense of release from their domestic problems. The daily need to be on guard against indefinable dangers continued to prevail in Moscow; but it seemed that there was no objection to thinking about Spain.

A cold draught invaded my literary solitude. I was invited to a full meeting of the foreign writers. The Comintern had censured the publication of a book which described in detail, with full arguments on both sides, the course pursued by a Trotzkyite who returned to Stalinism. This dialectical novel was condemned as a work hostile to the régime, on the grounds that the author had used it for furthering Trotzky's ideas.

A Hungarian had been commissioned by the State Publishing Trust to translate the book into German. I saw him seated at the head of the table. He had been sent to a sanatorium in the south not long before to be treated for serious heart-trouble. He seemed to have made a remarkably rapid recovery. I went up and spoke to him.

"Are you better?"

"Not in the least."

"Then why have you made this long journey?"

"Surely you must know what it's all about."

"Of course, but with your heart in its present conditions—to travel all the way from the Crimea!"

"But this is a matter of life and death."

I looked about me. All the faces wore the same expression, one not easy to describe. The eyes proclaimed uncertainty, and there was a hint about the tightly pursed mouths suggesting that any words they spoke would be dictated from outside. They were like soldiers in a beleaguered citadel, awaiting the drumbeat that might at any moment summon them to action. But the summons could only be to one man at a time, and it would be a summons to a court-martial. They had given up thinking about this.

The representative of justice on this occasion was a young workman who went under the name of Weber and had done under-cover work in Germany, a fact from which he derived especial prestige. The "home-front workers," as Koltsov had once called the exiled writers, deferred to the "front-line workers" in consciousness of their inferiority; not that this added considera-tion was of much importance, since they acquiesced anyway in the verdicts of all judges. Studying Weber's self-assured and dangerously positive ex-pression I thought of something Molotov had said in the course of a conver-sation in the VOKS clubhouse. An Englishman had raised the subject of justice, and I asked what would happen in Russia if a judge made a mistake and an innocent man was executed. Molotov replied:

"When that happens we shoot the judge."

The ice-cold answer of a book-keeper balancing the columns of debit and credit; and one which by its very promptness displayed Molotov's estimate of the people's readiness to accept the most ruthless justice. This readiness had indeed become a disease, as I realised at this meeting of writers. The "engineers of the soul" had become the concealers of their own souls. They went on foot to the carrion-pit.

I had a last look round. Schmückle was no longer there. Had he already been shot?

I went to Koltsov's office, taking my manuscript with me. I felt as though I were taking a child with an incurable disease to the doctor, and that I would return home alone.

Koltsov's secretary was strangely reticent. She told me that Koltsov was away on a special mission, but that was all she could say. He had left another money-order for me, in payment for the book. But I need not hurry over it. The publishing programme had been changed. She did not look at me while she was speaking.

I asked if I might take away a few foreign newspapers. She gave me a bundle, but advised me not to leave them lying about in the park. It would be better if I read them at home.

I sat in a small garden near the office with the pile of newspapers which, it seemed, I must read in secret; with my manuscript on Loyola, which I had come to love; and with the radio-script of our Volga journey, which in its censored form was like the work of an over-punctilious schoolboy. I looked at the picture of Loyola which I had pasted on the cover of the manuscript, and it seemed to me that he was grinning—grinning at the sense of triumph I had felt during those weeks of work, at all the wiles and subtleties which I

R

had insinuated into the book, which served no purpose, since modern dictators did not recognise wiles and subtleties; grinning above all at my attempt to show Jesuitism as the father of all evil, without perceiving how near I was bringing myself to the executioner's block in doing so.

If only I had been able to talk one last time to Kamenev and Koltsov! But "the programme had been changed." The phrase hurt me like the unexpected derision of a friend.

A man walked slowly past the bench on which I was seated. He had a grey beard and reminded me of Kamenev. Presently he came back, glancing sidelong at the bundle of papers beside me. I could see that he wanted to look at them, and I held them up; but at this he recoiled, looking to left and to right, and hastily departed. I thought of Ehrenburg's joke—"One of us is bound to be a member of the secret police."

I began to read the papers myself, and a thrill of joy ran through me. Perhaps one should say nothing about these grotesque reactions, but, however it may sound, I felt as though the grey sky overhanging the Russian town had suddenly cleared. The civil war had broken out in Spain! I read every line of the papers, down to the last detail, like a beggar who does not waste a single crumb.

"Telephone communication with Madrid cut . . . Military revolt in Melilla . . . Reuter learns from a reliable source that the political situation in Spain is very grave . . ."

The picture rapidly took shape: the rift ran through the centre of every town. In most cases the Republicans had been taken by surprise. The barracks of the disloyal garrisons had been transformed overnight into fortresses dominating all else. In some towns the masses had battered the doors down; in others they had been overwhelmed by the organised strength of the rebels, and had paid the price of their loyalty to the Republic and their often incomprehensible simple-mindedness.

Where they were victorious the well-to-do citizens lost whatever remained to them from previous confiscations, and often enough their lives as well. Quarter was not asked on either side.

The map of Spain was like a bullock-skin chequered with bloodstains. Madrid and Barcelona preserved their freedom while Irun and San Sebastian had lost theirs. The miners were fighting for Asturias, and the troops of a general from Morocco named Francisco Franco were attacking Badajoz. A force of 600 Civil Guards and 250 cadets had installed themselves in the Alcazar, in Toledo, with 300 women as hostages. Rebels were holding out in Alcalar de Henares, in the eastern sector of Madrid, and priests in Santa Maria and San Justo.

Every town had become a symbol. The nationalist Alcazar was a challenge to the republican capital, and the republican Badajoz was a bulwark between North and South. Upon the destiny of these improvised fortresses depended the faith of one side and the hopes of the other.

I now went to Koltsov's office every day. I discovered nothing more about where he was, still less about where Kamenev was; but one evening there was a letter asking me to go next day to the broadcasting studios to read my Volga script.

I read without much genuine feeling, but it gave me great pleasure to meet the negro singer Paul Robeson, who was there to read a paper written by himself on Pushkin, the mulatto poet. I stood in an anteroom watching him through the big, soundproof window, while his wonderful voice came to me by way of a loud-speaker in the ceiling. He spoke warmly in praise of the land where there was no race-prejudice; he gave thanks to Russia.

Finally he bowed to his invisible public beyond the microphone and came out on tiptoe. We listened together to the latest news-bulletin, read by a quiet-voiced announcer. There was apparently nothing new from Spain. I smiled at Robeson. Beside us stood the head of the broadcasting station, a small Polish woman named Frumkina. Her dark eyes were shining with satisfaction. She begged Robeson in a whisper to sing a few songs. Messages had been coming in all day asking him to sing. She besought him with the eagerness of a child, and although he raised his hands in protest it was plain that he was ready to give way. But then a messenger came in with some fresh news-reports for Frumkina. She murmured excuses and began to read them.

As she read the first her face drained of colour, and I thought at once of Badajoz. Had it fallen? Had the Spanish Republic collapsed? Frumkina, now white as death, did not look at us. She made a sign to the operator on the control-panel and whispered:

"Give the announcer a flash! He's to stop at once. There's an important announcement from——" her voice failed her for an instant—"from the Central Committee."

Her whole body was trembling, and Paul Robeson and I gazed at her in consternation. The door of the microphone-room opened, and she handed the bulletin to the announcer. A minute later the following came to us over the loud-speaker:

"The Central Committee of the Bolshevik Party announces that on the 19th of August, in the October Hall of the Trade Union Building, the Military Tribunal of the Highest Court, under the presidency of Army-Judge W. Ulrich, will try in open session the cases of Zinoviev, Kamenev and others, charged under Articles 58–8, 19–58–8 and 59–II of the Criminal Code with organising and participating in the preparation of acts of terror directed against the leaders of the Party and the Government. The prosecution will be conducted by Comrade Vishinsky, Public Prosecutor of the USSR."

A thousand things ran together in my mind—Sonya's embittered out-burst in the park, the unripe fanaticism of the boy Jan, the double-talk and double-think, the numerous arrests so discreetly carried out, my own ex-periences in the country and the factory and the suburbs of the town—all culminating in this trial, which emerged like a serpent from the swamp, and must, I was sure of it, bring other trials in its wake. I looked through the glass pane at the announcer at the microphone. Now I knew the reason for Kamenev's absence. Was my own manuscript to be regarded as high treason? Would Koltsov be the next one to be tried? Of course he would be! That was what the "special mission" really meant. He had been arrested; he was lost, like Kamenev and Zinoviev.

For the moment I had completely forgotten where I was; then I heard a sigh come from the mouth of Paul Robeson. He had laid a hand on Frum-kina's shoulder. He rolled his eyes so that the whites were visible, and his lips parted like those of a wild animal; he pressed a hand to his forehead as though to overcome a feeling of giddiness.

He loved the land of Pushkin—"The only country in the world where we can feel at home. Here there is no segregation, no foolish ban—we are all brothers." They were the words he had just uttered over the micro-phone, and he had sung the same message amid the shacks on the Mississippi, through Texas and Arkansas and to the coloured soldiers of France. Now his sensitive nostrils caught the scent of death, fratricide, the ugly smell of Judge Lynch. There was a look of such torment in his eyes that for a moment I forgot my own troubles; and a brief sentence broke from his lips as though it were a groan—"It must not be!"

As he turned to go the man on the panel called to him, reminding him of his promise to sing. Robeson looked sadly up at him, clearly marvelling at so little perception, and politely refused. It was no time for singing.

A car bore us along the bank of the Moskva back to our hotel. The towers of the Kremlin rose, aloof and unapproachable, against a starry sky. Near by, in their cells in the Lubianka, Kamenev and Zinoviev must be sitting, the friends of Lenin. All through that night I heard Robeson's voice saying, "It must not be—it must not be . . ."

The next evening Sonya rang up and asked me to meet her on the bridge. It was near the place where two years before she had pointed out Dimitrov to me. The Moskva flowed silently, the streets were empty, and there were very few lights to be seen in the government buildings. I pointed this out to Sonya, who had always taken pride in the fact, as something special to Moscow, that the high-ups worked late into the night. She spat at me:

"You mean that now they're afraid? They're all in hiding? You think we're all ostriches?"

I had never heard her voice sound so unhappy.

"I only mentioned it," I said apologetically.

"One doesn't 'only mention' things like that."

"Is that forbidden too?"

"I see. So you think we're all fools and slaves!"

"Sonya," I said, "I've come here because you asked me to—and because I can't sleep."

She took my arm with a friendly gesture and led me across the bridge. Then she said in a tone of mock-pathos:

"Keep moving. You mustn't forget, my dear, that to stand still is suspicious under a dictatorship. Shall we walk round our beloved Kremlin? There won't be anyone else doing it, so no one will see us. Or perhaps an even closer watch will be kept on us. Who can tell? This is a time of big laws, because now there aren't any laws. We're in the full tide of dialectic—do you know what dialectic? And incidentally what are you doing with your Loyola? Will you come forward as a witness for the defence?" She altered her voice. "I'm Regler. Comrade Kamenev is innocent. He commissioned me to write a book against the Jesuits, which proves that he values one-man rule."

I thrust her arm away.

"This is no time for putrid jokes," I said. "I shall throw the manuscript in the Moskva."

"Don't you see how funny it is?" she said almost calmly. "We've fed you for months, and now you're going to throw your work into the Moscow drain. These are the great days when nothing makes sense any more, when the wrong are held to be right, when thinking is a mockery of thought, when we're stripped naked and when one wants to be sick. . . ."

She stood still abruptly, as though her stomach were indeed heaving, and pointed to the Kremlin.

". . . Sick at the sight of that building, with all those guards protecting a single man who wants to rob a hundred and sixty million people of all protection. Oh, I'd like to be sick into the river, over the pages of your drifting manuscript! I'm sick at the thought of myself, because at this moment I'm ready to go to bed with the first man who asks me. I'm sick at the thought of your beautiful Marie Louise with her flower-pictures—sick, sick, sick, do you hear me? I can say it to you now, because now everything's falling to bits. These are what I call historic hours. We're beginning to devour ourselves. Tomorrow it will be routine again, but tonight everything has the true reek of Hell!"

She looked at me.

"And what's Maria Louise doing at the hotel? Has she finished her picture of the shells?"

I knew how it was with her. She wanted to hurt me, as though she were hoping to be beaten in return. She walked beside me, the little creature that she was, like a stifled cry of protest, that should be made to echo over the red, mediaeval walls of the Kremlin.

"You felt proud of yourself, didn't you, when you were talking on the air? All about the Volga, where Catherine's villages were! I listened to you, and I knew that in about ten minutes all your Potemkin villages were going to be shot to ribbons!"

"If you know so much," I said, "perhaps you can tell me if anyone else is going to be in trouble?" I was hoping for some reassurance about Koltsov.

She laughed.

"Anyone else? *All* of them!"

"Can you tell me any names?" I asked with an effort.

We were on the northern side of the Kremlin and could see the guards at the gate. She clung to my arm like a girl in love, and said in the tone of a child reciting a lesson:

"Bukharin and Radek, Tomsky and Rykov, Uglanov and Sokolnikov, Rakovski and Pyatakov . . ."

The names of all the old revolutionary fighters, a list so illustrious that I dared not ask after Koltsov. We turned our footsteps towards the Kremlin, seeing the whole landscape as a leaden dream from which, surely, I must awake to find that the young woman at my side had shed her face of torment, and that her voice was as light and happy as that of Marie Louise.

But the walls of the Kremlin rose massively in the moonlight, and we were obliged, by regulation, to make a wide detour to avoid it. Sonya suddenly began to talk in Russian.

It was the 15th of August. The trial was due to begin in four days. I took my daily medicine, the news from Spain, which did not seem to be too bad. The Republic was asserting itself. The rebels seemed to be realising that they must not strangle their own countrymen with colonial troops. Thus did I account for the momentary lull—until I bought an evening paper and read the report of the fall of Badajoz.

The tragic news broke through the heavy, suspicion-laden air of Moscow, evoking its grim vision of human hatred and violence—a peasant people manning the barricades, inspired by nothing but a simple and passionate belief in a form of government.

They had heard that a disloyal general was sending Moors to attack Madrid, and so they barred the way. Behind them lay the town where presently they would play *boules* again, and applaud the daring and elegant matadors. Presently . . . but in the meantime they flung their bodies against the dark-skinned troops of the general from Africa, the Tercio Regiment, in

which criminals from all over the world enlisted, when they could escape
the scaffold, the guillotine or the electric chair—how pure was their cause in
comparison! The cool shade beneath the trees on the market-place, the scent
of coffee and aniseed, the mock-bullfights of the children in the streets, the
voices of full-bosomed women cooking chicken with rice and saffron and
olive-oil—peace and equilibrium, and the land that must eternally be hus-
banded. . . . The men knew well enough what they were fighting for. Their
force consisted of 4000 civilians and 600 regular soldiers. For ten days the
eyes of the world had been upon them, so they thought; and now it was
over.

The report came from the American foreign correspondent, Jay Allen,
who had managed to get into the town from Portugal and had seen for himself the utter mercilessness of the conquerors. They had come resolved to
"strew the streets with bodies." There were more than three hundred in the
little Calle San Juan alone, lying beside their drinking-flasks, the blood
mingling with the wine, their simple passion for freedom cooled for ever,
their only crime that they had sought to bar the way to the homeless mercenaries from Morocco.

Jay Allen had found the bodies of two militiamen in the cathedral, shot in
front of the High Altar; it meant nothing to the mercenaries that those men
of the Left had in the last extremity fled to the Church for refuge. Did they
know nothing of Christian customs? According to Allen the Moors were all
baptised Christians, and he had seen some with gold medallions hanging on
their chests, stamped with the Sacred Heart of Jesus. The men were running
in the direction of the bull-ring, where the town's defenders were mowed
down with machine-guns. Those who sought in desperation to get away by
climbing over the tiers had been hauled back by the bullets. *Sol y sombra!*—
but in that arena there had been only shade. Jay Allen estimated the number
at 3000—the Sacred Heart of Jesus must have been drowned in the sweat of
the executioners!

On the evening on which I read the news I applied to the Comintern for a
recommendation for an exit-visa.

Four days later the trial of Kamenev and the other friends of Lenin began.

I saw the prison-vans, in which they were brought for trial, pulled up
behind the Bolshoi Theatre. They did not look very different from the vans
used by the Tsarist police. I saw Kamenev get out and stretch himself; he
was not bound. I thought of Strasser, marching past me to his death in
Munich, and putting a finger to his lips to warn me not to give myself
away.

"If you knew how abominably they treat people in the Lubianka!" Sonya
said when I went to see her. She began to cry, and I put my arm round her.

For the first time she abandoned all reserve. "Bukharin's wife gave way at the first interrogation. Those police officials are the most vile creatures you can imagine. Incidentally, have you made any kind of statement to the Comintern?" She seemed suddenly alarmed.

"I rate a-hundred-per-cent safe," I said. "Anyway, for weeks past I haven't talked politics with anyone except Bela Kun and you."

"Well, see that you don't. Perhaps you'll get away with it. But if they find that manuscript of yours——"

"It was burnt yesterday."

"Not in the hotel?"

"No. Koltsov's Catholic cook did it for me. I told her it was the story of a godless man. She will be silent as a grave."

On Sunday the 23rd of August, by Christian reckoning, Kamenev was condemned to be shot.

His last speech to the Tribunal was notable for its dignity; but he so overstressed the merits of Stalin and the misdeeds of Trotzky that any listener who was not wholly dull-witted could understand his intention—"For Brutus is an honourable man." For the last time he was using the methods of Loyola. The song was a means to an end.

It was the Russian Air Force Day. That morning the names of the accused in the next trial to be held were given out over the radio. They were the ones Sonya had already told me—Bukharin and Radek, Tomsky and Rykov, Uglanov and Pyatakov. The mass-murder had begun. Tomsky shot himself that same evening, when they went to his villa near Bolshevo to arrest him.

"Why is nothing said about Koltsov?" I asked Sonya, as we stood together on a roof overlooking the military airfield. She must have seen the state of torment I was in. She pointed to the sky and said, "Look, the parachutists are jumping!" and she added in a low voice: "I think they're all dead already.'

Some hundreds of white umbrellas opened beneath the roaring transport-planes and fluttered down on to the huge field. When they had all landed a force of fighter-planes flew over, and a gasp went up from the crowd, for the squadrons were in a formation that made the word LENIN.

"You see?" said Sonya. "Stalin is modestly keeping himself in the background today."

I felt suddenly sick. I pictured the Lubianka and thought of the bitterness Kamenev must have felt as he entered his cell.

The tall figure of Tretyakov, a literary acquaintance, approached and said *sotto voce*: "It's nice to be able to read the old man's name in the sky again."

"If the pleasure weren't so dearly bought!" said Sonya sharply.

Some other people were drawing near. Tretyakov bowed and made for the buffet.

"Now will you tell me when Koltsov's turn is coming?" I said to Sonya. She gazed at me for some moments in silence, knowing how strongly I felt; but I had no strength left for argument.

"If they have harmed him I shall hate them all my life!'" I burst out.

She saw that I was capable of any folly, and she smiled gently. I seemed finally to have overcome her mistrust. Her face relaxed.

"Koltsov hasn't been arrested. He has been sent to Madrid as the *Pravda* correspondent," she said.

I turned to embrace her, but she drew back. "You mustn't kiss me, this is not the day for it." She led me to a part of the roof-platform where there was no one else and said softly, "The great revolution died today." Then she said more loudly: "But we shall support the Spanish republicans. Stalin believes in revolutions—when they don't happen at home."

She gazed over the airfield. "Perhaps our salvation will come from outside . . ." She nodded towards the imposing row of high army-officers, seated in well-guarded isolation at the front of the grand-stand, not far from the civilian visitors. Their uniforms were plain in colour and not yet much adorned with decorations, but the figures had an air of self-sufficiency and terrifying finality. "There's nothing to be hoped for here," she said. "That lot won't man the barricades any more. Oh, if only I were a man!"

I stepped back a few paces, breathing deeply. I thought of the men of Badajoz, civilian-clad, true men, who did not make a business of death. The whole scene that was being enacted before my eyes, the generals and adjutants, the loud-speaker vans, the roaring aircraft, the incendiary bombs falling on cardboard villages, was a portrayal of power flaunting itself in the assurance that it was secure and indispensable. But Kamenev and Zinoviev, two of the founders of the State, were perhaps at that moment being consigned blood-stained to their coffins, while in the Kremlin a man who would let no other man near him sat sipping vodka and poring over the next list of victims.

Slowly I went back to Sonya. Now I knew the full extent of the danger, and that I would never drive out Satan with Beelzebub. As softly as possible, and with a Jesuitical—yes, Jesuitical!—smile I must steal away from this burning house. Tomorrow I would see Dimitrov and tell him how grateful I was. I would ask no one about Koltsov, but discipline even my subconscious thoughts and become the harmless visitor from the West. Only a few people should be allowed to know that I was going to Spain. I had no need to say anything to Marie Louise. The day before, when friends called to see us at the hotel, she had quietly unplugged the telephone; it was as though she were finally severing our connection with the Russian State, and

I had nodded approval. Even in Paris I would assume no political colouring. In Spain, I felt sure of it, I would breathe a different air. There, death was a protection against treachery and judges; one died at the hands of the enemy. How good it was to think of death!

The cardboard village, on which swastikas had been painted, was now burning brightly in the distance. None of the distinguished visitors were looking at it, but the densely packed crowd round the outskirts of the aerodrome clapped their hands.

The generals all had their binoculars pointed heavenwards. The loud-speakers had announced that a man was to make a parachute-jump from a great height, but without pulling the rip-cord until he was within a few hundred yards of the ground. It was a gamble with death, a circus-trick performed in the name of the world-proletariat, and to distract attention from the vile happenings that were taking place elsewhere.

Sonya and I, too, gazed upwards, knowing that the place where we stood was under observation, and that any suggestion of indifference to the proceedings would render us suspect. I peered into the sky, searching for the plane from which the acrobat was to jump, but could not see it. However, the excited gestures of the officers in the grandstand indicated that he had made his jump. The loud-speakers whipped up the applause of the crowd in a series of practised staccatos. There were cries of enthusiasm for the Government as well. But I still could not see the Soviet Icarus as he fell like a plummet towards us.

Then silence descended upon the airfield, among the generals no less than among the marvelling masses. "How weird it is!" Sonya whispered. "We might be in a capitalist State!"

Small sounds came from the loud-speakers, like the groans of a dying man, and I thought of Kamenev and Zinoviev standing helpless before the youthful soldiers whose business it was to shoot them. Had they told them who they were, or had Russian fatalism made them dumb? How much dignity does a man retain in the hour of dishonourable death?

"Keep looking up!" said Sonya. "Otherwise they'll see what you're thinking."

At this moment the crowd began to cheer. A general sprang to his feet, pointing, and now I saw the tiny human figure plunging downward from the sky and seemingly turning over all the time.

"I'm going to Spain," I said abruptly to Sonya; and she squeezed my arm and said, "That's what I hoped."

More cheers rose up from below us, and the generals levelled their binoculars and I saw beneath the clouds the white flower of the parachute with its daring burden swinging slowly to earth.

"We must clap like everyone else," said Sonya. "Greet Koltsov from me.

He must come home victorious, and then perhaps he'll be all right. Clap harder! Someone's watching us."

I clapped vigorously, while from the loud-speaker came a song that I had last sung in Berlin in 1932, when Russia was still the fatherland:

> Higher and higher and higher
> We rise despite hate and derision.
> Each whirling propeller sings:
> "We defend the Soviet Union."

Sonya's small figure was pressed against me. "How I envy you!" she said.

The uniformed giants were now also clapping and waving to the people. I thought for a last time of Kamenev, whose body was perhaps now on its way to the crematorium. I heard his voice saying, "Give us a Loyola for domestic use," and saw the smile in his grey beard, and the quizzical sceptic's eyes. I thought that I would speak of him in the outside world when the time came. I was going to Spain, but I would remember him.

An officer of the GPU went by. I said to Sonya in a loud voice, "What a magnificent demonstration of Soviet strength!" The officer glanced at us and smiled.

"You understand us wonderfully," said Sonya.

We went slowly down the stairs.

"I won't let them get me at the last moment," I said. "They're not Russia. I know how to lie to liars."

She smiled.

"Even if they interview me on the station platform, I'll go on saying it— the Party comes first—our great leader—traitors are all scum—higher and higher—defend the Soviet Union!..."

BOOK FIVE

13. We Defend Madrid

My life has been governed by an inward compulsion: the important decisions have never been the outcome of long reflection but rather of a desire for simplification. It seemed to me at that time that I was again taking the bit between my teeth, and I was terrified, as though a voice had called to me from the clouds; but it was really no more than the thought that no man has the right to live self-indulgently in the presence of suffering, to take refuge in privacy from the problems of his time, or to hedge himself about with cynicism against his duty to his brother, his sick neighbour, his threatened friend.

Spain was the threatened friend in 1936, after Russia had proved to be the friend fallen into evil ways. Perhaps my decision to turn from Russia to Spain was rendered easier by the fact that to do so was to face more obvious dangers. The risk of physical death is one that phrases cannot disguise. Nor could the enemy be easily dismissed. It was more difficult to put the decision into effect.

The crossing of the Pyrenees was in itself a matter calling for numerous compromises. I found that the International Union of Authors, of which I presided over the German secretariat, was prepared to send a token gift to republican Madrid. They proposed to send a small van, with a printing-press for leaflets, a film-projector and some suitable films.

By the end of September we had everything except a driver. A workman from the Paris suburb of Ivry offered to drive us on a zigzag route through France, thus covering our trail, for all exports to Spain were officially forbidden.

Only on the day of our departure did I disclose my plans to Marie Louise. I asked her to forgive me for not having discussed my decision with her from every point of view.

"There are no points of view," she said.

"You won't be too lonely?"

"You mustn't ask. It's not the time for asking."

She smiled and showed me her handkerchief, all ready to wave. I thought for an instant that perhaps she wanted to go home to Germany—home, I thought guiltily. But what did the word mean in those days? No matter where we turned, we were nowhere at home. Everything was slipping away, the walls were crumbling, north was south. "Ahead" was where friends and enemies clashed; that was where the light shone and the new geography began.

The small figure stood in the grey, morning light of the Paris suburb, knowing all too well how sundered she was from everything that had made her life. It was far too late to think of those things now, and she made it easy for me not to do so.

"Perhaps you'll win," she said.

I got into the seat beside the driver and she waved her handkerchief. A cat came out of a bistro and stretched itself, paying no heed to our departure.

Luck was with us in the Pyrenees. Seeing the figures of Spanish militia-men beyond the frontier-post, we were tempted to dash through and seek safety among them, but a sign from the French customs-officer obliged us to pull up. He spent a long time examining our papers. But then the hour of midday sounded, when every Frenchman of culture heeds only the voice of his inner man. Chimneys were smoking down in the valley.

Our official came out through the door of his little hut. "I'm off to lunch," he said. "What goes on here during the midday pause does not concern me." He chuckled. "*Il y aura des tomates farcies!*"

We crossed the frontier at one-thirty, and by evening we were in Barcelona.

Louis Aragon, who had come by train, took charge of our offerings for a few hours so as to display them to the Government of Barcelona and to have them and himself filmed. Then we went on to Madrid, where he again took charge of the gifts and handed them over to the poet, Rafael Alberti, and the poetess, Maria Teresa. He delivered a speech filled with promises in the theatre and went back to Paris. It was a most elegant appearance, but I soon forgot all about him.

I stood on the Gran Via without a *peseta* in my pocket and without knowing the language. I had no spare shirt and no letter of introduction to anyone. I was cast adrift in a way that would have induced panic in many people, but I felt happier than I had ever done in Paris or Moscow.

The exciting thing was that my state was exactly the same as that of Madrid itself. Only on this occasion have I known that sense of freedom, a feeling of unconditional escape, of readiness for absolute change; it was the daydream of a whole people. Everything was in readiness for the unexpected, and the unexpected happened. By midday I was guest in a militia-kitchen where they all stood up and sang when they heard that I was a foreign writer come to join them. After our meal they took me to a barracks and gave me a set of blue overalls, and in the evening I went with them to work on the fortifica-tions that were being constructed outside the gateways of the town. We came back singing in the morning.

There was a spirit of intoxication in the people, an infectious eagerness for sacrifice, a hot-blooded unreason and fanatical belief in freedom, which could never lead to the constitution of an orderly State on any earlier pattern. To judge by their outward aspect, the militiamen might have been pushed out into the streets by the French Revolution, and no doubt many of the acts of violence of the first days of the war had been prompted by unconscious imitation of the *sans-culottes*. Anarchist doctrines were far more widespread than one would ever have supposed. They loved to see flags waving, and they built barricades which obstructed traffic more than they served the revolution. They drove in requisitioned Cadillacs up and down the Gran Via with sashes round their waists and Phrygian caps on their heads. No one knew whether the war was going well or ill. When I grew restless amid the fortifications, and asked for a car to take me to the front, they provided one at once.

We drove westward by way of Talavera. No one stopped us. Children were playing in the village streets, and cats lay contentedly on the doorsteps.

"Where is the front?" I asked.

"Wherever they start shooting at us," the driver answered.

We were brought up presently by a grey-stone barricade set diagonally across the road, and a few armed men surrounded our car.

"What's the position?" asked the man in charge of our party.

"They may have reached the next village. We're waiting to hear."

No one seemed to be worrying. The whole war was like this. The enemy was imminent, a constant threat, like that of disease or any other danger, making all life unsafe but at the same time stimulating the deepest powers of resistance. As I came to realise later, this first expedition should have taught me the whole nature of the war; but at the time I only asked, in reasonable astonishment:

"Why do you simply put up barricades at the entrances to the villages? What's to prevent the enemy going round them? Are your flanks secured?"

They laughed without resentment.

"It's not the custom. We only fight on the roads."

I shuddered at this, but it was quite true. The enemy observed the same principle.

I returned to Madrid to try to find out how clear a view the people in government offices, the journalists and the people in the streets, had of the danger that was approaching from the west. The Foreign Minister, Alvárez del Vayo, drove from barricade to barricade enjoying the humorous equability of the militiamen. He had a very clear idea of how Quixote would have behaved as Foreign Minister, and he did his best to follow that illustrious example. The covered inner courtyard of the Ministry was filled with casts of classical statuary. Phidias had his ambassadors here, but there was

S

no Socrates to tell the widely-smiling Minister that any other ambassadors in the town were more likely to be enemies than friends.

Nor would he have taken any heed of the warning. He put his faith in two things, so he told me: first, the help that must surely come from Russia, and secondly, the revolver he kept in his desk, with which to shoot himself if the Fascists came knocking at his door. "But that's a long way off," he assured me, although I had myself seen the shells bursting on the horizon.

I went with him the same evening to visit the foreign correspondents. They were in a state of wild excitement. They loved the Spanish people, hoped for the victory of the Republic, and were all opposed to the official ambassadors of their own countries. On that evening they welcomed Del Vayo with especial vigour.

Owing to an error one of their number, an Englishman (I think he was the *News Chronicle* correspondent) had gone too far north and been captured by the Fascists. Alvarez del Vayo did not seem to attach much importance to the circumstance. He would probably be shot, an American said. I got away quickly; it was time for me to rejoin my militia company and go on with my trench-digging. Out in the street I signalled to a passing car. The only word I knew was *internacional*, but it was enough to cause a driver heading south to turn about and take me northwards.

And then there occurred something that I was to meet with over and over again in that war—the Spanish marvel, the outbreak of pure unreason.

When I started to try and tell them about the captured Englishman, the men and women who came to spend half the night digging trenches, after working all day in the factories, at once crowded round me to listen. A barber who spoke French came to my assistance. He seemed to possess remarkable eloquence. I had wanted to add that the Englishman was engaged to a Spanish girl, but a number of them had already snatched up their picks and such rifles as there were and were running down the slope to where I could see a stationary lorry.

I followed them as though in the grip of an irresistible compulsion. We drove northward, and each time we pulled up at a village barricade and explained the object of our excursion—which seemed to become more hazy and improbable each time the explanation was uttered—an additional man jumped on the lorry.

The Sierra was bathed in greenish-white moonlight. All the men had expressive faces to which Nature had devoted some thought, and these grew more eloquent as we drew near to the Escorial. When at length we had our first glimpse, from a mountain road, of that monstrously outspread and weirdly beautiful palace, built by the sick and tormented Philip II, and knew that the Fascists might already be installed in the mountain-passes we were approaching, they became as lively as crickets. The driver pushed the lorry at as much speed as the gradient would allow. We swung round the curves, jostling one another, laughing and hanging on; and suddenly we were going downhill into what must be enemy territory.

The driver went faster still, and everyone seemed delighted at the thought that we had passed that unnatural frontier. Or was it really a natural frontier, the only true one to be found in our century, the dividing line between peoples and governments; between those seeking freedom and those who wished to keep things as they were?

The pinewoods were swaying in a hard, gusty wind. The men were suddenly motionless. The sight of the endless woods had caused them to realise that they had embarked upon a wild-goose chase, and that the desire to rescue the Englishman had led them, like a will-o'-the-wisp, into dangerous hunting-grounds. The driver pulled up and they all jumped out, to stand, with their picks and rifles, like lost children in the green light of the moon. A wild but noble impulse had sent them plunging into the night, and it was touching to see them awaken from their dream. A whole division might have scoured that vast region without finding the prison-cell where one particular man was held captive.

I do not know what it was that caused me, as I stood there in the woods, to think of Moscow. I had been told that morning that a special Soviet mission had arrived in Madrid. The good Russia had arrived; would the diabolical Russia follow? I looked at the men around me. They had come in search of a foreigner who was no foreigner but a man in danger. They had come willingly, untroubled by any thought that they might be helping a suspicious character, with no picture of demigods in their open, candid eyes, but only the vision of the horizon to which their concept of brotherly love would lead them.

We got silently back into the lorry and drove back to Madrid. I asked them to drop me off at the Palace Hotel, where the Russians were staying. I was in a hurry to see Koltsov. The thing had become an obsession with me. I felt sure that he would not look the same as he had done in Russia.

I ran into him in the doorway of the hotel. His face was relaxed and there were wrinkles of happiness round his mouth and eyes. He uttered a cry and flung his arms about me and pressed his unshaven cheek to mine. He held me thus for a long time, and it was as though a cramp in both of us was dispelled. Then he said:

"Everything will come right. You'll see."

Some stretcher-bearers went past us carrying a groaning man into the hotel.

"Everything is very unreal," I said.

"It's a dream," said Koltsov, whom I had never heard speak in this way before.

The wounded man caught the sound of German. He heaved himself up on the stretcher and raised his clenched fist. "*Rot Front!*" he said, and then sank back groaning.

"Aren't they wonderful?" said Koltsov.

I let him lead me into the hotel. He had a big room with windows looking over the street. We did not talk very much, being overwhelmed by memories.

"If we win here," he said, "you'll soon be able to go back to Germany."

From time to time a young man came in with telegrams. After the fourth of these interruptions, Koltsov passed the message over to me; but it was in Russian code and I handed it back. He apologised and then translated all the telegrams he had received.

1. After the massacre of Badajoz the rebels had made contact with the North and were hurrying to the relief of Oviedo, upon which 3,000 Red militiamen were marching.

2. Toledo had been evacuated by the Reds. It was now known that a million rounds of small-arms ammunition had been smuggled into the town before the cadets had dug themselves in—the treachery of the officers was proved. Parties of Moors had entered Talavera armed with rifles equipped with German telescopic sights. ("How far is Talavera from here?" I asked. "Seventy-five miles," said Koltsov dryly.)

3. The Comintern had decided to form an International Brigade of volunteers in the province of Valencia, based on Albacete. The German formations already available would be sent from Aragon to Madrid.

4. Stalin intended during the week to send a telegram to Largo Caballero, the Spanish Prime Minister, proclaiming to the world that the cause of the Spanish people was that of anti-Fascists everywhere.

Koltsov stammered in happy excitement as he read out this last news, and I knew the thoughts he was suppressing. He clapped me on the shoulder. "That means weapons, tanks, aircraft!" he cried. Then he put a hand to his mouth and looked round in mock-terror. There was an element of self-satisfaction in his humour. I interrupted, as he went on talking about the Russian aid that might be expected, and told him about the captured newspaper man. He listened calmly, eating preserved fruit that he got out of his pocket. Then he said surprisingly:

"We know where he is. We've been shaking up the British Labour Party and the Foreign Office. The wires have been burning since yesterday. He's being looked after." He smiled. "We're the only people who can do that, you know—stir up the whole world on behalf of a single man. And at the same time no one knows that we're at the back of it. That's something else that only we can do."

I marvelled at his assurance. Had he forgotten the men immured in shameful isolation in the Russian prisons? Did he regard the two things quite separately? Was Spain another world—the true Socialist world? There was something depressing and at the same time attractive in his optimism. Sonya, too, had believed that Russia could recover her health only through the pressure of outside events. Now I was hearing the same thing in the heart of fever-ridden Madrid, a town that was perhaps in greater danger than any of us suspected.

The young man entered the room again, talked hurriedly to Koltsov and vanished as silently as he had come. Koltsov gazed fixedly at me for a moment, as though he were trying to determine whether I could bear to hear some bad news. Then he said:

"We have been ordered to leave the town. Things are getting serious, very serious. I shall stay here as a newspaper correspondent—last impressions before the débâcle, and so on. Do you want to come with me?"

"Who's in charge of this International Brigade in Albacete?" I asked.

"André Marty," said Koltsov, and looked at me with satisfaction, seeing what I had in mind. Then he picked up his spectacle-case from the table and put it in his pocket. "Let's go," he said.

When we reached the ground floor he nodded towards the hotel lounge, which was packed with wounded. They were all serious cases—amputations destined to turn gangrenous for lack of antiseptics, head-wounds, maimed men who had managed to escape from the Fascists.

"Perhaps they'll be killed in their beds by the Moors this very night," said Koltsov softly, gazing over the bandaged forms that lay so quietly. "But they won't know anything about it until the last moment. Come on, let's go."

Perhaps it was the helplessness of those wounded men that finally altered my mood. A Russian car bore me through the night to Albacete, where I at once reported at the headquarters of the International Brigade and offered my services. I was searched for weapons and then shown into the room of André Marty.

Marty was known to me for the part he had played in the Russian revolution. His French warship had been ordered to fire at the mutinous sailors of the Tsar. Marty had refused, and by doing so had considerably influenced the course of events.

I too thought, at first glance, that he really was the right man to assemble volunteers from all over the world and send them to the defence of threatened Madrid.

But it is not so easy to turn a mutinous N.C.O. into the commander of an army, a fact of which the last war furnished notable examples. Marty covered his forgivable inadequacy with an unforgivable, passionate spy-hunt; he was genuinely convinced that many of the volunteers who came to his headquarters were Fascist spies. He put all his energies at the service of his mistrust, and did not shrink from conducting day-long, soul-destroying interrogations, or even from sacrificing the tranquillity of his nights and his peace of mind by promptly liquidating doubtful cases, rather than harm the Republic by what he called "petty-bourgeois indecision."

Frenchman that he was, he permitted himself a certain use of irony in his proceedings. As he invited me to be seated in his office I felt that he had decided upon a cat-and-mouse game.

"Where have you been?" he asked. "What do you think of General Miaja? Are the Republicans going to win?" And then suddenly: "When did you leave Germany? Whom do you know in Paris? Malraux? Aha! Where is he now? Did you also meet any anarchists?" Then abruptly, this time like a pistol-shot: "Show me your membership card of the POUM!" (This was the Trotzkyite organisation of the Catalonian ex-Communists.)

At that time the POUM was quite unknown to me. I was opposed to Trotzky because I felt that his desire for revenge was overriding his reason.

Marty's game was suddenly too much for me. I wanted to jump up and hit him, although I know now that if I had done anything of the kind I should have paid for it with my life. But I controlled myself, considering the cause we were both serving. I produced the letter Koltsov had given me, stating that I was Spanish correspondent for the Moscow-published *Deutsche Zeitung*, and referred Marty to Koltsov if he wished for further information about me. Then I left.

Out in the street I met André Malraux, who I knew had organised a flying squadron. He led me to a café. He had something sensational to talk to me about. André Gide had sent him a proof of his *Return from Russia*. It was a sad, prophetic, incorruptibly impartial account of everything, good and bad alike, that he had seen during his tour of the Soviet Union.

"He wants us to say whether we think he should publish it," said Malraux. "It's a difficult problem in view of the Soviet help for Spain."

I well understood, and I remember how consoling it was to me that Malraux, who belonged to no party, should have invited me to share in this weighty consultation within the very hour in which Marty, the over-blown Party-member, had dared to treat me as though I were a spy.

The café was gloomy in its state of wartime impoverishment; flies were swarming over a patch of spirits spilt on the billiard-table. The furniture was old and worn, the wallpaper reeked of provincialism, yet the shabby place was filled with the spirit of the Europe of tomorrow. Malraux sat at one corner of the table with a packet of cigarettes, I sat at the other. We read the proofs. In the open doorway Gide's personal messenger was having his shoes cleaned by a lively, voluble *bolero*. In a little while they were absorbed in each other's company, communicating by means of gestures. Their laughter broke in upon my concentration as I read.

When we had both finished, Malraux and I drew closer to one another. It had been a great satisfaction to me to find that Gide, whom I greatly honoured, had endorsed the impressions I myself had formed of Russia. I did not want to say anything about the pros and cons of publication, but I was glad to hear Malraux suggest that this should be postponed until after the end of the Spanish war.

I had seen in Russia, in 1934, how Malraux suffered from these contradictions. I remembered how, in Stalin's Moscow, he had dared to speak of Trotzky. He had always sought to cast the balance fairly, never descending to any kind of opportunism, but striving to put events in their true proportion. The *bolero* had packed up his shoe-shining kit and was now listening, with a childlike delight, to the conversation of the messenger, which he could not understand. Outside a party of militiamen passed down the darkening street. The weight of the world, it seemed to me, had been transferred to Spain, to the west, where a writer like Gide took his responsibilities so seriously that he sent a messenger to the end of Europe to consult his friends, lest he should do something harmful to the cause of men of goodwill.

At this moment a man came into the café calling my name. It was a messenger sent by Marty to find me. I took hurried leave of Malraux and followed him.

Marty now received me with a shameless affability. He led me upstairs to his wife, who, when he left us alone together, spread out an array of pistols on her unmade bed, inviting me to choose the one that I liked best. I did so with a deliberate coolness, bowed to the very good-looking woman and withdrew, scenting a suspicious mixture of politics and sex. As I went downstairs I had reason to perceive the grotesqueness of the situation. I heard Marty telephoning beyond a closed door, warmly recommending me to someone. It occurred to me that someone might have told him what I had been reading in the café twenty minutes previously. The door opened and he came out and announced in a tone of hearty comradeship that I was to be sent as Special Commissar to the international battalions south of Madrid, which had suffered a severe defeat and were in a state of great confusion. "You will have *full* powers," Marty emphasised. I knew what he meant, and resolved never to use the powers in the sense he intended.

After a wearisome journey in the rain I reached the exhausted troops. At a road-crossing I met Paul Lukacz, a Hungarian who was in command of the unit and whose Political Commissar I then became. He had taken part in the Russian revolution as a cavalryman, had written novels about it, had remained in the Red Army and now, after weeks of pleading, had been put in command of this formation of German, French, Polish and Italian troops. I told him who I was and offered him him my papers.

With a tired movement of his hand he told me to put them back in my pocket. "This evening I can't even read," he said, and pointed westward through the mist to where a fortress stood on the crest of a steep hill. "We were ordered to take that place without any artillery preparation," he said, and I was glad to find that he spoke fluent German. "Naturally we were beaten off. If it had happened in Russia I should have called it sabotage, but here it seems to be nothing but stupidity. All the same, I mean to find out who was responsible."

He looked me over searchingly, and seemed content.

"So you're my Commissar," he said. "Well, you can wash the dirty linen. There are casualties as well."

By nightfall the "dirty linen" had been washed. The troops, although still somewhat disorganised, were ready to endure further trials; they were not arguing any more.

The French were standing about in groups beneath the overhanging roof of the barracks. I made no attempt to parade them in army fashion. I joined one of the groups and listened to what they had to say. They were convinced that they had been criminally mishandled; they cursed in every tone of voice; but I could see how reluctant they were to pursue the argument to its conclusion and give up. I said casually:

"When I'm afraid, the first thing I mistrust is my own arguments."

Ten pairs of eyes glared at me.

"Who says anyone's afraid?"

"Well, I certainly should be, if I were part of a civilian army and had had to put up with this kind of stupidity."

"Who are you, anyway?"

"I'll tell you that later. First I want to explain what is different about our army. We aren't tied to any one commander. We get rid of the inefficient ones and look for better ones. Our discipline is voluntary, not enforced. That is why we have Commissars, advisers, who don't let anyone get above himself."

"Well, but where's our Commissar? We haven't seen anyone who might have saved us from that mess?"

At this moment stretcher-bearers appeared bringing the dead into the barrack-yard. There were three, if I remember rightly. The rain had stopped. The wind blew back the groundsheet that covered one of the dead men. His face was already yellow; there was an exactly recognisable distance between us and him. His state of homelessness might at any moment overtake us. But there was a good safeguard against that kind of infection—to march on, to go forward.

I saw that the whole troop was now standing round me, noting my reactions. Did they expect me to show revulsion or become voiceless in the presence of those silent forms? I pulled the groundsheet back from another face and said:

"They can say no more. It is for us to speak and act for them. These dead men must have a reason. A mutiny among their comrades would make fools of them, meaningless sacrifices. I must also tell you that I am your Commissar, and that I want each company to choose a man who will keep me informed of your doubts and fears, your wishes and your complaints."

A motor bicycle came roaring into the yard. The rider jumped off and handed me a dispatch from Lukacz. All sections were to march immediately to the north of Madrid. The enemy had broken into the university quarter in the western part of the town.

I read it aloud. The men ran to their rifles. I left a small party to attend to the bodies and we marched off in silence. The rain had started again and a cold wind was blowing. No man had a coat.

Thus it began. For days the horses of the Apocalypse rode the clouds above Madrid. We saw the town only from a distance. We encircled it north-about, passing through poor districts filled with cheerful inhabitants, and halted for some hours in the outer suburb of Fuencarral. Lukacz sent out patrols which always returned without having made contact with the enemy. Lukacz began to curse. We had no better map than a plan of the town torn out of a *Baedeker*. Finally a tall, thin German appeared, introduced himself as Alexander Maass and said that he was looking for me and my general. Lukacz laughed at this lofty designation and asked him what he wanted. Maass looked at me, scratching his head, as though wondering whether to speak. I assured him that he might. He then said that so far as he could make out there was no proper Command in the whole blasted place, but that if the general would take the whole situation in hand he was ready to go out and explore the ground thoroughly and get back a report by morning. All he asked for was a pair of field-glasses and a few hand-grenades.

"A patrol is not supposed to shoot," said Lukacz, "but take the Commissar with you, and this young man."

He pointed at a dark, gipsy-like youngster of no more than twenty who as a passport showed his camera. I liked the idea of a reporter taking pictures of the front which we ourselves ignored.

The young man disliked the noise of the shells which soon whistled over us, though they exploded far in the country. Later he asked leave to change his pants saying with humour that it was his first battle and that his bowels had been weaker than his feet. His name was Capa. He later covered all the wars of our time, became the mascot of the Western armies and was killed by a mine in Vietnam.

So together we penetrated into no-man's-land. The scrubby woods on the left bank of the Manzanares were hung with rime. Once a hare crossed our path. When we came to the river we found built-up trenches but no one in them. We moved southward and found the same thing. Madrid lay as open to attack as a doe overtaken by hounds. The town had no walls. Its only defence consisted of a young German emigrant called Maass, presently to be joined by one Hans Beimler, the leader of the German contingent, who was stamping around in the bushes trying to establish a front line.

Lukacz was poring over his *Baedeker* map. The Battalion doctor, a German named Heilbrun, was searching for beds and an operating table, so as to be "ready." Ludwig Renn, the pedantic writer, was hastily studying Spanish grammar by the light of a shaded candle—an Archimedes whose cogitations were liable to be interrupted at any moment by an irruption of murderous Africans. The French were practising throwing the hand-grenades which the Spanish had contrived for them out of jam-tins, dynamite and a primitive fuse. Less than a mile away were the Moroccans, with German telescopic sights on their rifles. My Italians were organising themselves under Pacciardi's quiet orders.

Back in Madrid I expected to find universal despair and the still-unthreatened western and southern entrances to the town crowded with fugitives. But instead I found the cafés filled with men smoking, and a notice over the bar saying, "*No hay anis, no hay pastel*—no anisette, no cake." The men were playing chess.

In the militia-kitchen, where I was known, I was received with shouts of joy and some of them wept. They told me that Russian ships had arrived from Odessa with cargoes of grain, fats, rifles and field-guns, and Mexico had sent arms as well. Suddenly Maria Teresa Leon, the wife of the poet Alberti, appeared and told me that our printing-press was already in operation and that the film-projector was giving shows in all the suburbs. She was full of high spirits and talked optimistically about the situation: Madrid would now shine forth like a mountain of diamonds. She invited me to her car and drove me to the "House of Culture," a charming palace belonging to an absent grandee. It was filled with militiamen and workers who sat waiting in a small concert-hall. An orchestra occupied the platform, and a slightly built man with a baton entered amid loud applause. Maria Teresa explained that he was the Mexican composer, Sylvestre Revueltas, who was conducting his own works. By an almost comical chance a bomb fell near by just as he raised his baton. No one so much as started and the great little man, obviously stimulated by the danger, treated it as though it were no more than an appropriate opening chord.

The music was like a cascade of crystal balls. Then it grew harder, like cooling lava when the sharp edges rattle together as it sinks. It was like the play of lightning along a high-tension cable, and then the music of

Mexican songs crept in, to be suddenly resolved in challenging fortissimi which were like storm-bells and cries issuing from throats that had long kept silent.

I was shaken by its savagery, but the audience pressed forward to shake the composer by the hand and beg him to repeat the last movement of the symphony, as though this were an ordinary day and Madrid a town untroubled by problems or enemies. Then they went off, enlivened by the music that had adorned the steely harshness of the revolution with a mixture of vitality and nostalgia.

I got back to my battalions in time to take part in General Miaja's first brush with Franco's forces. Much was later said about Miaja. Republican propaganda needed a hero to put on a pedestal, and the enemy helped in this process, because if they had not ascribed exceptional qualities to their adversary the stemming of Franco's advance that autumn would have appeared an altogether too mortifying defeat. Miaja therefore "held off the enemy with a strong fist and broke the black tide"—so it was said.

As a matter of policy, as well as from a sense of tact, we endorsed this glowing picture when talking to the foreign correspondents and even to the Spanish people.

Only Capa would say bending over his camera: "Have you seen Miaja?" And the camera would say: "Not here."

The time may now have come when we should approach nearer to historic reality, and the simple truth is as follows:

When, in that autumn of 1936, Franco's Moors were on the verge of perpetrating unthinkable atrocities in the naïve, unarmed and daydreaming city of Madrid, they were stopped by those few battalions which were later named the International Brigade. The saviours had no names and will never have any. Their heroes, very different in character but united in their devotion to the cause of the Spanish Republic, were Paul Lukacz; Hans Beimler and Hans Kahle, the German Communists; the youngster, Alexander Maass, who was the first to make contact with the enemy; Ralph Fox, who was killed, and Ralph Bates, who survived, both British members of the brave Anglo-Saxon formation called the Lincoln Brigade.

A strong magnetic power emanated from Madrid and these voluntary units. They have called us adventurers and ascribed to us a considerable number of crimes. Koestler in his obituary of Orwell talks about the "sham-fraternity" of the International Brigade. But how could a troop exist and win the most difficult battles if their main duty were that of fieldgendarmes, their ambition plunder and their morale a sham-fraternity?

There were also reporters of the *New York Times*, the *Manchester Guardian*, the *News Chronicle*, *L'Œuvre*; with us were Herbert Mathews and Josephine Herbst, and, the most devoted of all, Martha Gellhorn, witty and humane, of the best St Louis stock. Her book *The Trouble I've Seen* had shown her sympathy with the unemployed masses during the depression in the USA. Now she saw our brigade in the making, strolled with Pacciardi in no-man's-land, provided the doctor with his first bandages, saw our amateurish weapons and wondered at the almost incredible modesty of our troops. I call her as a witness with special satisfaction, as her testimony can certainly not be called that of an agent of Moscow. And I give my reason for saying so: When in 1939 Finland was invaded by Russia she covered the Finnish and not the Russian front, leaving no doubt as to where her sympathy was and always would be.

Our forces were under the observation of the world. The Vatican viewed us with disfavour, quite unjustly, since the Brigade defended the churches and, as a politically educated body, made it a deliberate part of policy to respect the principle of religious toleration. The Vatican was never able to prove that any crime had been committed by the Brigade against any priests.

We were installed in the university quarter, in the western sector of the town. From behind barricades of book-shelves, from cellar-windows and sometimes from the rooftops of that very modern, uncompleted centre of learning, we poured our bullets into the night.

After the tall Moroccans had been surprised by our few battalions, and mowed down in battles as tragic as they were grotesque (for no one on Franco's side realised how few we were), we saw no more enemies, only here and there, at street-corners, the flame of trench-mortars. The black bodies lay unburied between what were called "the lines"—the philosophical and legal faculties. My volunteers displayed an indifference to danger which I find it hard to explain. No one knew exactly where the enemy was, and a surprise attack might come at any moment, obliging us to turn and fire in the opposite direction. Out of the uncertainty of the military situation there grew the certainty of gladiators. Men dedicated to life again discovered the meaning of life. Most of them were *emigrés* who for three years had suffered humiliation at the hands of the Paris, Prague and Swiss police. Some had been obliged to report daily (I repeat, daily) and apply for another day's asylum. Now they had arms in their hands and a city to defend. The constant threat of death, which they laughed at or at the least ignored, had restored their dignity. Many were Jews, and their bullets in the darkness were aimed at Hitler. They took pleasure in talking of mercy; this, too, repaired their wounded pride.

Once by daylight a Moor was pointed out to me, standing in the street below our roof. He had lost his way in the confusion of buildings and was running back and forth like a hunted animal, sometimes turning his back to us, sometimes pausing and sniffing with his nose in the air, but in the wrong direction. We could see him plainly from above, and an argument arose as to whether he should be shot. The majority were against it, because one does not shoot a man in the back, and because after all he was only a man, a victim of colonialism. This thought cropped up from the beginning, and had no small influence upon our methods of warfare. It was destined to lead to a notable victory at Guadalajara, in March 1937.

In this case the desire to destroy the enemy triumphed over principle. The volunteers did not shoot the less well because they had hesitated, and they were fortified in the last resort by the hideous memory of Hitler, or simply by the ruthlessness of the war.

"I've come out of Dachau," said Hans Beimler, the Bavarian leader of the Germans. He had got away to Prague and then had become a member of the Central Committee of the exiled German Communist Party. He had had reason enough for flight. Held in solitary confinement and certain of death, he had strangled the first SS man who came into his cell, exchanged clothes with him and thus made his escape. "The only way we can get back to Germany is through Madrid," Beimler said as we lay side by side on a mattress in Fuencarral. He had been in the fight for forty-eight hours and it was only with difficulty that we could persuade him to take a little rest. But when at last he was persuaded, his almost superhuman intensity and coolness fell away from him. He took my shoes off. "The Moors won't come as quickly as all that," he said, "and a foot can only rest when it can breathe." He awoke us at five. "We'll relieve the look-outs before daylight."

There was something gluttonous in his ardour, as though he were afraid of not getting his fill. He wore a wool-lined jacket and a grey militia-cap adorned with a red star. There was nothing unusual in his face with its high cheekbones, but within a few days he had become the magical centre of all the fighting in the farms round Palacete. There was a German thoroughness in his exercising of command, relieved by a care for the momentary weaknesses of his men, a kindness which was his Bavarian inheritance. He insisted that there should always be at least one stretcher available for his troops; he thought of everything, and he caused me to feel that after all this war could be won, for the example he set was worth battalions.

On the 12th of December 1936 I found him behind a machine-gun in the north-west of Madrid, among the farm-buildings of Palacete. The long forms of dead Africans lay a short distance in front of him. I was astonished by the lack of hatred in his face. With the cool detachment of a land-surveyor he turned the gun on an enemy patrol which was trying to get under cover behind some buildings. One of them tried to find a way out by rushing straight towards us, and Beimler shot him down within ten yards of our earthwork. Werner, the doctor, came creeping up beside me.

"You'll have to hold out until nightfall," he said. "I have three wounded to get away."

"All right," said Beimler and pointed to the man he had just shot. "What about him?"

Werner, to my consternation, got up and went forward to the African, knelt beside him, felt his pulse and then let the dark-skinned arm fall. Beimler cleared his throat and said glumly:

"A pity the poor devil had to be fighting for Franco!"

That afternoon he heard that there was a weak spot in our line near the river, and he decided to go and investigate. He came to where I was stationed and said that he wanted to try and re-establish the line. Werner pointed to a stretcher that had just arrived. "Fine!" said Beimler, and climbed out over the earthworks. I warned him of the snipers that were in the red house in front of us, but he only laughed. "I'm bullet-proof," he said.

Ten minutes later two Germans whom I did not know appeared, picked up the stretcher and dashed off with it. I heard tanks firing from the direction of the Manzanares, evidently to cover Beimler, who must have got through. Greatly relieved, I ordered the men to open fire across our shell-pitted sector. The wood echoed with explosions; the sun broke through the clouds and lit up the birch-trees; and then the two young Germans reappeared, coming slowly and almost solemnly round the end of the earthworks. Beimler lay on the stretcher. His face was colourless; his wool-lined jacket was open, and there was a small hole in his sweater above his heart.

Werner knelt beside him and quickly rose again. "Is it bad?" I asked, voicing the foolish question although I knew what had happened. No blood was coming from the wound because the heart was no longer beating. I wept, and Werner passed me his handkerchief. Then I went through the dead man's pockets. He still carried the hunting-knife he had taken from the SS man he throttled. I found a newspaper-cutting of Stalin's speech promising help for Spain. He had left nothing else behind. I took his jacket and put it on, and was only parted from it in 1940, in a French concentration-camp.

He was laid in state in Madrid, and I delivered the funeral oration. His comrades then bore his body to Barcelona, taking days to do so, because in every village they were held up by peasants and citizens desirous of honouring the foreigner who had died for Spain.

Over-zealous opponents of Communism have since asserted that Beimler was "liquidated" by the GPU. The thing was not impossible in principle; but in fact he was killed by a Moorish bullet.

We had no feeling that we must be revenged. Each of us reckoned with a similar end, and it was very much more agreeable to contemplate than, for example, the prospect of lying sick in a Paris hospital, begging alms from some charitable organisation.

Our war was narrowed down to the defence of Madrid. Slogans determined the strategy on both sides. *Madrid sera la tumba del fascismo.* Franco, for his part, boasted of his "fifth column," which remained powerless throughout three years. But despite this, Madrid did not become the "grave of Fascism."

Large outflanking movements were attempted and failed. For the most part they led to an increase in the enemy's strength. It looked as though it was only after those attempts that the Fascists took us seriously. We lay overlapping like two angry sickle-moons, but neither could break the other.

Thus we were left to fight for weeks among the farm-buildings at Placete, where Beimler was killed. At the end of December we threatened the enemy flank at Pozuelo, and in January we moved to higher ground to the eastward, where Pacciardi had established a solidly constructed line less than a mile long between the villages of Almadronas, Mirabuano and Algora. We abandoned this, after a theatrical display of fighting, to relatively weak Spanish forces, so as to hurry westward to Majadahonda and, amid the mists of the Sierra, give the unsettled enemy the impression that we could break through whenever we wanted to. These were feints and stratagems which had considerable success. But in February the Moors descended from the plateau in the south-east on a similar manoeuvre, and crossed the Manzanares to cut off the Arganda bridge and the road to Valencia.

They surprised our French Battalion in the foggy valley, and it was all over before Lukacz was able to send help. The battalion used up its last bullet of machine-gun ammunition, and none fled when the Moors swept down on them with knives between their teeth. They were a battalion much given to complaining, who had sometimes seemed to me to be thoroughly demoralised; but when it came to the point, and they knew that the southern approach to Madrid was threatened, they forgot their grievances and their anarchist self-righteousness.

Werner, the doctor, lay in helpless despair on a nearby hill, watching the last of the engagement through field-glasses. When I got back to Arganda after a night of heavy fighting on the Polish sector he told me about it:

"They were better than any creed deserves. Perhaps the certainty of death makes men greater than they really are. Schaefer, the Alsatian, stood firm until a shell-splinter got him in the stomach. Bouman went on firing his machine-gun until he ran out of ammunition. Thanks to Léon Blum, eh?—and Attlee, too, and all the fools who can't see that it will be their turn next! Bouman went on using his revolver until he was bayoneted. He was lucky that he didn't live to see what happened at the end. The wounded were lying on stretchers on the road to Chinchon. I wanted to get them away, but at the last minute I was warned not to try. The Moors slaughtered the lot. I saw it happen! One or two tried to crawl away, but what chance had they against those animals? How can one go on living after a day like this?"

From that day Werner accompanied me everywhere. He could not rid himself of that hideous picture, and he hated to be alone. Also he wanted to ensure that every battalion was supplied with adequate transport, so that the wounded could be removed to safety with the minimum of delay. The troops soon realised that they had acquired a new protector, and they came to have a great affection for him.

He moved among them, with his cap tilted sideways on his shock of black hair, like a weary beggar-monk; but he worked day and night, his deep-set eyes glowing with the sense of his mission. He had come to Madrid as a psychiatrist, but, being obliged to return to general doctoring, had very soon adapted himself to his new duties. He saw through the childishness of the Spaniards, their fondness for make-believe, their slight sense of reality. He did not allow them to be carried away by this, but at the same time he brought an easing of the stiffness, the apparent indifference, which they needed. Without his help, Lukacz and I would not have been able to build up the Brigade; and I must again remind my century that this embodiment of humanity, kindness, prudence and courage was a German Jew.

Werner and I were by turns optimistic and pessimistic. Our lives were merged together; often I would be organising first-aid posts while he was talking to the dispirited troops. He had the Jewish instinct for danger, and for the moment when fear takes refuge in lies. No one could deceive him for long. He would inspect a contingent of wounded brought in after an action and instantly gauge from them the extent of the attack, and from the wounds he would judge the capacity of the officers. Leaving the groaning victims, he would turn like a judge upon those who had irresponsibly risked the lives of their men; and the accused would hang their heads and utter no word of protest. I first really understood the reason for his influence on a day in the Pozuelo woods when he pushed past me, sprang over the parapet and ran towards the enemy. Thirty yards from the enemy line he knelt down and went to work on a wounded man, hastily bandaging him while the bullets whistled past, for in that war no notice was taken of the Red Cross. He heaved the man on to his shoulder and came staggering towards us. He was under heavy fire, and I ordered mortar-fire on either side to cover him. The enemy fire slackened. Werner reached our trenches, tumbled in and shouted for ambulance-men. I had seen him do the same thing in the case of the Moor whom Beimler had killed, but I had supposed this to be exceptional. Now I realised that it was what he normally did.

For him there was no such thing as a danger-zone. He had made his compact with death, and sooner or later it would cost him his life; but until then,

WITH THE FRENCH VOLUNTEERS IN SPAIN, 1937

as an advance payment, it gave him indifference to danger. So he went out to bring the wounded back from no-man's-land, teaching friend and foe alike his conception of this war.

He was not trying to prove anything. Hitler would never have been able to trap him into any kind of apologia. He regarded the Führer as a fool who knew nothing whatever about the Jews and had been successful only because the masses were so immeasurably uneducated. His courage was born of his longing for a faith. We possessed that faith, we, the innocents—Hans, Lukacz and I. Werner was too old. "Nothing will be changed," he would say; but he would accompany the words with the heart-warming smile that our protests called for. I might call him the agnostic among us, the most lovable I have ever known.

"When I saw the Moors falling upon the wounded yesterday," he said, after reporting on the disaster of Jarama, "I wanted to pray. But to whom? Can you tell me? Franco is fighting for the Christian God, and for Franco's sake the Moors cut the throats of young Frenchmen. I am sure the Pope will soon come out publicly against us. Should I pray to Mohammed?"

During the night that followed the disaster, Pacciardi and his "Garibaldi" battalion drove the Moors back and secured the road to Valencia. In the hastily-dug trenches by the river I found a strikingly full gathering of the Italian leaders. Nenni was there for the Socialists, Vittorio for the Communists. It was as though they were seeking to outvie one another displaying their courage to the men in Rome. Pacciardi was everywhere and master of them all, like a proconsul untroubled by nerves or fear.

Franco's artillery poured shells into the valley from the hill. Pacciardi first took the bridge on the Moors' flank, then he advanced in the centre so rapidly that the guns could no longer fire because the lines overlapped.

I still marvel at the fact that the Italians seemed to suffer from no feeling of oppression or exile; they were truly on the road to Rome. With all the other contingents—the Germans, readily obedient in their masochism, the melancholy-virile Poles, the eternally grumbling French—I was never sure how long they would put up with the weaknesses of the Spanish, the amateurishness of the leadership, the defeats and the long periods of inactivity. They were never quite at home, perhaps also because the leadership was so largely Communist, oriented on Moscow, and often acted without consulting me, thus dividing their loyalties.

But the Garibaldi contingent, composed of all the left-wing parties and possessing in Pacciardi a leader of exceptional intelligence, vigour and understanding, was a well-knit body. They had a quality of true Roman pride. They were by no means uncritically docile; their decisions were the outcome of conflicting opinions. They would argue as though they were on the

T

Corso in Rome, and the self-assured and truly dominating Pacciardi would knit the arguments together. He was never dismayed by human failings; he drove his men to forget their own small egos, was patient with their talkativeness and knew the precise moment when talk should give way to action. He was the one who decided. "Democracy should not paralyse," he said, "or reduce everything to platitudes."

His counter-attack that February was a foretaste of the victory achieved by the Brigade at Guadalajara in March 1937; but even more important was its demonstration of the unity achieved by a variety of political parties. I was happy to find, when I went to visit him in the trenches, where he was resting with a wound in the leg, that he remained modest, listened to all reports, did not assert himself unduly and stressed the fact that his victory was shared by everyone. He was in pain and grumbling at the stupidity of Miaja, whose intelligence service had failed; but he never went further in his open criticism than was permissible if respect for the higher command was to be maintained.

It was a remarkable chance that at just that time, when we were in urgent need of a sympathetic world-opinion to explain our defeats, Ernest Hemingway should have appeared as a war-correspondent on our front. I at once took him to Pacciardi's battalion. I did so for a purpose. In *A Farewell to Arms* Hemingway had written about the disaster of Caporetto in 1917. He was convinced that the Italians always ran away when the fighting got too hot. It was in his nature to despise them for this, just as he despised men of letters and intellectuals because he caught in them the scent of cowardice. Courage was the quality by which he first judged a man. I took him to the muddy trenches by the Arganda bridge. He met Nenni, the parliamentary fox, who stamped into the attack as though he were on his way to the speaker's tribune; and Vittorio, who later became the head of the trade unions in de Gasperi's republic, and who at that moment was cleaning a machine-gun in view of the enemy. Then he saw the wounded Pacciardi, who was being helped on to a motor cycle, to be taken as quickly as possible to a first-aid post, so that the battalion should not be left too long without a commander. Hemingway was amazed to hear them all talking Italian.

Finally he saw Werner, the "intellectual," at work. "Only the best bullfighters," he remarked, "are so detached in the presence of death." Werner was joking, making all those about him laugh. He greeted the visitor briefly, although he had been delighted on the previous day to hear that Hemingway was coming to us. "He could have earned much more fame and dollars on the other side," he said.

A wounded man was brought in; Werner invited him into his car. Shells were whistling down from the hillside. "You can't go now," said Hemingway. Werner got in and beckoned to me. He wanted me in the hospital. He was not sure of some of the nurses, who might be Fascists, and he wanted me to interrogate them. Another shell whistled past, exploding in a nearby tree. I took leave of Hemingway and got into the car. "We shall be back in an hour," said Werner in his most casual voice. "You aren't afraid, are you?" Hemingway laughed. Like the work of evil magicians, the surrounding swamp erupted in chalices of mud under the shellfire.

We turned on to the lane which my Frenchmen called *l'avenue de la Mort*. Hemingway was climbing down the river-bank.

The next day he brought with him Joris Ivens, the Dutchman with whom I had made the film in Moscow. I greeted him with considerable reserve, remembering where we had last worked together. Did he propose to make another film of self-deception? It would be hard on my Spaniards.

But the smiling Ivens was full of stories. He had been visiting villages behind the lines where they were in the throes of dividing up the land. "I've been filming it," he said, tapping his small camera, the same which he had used on the Red Square. "Wonderful faces!" He made a sign in the air. "They've grown young—and you've grown younger, too," he said, and at once regained my confidence; for what he meant was, younger since the great betrayal in the east; grown younger and with faith renewed by the peasant people for whom we were fighting. I felt that I wanted to show him the front at once. He said that Hemingway was going to write a commentary for his film—"and you and the peasants will be the heroes, you, the nameless, and they who until yesterday were landless." He was once more as convincing as the dykes of his homeland.

He filmed the bursting of shells from a dangerously short distance, and said that he intended to follow these with explosions of a different kind, which were to make it look as though the shells in this war had tapped new springs, causing water to flow through land that for centuries had been neglected by its wealthy owners. The owners were gambling away their money in Hendaye, and Ivens intended to go there and film them as they were, overfed and weary with idleness. He was still not afraid of plain black-and-white. "The world *is* black and white!" he said. "Look!" And he produced photographs out of his case of peasants kissing the soil that was at last to be rendered fruitful again—seared and wrinkled faces now wreathed in a new smile. "Faces like the earth itself," he said.

When we awoke the moon was still shining.

"There won't be a dawn attack," I said.

Ivens already had his camera ready.

"I wanted to show you another picture," he said, as though our last night's conversation had not been interrupted. He handed me one that he had taken a few days before in Madrid.

It was a picture of the open space in front of an hotel, under a bright sun. Beside a black hole in the plaster a man lay with his face to the ground in a dark pool—and at once I was painfully reminded of the artilleryman on the Chemin des Dames who had drunk his own blood with his last gasping breaths.

"They deliberately only shoot one shell a day into the town," said Ivens. "Cunning, isn't it? They want to keep everyone in a state of fear. Naturally the Madrid people take no notice, and then someone cops it when he's engaged in some harmless occupation. Hemingway will explain it. It's all so simple, so clear-cut—a truly vulgar death that they want to inflict on Spain."

"I've known that ever since Badajoz," I said.

Ivens stood up.

"And now I'm going to photograph the peasants, over there behind Arganda. Perhaps I shall be able to get some of the ones who dare to come out and do their ploughing at night. That will be another symbol of the dirtiness of this war—ploughing in secret, as though it were a crime!"

In the streets of Arganda I assembled the remains of the decimated French battalion. It was a wine town, and they kept returning to a deserted cellar and broaching the casks; they had much grief to drown.

Marty had heard through his spies about their looting forays, and he sent an express messenger to me to ask what I intended to do. In the innocence of his sergeant-major's soul, he had ordered that they should all be arrested and tied to trees, to sweat themselves sober in the sunshine. If there was any resistance I should shoot a few in the presence of the others, to make an example.

I was tempted to reply that we were no longer living in the days of Frederick the Great, but I did not do so. I had heard a few days before of the interpretation he put on my methods of education, and I still shuddered when I thought of it. It was a cynical tale. I told Hemingway about it as he accompanied me to the Town Hall, where the French had of their own accord offered to meet me for a discussion. Two volunteers had lost their heads in an engagement near the Escorial, seeing enemies everywhere in the mist, and had shouted to the others to run. I had had them arrested and brought to headquarters. They were professed anarchists, suffering from our lack of success and from the climate. I decided to send them to a sanatorium, and I reported this to Marty. He replied promptly that he knew of a suitable place, near Alcalá de Henares. They were taken there, and two days ago I had heard that they had been shot in the castle by a Russian execution squad.

"Swine!" said Hemingway, and spat on the ground.

The gesture made me his friend, and thereafter I lost no opportunity of proving the fact. I told him the inside stories of operations and crises which

I had witnessed earlier. I let him know our losses and gave him advance information whenever I could, feeling certain that he really understood what it was all about. I gave him secret material relating to the Party, which he respected, because it was fighting more actively than any other body, although he despised its Martys. He used my material later in *For Whom the Bell Tolls*, and countless readers learned from the brutal interpolations in a work of romantic fiction about things that they would not listen to in real life. He depicted the spy-disease, that Russian syphilis, in all its shameful, murderously stupid workings, writing with hatred of the huntsman for the poacher.

As we entered the small Town Hall in Arganda I asked him to say a few words to the demoralised men. They recognised him at once as one of themselves. He started by offering them a flask of whisky. Then he asked about the battle.

They answered him without hesitation, and Hemingway listened as one does to the forerunners of a catastrophe. He stood with his flask ready beside each speaker in turn, snorting to show that he understood. The knives of the Moors seemed to flash again, and the survivors raised their faces to the square-figured man in the shapeless woollen jersey and the absurd cap. "*C'est défendu, n'est-ce pas?*" they asked, and he nodded and gripped their shoulders reassuringly and repeated with an almost childish gravity, "*C'est défendu.*"

Finally, they invited him to accompany them to the bridge. They wanted to go back into the line of their own free will, to show that they were good comrades—*et merde!*

He asked me if this was in order, winking at me as though to indicate that he realised that it was the necessary conclusion to the business of restoring their morale. I was so surprised that I only nodded and hastily departed. Later I saw them go off. Some were still without rifles and I should have called them back, but it was more sensible not to disturb their mood. They passed in straggling formation through the entrance to Death Alley. They would not let him march at the head of the column; he followed them as though he had just been drafted.

I sat in the windowless staff building trying to recover my equanimity. I did not begrudge them their Hemingway, even if there was an element of treason in their accusations against the general, against myself, against Miaja and against the Russians, who were not sending enough arms. I plucked the remains of the glass-splinters out of the window-frame. Who would rescue me from my visions? I thought of the hotel where the Russians were installed; Koltsov would distract me. I would have a bath and get my thoughts in order. Perhaps Ivens had confused my mind.

I called to my driver, Jesús, and we followed a northern road into Madrid.

I avoided Death Alley, although the possession of the bridge still enabled us to go by the direct route. But there was no suicidal impulse mingled with my melancholy. This changed during the same night.

Koltsov received me in the dining-room of the wing formerly reserved for Court circles. I saw strange faces; the Russian generals were often changed —"When they have learnt enough about defeat," Koltsov had once jested. He was now full of sympathy.

"I know all about it," he said. "The troops guarding the bridge were surprised. The Moors crept up on soft-soled sandals. You did not know what large numbers had been assembling on the plateau during the past few days. They knew every footpath, and they had had three days' rest."

I was amazed at his knowledge of the details. He went on without raising his voice, polishing his glasses as he did so:

"The valley was asleep, you were asleep, the whole staff was asleep. You should have tested the telephone-lines—but you hadn't enough wire to carry out repairs. You should have sent a reconnaisance plane by daylight over the hill—but you hadn't a plane. You should have kept the hill under constant fire—but you only had one field-gun, because the other's being overhauled. I know it all. I'm talking like a Pharisee. Why don't you shout at me? We should have sent you a tank-squadron—am I not right? Isn't that what you're thinking?"

He put his glasses on and looked at me again.

"Without glasses everything looks black to me." He uttered the short laugh which I remembered from Russian days, and which was like a manifestation of slight insanity. "If they ever shoot me I shall have to ask them not to take my glasses off first."

"How morbid we have become!" I thought, and he guessed what was in my mind. "I'm going to take you to a party," he said, and seized me by the arm.

He led me into a room where a dozen high officers of the Russian delegation were assembled, clad in civilian clothes.

Gorkin, an engineer, was the first to greet me. He had set up searchlight installations for us, the only defence we possessed against night air-attacks— the A.A. guns had still to be bought abroad. Now he had been recalled to Russia, and this was his farewell party. He was beaming with satisfaction. His work had been approved of, and in Moscow he would get his reward.

There was something that rang false, something over-childish, in his demonstration of delight. He showed us the presents that he was taking home with him—a fur jacket, photographs from Granada, where our troops had never been, but he displayed them as though they were pictures of a conquered land. Finally, he operated a scent-spray, and everyone laughed, for this was a quite un-Bolshevik present.

Their laughter went beyond my patience; I quickly drank a vodka, but then steadied myself. Why should Gorkin not take his wife a scent-spray? What was far more important was the genuineness of the atmosphere that prevailed among these men. Here there was none of the slavish terror of the Moscow intellectuals. Under the hail of Fascist bullets they forgot the bullet in the back of the neck, the secret executions of the GPU. Their talk was relaxed, uncharged with double-meanings, un-Asiatic. I thought of Marie Louise disconnecting our telephone in the Moscow hotel. Here the revolution gave men confidence.

Then the telephone rang. Gorkin took up the receiver, listened, bowed, hung up and told us that Maximovich, the leader of the Russian Delegation, was coming to the party. His voice trembled with pride.

Maximovich arrived soon afterwards, a thick-set, clean-shaven man of fifty, who at once reminded me of the generals at the Moscow air display. I had an uncomfortable feeling in my stomach, but I treated it with vodka. The whole company had sprung to their feet. A waiter filled our glasses with champagne and Maximovich toasted Gorkin in a little speech which moved him to tears.

All my depression was swept away in happy astonishment. I watched the men embracing one another as though it were a New Year party, and I thought that in becoming partisans they were made whole again—they became new men! The stink of Moscow was blown away by the winds of the Sierra and this heroic Spain.

It was late when I returned to the front, and I ordered my driver to go by Death Alley. It was under fire, and Jesús recommended waiting a little. I agreed, and we ran to take cover in the trenches under the bridge. Ivens was there, waiting for sunrise so that he might take more pictures. I told him about my evening with the Russians, and he joined in my optimism. "That's what revolution does," he said.

When the firing had died down we climbed up to the road again and found the little Opel on fire. It had caught a direct hit and was past saving. Jesús crossed himself; he was a Socialist, but the traditional gesture was automatic.

The next day Koltsov visited Arganda. He found me on the balcony of the staff-building. Pointing to the searchlight beside me, he asked, "What's that?"

"A legacy from Gorkin," I replied, still in the best of spirits.

He laughed cuttingly and said: "A legacy? That's the literal truth!"

"Has something happened to him on his journey?" I asked.

"No," said Koltsov, and looked towards the ridge of Chinchon, where the unburied corpses of the murdered Frenchmen lay rotting. "On the journey? No. But something will happen to him when he arrives." He passed a hand caressingly over the searchlight. "He'll be arrested when he reaches Odessa."

For some moments I was dumbfounded. Then I asked:

"How do you know? Is it something political?"

"Yes," said Koltsov, and it was as though another world was speaking as he went on: "Why are you so surprised? Because of the farewell party? We knew all about it. In fact, that's why we gave him a party. It's why Maximovich came."

I was feeling slightly giddy. I moved nearer to the balustrade at the edge of the balcony.

"The French give a man rum before they lead him out to the guillotine," said Koltsov. "In these days we give him champagne."

The sound of machine-gun fire came up to us from the valley; Pacciardi was keeping the Moors on the alert.

"I'm going into the line," I said. "I don't feel well."

"It's not easy for a European to get used to Asiatic customs," said Koltsov.

"I prefer American customs," I said. "I'm going to join Hemingway. He and Ivens are with Pacciardi. One can breathe more freely in his neighbourhood, if you'll forgive my saying so."

"I'll come with you," said Koltsov, and he muttered as he straightened his revolver-belt: "Perhaps I need a breath of western democracy too!"

(I assume that it was this humanity which in 1940 caused his death in a Stalin gaol.)

I called to Jesús. Koltsov was again stroking the searchlight, as though he could not restrain himself from doing so. I said:

"Hemingway is not western democracy but jungle, the green hills of Africa, the ocean off Key West. In those places there are certain things you can be sure of."

"Well, let's go and visit your jungle."

Jesús appeared, smiling all over his face.

"*Ya tenemos otro coche*—we've got a new car," he said.

I had not been exaggerating with my talk about the jungle. Hemingway had the calming effect of a buffalo straying shaggily over the tundra, knowing its water-holes and its pastures. For him we had the scent of death, like the bullfighters, and because of this he was invigorated in our company. We had achieved a certain familiarity with death and had gone beyond all normal calculations. Hemingway came from a country whose standard was material success, and whose consuls asked people applying for visas what they were "worth," meaning how much money they had in the bank. There could be no more absolute contradiction of this attitude than the one he now encountered, among the poorly clad volunteers from sixteen nations, under a bridge in a civil war. God knows, none of them carried life-insurance, and they were all tolerably sure of having to sacrifice their present so that Spain might have a future.

As early as the third day I came upon Hemingway lying in the mud beside a young Spaniard whom he was instructing in the use of his rifle against the *caprones*, the Fascists. If he had been captured in a sudden counter-attack he would have been stood up against the nearest olive-tree and shot, for no mercy was shown to members of the International Brigade.

His devotion to our cause has often been misrepresented. It has been called blood-thirstiness and worse. He loved the Communists, who were capable of rebelling against the stupid orders that came from Albacete. He loved the commander, Hans Kahle, for reasons which went so deep that he proposed to write a whole book about him. However, I have not mentioned Kahle solely for this reason, but because he played a great part in our victory at Guadalajara, and because he lessened my dislike for the self-assurance of German officers through the friendship which he inspired in everyone from the first moment they met him. He was a Communist, commanded the Eleventh Brigade, was precise in his orders, understood the unstable Spaniards, mingled the methods of Potsdam with those of Alcazar, obeyed his Party, because obedience flowed downwards to the troops, but leavened it at staff meetings and conferences with an almost French irony. He resisted onsets of melancholy with a formal bearing which dominated all staff activities and meals. He liked looting, but handed everything he found in the castles over to the legal Government, departing from this principle only with a big china vase which he took with him from one field headquarters to another in a packing-case. He wore silk shirts and during lulls in the fighting went to Madrid, where he slept in the Empire bed of a film-star who had fled, swam in her pool and slowly drank her cellar dry. During critical periods he scorned all feminine consolations, but as soon as things eased up he was to be seen again at Gaylord's or at the theatre, which was kept open despite the bombardment. Hemingway would have been hard put to it to say which he loved more, the towering German or the thick-set Hungarian, Lukacz, who mingled war and peace, self-sacrifice and pleasure, in quite other ways. Hemingway wrote later:

I think I cried when I heard Lukacz was dead. I don't remember. I cried once when somebody died. It must have been Lukacz because Lukacz was the first great loss. Everyone else who had been killed was replaceable. . . . And about crying let me tell you something that you may not know. There is no man alive today who has not cried at a war if he was at it long enough. Sometimes it is after a battle, sometimes it is when someone that you love is killed, sometimes it is from a great injustice to another, sometimes it is at the disbanding of a corps or a unit that has endured and accomplished together and now will never be together again. But all men at war cry sometimes, from Napoleon, the greatest butcher, down.

A shy declaration of love! Of course it was for Lukacz, the son of the Russian Revolution, who had not let himself be frightened by it; the rider who appeared on the Castilian plateau like an emissary of the army which in 1919 fought another Franco. When Hemingway first visited us in the mess Lukacz sent a messenger to the village asking all the girls to come because he had a great writer as a guest. Twenty came, and Lukacz introduced them all to Hemingway. None of us wanted to choose, so they all stayed and waited on us. The meal was of the plainest kind, but they all wore their best clothes and served it as though it were a royal banquet. One of them, Paquita, fixed a high comb in her raven-blue hair and danced a tango after the tables had been pushed aside, and everything was human dignity and beauty, and the cries of *Olé!* were tomorrow's music and Hemingway was no longer a guest but the homecoming brother of everyone in the room.

In 1938 he gave up reporting the war, returned to his hurricane-proof house on the Gulf of Mexico, exercised with the punch-ball before breakfast, drank his bottle of Hennessy while he thumbed over his sheaf of "true stories," fished off the Florida keys, danced with fair-haired girls in Josie's Bar under the admiring gaze of his wise, polio-stricken friend, Canby, and pushed him home in a wheel-chair through the peaceful palm-avenues of Key West—was all this a final farewell to arms?

By that time I had been discharged from the Spanish service with severe wounds and was busy, in a beautiful castle in Brive-la-Gaillarde, writing my book on the Brigade, which had now, in conformity with international orders, been withdrawn from the fighting. But in the evening I switched on the radio and listened to news of Belchite and Madrid, the Ebro and Teruel. My wounds burned (it is no superstition, they share my feelings!) whenever a Republican counter-attack was bled to death—how else should one describe it? Did the world not understand that it was not merely a matter of Spain? Was the century bogged down in indifference?

Then one evening, when I was pacing up and down like an exile in front of the stove in the big dining-room, planning a manifesto (but who would read it without asking, "Why is anyone still talking about Spain?") a brief announcement came from the radio:

"The writer, Ernest Hemingway, has suddenly left his home in Key West. He was seen in New York boarding a ship, without hat or baggage, to rejoin the Spanish Republican troops at the front."

"Without hat or baggage." I repeated the words in sudden wonderment as I stared into the fire. The gesture restored the feeling of certainty which for many months Madrid had given me. Not everything ended in banality and betrayal. "Without hat or baggage." Thus had Tolstoy walked through the darkness over the steppe. "Without hat or baggage." Who thinks of a secure house while the people of Spain are in danger of being rendered voiceless by dictatorship? "Without hat or baggage." Who takes his Sunday suit with him? It is the hour of destiny, the frontiers are on the Ebro and all men are at the beginning of all things.

14. The Battle of the Loudspeakers

WITHOUT hat or baggage—that meant that this was a very special war. A battle in March 1937 proved this bold theory to be true. It was the Battle of Guadalajara, through which blew the snow and the icy winds of the Sierra; the battle of the eleventh and twelfth International Brigades and their commissars.

It began with the Pope. Alvárez del Vayo, now political commissar of the Republican Army, arrived on a friendly visit at our headquarters in the mountains north of beleaguered Madrid. Werner appeared, saw him and went into the kitchen to prepare a fuller menu; then he ordered guitar-players. Lukacz was the last to appear. He had been in Valencia begging for more troops, and had had his appeal haughtily dismissed by the Chief-of-Staff, General Rojo. He was very bitter at the rebuff, consumed as he was with his dream of forming a division. He looked older. At the sight of Paquita laying the table his face lightened, and she saw this and kissed him. Alvárez del Vayo clapped his hands, and the staff-officers joined in the applause. Paquita promised to dance by torchlight in front of the church after the meal was over, but first the general must laugh and sing a Hungarian song.

"Where are we?" asked Lukacz, seizing the guitar and setting his foot on a chair.

"On the Volga," I said, but then I remembered how desolate that countryside had been. I had a better idea. "In Castile, the land of Quixote."

Alvárez del Vayo showed his white teeth. Lukacz began to sing a gipsy song, melancholy at first then abruptly breaking into wild cadences. We all shouted *"Olé!"* at the frenzied refrain. Lukacz sang several verses, then put down the guitar, took his seat at the table and called for food. Paquita poured wine into the glasses.

But Del Vayo rose and proposed a toast to the International Brigade. He said that we had thus far made the greatest sacrifices, but that one day we would be compensated. Then he described the present situation. He took a rosy view of it: the ring round Madrid would soon be broken, and the sub-dued north would rise again. He executed a bow, having just noticed the visiting Russian attaché at the table. Had not Red Russia been completely encircled in 1919? He smiled at this diplomatic inspiration and recited the names of the white generals, Denikin, Yudenich, Kolchak. The Russian nodded his appreciation and Del Vayo turned to Papal politics, saying that the Vatican was bringing pressure and even blackmail to bear on Roosevelt— "No arms for Red Spain, or the New York Irish won't vote for you!" Del Vayo grinned. "But we'll flavour the Irish stew with vodka!" The staff-officers clapped, and Lukacz, too, beat his hands together, but he was frowning. He knew, as I did, that Russian supplies were falling off; for Comrade Stalin wanted gold in payment, and gold had become scarce in Madrid.

I murmured an excuse to Werner and crept out, shaking myself when I got out into the air. A snowy wind was blowing from the Sierra, and far below me lay the Escorial. The sombre, deserted palace suited my mood. I went down the mountain-path towards it, and asked the guard to open the door for me. Inside it smelt of decay.

I wandered along the chilly corridors and came to the chapel and the Royal Sepulchre. The coffins were in niches rising to the roof. It was said that only one niche remained unoccupied—the Monarchy had got itself driven out just in time! Was this due to accident or the working of a Higher Power? "What does a Higher Power mean?" I growled, thinking of the Pope's interference in our struggle. Then Werner appeared.

I do not know how he had found me. As ever, when he was agitated, he had pushed his cap on to the back of his head. A candelabrum with half-burnt stumps was standing at the edge of the crypt, and he got out his lighter and lit two of the candles. "For the soul of Don Julio Alvárez del Vayo," he said as though to himself, but I knew he was telling me that he understood the reason for my own frame of mind.

"We shall soon all need a candle," I said.

"You can't even read the paper by them," said Werner.

"I don't want to," I said. "I know we're done for."

How far the losses at Arganda and the gruesome farewell-party for the wretched Gorkin were responsible for my state of inner weariness I cannot now tell. Perhaps it was my consciousness of the power of Rome, which is again and again victorious, whether it is right or wrong.

"Forget your Pope," said Werner, and gazed at the coffins, which by the light of the candles looked more solemn and gloomy than ever. "He belongs to the past. The world no longer wants a religion that is inspired by a single man. And it especially doesn't want priests that interfere in politics. As for your Russians," he went on, and his sudden emphasis was like a warning, "Spain is older!" He blew out the candles. "Let's go. Hemingway has left a bottle of whisky for us to drown our sorrows in. I'm sure he meant the Pope, but he doesn't say things so precisely."

I stared at the white smoke rising up towards the coffins from the extinguished candles. I was not convinced, but I felt that to give way would only make things worse.

Half an hour later, at about midnight, when we had emptied Hemingway's bottle, Lukacz came storming into our room. He said without any preliminaries:

"I've come on an official visit to my commissar. What's all this about the Pope? Why's he trying to turn the Americans against us?"

Werner went quietly out. Lukacz sat anxiously awaiting what I had to say, like a man who has come to consult his doctor. I sought to stifle my own misgivings.

"The American Catholics are very influential," I said. "They can bring a lot of pressure to bear on Roosevelt."

"But we aren't persecuting anyone."

"Don't deceive yourself, Comrade General!"

"All right, so I'm deceiving myself. But is this Pope so important?"

"He offers a life beyond the grave. We can't do that."

"I'm offering life here and now."

"That's not enough. He builds on our primitive fears."

"Our what?"

"Our primitive fears." I had to repeat the words. Lukacz's eyebrows were knit more closely than ever. He stood up, straightening his belt, and I did the same. It was as though he were asking me to convey his gauntlet to the Vatican as a challenge.

"Thank you for the explanation," he said. "That kind of fear comes out of a hollow belly. But mine's full, and I want the Spaniards to have full bellies. . . ." He was calm again, filled with the self-assurance that foursquare ideologists bestow upon their pupils. Then out came the copybook maxims, like bullets fired at a crumbling fortress. "Religion is the opium of the people. A man with a full stomach does not whine for God. The Pope is the accomplice of capitalism. Twice two is four. Wherever there is a carcass, there you will find vultures. Marx knew it all. Long live Stalin!"

He went out so quickly that I did not realise how deeply he now mistrusted even me. I could understand the state of tension he was in. He had not yet recovered from the defeat at Jarama, and now I was confronting him with a new problem. But was it really I? This talk about primitive fears, the Pope, the future life. . . . Such things were never discussed in Russia, but here they were present in every militiaman, every ministerial decision, the conquest of every village, the capture of every Fascist priest, the death-agony of every wounded man.

I started to go after Lukacz, but then Werner returned bringing with him a bottle of claret. Werner, who seldom drank, grew merry and told me that

I was talked of in the Brigade as a saint because I never slept with a woman. Was it for some reason to do with magic?

"You might say that I'm superstitious," I said, "and have an idea that we shall lose if I'm unfaithful to Marie Louise."

"But that *is* magic!"

There was a knock on the door. To my astonishment three battalion commissars were outside, having been ordered to report at midnight for political instruction. I learned later that Lukacz had sent them.

Werner tried to get rid of them by saying that I was not well, but I told them to stay. I drank another glass of wine. How much did I need to drown the unhappiness of that day?

"I'll tell you the truth," I said to them. "What you pass on to the troops is your own affair. All right. There's a permanent government crisis in Valencia. Caballero is resisting Communist influence and the Russians are withholding arms. Their food supplies have stopped too. The whole thing is a deal, and we're nothing but pawns in the game. The Russians want to win the war first, but the anarchists want to see positive results right away—co-operatives, land distribution, a charter of rights, a new world. Caballero's in the middle. He'd like to come back to Madrid, which our Brigade has saved for him, but if he did he'd be the prisoner of the Communists. They're trying to form a trade-union Government as a way out. Catalonia has threatened to break away. That is the internal situation."

"But other countries have something to say!" cried the French commissar, and they all looked expectantly at me, hoping for better news. But I had nothing encouraging to offer. The overall picture was too bad.

I gave them the harsh facts.

"Léon Blum is rigidly applying the arms embargo. Everything that gets through to us is smuggled; it's poor in quality and three times the proper price. The right-wing parties in France are proposing a settlement which would give Franco the greater part of the country and all the mines. At the tenth International Trades Union Congress in London our Spanish delegation was applauded and then forgotten. The Spanish claimed the right to buy arms and they demanded that all foreign ships and troops should be withdrawn. More applause, but nothing was done. Instead, the Fascist Grand Council in Rome decided to send Franco a few divisions."

"Well, I'd call that good news," said Werner dryly, trying to lessen the tension.

Others now spoke up.

"The Russians are bound to help as the danger gets greater," said Maniou, the Frenchman.

"If the Duce really sends troops," said Barontini, "we'll get them all to desert to our side."

I was astounded at the hopeful view they took of everything. They talked like their own propagandists. The Pole, Henri, said:

"That was a good, truly Bolshevik report. We are grateful to the Brigade Commissar."

I stood up. There was a knock at the door and a motor cyclist appeared with a dispatch. Werner took it from him.

"That's all," I said, feeling somewhat humbled by the coolness of my three commissars. Werner was reading the dispatch.

"Just one more trifle," he said, and handed it to me. But before I could read it he went on in his drawling voice:

"The Italians are advancing from the east along two roads. Brihuega has been taken. So our hospital will be at Guadalajara. Better let everyone know. It's just as well to know where the hospital is. There are first-rate operating theatres and a few Fascist nuns whom I shall have to throw out. But otherwise everything's fine! . . ."

Thus began the Battle of Guadalajara, in March 1937. The "papal" Italians appeared in considerable numbers. When I received the report I wondered how much I should reveal to my officers of the immense danger that threatened us. I drove with a tolerable rapidity eastwards from Madrid, collecting local reports and fitting them into the overall picture.

One Littoria Division, one division of Blackshirts, two special brigades, a Spanish division, a German unit and thirty-six guns per division—it added up to a formidable fire-power. My blood ran cold as I reflected that our German contingent possessed only three guns. We seemed to need the protection of Heaven. But was not God on the other side?

"No, only the Pope!" I cried aloud.

"Beg pardon?" said Jesús Hernandez, my normally silent driver.

"It's all right, Jesús," I said. "Everything's all right."

We pulled up at kilometre-stone 74. Torija, the mountain village, lay behind us, and before us two roads from the east came together. One came from Siguenza, and the other curved over the plateau towards Brihuega. The enemy was in both places. He was advancing along both roads. What had been done to stop him?

I gathered that all the field-kitchens were out of firewood, that the men of the International Brigade were at their posts, but that the Spaniards were holding a debate, and that no field-telephone had been laid.

There was nothing very new in this. All our battles had started in the same fashion—in chaos. We were all amateurs, Russians, Spaniards and "internationals" alike. But this battle was more vital than any. Here we were up against the troops of the Duce and the Führer. There were ticklish political considerations, and the overriding consideration, which was the reason why my title was that of commissar and not commander.

An African from the Garibaldi Battalion came up to me. He was a man I knew, an Abyssinian whose father had been hanged by Mussolini's soldiers. He greeted me and said, drawing his hand across his throat, "*Mio giorno*— my day." He had vanished in the direction of Brihuega before I quite grasped what he meant.

But his gesture frightened me. This was exactly what must *not* happen! It was here that ideology cut across purely military considerations. This was a battle that had to be decided as between officers and men, between the Duce and his troops.

The object was not to cut their throats but to win them over. That was what we were here for. That was what I had come for—to point out the new frontiers and abolish the old. The revolution in ideas. The true civil war in all its tremendous novelty—to bring about the disintegration of the enemy, to unmask the lying propaganda. To restore humanity in the midst of murder.

I telephoned Madrid from the half-demolished staff office. The Italian commissars were already at work and would be sending a motor cyclist in an hour with the proof of a leaflet for my approval. I was so excited that I could scarcely control myself. I had waited so long for this moment! "Approval?" I cried. "Don't wait for that! Consider that you've got it. Run them off at once and send me a supply. *Imprimatur, imprimatur, imprimatur!*"

I repeated the clerical word, sanctioning publication, with especial delight.

And then began the drama of the leaflets. For days on end I struggled through all its human and sad phases. I remember that for nine days I scarcely slept.

Snow fell upon the roads, upon the fortified castle of Ibarra, before which our French and Italians lay, and upon our right wing, where the Poles were working their way forward in a series of short, rapid advances. Machine-guns were installed under the bushes, at the park-gates and the holes in the walls, but they still kept silent.

It was for the loudspeakers to speak first, to proclaim their heart-warming message through the cold air. I looked up at the black gaping mouths in the white-clad trees. The first was already speaking. I stood directly beneath it, a hundred yards from Ibarra Castle, listening to the men of Garibaldi calling to the men of Il Duce:

"Italian brothers! Marshal Graziani, whom you call the Libyan hyena, and whom the Ethiopians christened 'General Yperite,' has been overtaken

U

by their revenge. He was seriously wounded in an attempt to assassinate him. You too, if you stay where you are, will be in danger. The hatred of Spain will sweep over you! Italian brothers, the Spanish people are fighting for their freedom. Desert the ranks of their enemies! Come over to us! We will welcome you as comrades-in-arms, we, the men of the Garibaldi Battalion."

A bullet burst against the wall where I was standing with the French, waiting to see what effect this would have.

"Not a bad full-stop!" said Boursier, their youthful commander. He said it so grimly that I suspected something.

"What was so special about it?" I asked.

"It was a dum-dum. They cut the nose off the bullet and——"

"I know what a dum-dum bullet is."

"And what are we supposed to do? Answer them with love-letters?"

"*Ta gueule!*"—but he must have realised from the sharpness of my voice that he had scored a point. But had he? The Garibaldi men did not give up so easily. The loudspeaker cleared its throat, and quoted from a speech by Pacciardi, their commander, who had been in Paris, buying arms, but had been ordered to return the previous night, since this was the moment he had been awaiting for years.

"In the mud of the trenches, amid the thunder of the guns, an ideal of peace smiles upon us. . . ."

The Italians around me wept, but they were happy tears. Their exile was ended! They could talk now with a very different voice. There was no longer any police to humiliate them, no scurrilous reports to distress them. They were fighting on level terms, no longer like the fox pretending that the grapes were green. The self-imposed silence of the Paris cafés was lifted; they could answer back, say what they really thought, prove that they were in earnest with their humanitarian ideals. The struggle was extending its frontiers, which hitherto had been directed against the police, the torture-chamber and starvation. Now the new demigods were being challenged, the Imperium Romanum and the Third Reich. This was the new frontier, before the dilapidated castle of a Spanish grandee, and the loudspeakers proved it.

"You gave us this chance!" said the Italian, Barontini, to Augusto, the tall, universally popular Spanish captain. Augusto smiled. "The honour is mine," he said modestly and looked over the sights of his machine-guns towards the castle from which presently an answer would come. But when, oh, when? *Quien sabe?* Augusto had no faith in leaflets.

"If they were all like you, Augusto," said the Pole Janek, "there would be no need for us 'internationals.' "

Augusto smiled again and signalled to the left wing of his company. His young men dashed forward twenty yards, advancing with him towards the chapel. A machine-gun opened up, but they were already flattened to the ground.

Another report came from the Italians. "Augusto is thirty yards from the chapel. It is time to frighten the Fascists again. Loudspeakers!"

The loudspeakers sang the Italian song, "*Fratelli nostri . . .*" Augusto got within ten yards of the castle. Which would win, reason or courage?

The bullet got Augusto as he was making his final sprint to the doorway. He clutched his heart, opened his mouth, then fell on his face in the snow.

His fellow-countrymen fell silent when the news went round. Some of his own men carried the body back, and the whole company went with the bearers, weeping; they did not ask who would take his place. Had not the world stood still?

I met them with the dead man on the road to Trihuecque. Augusto seemed even taller under the sheet that covered him. I had often looked at him when I was giving him instruction. Now I bent down, uncovered his face and kissed his forehead, on which the melting snow lay. The bearers wept.

"Murdered by an Italian!" one of them cried.

"*Caido*—fallen in battle," I corrected him.

Mortar and machine-gun fire was now coming from the castle, and the boom of tank guns. The battle was again in full swing, and the loud-speakers were silent as though ashamed. The first day of ideological warfare had ended in defeat.

But I did not give up. The next day I took the yellow leaflets along to the Poles who were working their way forward through the rocky ridges. Commissar Henri translated them while we crouched on the rim of the Brihuega valley. The men protested violently, and Henri translated their remarks for my benefit. "Why had no one dropped any bombs on Mussolini? If the Italians on the other side are so ready to desert, why aren't they shooting their officers? We aren't the Salvation Army!"

The men who protested were all Communists. Finally, not knowing what else to do, I adopted Gallo's technique and said that the distribution of the leaflets was a Party order.

That night they took them over to the enemy lines.

I did the same with the Italians. We wrapped the leaflets round stones. "Scissors cut paper, stones sharpen scissors, paper wraps stones . . ."—the old children's game. We flung our messages of peace into the trenches where Mussolini's soldiers lay sleeping, and then crept back. That second night was a victory.

I said so to Augusto, when we buried him on the morning of the third day.

And on the third day some of our Italians rebelled. They hadn't come here for this sort of thing. They wanted to be revenged for the shame of exile, the years in foreign cities where there was no Corso and the people talked ugly languages, and where one could only dispute with other *emigrés* and not with one's own kind. Verona, Perugia, Florence, Rome . . . they wanted to be revenged for the life of which Mussolini had robbed them— and now, there were his officers, within reach! Well, blow them to bits with mortar-fire! Let's have more guns, to teach them what we really mean! Leaflets? You must be mad! The sort of thing only a highbrow would think of (they had just discovered that I was a writer)! Why don't we attack Brihuega with knives between our teeth? They captured Luigi today, the light-hearted Luigi—God knows what they'll do to him in Brihuega!

It was hard, I must admit, to stand up against this. But again the Communists helped me.

They announced that the enemy was on the verge of surrendering; and in fact the fire from Ibarra died down that afternoon. The loudspeakers got the upper hand. "*Fratelli nostri* . . ." Our speakers put more emotion into their voices. We were all full of hope until, in the course of the rainy evening, a patrol found Luigi. He lay in a furrow near a tent that had been hastily abandoned by the enemy. His wrists bore the marks of torture, and all the teeth had been battered out of his head. He was scarcely recognisable, but the Garibaldi men knew him. They did not weep.

But if I had gone to them with more leaflets on that third night, while they were talking about Luigi in the fox-holes of Brihuega, under the walls of Ibarra, amid the furrows of the fields and in the caves of Fuentes village, I might have been met with such contumely as no commissar can encounter without being punished for it. Perhaps they would have thrown grenades at me.

So I bided my time and helped to bury Luigi.

Then a red rag was waved from one of the windows of Ibarra. When it was noticed we all held our breath. And when shortly afterwards a number of blackshirts emerged from the castle and came towards a tank hidden amid the bushes, the young Spaniards sprang to their feet like delighted children, swarmed round the deserters, overwhelmed them with greetings and offered them cigarettes.

It was nothing but a trick! Suddenly the machine-guns opened up again and swept the field of reconciliation clear. But half an hour later I saw a hand at the same window groping for the red rag. I turned my field-glasses on it just in time to see it quivering in a death-agony. An officer had punished the presumably genuine gesture of some dispirited soldier with a bullet in the neck. But the sight of that quivering hand gave me strength to continue the "battle within a battle."

More loudspeakers were brought into action. Our Italians drafted fresh texts. Loudspeaker vans were brought from Madrid as close as possible to the front. Actors spoke to the soldiers of the Duce, appealing to their pride, invoking their home-sickness, and, as though talking to children, reminding them of the danger in which they stood. "*Ritornate alle vostre case, non dovete morire*—go home, you must not die!"

That night the Fascist commander departed from the castle, accompanied by the officers who were Party-members but leaving behind a number of career-officers and sergeants to keep the demoralised troops in hand. As he vanished into the night he may have heard the voice of Garibaldi crying:

"They promised you the earth, but they are giving you death."

The snow fell, covering the bodies of their dead and ours with its merciful, white shroud.

The next day the commissars won. I had the "Internationale" played. It might shock the Catholics on the other side, and harden the hearts of the Fascists, but it seemed to me that after so much talking we needed music, the message without words, and that it must be a chorus that would swell and warm the heart like a symphony. It seemed to me now, as it poured out over the countryside from the hidden loudspeaker van, that the song, that had filled me with terror in Russia, had again acquired the purity of superhuman striving.

I remember that I came upon a young White Russian named Mishka standing in the undergrowth outside Ibarra. He had come from Paris, and had joined us so as to work his passage back to Russia. I had made him the general's orderly, but in view of the reports of the Moscow trials I had to warn him that his chances of being admitted to the land of Stalin were very slim. He was intelligent and understood this; but at the sound of the workers' hymn all his longings awoke like a wound. He saluted as he listened, and I saw tears in his eyes.

The Poles no sooner heard the song than they fixed bayonets and pressed forward to the walls high above Brihuega. They did not want to arrive too late.

Barontini, the Italian commissar, whose companies were having to stand up to the fire of the Fascist artillery, was cursing when I scrambled down into his quivering dug-out. Shells were bursting all round, and the notes of the hymn reached us on gusts of wind.

"Theatre!" growled Barontini. "Mass-murder of volunteers with musical accompaniment!" He snorted in disgust. "Another headquarters notion!"

"What do you mean by headquarters?" I asked. "I'm *here!*"

He was silent. A shell exploded above and a heavy man came sliding down the steps. It was the Abyssinian. "Cut their throats!" he said and started to climb up again, but I gripped him by the arm. "Not to touch the wounded, do you hear? All comrades, understand? All Abyssinians, do you hear?" I felt that the last words had impressed him.

He did not wait for the shell-splinters to stop falling, but vanished into the hell above.

An hour later Ibarra surrendered. Mussolini's soldiers came hesitatingly towards us, but this time there was no deception; they all had their hands above their heads. They were rapidly searched for weapons by the commissars and then allowed to put them down.

They came in hordes to our headquarters. We did not count them. Lukacz beamed and then pointed to the men of the Garibaldi Battalion, who were looking almost shyly at the prisoners.

"It's almost as though they were ashamed," said Lukacz.

It was, I thought, symptomatic of the confusion of our century. Then the Abyssinian pushed his way through the crowd leading two Italians, their wrists tied with cord. He came up to me and saluted with a broad smile, and the men all around laughed, happy in his triumph. Even the prisoners were laughing.

"Well done!" I said, and embraced him. "And now take the rope off them."

It was our most significant victory.

Hemingway in his preface to my book *The Great Crusade* wrote of the Twelfth Brigade, who won the battle:

> The Twelfth Brigade was where my heart was. There was Regler, who is the commissar of this book. There was Lukacz, the general. There was Werner, who is the doctor in this book. There were all the others. I will not name them . . . They are all in this novel of Regler's and most of them are dead now. But until they died there was not one of them (that's a lie, there were a few) who could not make a joke in the imminent presence of death and who could not spit afterwards to show the joke was real. We introduced the spitting test because it is a fact, which I discovered in early youth, that you cannot spit if you are really frightened. In Spain I very often could not spit after quite a joke.
>
> The jokes were never bravado. The jokes were because really brave men are nearly always gay and I think I can truly say for all those I knew as well as one man can know another, that the period of fighting

THE AUTHOR SPEAKING TO THE WRITERS' CONGRESS IN MADRID, 1937

when we thought the Republic could win the Spanish civil war was the happiest period of our lives.

Was it the happiest? Lukacz was happy. He had achieved his dearest wish. After weeks of haggling he had got reinforcements. He had been able to give Pacciardi a whole brigade; he had prevented my recall by Marty; he had enough arms for everyone.

We were a division! The International Brigade had become famous. But no one knew the losses we had sustained. Seventy out of every hundred of the volunteers who had saved Madrid in 1936 now lay beneath the ground. They had been replaced by Spaniards; but the brigade still called itself the "International," and the young sons of Spanish peasants were proud to belong to it.

Lukacz had drilled thousands of recruits. No longer doubtful of victory, he was formulating the most daring plans. He almost infected me with his confidence. I talked to the troops about the decisive battle—Huesca was to be captured.

It was the 11th of June 1937. We had occupied the surrounding country by forced marches, taking up our positions at night. The town was to be taken by surprise.

I sat high up in the mountains whose hidden roads we had used so as to get behind the town unobserved. Werner was with me; it was the last time I was to see my dark-eyed, tender and wise friend. Far below us the town with its towers and spires lay like a plaything, surrounded by a mediaeval wall.

"When we've won," said Werner, making me happy with the words, for he had never been optimistic, "when we've won I shall accept Hemingway's invitation to Key West. He has told me about his boat, and about landing two-hundred-pound fish. I've never done any fishing, but perhaps one can just lie on deck and watch the fins cutting through the water, and then turn over on the other side and see the bottom and the coral growing."

"And smell the scent of distant orange-groves mixed with the tang of the sea. Ernest says it comes in sudden waves."

"Spain will be free by then," said Werner, "and they'll have forgotten all about us. But who wants to be remembered too long? It makes one old."

A gun was fired from the town below, and a white puff of smoke rose up from the wall. Then another cloud of smoke appeared over the road where it ran through our positions.

"The usual evening excitement," said Werner.

"If anything should happen to me," I said, "will you see to it that the battalions don't hear about it for as long as possible?" The thought had suddenly entered my mind.

"Nothing's going to happen to you."

"It was just a thought," I said.

We separated without looking at one another.

The shell got us just as we were driving past the anarchist battalions. Our car was lifted into the air, to drop with a thud. I felt a savage blow in the back, and my hands were covered with splintered glass. The driver, beside me, was dead with his hand clutching the brake. The Russian interpreter behind me was leaning forward, motionless. Lukacz was lying with his grey head against the upholstery; his brains were exposed. I tried to get the door open, but it was jammed.

"*C'est ça la fin,*" I said. I thrust an arm outside the car and, clutching the roof, dragged myself up. The sun was shining, and a soft carpet of grass ran up the hillside. I was now conscious of the tepid pool of blood in which I had been sitting, but I went on pulling myself up. When I had managed to get halfway through the window I let myself fall. A shell whistled over me.

"*Nous sommes les premières victimes de la division,*" I said, and gave a last glance at the groaning Lukacz.

I recovered consciousness only twice in hospital. It seems that the first time I shouted, "You must take Huesca!" The second time I asked for Marie Louise to visit me. This was shortly before the blood-transfusion. In the next room Lukacz was on the verge of death.

They found a bullfighter who had the same blood-group as I. As he lay beside me I thought of Marie Louise. It is not true that when one is near to death one sees a rapidly unfolding picture of one's life. One is preoccupied with a single problem, one that one has never really faced; and for me it was the thought of this woman whom I had spirited out of Germany in 1933, and rendered homeless and was now deserting. My heart beat weakly between life and death, and seemed sometimes to be giving up altogether. So I asked for her, and indeed ordered that she should be fetched.

I did not know that owing to an error I had been reported dead in Paris, or that Werner, on the morning after the attack, had gone from battalion to battalion denying the rumour that something had happened to Lukacz and me. After bringing this reassurance to the last of the units surrounding the town, he had got in his car and driven towards the Pyrenees. He must have been tired of the many white lies he had told, besides being convinced that neither Lukacz nor I would live through the day. An enemy plane spotted him and emptied its guns into his zigzagging car, and a bullet cut one of his arteries and he died.

15. The Exodus

It was a war of attrition, and so the Spanish consuls in foreign countries thought twice about allowing anyone to enter the fortress of Spain. Moreover, it was a war subject to controls. Moscow, suspicious and never generous, examined every would-be visitor down to the last wrinkle of his brain to see if he could be relied on to remain faithful to the Party-line.

Marie Louise returned the most astonishing answers when she applied for a visa to the fusty-minded functionaries of the German Communist Party in Paris.

"What do you think of André Gide?" Gide had, after all, published his account of his Russian journey.

"There are friends of Gide with Gustav in the trenches. Do you want to arouse discontent at the front?"

The official: "Gide is worse than Franco!"

Marie Louise: "That is something I will not listen to."

And she walked out.

The report of my death had by this time been amended to one of "seriously wounded."

"I have a right to go to him on his deathbed," said Marie Louise, paying a second visit. "If you don't allow me to I shall let all Paris know of your hardness of heart."

They stamped her papers and she set forth, not expecting to find me alive. But the frontier was not so easily crossed. Mistrust prevailed on both sides. Wrapped in a dark cloak, pursued by searchlights and threatened by machine-guns, she passed over at night, by way of the tunnel at Cerbère.

"I came to join my lover," she declared proudly when she reached Madrid in August 1937, and sat at my bedside holding my hand.

She wanted to make herself useful—"Even the dirtiest work," she said. But at the sight of my wounds her nerve failed and she fainted.

A sensible Spaniard then took her to the hospital for the Germans and French. She visited them after the bandaging or before the operations. She visited those with terrified, staring eyes, and those who were blinded and those whose sight was failing and who wanted for one last time to hear a woman's voice; and her clear, steady voice gave them confidence and never uttered a false word, such as priests and nurses so often do.

She told them of her native moor, the drone of bumble-bees over the lilac, and to those dying in unhappy Madrid, lying until the last minute in terror of a bomb that might blow them out of their beds, the bumble-bee became a benevolent pilot filling the sky and catching the bombs as though in a butterfly-net; and many died smiling, as though at the last they had been borne through the air to their homes, to lie on the warm turf with the grass brushing softly against their chilling hands in a childhood caress.

For four months Marie Louise sat at the bedsides of the many who died too young. What she thought about it I learned later, in a dramatic hour.

It was four months before Julian, the hot-blooded, well-read surgeon, whom Franco later shot, had more or less patched me up. There were still splinters in my back, but my kidneys and backbone were usable. However, the Army could make no further use of me, and so Dr Negrin, who was then the Socialist Prime Minister, proposed that I should do something to help the hospital service. He made me officially a Spanish citizen and sent me with a diplomatic pass to the United States to appeal for funds.

In December 1937 my driver Jesús drove us to the frontier. They had just started shelling the little town of Port Bou.

During the next twenty-four hours we experienced in all its agonising sharpness the contrast between suffering and joy in this world, a contrast which we never forgot, and which has been a warning to me ever since. By candlelight, in the cellars where we took shelter, we saw children with their bellies swollen with hunger. The mothers sat silent against the walls, only weakly clutching them when a bomb caused the earth to tremble.

Fourteen hours later we got off the train in Paris. Here the night was trembling with the brilliance of the lights. We thought of the candles in Port Bou, and spoke of them as though in apology.

The area around the Trocadéro was especially bright. Official Paris was there celebrating the end of the World Exhibition. We first walked along the narrow streets behind the station, almost in self-protection, so as not to be overwhelmed by the unaccustomed feeling of riches and plenty. But even those humble shopping-streets gave us the same sense of shock, which was to remain with us all our lives. It must be borne in mind that in struggling Spain only the Army got enough to eat. There were communal kitchens and co-operatives, but they could not stem the steady onset of starvation. Children died of hunger in the bombed towns, and mothers had cried out to us in their despair.

And here, separated by a mountain-range, a hand's breadth in the eyes of

God, were the shops of the provision-merchants with their loaded shelves—
the steak neatly wrapped in paper and adorned with a sprig of parsley to
please the eye as well as the stomach. We stared at the long French loaves,
the mounds of butter, the sausages and hams, the creamy rounds of Brie, the
piles of eggs that were in no danger of being shattered by a bomb. The contrast was more than we could bear. Could one nation know so little of
another? Where was one to turn? Must one acquiesce—or turn back to
Port Bou, to Madrid, wounds or no wounds, and at least take comfort in the
unity of suffering?

We travelled to the United States, I as a member of the mission sent to
raise funds for the needy hospital-service of the Spanish Republican Army,
and Marie Louise as the guest of Ernest Hemingway, who would not hear
of my going without her while I was still convalescent.

The sea-passage afforded us a first glimpse of the world we were entering.
President Roosevelt's mother was collecting dollars for polio-research.
Money was showered on the old lady. It seemed, then, that the people were
concerned with suffering. They were also realistic and natural in their
bearing.

I spoke in Washington and New York, in Buffalo and Detroit, always to
the same sort of people, attentive, ready to be won over, opposed to dictatorships and therefore in favour of the Spanish Republic. They wanted it
to have its parliament, and they wanted to restore to Spain everything that
literature, the cinema and painting had made famous—the pride and the
colourfulness, the passion and the dreaming, the bullfights and the flamenco
songs, the dancers and poets. Money was showered on me too, dollars were
thrown on to the stage, and there was nothing humiliating about it; one
handed it over to the pretty girls with collecting-boxes, with their very short
skirts and long, silk-stockinged legs, but there was nothing obscene in this.
One man was so moved by my speech that he came to the rostrum saying
that he had not enough money on him, but here was his winter overcoat,
quite new, and would I please have it sent to a hidalgo in Madrid.

Hemingway had written an introduction to this lecture-tour, and a well-
known journalist, Marquis Child, read it to an audience of socialites and
senators in Washington. When a senator sniffed in his emotion he shouted:
"No tears, Senator, however rare yours may be! Money is what Regler
wants. Spain needs dollars!"

Something of the blunt, unsentimental realism of the covered-wagon days
was present in all these people, endearing them to me and making their
riches tolerable.

One evening a young woman who was pregnant cried out that I was Anti-
Christ. I had murdered monks, she screamed, violated nuns and set churches
on fire. Her voice failed at the end, and she was led out of the hall, exhausted.

We calmed the audience, and since most of them sympathised with us, the incident was soon disposed of.

"That could have been your moment," said Marie Louise, as we took leave of the committee, happily counting the takings, and set out on a walk through the unknown town.

I did not reply to the especial emphasis in her voice. I was oppressed at that moment with the thought of our isolated state, without home or country or family. The sound of strange music came to us from strange houses. All the public notices were in a language which as children we had not known. My diplomatic pass was valid only so long as the struggling Republic Government continued to exist in Barcelona. We were without money and without friends, except for Hemingway, who stood like a rock; but the very existence of this single rock showed the emptiness of the landscape.

"I have never felt so much an exile as I do tonight," I said to Maria Louise, who had stopped to look in the window of a shoe-shop—shoes were her passion.

"Why?" she said. "It's just the same as Paris. Hundreds of pairs of shoes, and four that I like; but I'm not telling you which they are because you can't buy them for me."

"You must tell me!" I said. It was our old game, but this time it did not work. She turned away from the shoes and, repeating her original remark, she went on to explain it, speaking with the same note of passion that I had first heard in Berlin, when she made her pepper-pistol. She looked the same, except that her small face was even more intense, her walk more decided, as she told me things that she had long kept locked within her bosom while we walked, like lost children, through the unfamiliar streets of that American town where no one knew who we were.

"It was your first big chance," she said. "You had everything in your favour—your wounds, your popularity, the sacrifices you have made; the dying men to whom you want to send morphia, and the overwhelming strength of the other side . . . Let me finish what I'm saying. You're going to be beaten. You all know it, but you won't admit it. Russia is withdrawing her people. You told me so yourself. Koltsov, Kleber, Walter, Gorkin— they all go. Russia is not interested in a State where she has to come to terms with Anarchists and Socialists. And Negrin's 'Thirteen Points.' Respect for Religion! What do they care about that in Moscow? It is only one point, but an important one. That woman tonight, she was hysterical, certainly—but wasn't she right? You should have said so. Tonight they would have listened to you. People always listen to the prodigal sons. . . ."

She had begun to walk faster. A burst of jazz came from a bar, drowning her voice. We turned a corner and found ourselves in the Negro quarter— wooden houses with balconies, and washing-lines strung across the unsurfaced street. A man was singing a spiritual as though it were a lament, and Marie Louise exclaimed:

"Like your Pope John XXII of Avignon! He couldn't bear the contrast either. How can the blessed live in eternal bliss while children are starving in Port Bou?"

"But I said that!" I protested, although I knew what she was driving at.

"But there are children starving in Moscow—Lebedev's children, for instance, because their father held the wrong views. You should have said that Marty shot comrades in Albacete because their opinions differed from his own, and that you couldn't save those two Frenchmen who had had enough of it, and that the Russians were the executioners in the background. You should have said that although your brigade protected the church in Brihuega, you hate the priests. You hate them because you need to hate, because hatred is a part of you. You look for the sins of the priests, and there are plenty to be found in Spain—but you should have admitted that you're no better yourselves. You've brought no new life to the churches. Madonnas don't smile in museums. You have torn them out of their rightful place, just as you have the jewels!"

"The jewels have been declared public property," I said.

"Yes, and your Communist generals and politicians will go off with them hidden in their boots when the defeat comes!"

This was too much. I shouted:

"We aren't defeated yet!"

Marie Louise stopped and turned to face me. Behind us the Negro was singing as though in a delirium.

"Gustav, you were defeated this evening by that woman. She was the portent, but you did not accept it. You should have said to them, 'I'm not going to give you any more propaganda! You have trapped me into speaking for an untrue world. I have been seduced by the publicity in your newspapers, the passage across the ocean, the flattery of women, all the thousand things which in the midst of the struggle I could not see. But now I mean to see them and to warn you. This is no betrayal and no surrender. It is my hour . . .'" She broke off.

"Go on," I said.

She paused for a moment, listening to the singing of the Negro, and then said collectedly:

"You think I should have said all this to you before. It's no use speaking until the time has come. While I was visiting the wounded in the hospital I watched you, waiting to see when your hour would come. It has come now. Look, we're in the midst of Negroes, among the despised, the poor in spirit. But they're nearer to the truth than any of us. They don't set up as missionaries. That is the evil of evils. Franco wants to convert people. Hitler,

Stalin, Negrin and you too—you all want to make other people like yourselves. It is scarcely perceptible in you, but *I* can hear it and I wish you
would be silent. I wished it when you were very ill; and when I heard how
Werner went from battalion to battalion assuring them that you were still
alive and that they must go on fighting, and then went off by himself and was
killed—I wished it then. I wanted you to stop deceiving yourself and give
it all up, the fame and the applause of others, the calculation and the argument, all the trumpery of heroism that smells so sweet and yet stinks. I
wanted you to leave the ranks and retire into obscurity, where we might
be alone together and find ourselves. My father has taken shelter in the
community, Bill Moll has fled—Koestler, all the ones I saw around you, none
has grown larger. They all turned into something else, something indefinable; and you have it too, a sort of varnish, a cocoon spun round you
which I can't get off. You were near to shedding it yourself in Russia, but
now you're wrapped in it again, and that's why I'm saying all this. We have
found a place that is so wonderfully neutral, such as we shall never find
again. . . ."

She fell silent and touched me on the shoulder. A Negro had appeared on
a balcony, raising his handsome head as though he wanted to breathe in all
the scents of the street. He glanced at us, saw that we were preoccupied with
some critical matter and looked quickly away, without, however, quite
letting us out of his sight.

I thought of the Abyssinian who had so touchingly controlled himself and
refrained from murdering his prisoners. Was he to be defeated too? Was
the Pope again to triumph, the only sovereign in the world who had approved of the attack on Abyssinia, and indeed supported it with gold and
silver and bells?

A stream of terrible facts raced through my mind while I stood looking at
the small figure confronting me. For months she had been thinking on quite
other lines, and I had not noticed. Could I catch up with her, ought I to
follow her? Her attitude was clear, but responsibility spoke against the stern
demand she was making. The compromises I had accepted were those that
had been accepted by hundreds of thousands of other men. Why did she
demand this sacrifice of me, that I should submit to a holiness towards which
I had never felt any inclination? How remote she was, but at the same time
how brave, since she did not fear to find herself alone in a world from which
she was cut off, and one without understanding.

Should I put my own case, and remind her that before the revolution there
had been one priest to every nine inhabitants of Madrid, infesting the town
and having to be fed? That Primo de Rivera, the dictator smiled upon by the
Church, had spent 68 millions on the Church but only 33 millions on education? That in 1912 a third of all the wealth in Spain, railways, mines, ships

and fruit-plantations, had belonged to the Church, which had kept the masses illiterate but set them such a bad example that as early as 1910 two-thirds of the population were no longer practising Catholics? In 1936 they had put the Popular Front parties in power with an overwhelming majority. Were figures valid as arguments—267 Reds to 132 of the Right? Should I remind Marie Louise of them, now that she was trying to overthrow me with quite other arguments? How many people would listen to me in this country? These were not people given to confession—or so I thought at that time.

"Don't think of the effect, think of yourself," said Marie Louise, as though she guessed what was in my mind.

"I'm thinking of the priest in a village near Brihuega," I said, and glanced up at the Negro, who was still covertly observing us. "He was hated. In Primo de Rivera's days he had betrayed all free-thinkers to the police. He was as fat as a pig. When the revolution broke out he barricaded himself in the church with the Fascists. The peasants who attacked it were mowed down, and when they ran they were overtaken and slaughtered. The village became a hell. When we captured it I gave orders that the church was to be safeguarded and that the priest was not to be harmed, but they shot him before I arrived. Should I have told that woman tonight about this? Should I have told her the whole ugly story? They took the priest to the bridge, where a row of machine-guns were trained on the other bank of the river. The wretched creature was trembling and howling for mercy. They said they would spare his life if he would run across the bridge cursing the Holy Virgin and the Sacrament. He didn't hesitate for an instant. He ran blaspheming against his God as no unbeliever would have done—and a machine-gun opened fire and blotted him out like the louse he was. One of the militiamen hadn't been able to stand it any longer. I spoke to him, and he was quite unrepentant. 'I wanted to send him to Hell in deadly sin,' he said."

"How ghastly!" said Marie Louise, and drew a little away from me. "The man's faith was more terrible than the priest's unfaith." She said it with horror, and then looked sharply at me. "But you liked telling the story! Can't you see that they were both devils? That Hell has nothing more to do with God than your Socialist heaven—my father's heaven, and Marty's, and the Passionaria's and Negrin's!"

It was the most critical moment in all our union, which had now lasted ten years. There were to be similar moments in Mexico, when she begged me not to reply to the slanders of the Communists, but simply to let them know that I was no longer either for them or against them.

I felt that she had gone farther than I, and would no longer acquiesce in any illusion based on sentimentality, loyalty, stubbornness, indolence or uncertainty. But there was too much asceticism in it all, too little forbearance for human weakness.

We stood in the dusty street with a gulf between us. I was suffering more than she. For me such moments are always a kind of death, and from my youth, owing to my Catholic inheritance, the finality of such a death has always been brought home to me as the greatest of human failures. But she was a Protestant, and when an issue had finally been resolved in her mind she could cast out all feeling and all tenderness.

But that evening no final decision was reached because the Negro intervened. He leaned down over his balcony, as he stood there so rigidly, and asked:

"Looking for something?"

I nodded, but Marie Louise smiled in sudden relief.

"Hope you didn't lose anything," said the Negro. Everything had suddenly acquired a light-hearted symbolical significance. Marie Louise felt it too. He was trying to help us.

"Ask him to sing something," she said.

I did so, and he understood at once and laughed, as though he were sure that all our troubles could be dispelled with a song. He raised his head to the night sky and sang, "Nobody knows the trouble I've seen . . ."

At the end of the first verse I took Marie Louise in my arms. The song had relieved the cramp in both of us. After all, there was no need to despair. Nor was there any gulf between us. We could each think our own thoughts, and we would not let this mad, merciless century drive us apart.

But I did not say this, neither did I want to make the effort to grasp what she was thinking. How much recognition is thus drowned in the waves of emotion? Our embrace was the only reality, and the Negro's song, enfolding us like a cloak.

A year later, in March 1939, the war in Spain ended with the defeat of the Republicans. The Fascist superiority in numbers and equipment, which had been unavailing at Guadalajara in 1937, triumphed after a winter of starvation. For a year the members of an international commission had been paid salaries to supervise the withdrawal of foreign troops on both sides. The remains of our brigades were shifted aimlessly from one base to another. Sometimes they rebelled and were allowed to take part in a battle. But Franco's Condor Legion kept its artillery always ready for action, while the German generals sat in famous castles making their plans and the Junkers and Messerschmitts made daily sorties. Now they could fly over Barcelona without encountering any opposition. The Spanish sky was theirs, and presently an officer of the Falange appeared in Port Bou, where two and a half years earlier I had smuggled in the printing-press and the film-projector in my van, and raised the hated flag of dictatorship.

I heard in Paris of the fall of Barcelona, and was filled with rage and despair. Where were the remains of the brigade? The Commission would not worry about them any more. Events had done their job for them, and they would now depart and apply to the League of Nations for their expense money. But the men of the brigade would fall into Franco's hands and be summarily executed. This had happened throughout the war. We were held to be worse than the Spanish Communists, since we had interfered in Spain's "domestic affairs." No mercy was shown us. I felt that I must search for the brigade and render it my last service as commissar. I did not know how grotesque and grave were the circumstances in which I was to find it.

In the Grand Hotel in Perpignan I ran into the Correspondent of the *New York Times*, whose name was Matthews. On the table lay a telegram from his editor warning him not to send in any sentimental stuff about the (impossible) refugee camps.

A gramophone was playing in a corner of the room— ". . . for we have not lost our home, our home today is before Madrid." It was the record which the singer Ernst Busch had made with the German volunteers in 1937.

"Come with me," said Matthews, switching it off. "Come and see for yourself. Perhaps you'll find out something about your own lot."

We drove to the frontier. It was as though we had arrived too late at a vast public meeting which was just breaking up. We threaded our way through the crowd hurrying homewards. The landscape was a tragic one. Beneath a flowering shrub a man lay dying, his face yellow, his eyes staring up at the blossoms. Men lay huddled together, drinking at a stream. A shaggy-haired man with a donkey, which had apparently refused to go any farther, was seated on the ground, waiting.

The frontier, when we reached it, was like a mediaeval picture of the Crucifixion. Groups of men in civilian clothes were streaming down from the hills. They bore themselves with dignity, advancing with evident trust towards the fate that awaited them on the guarded plain teeming with soldiers.

Some still had earth clutched in their hands which they had snatched up as they left their villages. When I saw one of the *gardes mobiles* forcibly open one of these clenched hands and scatter the soil in disdain I knew that the soldiers of France did not understand the meaning of the word "home," and I wished that one day they might pay for it. It was an impermissible wish, a meaningless one, but at that moment rage at defeat, not reason, filled my heart.

Others came singing. Just as the dying are sometimes seized with an over-exalted lightness of heart, so did these fugitives display a boisterousness which caused us who watched them to marvel and which added to our grief. Had they already an inkling that before long the people of a dozen European nations would tread the same road? That is not an afterthought. Standing in

x

the stink of the chloride of lime that had been strewn on the road, I seemed to catch, with the heightened sensibility of the defeated, the stench of tomorrow's corpses. I said so to Matthews.

"Smells like it," he said dryly.

At that moment I saw the Frenchman, Aragon, coming down the road towards us with another group of journalists. It was a tragi-comical interlude, and to me it was as though a diabolical Puck sought jeeringly to remind me of the ass's head I had worn for two years. Nothing had changed in the attitude of the writer, who during that time had become the doyen of the French Communist array of half-talents. Here too he seemed unable to control his own arrogance. Like a peacock he walked a few paces back and forth, recoiled from the chloride of lime, glanced with theatrical contempt at the *gardes mobiles* and then went back to his car. I did not see him again in the town; he had left. Two days later I saw his picture in *Ce Soir*. He had been photographed surrounded by Parisian women who, so the caption said, had come to thank him for all he had done for the fugitives in Perpignan. The hundred eyes of the peacock! Even in the presence of despair they remained wide open in vanity. Like a circle—truly a vicious circle—the course of this lamentable man between September 1936 and that March of 1939 was rounded off. To me it was as painful as the snapping of handcuffs, but the steel springs closed on my heart.

Women came with children in their arms, others carrying small dogs, and one was carrying a hen in her apron. The Quakers had sent cars with milk and cocoa up into the hills, and some had picked up women they found on the way. One woman discovered, just as she was passing us, that the child she was carrying was dead. She covered it with her apron and pressed it the more tightly against her. A policeman thought it necessary to ask her name and age, and what brought her here. She did not answer, but after a pause another woman said, "Anything is better than Fascism."

That afternoon the Republican troops came. They were received as though they were tramps. We saw them in the distance marching towards us, with their rifles over their shoulders, still with a mile or more of Spanish soil between them and the frontier which represented the death of all their hopes —rifles of Madrid and Guadalajara, of Belchite and the Ebro—rifles of so many despairing victories. . . . There were five of us helpless onlookers, two Englishmen, Matthews and an elderly Frenchwoman from the League of Human Rights.

The international bridge, the no-man's-land between the two republics, lay in a gulley. We had been given permission to go as far as this. The Prefect of Perpignan was standing on the other side of the road with some French generals and a young Spanish officer who recognised me and came over delightedly to greet me. I warned him that I was in danger of being put in a camp myself. Perhaps for the first time he realised what the position was. He told me with tears in his eyes that he had been appointed to act as liaison officer between his army and France.

The soldiers were now approaching the bridge. They knew what the contingent of the *Garde Mobile* signified. As the first of them laid down his rifle I saw Matthews turn away his head. "I can't bear to watch it," he said. But I watched steadily, and I hope to be understood when I say that I have never felt such close feelings of comradeship for any army as I felt for those defeated soldiers of Spain. There was something of tenderness in the man's attitude as he bent down over the rifle which he was relinquishing to the "friendly hands" of France. Before moving on he picked it up again, and for the last time ran his hand caressingly over stock and bolt and barrel. And this was too much for the *garde mobile* who stood facing him. He snatched the rifle from him, and it looked to us as though he was afraid that he was going to shoot.

Then came the search. The Spaniards were asked what was in the haversacks and ditty-bags they carried, and they answered that in surrendering their rifles they had given up all the arms they possessed. But the French tapped disdainfully on the haversacks and demanded that they should be opened.

The Spaniards did not understand. Until the last moment they persisted in the tragic error of believing in international solidarity. "Madrid, capital of anti-Fascism, stronghold of courage high as mountains, and of faith deep as an abyss!" But here there was another kind of abyss. The dirty road on which the disarmed men stood was not merely the frontier between two countries, it was an abyss between two worlds. Under the eyes of the Prefect and the generals, the men of the *Garde Mobile* took away the bags and bundles containing the Spaniards' personal belongings and emptied their contents into a ditch filled with chloride of lime.

I have never seen eyes of such anger and helplessness as those of the Spaniards. They stood as though turned to stone, and they did not understand.

Matthews lost all self-control and shouted, "Don't you know that Spaniards never lie?"

Underclothes and fragments of food were scattered in the ditch. The first of the Spaniards was still standing there, his face pale with shock. The *garde mobile* turned to the next, while the Prefect and the generals chatted together, puffing cigarettes. And then Herbert Matthews, with a gesture that I shall never forget, bent down and began to pick the things up.

The Prefect frowned and sent a lieutenant to tell the guards to show a little more courtesy. Then he lit another cigarette. Matthews straightened himself and tapped the Spaniard on the shoulder. *"Lo siento,"* he said, as though he knew that his action had changed nothing. *"No hay de que,"* said the Spaniard and smiled again.

"I need a drink," said Matthews to me.

"So do I," I said, and we took leave of the Spaniards and went to our car.

"I have to find my boys," I said.

"You will," said Matthews.

We drove slowly back into the valley, past the silent procession of a people going into exile. Laughing faces were often turned towards us. It was as though the Spaniards wanted to comfort us.

After half an hour we came to a cross-roads of which one side was barred by the police. "I know how to deal with this," said Matthews, and leaning out of the car he signalled to the officer in charge of the guard.

"Where can we get something to eat around here, Monsieur le Capitaine?"

The scene changed as though by magic. The captain came to the car and told us in the friendliest fashion that there was an excellent restaurant half a mile away. The fish, *rouget à la provençale*, was especially to be recommended. He waved his men aside and we drove through the barrier, while the Spaniards were being herded in the opposite direction, towards a concentration camp consisting of primitive trenches in the sand of Argelès.

Matthews trod furiously on the accelerator.

"Voilà le cœur français—l'estomac!" he said.

At the restaurant of the widow X, I met a member of the International Commission which had been charged with looking after the Brigade. He told me that nothing special had been done. I stormed at him and his whole League of Nations, and he soon departed. Fortunately Matthews had kept calm, and found out from him, before he left, where the remains of the Brigade had last been seen. Shortly afterwards I met a member of the Society of Friends who took me with him.

Near a village in the mountains, of which I have forgotten the name, I came upon the last handful of the Brigade. There were about seventy-five of them, seated in a circle on the ground, facing outwards. They had formed themselves into a phalanx, and with weary eyes and rifles in their hands were confronting a group of about ten men who faced them from across the road, also with rifles ready to shoot.

I thought at first, as we approached, that the smaller group was composed of Fascists who had captured our men at the last moment but did not feel strong enough to disarm them. With my Quaker friend I withdrew behind the cover of an olive-tree and tried to recognise faces. Suddenly a man in the larger group waved to me. It was Klaus Becker, an artillery officer who had worked with André Marty in Albacete. Scarcely had he raised his arm, without leaving his place in the circle, when a tall figure arose from among the smaller group and looked towards us. I saw that it was Marty himself. Throughout the war he had never visited our headquarters. I had only met him once, in the autumn of 1936, and now he did not recognise me but merely took me for a foreigner, presumably a press-correspondent. He gave orders in a low voice to the soldiers crouched on the ground around him. They returned their revolvers to their holsters, let fall their rifles and followed Marty, who, without looking at us, led the way down a side-path to the lower valley. I looked at Marty's dark-faced followers. They were all Communists, reliable Party-men, who until yesterday had probably been his prison-super-intendents and worse. I had interrupted them in their last act of blood.

Klaus Becker sprang to his feet, ran to me and embraced me. The others also got up, some staggering with exhaustion. They had been sitting there for hours.

Marty had been well aware that they all knew about his corrupt administration and summary executions in Albacete. He must have thought that now they would weaken and make disclosures in France. The bourgeois Press would pay them. Such things had happened before—the world was full of treachery!

I am convinced that his thinking was as naïve as this, for anything more subtle, or even human, was not in his nature. He had probably meant to machine-gun them without warning, but Klaus Becker had suspected his intention and had passed the word in a whisper from man to man as they marched. Finally, they had come to this small plateau. The condemned majority of the troop had, by arrangement, suddenly broken away from the rest and formed their defensive circles on the grass, with their rifles ready.

"At first I wouldn't believe it," said a young Jewish boy who had once been in my signal-detachment. "But then Marty started cursing like mad, all about Trotzkyites and counter-revolutionaries. So then we knew for certain that he wanted to liquidate us. He nearly got away with it!"

"I should have shot him at once," said an older man.

"Why didn't he shoot?" asked the Jewish boy.

"Because he is a coward. Because he knew he'd cop it himself. Executioners are always cowards. It's a cowardly calling. Adolf's a coward, and so is Stalin."

The Quaker broke into the conversation.

"Are you all Germans?" he asked. Apparently he needed to know this for the purpose of his report.

"International," I said. It was the last time I could identify myself with the Brigade, and I knew that we should have to leave the pine-woods around us, the meadows and the mountains, and that tomorrow the Spanish country-side would be under Nationalist rule.

The Quaker went to the car and came back with a parcel of slabs of chocolate. At once they all lined-up.

"I can see you're Germans!" said the Quaker laughing.

"This is the last pay we shall get," said the young signaller with a choke in his voice. He put the slab of chocolate in his pocket, but then, when he saw the others eating, his hunger overcame him and he got it out again.

I learned that evening that the Spanish poet, Antonio Machado, was among those lying in the sand of Cerbère. One of his verses came to my mind:

> *Sabe esperar—*
> *aguarda que la marea fluya*
> *asi en la costa un barco*
> *sin que el partir te inquieta.*

> Know how to hope—
> await the rising tide
> like a boat ashore
> and do not fear for the departure.

Then the messenger went on to say that Machado had fallen gravely ill, and he added in a matter-of-fact voice that his heart was broken.

I asked Matthews to drive me there; but at Argelès we were held up by Senegalese soldiers who told us in bad French that we should be arrested if we went any farther. I saw only their faces, which looked very self-assured. The white of their eyes and teeth gleamed in the light of the searchlight by which they were standing.

I thought of the dead of Badajoz, whom Jay Allen had seen, of Hans Beimler, killed by a Moor, and of the wounded at Chinchon, slaughtered by Moors as they lay on stretchers. I thought of the Abyssinian of the Garibaldi Battalion who had mastered his own impulse, and I thought of Franco, who would now ride in triumph through the streets of Madrid, accompanied by mounted Moors in white cloaks and red caps. And somewhere in the night, sick and tired, ill-used by the murderers of his republic, lay the republic's greatest poet, watched over by the Senegalese, ill-used Africans.

"It doesn't make sense," said Matthews, and started his engine again.

"No, it doesn't make sense," I repeated.

We sat on the terrace of the hotel waiting for news. Matthews had telephoned the Préfecture. We were drinking whisky. "I'd like to recite a verse," I said to Matthews, and he knew at once who the author would be.

"It's stoical," I said. "Perhaps it will help him:

"Y si la vida es corta
y no llega la mar a tu galera—
aguarda sin partir y siempre espera
que el arte es largo y, además, no importa.

"And if life is short
and the sea does not reach your boat
wait still without departing and be patient
for art is large and that is all that matters."

A donkey-cart rattled past. The lines sounded like the ebbing of the tide. We had no more news that night.

It seemed the next day as though someone in Paris had intervened, but we learned that no doctor had yet been allowed in the camp. Matthews drove out there and came back very depressed.

"Nobody knows anything. How can all those thousands be expected to take any notice of a sick poet? They dug trenches for latrines, and the wind blew the whole contents over them as they lay asleep. It's shameful!"

The next morning he brought me a newspaper, pointed to a marked passage and went out again. I read that a lady had called at the editorial offices to complain that "the Red bandits" had brought a dying man to her empty house on the beach. She demanded that the body be removed at once.

I did not ask Matthews who it was that had died. I knew he had found out before showing me the paper.

Thus ended our war for freedom. Six months later the second World War began.

BOOK SIX

16. The Undesirables

AUTUMN light lay over the Riviera, and Provence was the denial of all rumours of war. The air was filled with the scent of harvest and grapes, lavender and rosemary, and the *frutta del mare* which the gaily-painted boats brought back from the enchanted isles off the bight of Sanary and Saint Clair.

I sat at breakfast on a restaurant terrace with an English friend, Paul Willert, and his wife Brenda. A youthful waiter came to our table with a darkened countenance and murmured as though to himself:

"Comme il nous a trahi, le grand Jo!"

"Pourquoi trahi?" I asked.

"Il a fait un pacte avec Adolphe."

I remarked to Paul that even the most fantastic rumours found someone to believe them. But presently the papers came, and we knew that it was no rumour.

We drove rapidly to Paris in Paul's Bentley. Paul offered to take me with him to England, where he was joining the R.A.F. He was sure there would be something useful for me to do.

"I owe too much to France," I said.

The next day I went to the Mairie of my arrondissement and volunteered for the French Army. Hitler was not Germany, and Russia was no longer a friend.

They thanked me and asked me to return when my number came up. Fourteen hours later, at exactly six o'clock in the morning, six *agents de police* burst open the door of my flat. The night had been hot, and I confronted their pistols stark naked. As I turned to reach for my trousers they saw my wounds, which were not yet completely healed. One of them pressed a handkerchief to his mouth, fighting a sudden nausea.

On my way to police-quarters, I invited them to drink coffee and rum with me in a Montparnasse café. They would not let me pay.

Hundreds of people were waiting in the big Salle Lépine at the Préfecture. An elderly rabbi, troubled by a physical need, tried to explain to an *agent* in Yiddish. When I ventured to interpret the policeman hit me on the jaw and told me there was a war on. Then I was taken to the cellars under the Palais de Justice, where, as I recalled, Marie Antoinette had also been confined.

There were thirty of us. We were given nothing to eat. The French become astonishingly disorganised when war breaks out. Prostitutes were brought into our cellar, but before long they were invited to join the guards and we heard the sounds of laughter echoing through that dismal labyrinth.

After four days' fasting I was taken to a stadium in the suburbs where I came across Arthur Koestler. He told me that Paul Nizan, the Communist writer, had rejected the Party's pacifist policy and joined the Army; also that the German Communist Party in Paris had sent Prime Minister Daladier a grotesque document promising its co-operation if he would cease to call the Nazi–Soviet pact an act of betrayal. "But Daladier has no sense of humour. He had them all arrested. They're here now."

We slept in the open air. There was no water and the latrines were utterly unusable. After forty-eight hours most people were either badly constipated or in a worse state. The liberal paper *L'Œuvre* announced with emphasis that Paris had now got all "bad elements" under lock and key.

Marie Louise came in the twilight wearing a smart green costume and threw a parcel of food over the high wire fence. A guard helped her.

After a few days of this we were taken to the station and politely invited to board a train; there were not enough troops available to prevent a mass-escape.

It was a goods train. I made the endless journey in a brake-box, consumed with bitterness and premonitions. Finally, we pulled up on a plain which I did not recognise. A camp of shabby hutments was spread out before us, and in the distance gleamed snow-clad mountain-peaks.

The first person I saw emerge from the train was Hans Schulz, the tall, youthful secretary of Willi Münzenberg. He came and climbed into my small compartment.

"I've had wonderful news!" he said. "Münzenberg isn't to be arrested. He's even going to be allowed to go on producing his paper. Isn't that marvellous?"

I was touched by so much loyalty. He stared at me and asked:

"Have you been sleeping on a sack of flour?"

"Why?" I asked.

He got out a small mirror, and I saw that my hair had turned completely grey during the night!

A party of armed *gardes mobiles* marched along the platform. We formed up in front of them. The utter senselessness of my arrest was causing me to shake as though I had a fever.

"Why are we here, Hans?"

The sanguine young man laughed and put a finger half-seriously to his lips.

"Better not say too much. It's protective arrest. They know we're against the Nazi–Soviet pact, and they were afraid Stalin's people might murder us

in Paris!" He was in a mood of boisterous high spirits. Pointing to where
the Communist leaders were standing, Dahlem, Merker, Rau and Eisler, he
cried out loudly:

"The great thing is that we have our leaders with us!"

"Shut up!" said one of the guards.

We were marched into the camp.

The first (and, as the event was to prove, the only) prisoners-of-war of the
French Republic were now safely behind barbed wire. They amounted to
560 fugitives from every country in Europe. For years they had found
asylum in Paris; their shelter now was a collection of ramshackle wood huts at
the foot of the Pyrenees, without beds, without light and without heating.
There were possibly a few dozen profiteers among the prisoners, as well as
the full strength of the Central Committee of the German Communist Party;
but the great majority was composed of opponents of the Third Reich. Not
a single National Socialist had been arrested, or any Italian Fascist. Many
carried papers showing that they had reported for service with the French
Army.

We lay on planks and were forgotten. At first the camp commandant
treated us as riff-raff and spies. After some weeks our dossiers came through
from Paris, but by that time we had become changed men and our hair had
been shorn down to the roots. Slowly it grew again, together with beards,
which made some of us look very old.

I was elected spokesman for my hut, number 33. In the next hut were the
remains of my brigade. My former comrades, now in rags, did the washing
for the wealthier inmates of the camp, who paid them with dried peas which
they did not themselves want, since they contrived to procure much better
things. There was a story about those peas. The defeated Spanish Army had
brought this food in the spring, not wanting anything to fall into Franco's
hands, and had presented the peas to the French, who, without showing
much gratitude for the offering, had put them in store. They were now
being issued to feed the remnant of the Republican Army. There were
maggots in them, and thus everything was logically rounded off.

There was a strange man with us whom I will call P.

He was frequently to be seen sweeping out the doorway of his hut and
occasionally raising his broom to threaten anyone who dropped paper about.
He was said to have been responsible for sending fugitives to South America,
promising them an earthly paradise when they got there. But we never got
to know anything about this because he spoke to no one except his two
associates, a dealer in forged passports, and a white-slave trafficker who was
fond of displaying photographs of his victims. P. liked his hut to be clean.
He was a "patriotic Frenchman." On New Year's Day he decorated the

front of the hut with branches forming the letters RF—République Française. To others the letters meant *résidence forcée* or *revolutionnaires foutus*, and to Gründler, a metal-worker from Dresden, they stood for *Ratten-Friedhof—* rat's cemetery.

Gründler came nearest to the truth. Vernet was an eerie cemetery. The huts stood like great coffins on the plain. Every morning the dead crept out of their graves to form up in rigid squares, a pathetic soldiery, and then, under the orders of uniformed men, went about the work of clearing paths, digging drains, stopping up rat-holes, burning foul straw and cleaning their coffins. It was a busy scene, as though someone had taken the lid off a churchyard to watch the dead at their squalid employments. But sometimes one of the dead, unable to endure the cemetery, would kill himself a second time. When we cut him down from the beam from which he hung we had a feeling of picking a ripe fruit, and we felt something like envy when we laid him to rest in the real cemetery of the camp. Everything, the box and the empty grave, had a look of dignity, privacy, cleanness and even homeliness. Death restored men's private lives. A man was by himself again.

There were some who were always by themselves. These were the leaders and officials of the German and Italian Communist Parties, who for some weeks were imprisoned with us. They could not be called dead.

They had lived in hiding for years, like creatures under a stone. They loved the darkness, or at least found it desirable. They gnawed at the roots. They were extremely industrious and even over-eager, for they believed the day to be near when their work might be openly displayed.

And then the catastrophe had come that changed everything. The war came, sweeping away the stone like a giant hand and stripping them of their cover. They might well have been terrified, as the rest of us were; but they were not terrified. We never ceased to wonder at this, and we do so still. That self-confidence is a mystery. Like the rest of us, they had been driven in open trucks through the streets of Paris to the railway station, and no worker had sought to prevent it, nor had any protest followed. But the Communists went about the camp at Vernet with the assurance they had always shown, and in the evenings they discussed leading-articles which would never be printed. Perhaps their attitude in reality concealed a deep dismay, and they were nearer to despair than we knew. Perhaps they stuck to their old habits so as not to have to admit to themselves that they had lost their imaginary supporters.

Every Thursday, with the punctiliousness of devout churchgoers, they would take the evening off and stroll about the camp instead of holding their usual cell-meeting. It was impossible not to admire the fantasy which sustained them in the depths of defeat. Basically they were only five, a political leader, an administrative leader, a treasurer, a controller of propaganda and agitation, and—the fifth man, representing all the rank and file, the masses: truly the fifth wheel of the wagon! They were Quixotes enacting a daily chapter of their romance of chivalry, and their Sancho Panza was the battered proletariat of the twentieth century. They flattered the masses and did not allow them to follow their own inclinations; as the possessors of the Book of Wisdom they knew what was good for them. They tilted indefatigably against windmills. What they lacked, to be true Quixotes, was the charm and gallantry and gentleness of heart of that Castilian knight. But one cannot have everything.

Instead they had an iron discipline. For the purpose of forced labour in the camp they fell back into the habits of their fifth member. Four leaders and one man of the people, carefully checked to ensure his loyalty to the Party-line, constituted themselves a working squad. They procured plaster-board and lined the huts with it to keep out the biting winds of the Pyrenees, displaying much more aptitude for this work than for politics. The camp, that perfidious and ironically revealing school, had restored them to their former way of life.

We watched them for any spontaneous show of feeling, ready to forgive them the crudest outburst of rage and despair. We should not have blamed them if they had talked the utmost nonsense about the Ribbentrop pact, the Communist Party and the ruthlessness of their Russian friends. On the day when the news came through of the Russian attack on Finland, a Finnish inmate of the camp, who was also a Communist, went and beat his fists against the barbed wire until he had torn his hands to shreds. He never said why he did it, but from that day we felt nearer to him. He had shown that at least he was human. But the Party-leaders on their Rosinante, that hobby-horse of theory, allowed themselves no human weakness.

We differed from them in that we were often silent in our despair. We would sit huddled in a corner, and after a long interval perhaps someone would say that we should never get out of the camp until we were carried out feet foremost to the grave. Then there would be silence again, but we would not move, not even when the White Russian general chose to air his bed and the stink made the atmosphere almost unbreathable. We would sit staring at the straw and perhaps thinking of our wives, who might at that moment be strolling in the Luxembourg garden, and then we would be en-raged with ourselves for thinking about them. We were nothing but com-mon humanity, itching in body and soul, and we talked nonsense when the mood was on us. And some had the courage to cast all inhibitions aside.

One man broke into a frenzy, while he was standing eating his peas, at the sight of a group that included the former Georgian Finance Minister eating a smuggled goose. "I shall hang myself!" he yelled and ran screaming out of the hut.

Another man knocked over the chessboard on which two men were playing with pieces made out of kneaded breadcrumbs. He had no reason for this savagery. He simply knew that in doing so he would make them his enemies for life, and that was why he did it.

The little Jewish journalist, Kurt Löwenthal, stood confronting the tall figure of the German engineer, Wilhelm Bock, and shouted:

"Even your face is Nazi! It's no use your telling me that you fought the Nazis and that they ruined your business because you wouldn't have a Nazi manager in the works. Did you ever put in a word for us Jews?"

He laughed and laughed, and the laughter turned suddenly to coughing and he clung to a post and spat blood. "I beg your pardon," he murmured and stumbled through the darkness to his bed.

There were others who defied the whole company. The more they felt that sheer necessity called for indulgence for their neighbours, the more implacably selfish did they become. And, on the other hand, there were some who were saintly in their patience. Everyone admired them, but once a man spat at one of them, finding it intolerable that anyone should possess so much self-control.

But the outbreaks occurred most often when a man had put his neighbour under some obligation. There was constant repudiation and fighting among friends. Feelings were relieved by sheer baseness; it was a dysentery of the soul.

There was one, a former Berlin advocate named Kunitzky, who sought relief by deliberately enhancing the vileness of our condition. He was a member of the old German nobility, an ex-officer in the Prussian Army. From the moment of entering the camp he never washed, and he took pleasure in seeing people turn away in disgust from the sight of his filthy, naked body when he exposed it to the daylight. He wallowed in his own abjection, tending it as others tended their newly-growing hair.

There was a Bulgarian terrorist who after living in friendly comradeship with a deaf-mute Pole, with whom he shared his meals, suddenly flung his bedding out of the window and threatened to fling him after it if he did not stop exasperating him with his dumb gesticulations. The Pole wept bitterly, staring at his straw mattress, on which the rain was pouring down.

In the middle of the hut there hung a single stable-lantern. We had bought it with our own money, but we could not afford to keep it burning all night, despite the danger to the limbs of those who were obliged to climb down from the upper story in pitch darkness. When I went to put it out, saying good-night as I passed down the centre of the hut, and being answered in a dozen languages, I thought of Europe. We had simply been forgotten.

I always hesitated before putting the lamp out, as though in doing so I were consigning the whole hundred and fifty of us to perpetual darkness.

But we had time for thought as we went about our daily tasks of sweeping and cleaning and mending and wood-chopping. We were back at the heart of things, seeing mankind stripped naked and seeing ourselves as we were. We did not, like Job, heap ashes on our heads; our hair had been shaved off, for one thing, and we had no inclination to play the penitent sinner. We sought to understand our time. No kind of evaluation could have withstood our grief at our imprisonment. For a time everything seemed to us mere senseless chaos. But presently we came to understand that it was not due solely to accident that we who had fought in Spain were confined in the same camp with arms-profiteers. We thought we knew why the French Government was imitating Nazi anti-Semitism and sending along Jews by the truckload. Scapegoats were needed.

We had other mysteries to unravel. Vernet was like an epitome of police blunders. But were they blunders?

There was a thin man who kept to himself and was the only one whose head had not been shaved. I saw him reading and softly quoting; he kept his books hidden under his mattress. He wore the red button of the Légion d'Honneur, and it is strange that no one remarked upon this anomaly in our present surroundings. One evening I quoted a line of Baudelaire to Klaus Berger, the art-historian. I quoted it wrongly, and suddenly an arm reached down from the upper bunk with a copy of *Les Fleurs du Mal*.

"If you would care to consult it," said the thin man's voice, which I had never heard before.

His name was Dzelepis. We became friends. His tale was as simple as the times were mad. He had been in the Greek diplomatic service, but had resigned in 1938, outraged by the events of that year. He had said to Paul Leger, the *eminence grise* of the Quai d'Orsay, who was sympathetic to Fascism, "What is the difference between you and Hitler?" In 1939 he published an article in which he said that Britian had sold the Spanish Republic for thirty pieces of silver. It went into his dossier, and six months later, such is the strange shape of justice in our time, it was used in evidence against him. He was arrested because in March he had attacked the ally of September.

He strayed about the camp, turning over the pages of Plato and Baudelaire with his long, aristocratic hands, and for a time he talked to no one but me. Eventually he made another friend, an Austrian count, the representative of a group of British hotels, who had been on a visit to Paris in autumn 1939. The Count had stayed a little longer in Paris than his papers allowed, and he went to the Préfecture de Police to ask for an extension. He got there at the precise moment when the lorries were waiting to take us away, and was

Y

promptly put on board one. No one could prevent it, since none of the arrests was carried out in legal form. As a result of a technical infringement of passport regulations, he fell a victim to French administrative bungling which was later complicated by the German occupation. In fact, he was in trouble for nearly seventeen years. He told me this himself long afterwards, when I met him again in Paris.

But he had no inkling of his fate when, at Christmas 1939, he offered to cast my horoscope, and did so in strikingly shrewd terms. It was a strange fruit of that grotesque imprisonment. The Count, whom no one outside protected, cast the horoscopes of freedom. It did not matter to him where he was when he consulted the stars. He was given food in exchange, and despite his poverty, his gesture, when he handed over the document, was that of a monarch conferring honours. I loved him for it. He stood for values which had nothing to do with force.

Klaus Berger, the art-historian, gave us a talk on early Gothic, perched on the upper story by the hanging lantern, while the rest of us each took a vitamin pill from the box that Marie Louise had sent.

"Nothing in the world can justify the destruction of the Gothic cathedrals," said Klaus. "Do you realise that Chartres, with its incomparable glass, is only separated by a narrow valley from the biggest airfield after Le Bourget?"

"I'll exchange all the stained glass on earth for a new social order," said Walter, the former German artillery officer.

"But nothing could replace those windows in Chartres cathedral. It would be a gap in civilisation, a permanent loss. It would be death!"

"Rubbish!" Walter said.

The next morning Walter volunteered for the job of emptying the latrines. I knew his ways and went with him. He had imposed this chastisement on himself. He staggered in front of me beneath the yoke from which the heavy buckets hung. The raven, Jacob, which one of the prisoners had tamed, perched on his shoulder flapping its wings. We went from one small house to the next, filling our tub, and a White Russian helped us, but none of us spoke.

Then the gate in the barbed wire was opened and we rode on small trolleys down the poplar avenue to the river. The raven was still swaying on Walter's shoulder. The trolleys rolled slowly down the slope. Suddenly Walter got a letter out of his pocket. The raven cawed and pecked at it, but Walter pointed warningly at the cess-tub and it was silent.

"I'll read you a letter," said Walter. "It's from my girl. Ruth Forster her name is. It was written in 'thirty-seven. Mind you don't fall, Jacob." He had spoken to the raven because he was trying to behave as though I was not there. "She wrote it in one of Hitler's prisons. She'd been doing under-cover work. They locked her up just when they let me go. One in and one

out, that's the way it was with us. But we loved each other very much." He
stroked the raven, which pecked at him. "Well, this is what she wrote:

" 'Dear Walter,
        I have had to desert you at the last minute, but please don't be un-
happy. They came for me quite unexpectedly. You see, you aren't allowed
to be one up on me, darling! Even before I was brought here I felt that we
were scarcely separated, and now I feel it more than ever. The same daily
routine to be lived through, and the warm and happy dreams to bring back a
thousand memories. Do you know, there's even a pear-tree outside my cell,
and in your last letter you said you had one there!
        " 'But you want to know how I am, and of course you're worrying. Well,
naturally I have pains and difficulties with food, just as I used to have. But
now we're getting a supplementary parcel every Tuesday, so I expect I'll
manage. Otherwise I'm very calm, and I shall go on being calm so long as I
know you're free. It's a shame that I couldn't be waiting at the gate when
you came out. I hate to think of you finding your way back into life all by
yourself. But perhaps it won't be long before they let me go too. The first
book my sister sent me was Felix Timmermann's *Pallieter*, the one about
Flanders. Do read it again if you can get hold of a copy! It's wonderful. I
should love to make that journey with you, and spend a fortnight in a ship,
like he did with his Marie, away from everything. But meanwhile I can be
happy knowing Rilke's *Winter Stanzas* by heart. Remember them now that
you are free, and then we shan't be separated at all. . . .' "

"Free?" exclaimed Walter and laughed bitterly. Suddenly he started to
quote the verses of Rilke:

> "Did you feel fully all last summer's flowers?
> The roses? (Oh, be honest—it repays!)
> The re-awakefulness of morning hours?
> The light-foot walk down spider-woven ways?"

The little train stopped. Walter put the letter hurriedly back in his pocket.
The guards were shouting orders. The raven spread its wings and flew to
the top of one of the poplars, thence to take a bird's-eye view of our dirty
work. I sat for a few moments under a tree amid the stench, fighting back
the tears that had risen in my eyes. Walter emptied his tub and went back to
help with the others, working with a furious energy as though to apologise
to the cathedrals for what he had said the night before. Poetry had come to
him as an admonishing angel.

Humour helped us as well as poetry, the humour of suffering, which has
a curative effect, however wild or raw or childish it may be, and how-

ever incomprehensible to those who have not undergone similar tribulations.

I recall Max Dessauer, a Jew, of whom I knew nothing else at the time,
confiding one night as he lay beside me on the planks:

"Now I can tell you too—the others know it already. I happen to have an
artificial arm. You have been tactfully not noticing it, but it hasn't understood. Let me introduce you."

He performed solemn introductions, and I bowed, no less solemnly.
Then he tapped me with it on the shoulder and said:

"You can swear any oath of allegiance with this, because of course it
wouldn't count. Very useful for Hitler and other statesmen, except that they
seem to manage pretty well with real arms." He was unstrapping it as he
spoke. "Would you mind putting it up on the beam for me? Thank you.
Now it's safe for the night, and we can go on a journey. What sort of things
do you dream about?"

I had no time to answer him, for the evening's entertainment was about
to begin. It was performed by Emil Berger, formerly Münzenberg's chauffeur.
We all knew his tale of the young bride who on the eve of the wedding con-
fesses to her mother that she is in a state of great alarm. The somewhat
flustered mamma thereupon embarks on an account of the facts of life, using
great tact and words of womanly encouragement, only to be cut short by a
peal of girlish laughter—"But, mother, I know all about *that*! It's the cooking I'm afraid of!"

The hut was settling down for the night and Dessauer arranged his pillow.
What we were waiting for was Emil's dramatic enactment of the tale, which
reached its climax with the words, "Oh, mother dear, I'm *so* afraid! . . ."
Emil repeated them in a rising falsetto embracing all the range of virginal
apprehension, fluting, quavering, mooing like a love-sick calf, his voice
resounding through the pitch-dark, wind-shaken building, enlivening the
spirits and stirring the senses of a hundred and fifty lonely and dejected men.
"Oh, mother dear, I'm so-o afraid! . . ." and other voices would join in,
neighing and braying, laughing and mimicking, and the bodies would stir,
and a convulsion would sweep through the hut to die down at length in
silence, so that one could hear a rat nibbling in the straw.

It was while I was on my way to Emil's sleeping-place that I discovered
that Eisler, the Communist, was secretly eating his goose-dripping. It is a
sad story, but one that deserves a brief mention. Three of our womenfolk,
Koestler's and Eisler's wives and my own Marie Louise, had clubbed together in Paris to buy a goose. Brenda Willert had contributed generously
to it. They had run off all the dripping and sent it to us in tins. I had sought
out four of the poorest prisoners, Fröhlich the Socialist, a Negro, an Arab

and a Chinese. We shared the fat, which was so lacking in our diet, and for three weeks we felt well. Koestler had done the same with his Hungarian friends. But we wondered what Eisler, the fanatical Communist, was doing with his portion. Did he mean to keep it until he was released? Was he ashamed of being better off than the poorer men around him? We saw the tins on his sleeping-place, but he continued to eat his usual ration without apparently touching them. Now, however, as I was making the last round, I heard a suspicious sound in the darkness. I switched on my torch, pointed it in the direction of the sound and saw the startled face of Eisler in the act of putting a piece of bread-and-dripping in his mouth. The under-cover technique of the propagandist of world revolution applied even to the filling of his stomach.

I wished him "good appetite" and returned to Dessauer. Pity for this night-time eater oppressed me like a weight on the liver. Conscious of the contradiction between his teaching and his behaviour, he was hiding it in the darkness of the night.

But the next day I lost all sympathy.

I was crouched over the hole in the latrine when the conversation began on the other side of the partition.

"You have the word, Comrade Gerhard!"

Eisler's voice came through the boards. "Friedländer has confessed," he said.

Friedländer was also a "chief" and had presided in Paris over one of those disguised international pacifist committees. He was a sensitive, obedient man who had finally seen the light when he was in prison.

Eisler went on: "He said that he has been keeping a diary in prison, and that it contains a great many criticisms of the Party leadership. He emphasised that he had been in the movement for thirty years and has seen too much. Those were his actual words—'seen too much'! He wrote it all down in his cell in the Santé in Paris, and the manuscript was taken away from him when he was searched on arriving here. He regrets that the book has fallen into the hands of the camp police. I asked him if he did not regret having written so critically. In reply he cursed and called me a fool. I wish to put that on record. Since he is a traitor he naturally could not insult me."

I kept my ear pressed to the wall. From the compartment on my right I heard the sounds of a man with dysentery. I forgot to rise from my squatting position. I completely forgot I was in the latrine. The court of inquiry behind the boards riveted all my attention. The first voice on the left now spoke again. It was that of the Party-leader Paul Merker.

"What is the opinion of the other comrades?" asked Merker.

I was astonished that there should be so many of them. It was a grotesque place to hold a court of inquiry. I crumpled the paper in my hand. Another voice spoke, again that of Gerhard Eisler:

"I naturally regard the whole thing as proved. Friedländer deliberately used this method of conveying his counter-revolutionary views to the bourgeois police."

"That is my opinion too."

Paul Merker said: "Well, then, we seem to be in agreement. Who is in favour of expelling Friedländer from the Party and not speaking to him any more, as from today? . . . Unanimous!"

Boots scraped over the cement. Their brushes swept the human muck into the buckets.

"Man overboard!" said a voice ironically, and I recognised that of Gerhard Eisler.

Then there was silence and I remembered why I was crouched over this hole in the cement. It afforded me a good opportunity of expressing my disgust in drastic terms.

We soon had other things to think about. The wind whistled through the boards of the huts, which had been built in the summer and did not even begin to be adequate as winter accommodation. An old Jew passed from high fever into a coma, and was taken to die in hospital only at the last minute. A young Socialist tottered out of the ranks at roll-call, leaned against the wooden wall and spat first blood and then gall. The next day news reached us that he would never again return to the hut.

At night the doors of the hut banged with the tempo of flails. There was no pause. The wind whistled through the straw. Shivering hands grasped the door. Despairing hands slammed it shut when sufferers returned from the latrines. The icy wind had frozen everyone's entrails. The huts writhed in cramp when evening came.

We wrote to Willi Münzenberg, the organiser of *The Brown Book*—how long ago those days of struggle seemed!—and asked him to help us. He had broken with the Communists and, as Hans Schulz had told me, was really free in Paris and in contact with the Society of Friends.

A week later bundles arrived containing blankets, boots, scarves and even gloves.

A cry of joy rang through the vast coffin. Thereupon the professional revolutionaries held another meeting and reached a new decision. As I was about to start dealing the things out, I was drawn aside by Merker, the envoy of the professional revolutionaries. He handed me a list of the names of those who were first to receive blankets; they were all Party-officials. Only after them were all the other "ordinary prisoners" to be considered. Thus had the professional revolutionaries decided. The words "preservation of the cadre" were used.

To this day I cannot bear to listen to those words. I threw the list in the dustbin. Perhaps I was already corrupted by the generous attitude of the Quakers, who had attached no political conditions to their gifts. Perhaps at that moment I realised for the first time, *really deeply*, that these lying and egotistical clerks would never better the world by one iota. Or did I secretly hope that this little cluster of professional revolutionaries would fall ill and their numbers diminish?

But they were not likely to die. I inspected their sleeping-places; they all had warm blankets! All they wanted, they impudently declared, was a third blanket to add to what they had already.

There were the disciples of another Allah in our camp. They called themselves Jehovah's Witnesses. They talked about Armageddon the way we talk about Marseilles or Miami.

Grotesquely enough, they had more success than all their political colleagues. Was it because they were non-political, or because they were right and the end of the human race is near? They arrived one evening. I was returning with Heiner, the first-aid man, from the wash-house which he had had cleaned out so that the prisoners of the French Republic, after three months' confinement, might for once have a shower.

Heiner grinned. "Sometimes laughter is the only thing that helps!"

Down the path came Hoffmann, the Hungarian with the Christlike beard and the melancholy eyes. Formerly the representative of an armaments factory, he had been as elegant as a gigolo when he came to the camp and had at once started to ruin himself by neglect. A beauty-strike. Only in one respect did he do the exact opposite: he wanted to remain aristocratic in the latrines. For this purpose he had had a sort of bar-stool made for him, a high seat with a round hole in it, so that he did not have to squat over the latrine, as all the rest of us were forced to do.

Heiner laughed disdainfully as he watched Hoffmann disappear into the little building with his stool.

The sun was now resting on the crest of the western hills, and glowing red, as though it wanted to burn out before sinking into the grave of the horizon. A stream of light flooded across the river-valley to the huge coffins and the little house into which the arms-dealer had vanished with his aristocratic wooden stool. I went quickly round the corner and saw a small group collected on the steps of the latrines. On the top step sat a red-headed youth whom I had never seen before. He was a Pole who had arrived with seven other youths that afternoon from Douai. He was talking and gesticulating with powerful workman's hands. Around him stood at least a hundred prisoners. The red-headed youth was speaking in German. He said:

"'But when ye shall see the abomination of desolation . . . then let them that be in Judaea flee to the mountains: And let him that is on the housetop not go down into the house, neither enter therein to take anything out of his house: And let him that is in the field not turn back again for to take up his garment. But woe to them that are with child, and to them that give suck in those days! And pray ye that your flight be not in the winter.'"

Never had the Bible been distorted in such fashion! Where in this place was the roof from which one might escape straightway into the fields? Who could here take flight, without at once getting a bullet in his body? What impudent mockery it was to pray that the flight should not take place in winter! We were still shivering at nights with the bitter frost, and winter was in all our hearts.

The young man then gave the reference for the text he had quoted—St Mark, chapter 13, verses 14–18. The figures were like a talisman. They afforded positive assurance that what he had said was true.

Oh, white land of Palestine, proud Jerusalem! Here is a Polish miner, a prisoner of the French Republic, again prophesying your downfall! He stood on the steps of a latrine saying it, and as at the Sea of Galilee they listened to him—the metal-worker from Dresden, the Ullstein editor from Berlin, the White Russian painter from Montmartre, the homosexual Turk who had been converted to Christianity, the betrayed officer of the Czech Intelligence Service, the Italian gambling cheat, two professional revolutionaries taking note of the proceedings, the young terrorist from Sofia and, a little apart, the distinguished Greek diplomat, the lover of Baudelaire, with the rosette of the Légion d'honneur in his buttonhole, smiling, sceptical, as astonished as I was.

"He couldn't have a better place for it," Heiner said. Indeed, the latrine, as opposed to the rest of life, stood very much in the foreground of our existence.

The Pole seemed to have smelt it. His prophetic utterance was as much surrounded by foul air as it was by the scent of decay that belonged to it. An angel of the latrines! A horseman of wrath seated on a cess-tub!

"He has the advantage," said Heiner, "that he can utter his threats aloud."

"He's exaggerating and will have no success," I said. "The chaps don't want to know it so exactly."

"Adolf was successful with the same methods," said Heiner, who that evening was as bitter as his own medicine.

The Pole on the steps had now reached the climax of his perverse, wrathful Sermon on the Mount. He warned us that the Judgment was near and that all statesmen would be summoned to appear before the judges—

Daladier and Chamberlain, Stalin and Hitler, Franco and the Pope, the trade-union leaders and the preachers in the churches.

"How he wallows in blood!" said Heiner.

There was a shuffling sound behind the prophet, and through the door of the latrine came Hoffmann, the arms-dealer, gazing absently over the crowd while with one hand he buttoned his trousers and in the other held the stool which was intended to make him superior to the rest of us. He was greeted with cries, and one or two pretended to box the provocative stool. The Pole saw that he had lost and that an element of comedy was fatal. Darting furious glances, he withdrew.

But the next day the prophet recovered his prestige when, with all his seven brothers, he bared his breast to the French Revolution and himself grasped the martyr's crown.

Our camp had been allowed the "privilege" of saluting the flag at dawn, with a company of the guards, when it was hoisted above the giant coffins out of the thicket of barbed wire to become visible to the surrounding villages, which we could not even see. We thirty civilians stood freezing in leaky shoes at the edge of the pathway by the exit-gate, gazing at the faces of the French peasant youths in uniform who stood opposite us, waiting to present arms.

We had to stand stiffly to attention; it was a humiliation. We first fully realised this when those primitive Polish wandering preachers refused to adopt that attitude of reverence. At the solemn moment of the farce, as the officer across the way shouted, *"Aux drapeaux!"* the Poles sprang backwards out of the rigid rows—it was as though they were recoiling from an infection.

They stood there in a furrow of the field and waited for the end of the ritual. Later one of them told me that he had expected to be shot on the spot.

Half an hour later the chief sergeant sent for me. I found him in his small office, with all his men around him. Outside the door, against the wooden posts of the barbed-wire fence, stood the eight Poles as though lined up for execution, except that their arms were not bound. I entered the wooden hut in alarm. The chief's glance calmed me somewhat. He was sweating and hurriedly turning over the pages of a book which I saw to be *Petit Larousse*, an illustrated dictionary. He was looking for the name of Jehovah, which the Poles, using Russian pronunciation, had called "Yegova." I was able promptly to enlighten him and further to assure him that it meant the familiar God of the Old Testament.

One of the guards cracked his whip impatiently. I remembered that I must do something to save these remarkable testifiers.

It was a battle such as Jacob fought. I had with me my small pocket-

Bible. I got it out, and for the benefit of the plump sergeant, already sweating under the weight of the problem, I translated all the Biblical texts relating to the end of the world.

"Show us where it says about revenge," said the sweating sergeant. I pointed to St Mark, chapter 13, Christ's visionary discourse on the downfall of Jerusalem, of which the Poles from Paris had made use. I translated the verses. The Corsican went out to have the words of the Bible repeated to him. Through the window, in much better French than mine, came the words of the Evangelist:

"But take heed to yourselves: for they shall deliver you up to councils: and in the synagogues ye shall be beaten: And ye shall be brought before rulers and kings for my sake, for a testimony against them."

The effect was immediate. The monotonous repetition of the verse from the yard was like a voice from Heaven. The guards were superstitious, like all policemen; they were religious out of fear. In that place where only blows were dealt, where innocent prisoners were assailed with filthy oaths, where the smell of Heiner's medicine-chest reminded half-starved men of repellant diseases, and where the tools of the road-mending squad stood about like instruments of torture, the holy words were striking in their denial. That they should thus be repeated, like the judgment of God, had the effect of a small miracle. The Poles had won.

They were taken off to prison and made to serve a ten-day sentence because—*tonnerre de dieu et quand-même*—God the Father had never said that one should not salute the *tricolore*. Drunken warders beat them at night. But when the Poles returned from prison they walked along the alleyways like canonised martyrs.

Then Weil, a German Jew, died. When I heard how he had died I felt as though I had been beaten over the head, and I did not know how to calm myself except by running out into the rain until I was soaked to the skin. There was so much stupidity in everything. This death was a master-stroke of the chaos in which we vegetated. It was stupid, ludicrous and shaming. I resolved, after an evening of profound depression, to endow the event with another semblance—Weil should be given a religious burial! I knew by then that Max Dessauer, before his right arm and his faith had been carried away by a shell at Verdun in the First World War, had been something in the nature of a Rabbinical assessor. Now, over this grave at the foot of the Pyrenees, he should sing the funeral dirge that certain shepherd tribes had sung two thousand years ago over the grave of David and over the grave of the heroes of Jericho. The camp-commander gave permission, "*à condition que vous trouvez un prêtre . . .*"

I turned to Dessauer. "Nothing of the kind!" he said, and shook his wooden arm against any temptation to renewed pious practices. Feeling my determination, he changed the subject and said, "But I can tell you a Jewish joke!" I sat down beside him on the straw and he began.

"For twenty years Samuel had refused to buy anything from the seller of lottery-tickets. Then one morning he bought number thirty-seven, and the same evening he won the big prize. 'How in the world did it happen?' cried the ticket-seller. 'A miracle,' said Samuel. 'I dreamed that a ladder descended from Heaven and a voice said, "Six—six . . ." The same thing happened three nights running. I was very puzzled, but my wife asked, "How many times did the voice say 'Six'?" I counted up. "Six times," I said. "Well then," said my wife, "you must buy six times six." And so,' said the worthy man, 'that is what I did. Six times six is thirty-seven, and thirty-seven won!' "

I laughed appropriately. After a pause I said, "Do you know why Weil died?" Dessauer wanted to know. "Because the head doctor said he should have *bouillon* every hour, and the orderly thought he said *bouillotte*, meaning a hot-water bottle, and that's what he gave him, and Weil starved to death. The most idiotic death one can imagine! Am I not right? Without Hitler there would have been no such confusion."

Dessauer stood up. "It's a reason for becoming a Rabbi again," he said. "Get the things for me!"

I got him the hymn-books and the cloak, advising him first to put it half on, and then wholly on, the way I had seen it done by Rabbi Tannenberg when I was a child.

A donkey-cart was procured, a coffin of rough boards, and the ceremony of washing the dead was carried out, although Weil should really have been washed before *rigor mortis* set in.

The camp-commander gave permission for the Jews and the dead man's close friends to accompany the coffin to the cemetery outside the barbed wire. Dessauer walked round Camp C saying, "Is anyone not a close friend of a Jew who has died of starvation in a concentration camp?"

At the appointed hour the whole of Camp C was assembled behind the donkey-cart. The guards did not dare to send anyone back. The gates opened. At the moment when the cart started to move I knew that I must escape.

The wind blew cold from the Pyrenees as Dessauer started his song. Perhaps he did not guess that his own voice would bring him back to God. Never did I hear such a Promethean *kaddish*, such a plea go out over the barbed-wire fencing, the frontiers and the fortresses. It contained none of the hysteria of the apocalyptical Pole. Dessauer did not make it easy for Him to whom it was addressed. Those standing round that hole in the ground were all the victims of human stupidity.

The grave was like an eye opened wide with reproach, staring towards

Heaven. Would Heaven answer, or, as the unspeakably silly Jehovah Witnesses proclaimed, must millions of such graves open before the great folly of death ended?

Dessauer asked no such question. He sang a Jewish *De Profundis* as though he himself lay below the ground and had been deputed to speak in the name of all those who were in danger in Germany.

His second hymn seemed to be a renunciation. "The Lord hath given, and the Lord taketh away . . ." But then, as his third hymn, he sang the true funeral dirge. This was no song dictated by the times. It was the submission of all Creation, it was the justified lamentation of the individual, who is allotted so short a span; at the same time it was a quite private lamentation of the man of Jewry, who truly has many questions to ask.

Shivering with cold, but happy to be able to stand for a little while on a free expanse of earth, I kept looking at Dessauer; he doubtless had a personal issue to settle with his God.

He went on singing, and I suspected that he sometimes sang the same thing twice over. He paid no heed to the shivering men round the grave; he ignored the lieutenant and the guards, who were watching the scene with increasing fury; he was communing with another Power which for years he had not invoked. Whether it returned an answer I do not know.

Finally, he bowed before the grave, picked up his cloak and folded it as I had advised. (Only later did it occur to me that this was a Catholic, not a Jewish, custom.)

We turned back with the donkey-cart. The gates of the camp stood wide open. "Too wide," I said to Gründler, my neighbour. Then Lieutenant Cons shouted to us to march in step. He had seen the camp-commander in the distance, standing outside his wooden house, and he wanted to show his zeal.

"Well!" exclaimed Gründler in surprise.

"You don't have to march now!" I shouted, and it was as though I were back in Spain and once more a Commissar putting an over-officious, tactless officer in his place.

"*Un—deux! Un—deux!*" the guards shouted and drove us into line with their fists. Dessauer, in the consciousness of his new dignity, walked at the side. Everything was in great disorder.

"*Pourquoi?*" I shouted, but then a fist caught me at the base of the spine, near my Spanish wounds, which were not yet healed. I cried out, but the "*Un—deux! Un—deux!*" was louder, and now the marching comrades had become a stream that carried me forward.

The guards ran like barking sheepdogs up and down the length of our column. They were taking revenge for having been compelled for a whole hour to think about death. They shouted down Dessauer's protests. They forced us to trample our hour of awareness underfoot against the hard-frozen mire of the road.

Why did I not spring out of the ranks and address them? I know that for an instant I thought of it, as the pain of my wounds eased; but then I thought of the Jehovah Witnesses—I could have nothing to do with their misuse of revelation. Still less could I have anything to do with the routine protests of the Communists. They advocated protest for its own sake, making of every injustice a "revolutionary action;" they lived on resistance and proved their theories with it. All that was over. There was another way—to break out into a new freedom. I would literally snatch my freedom. Away from these guards, from the barbed wire, into France, where somewhere there must be a hiding-place for me. And from this hiding-place I would send word to Marie Louise. Why should we not live somewhere in the mountains until everything was over?

I now wrote daily to Marie Louise. She busied herself with trying to procure an overseas visa, sat for hours in Paris consulates, wrote letters and, protected by an unusually good-natured young concierge, walked un-molested past all the poisonously glaring Frenchwomen in the big apartment house in Montrouge. Paul Willert and his wife Brenda most generously made sure that she did not want for anything, and Marie Louise especially valued the idea that our English friends had no nationalistic prejudices in this time of war. She was a fair-haired miracle that made its own way—but what good did this fairness do me in the mire of Vernet? Chaos had ap-proached too near with the stinking latrines, the silent hanged men, the beaten false prophets, the gnawing rats and our cheated love for France.

"You're going mad," said Walter. "You think. In times of crisis one has to distract one's mind."

Gründler, the Saxon, told me that he had come to the same decision. One might escape by joining the party which every week cut twigs for brooms in the Ariège. We would take money with us. My French was good, I could talk the guard into having a few drinks. He would not count us on our return, and so we should have the time from three o'clock in the after-noon until roll-call the next morning.

We revelled in the details of our escape. How long would we be able to survive in hiding without food? Where should we procure other clothes? Would God send people to our help? Would God . . . and there was the word again which we had not spoken—did He even remember us? We were a little ashamed, but then it rained for days and shame gave way to utter despair.

I continued with my work as chief of the hut. Thought for others helped me to master my own despair. From the first it had been a help to me, in this grotesque place, to be able to go on with the work I had done in Spain. What was a hut-leader? Generally an informer serving the camp-commander. But in our very intellectual "coffin" the officer of the *deuxième bureau* had thought it well to let the prisoners choose their own spokesman. The choice had fallen upon me; it was no light task.

Complaints, petitions, depressions, misunderstanding, bitter criticism, outbreaks of fury—everything came my way. To me it was like the prolongation of the Madrid days, although the office was lacking in all distinction. Too often it was merely comic and painful.

In the first place I had protested against the shaving of our heads. We had drawn up a petition, which had, however, been rejected. We had been herded like sheep to the shearing, and I remember that the humiliating nature of the proceedings was relieved only by the fact that Arthur Koestler, who was otherwise very reserved and furious at his arrest, had snatched the scissors from the barber before it was his turn, and in wild delight had cut great handfuls of hair from his splendid crop. "I've been wanting to do it ever since I was a child!" he cried, and then went quietly back to his place.

Another Jew died. I discovered that he had starved to death because he had simply refused to touch our rations, which were anything but in accordance with Jewish prescription. Silent and "fixed" in faith, he had ended his life in a corner.

I caused the camp-commander to be informed of what had gone on under his nose, explained the word "kosher" to him, and at once received permission to buy white bread and milk, two articles of diet which even the most rigid Jews could accept.

Then we found that we were becoming scorbutic. "Another petition!" cried the camp-commander. "You're boring me!"

I threatened: "In the first place we'll pay for the extra food ourselves, and secondly, you probably don't want the distinction of seeing the small cemetery in Ariège filled with the corpses of your prisoners!" He started and then gave way. We were allowed to buy potatoes and vegetables. We told the cook not to cook the harmful beef-suet any more, and bought it from him to fill our tallow-lamps.

All this was achieved by peaceful persuasion and without political demonstrations, and was decried by the Communists, whose principle it was to make a scandal of every deficiency. Even Koestler, who lived withdrawn in his own hut as a private person, regarded my methods as soft-handed opportunism, in this showing that certain tactics of his former Party still pleased him.

I ignored the black looks. I took no notice of the criticisms of the ceaselessly protesting professional politicians. I had now got so far that I could inwardly free myself from everything and prepare for flight.

Outside the camp I would again meditate on the dubious politicians, on their law of hardness, on their intransigence, on all their carefully considered inhumanity, on my own "opportunism," which relieved suffering, and on their "revolutionary tactics," which promoted suffering.

I now did nothing but plan my own and Gründler's escape. He wanted us to await the melting of the snow, and I discovered that he was contemplating an escape over the Pyrenees. "I should be shot there," I said. "Franco regards me as a war-criminal." He apologised. I proposed that we should make our way to Marseilles, and thence through Aix to Cézanne's Tholonet, where my friend Guilbert, the keeper of the Zola dam, would hide us for the whole war in the same place where he had hidden himself in 1914.

We talked enthusiastically for weeks. We stood every evening by the fence, our eyes hot with longing, until one morning, in the spring of 1940, a party of men approached from the valley through which we meant to escape at the next full moon. We knew at once who they were. I stiffened and clung to the barbed wire. The party came nearer. It looked sinister. They were bringing back a man who had escaped from one of the camps, leading him by a rope tied round his neck. There were wounds over his temples, and his face was caked with dust; he must have been knocked down more than once into the filth of the road. He staggered past us empty-eyed, like a beast being driven to the slaughter.

We remained standing by the fence long after the party had vanished into the camp. We did not speak a word. But too much was piling up in me, and presently I burst out: "I'm going all the same! I'm going tonight!" Gründler merely said, "Look who's coming!" It was a new vision of terror. From everywhere black guards appeared, like figures on a hellish stage, and shattered our world of illusion with inconceivable, ponderous force. Scarcely had they taken up their positions, with fixed bayonets, than a voice announced from the throats of the loudspeakers: "Whoever goes within two yards of the barbed wire will be shot!"

I slowly withdrew my hands from the wire which meant death.

So God was not with us, I thought. Why had I burdened Him with it? Why involve Him in this chaos?

I was sitting on my straw on the upper floor of the hut, absorbed in my quarrel with fate, when Count Schönborn climbed up, sat down without looking at me and cut himself a slice of my bread. He smeared dripping on it and reported that my horoscope was particularly favourable.

Someone called my name from below. The Count grinned and again reached for the loaf. I went down and found that a guard had been sent to take me to the commander's office. There I was informed that the Minister of the Interior, Mandel, had ordered my release. He had learned that the previous year, in Boston, Justice Frankfurter had received me in the most cordial manner. Justice Frankfurter was the Jew whom Mandel most greatly honoured. In addition to this, Hemingway, Lady Willert, Mrs Eleanor Roosevelt and Martha Gellhorn had intervened on my behalf.

I am sure that I flushed red. It was such a blow to the heart, as though one were again accepted into a family which one loved.

"This is all very indiscreet of me," said Nougayrol, the officer from the *deuxième bureau*. He was an archaeologist from the Louvre who specialised in Assyrian culture. "Another admission," he went on as he saw my agitation. "English newspapers were sent to you from London, but I was forbidden to give them to you. A second paradox—in September last year you volunteered for the French Army. That made you a suspicious case. Curious, isn't it? It cannot have been easy for you to volunteer. I see from your dossier that you have a son on the other side. A third paradox—and this concerns your future. At first we were told that you were still a Communist. Our dossiers sometimes dabble in remarkably muddy waters. The Communists in this camp have decided to get you at the first opportunity. You should beware of your former friends!" He was visibly moved. "And thank you for having been patient with us!"

A bugler somewhere was blowing the *"Aux drapeaux!"* as I left the hut. The snow was melting beneath my feet, and in the nearby field I saw the thin mist of the winter sowing. I do not know what it was that turned my head to look up at the spring clouds. "Thou hast again invited me in," I said aloud. Then the guard gave me a shove. I had to go to my hut and pack.

The next day all the inmates of Camp C stood by the exit-gate, through which the Negro Moia and Arthur Koestler had passed a short time before. Everyone wanted to carry my case, but Heiner, the first-aid man, insisted on doing so. He had been closest to me, and so he had a right to perform this service, which according to all superstition should bring good fortune.

At the last moment Dzelepis, the Greek with the rosette of the Légion d'honneur, stepped out of the ranks, cleared his throat and handed me a farewell address signed by all the comrades. It was like a school report on the examinations passed during that hard winter. It mentioned my protest, at the risk of my life, against the hair-cutting; my care for the diet of the Jews; the latrine-columns, and the beards which I had invented as a protection against work; the unpolitical blankets and the political peace; the chess competitions in the dark and the saving of the Jehovah's Witnesses; the driving out of the rats and the Christmas feast. But the last sentence brought tears to my eyes. "By your departure, Gustav, the camp is impoverished, but liberty is enriched."

The small, creaking door of timber and barbed wire opened almost solemnly. I felt giddy as I stepped forward and felt on my back the gaze of all those who would go in living in mire and indignity. I should see scarcely one of them again. During the winter, when Arthur Koestler had seen me running about trying to save the lazy ones from the wrath of the guards, he had often shouted mockingly at me, "Why do you worry about the *clochards?*"

Now the rejoicing of the *clochards* ran down my back like a warm wave. They did not grudge me my freeedom. Arthur Koestler had been wrong.

The road to the outside world ran past the part of the camp where for some months the Party-loyal Communists had been isolated. On the previous day, at a secret communication-point between the two camps, they had handed me a strange petition. They wanted me to work in New York for the freedom of the "cadre." They did not know how I had come to hate that word since the business of the blankets. They declared in their petition that they were liberals. I read it again and again, wondering how far they were aware of their own lies.

I asked for further explanations, and at the appointed time I went again to the place where the barbed wire was not watched. To my astonishment, the man on the other side was the Yugoslav, Theodore Balk. He was a good messenger, but his mission failed in ten minutes.

I liked him very much, this sceptical doctor of the Fourteenth Brigade who with an almost superhuman fearlessness had carried out his bloodstained work of rescue in the trenches round Madrid. The men had greatly admired him. He never displayed any personal vanity. He understood self-sacrifice, which was part of any Communist—indeed, this inspired him, who had so often been desperately poor and in need of support. He did not question the Party's right to call him to account at any time. But one day in July 1937 he appeared on my sector, pale-faced and with staring eyes. His wife, who had travelled over all Europe as an agent of the Comintern, had fallen into disgrace in Moscow. André Marty, the highest controlling official in Albacete, had at once sent an order recalling Balk from the front. (Family suspicion and family atonement was no invention of Himmler!)

Balk clung to his brigade as to a raft. From the beginning I had had the deepest contempt for Marty's theatrical performance with police power. I offered Balk work and the protection of my brigade, to which Marty did not venture to come. Balk had a meal with us, grew calmer and spent a whole afternoon bandaging the wounded. But he must have been overcome with fear during the night. He vanished and returned to his battalion.

Now he stood there in the mud, knowing that the Russians, in accordance with the Pact, would hand his wife over to Himmler. He should have cursed the Party, but he clung to it with a masochistic tenacity. He tried to explain to me that the pact between Ribbentrop and Molotov had prevented the outbreak of real war. Surely I could see it. No army was in motion. It was a pact of peace, all for the benefit of the proletariat. What difference was there between Wall Street and Hitler? Churchill was a warmonger. But it would not come to war. Germany and Russia would revolutionise the world.

I interrupted him sharply. In the distance behind him were the mountains of Spain, which we had lost because Russia had deserted us and German aircraft had shot us down.

How far away from me he has gone, I thought, as I stared at the pale-faced man who was trying to sell cheap Party stratagems as though they were moral truths. A verse from the book of Job occurred to me—"He shall suck the poison of asps: the viper's tongue shall slay him."

But I spoke the words into the void, for he had departed and the same afternoon I was told that he had reported to Dahlem, the leader of the Communists, that I had gone mad in the excitement of my release. (The Bible has a strange effect on Marxists.)

But still a third attempt had to be made that same afternoon by the conspirators in isolation. Oh, it was very understandable! I had so acquired the scent of New York, of freedom, of the world where conspiracy was possible, that they could not lightly let me go!

A third emissary was sent, the actor, Ruschin.

He came to the barbed wire with a joke on his lips and assured me that the case of my "weakening" would be deferred for a later Party tribunal, *provided* I would undertake to do what they wanted in New York. I answered that I was not Esau. He shouted back: "Your life will be like that of Cain! In no country will you be at peace!" I thought of Poland, occupied by the Russians. "Why Cain?" I asked. "It is you who are your brothers' murderer!" Ruschin spat and went away.

As I now finally left the camp he gathered at the barbed wire with the Party-leader, Dahlem, the writer, Rudolf Leonhard and Gerhard Eisler, so as to punish me with a last demonstration. They turned their backs on me, and Ruschin, the actor, did more than this: he raised his leg in an obscene gesture and broke wind.

That afternoon I boarded the train for Paris, and five minutes later went past the camp. Behind the barbed wire there stood in the mud, like a solid black block, the entire population of Section C.

I could not recognise any. They waved to me with a concerted movement of their hands. For two days they had laughed and showed their delight. Now I had become a stranger at the small window of the compartment. I waved back as joylessly. How could I have dared to display any joy? I think I even wept.

17. Coda

SEVENTEEN years later. The *Arosa Sun* has just let her anchor rattle down in Plymouth Sound. The chart on the promenade deck is marked with eight little red flags—eight stormy days since snowbound Halifax! The ping-pong bats lie idle on the green table. The passengers are German emigrants returning from Canada, Nato flying-personnel ordered back to England, missionaries on leave from their Eskimo life. They are now leaning over the rail impatiently contemplating the veils of fog slowly descending over the islands, the forts and the crane. The calendar under the ship's clock shows the date to be the 28th of March 1957. The pilot who is to take us into harbour is due in an hour.

I hold in my hand a glass of rum offered me by the French missionary. People around me are talking German, Canadian French and Neapolitan Italian. Nobody knows me; even my friends on the quay would not recognise me; but it is a soothing loneliness. It is like a cave, and I am tempted to stroll through its twilight and recall the past seventeen years.

I seat myself on the bench on the after-deck, under the closed window of the isolation ward. I notice the name-plate for the first time. It makes me feel as though I myself had been this day discharged after a long illness and were awaiting my own pilot. A good moment to think back and sum things up.

May 1940. The war had brought our seven-years' exile in France abruptly to an end. We got away from Paris to St Nazaire at the last minute. There were Belgian fugitives on the train to the port. Sawdust ran out of their children's dolls. German pilots had machine-gunned the fugitives from the air. Marie Louise looked shudderingly at the rents in the dolls, and when she began to play with the children their father asked where we came from. We exchanged glances and lied together, saying that we were Spanish. Marie Louise blushed like Peter at the crowing of the cock—but had she really betrayed anyone?

A week later we reached Ellis Island. A prison, but with no more air-raid alerts. Iron bars, but no more machine-guns outside them. Manhattan shone like a promise. Luxury food, clean bedclothes at night, hot baths in the morning. After two days we were free! Our friends gave a party for us on Washington Square. Mrs Roosevelt rang up—"I'm so glad you have reached our shores safely." They all wanted us to forget, and that afternoon they took us to the World's Fair. The town of pavilions had a look of un-ruffled peace. A Palace of Jewels rose before us. A robot walked in a house of glass and shook us by the hand. I thought of Vernet, the pale faces be-hind the barbed wire, the cess-buckets, the rats. We glided through the ex-hibition on one-seater electric cars. Marie Louise steered a dancing course through the crowds, like another Alice in Wonderland. A waterfall splashed outside Mussolini's pavilion, an invisible organ played Wagner. We had a sudden idea—we would get married. After thirteen years of illicit harmony. "To another eternity, Marie Louise!" Our friends gave us another party. Jay Allen, the Irish journalist, was best man; he was enormously kind. At the end of the ceremony he bent down under Marie Louise's broad-brimmed hat to kiss the bride. For a dollar a head we were able to go up to the roof of the Woolworth Building. A honeymoon journey above the skyscrapers! Time forgotten, the century forgotten! We looked down. Below us in the harbour lay the *Normandie*. We waved to her. The enemy had not yet reached his objective, Paris was still free. But suddenly the flag moved; it slid downwards and remained at half-mast. Marie Louise understood at once what this meant—Paris had fallen! She crouched in a corner and pulled her hat over her face. Jay and I stood in embarrassment gazing at the sky-scrapers. Marie Louise's shoulders shook, she was quietly sobbing. What a wedding-day it turned out to be!

Mexico, 1941. We lived behind a high wall in a small house near the lava-field of Ajusco. Cacti bloomed for a night, having taken seven years to burst into flower. The lava outside the door was five thousand years old. A round pyramid, which we could see from the roof, was even older. On the horizon rose the snow-clad mountain Ixtaccihuatl, the Sleeping Lady; she gazed into the blue sky without deigning to cast a glance upon the huge town. "Nothing here has any date," said Marie Louise happily. She loved the timelessness and soon began to paint. Her themes were neutral fairy-tales. She painted the fringes of the white corals, the bees at the edge of the oasis, the cinnamon-red fire-flowers of the icy-cold Lake Nevada—she raised her pictures protectively against the burning stage of Europe, which we all had in our mind's eye. She sought to convey the enchantment of the eternal spring which lay about us. Humming-birds one morning descended on one of her still-lifes of pomegranates.

This was the Promised Land! One took leave not only of yesterday but also of today; one could cast aside one's memories like soiled bandages. We lived for many months in this happiness, but then the ship brought my former friends to the safe shores of Mexico, and everything was changed. The Communist Party issued a secret order—"Regler is no longer with us, therefore he is against us." The Bible-true Communists! They had some success. By the next day I had become an agent of Himmler. On the following day I saw a cartoon in a newspaper which depicted me as a snake, sprinkled with swastikas, writhing out of the "tree of treachery." The tree, however, grew out of the split skull of the dead Trotzky. It was an incitement to lynch-law! Our house was watched by unknown youths.

"Let's go into the wilds," begged Marie Louise.

"Why should I run away from them?" I asked.

"I don't mean run away. Just go away!"

"They would call it running away."

"Does their opinion matter to you?"

The argument ended in the bitterness which began to poison us both.

Hemingway came from Cuba to see the bullfights. We had drinks at the Tampico Club. When we were out in the street again he clapped his hand on my shoulder and thrust me against the marble façade. "Why did you leave them?" (He meant the Communists.) Marie Louise tried to intervene, but he would not let me go; he was in an alarming state of emotional confusion. "Why did you believe them in Spain? There has to be an organisation, and they have one. Go back to them! Beat the slanderers in their own house!" After a time he turned away from me and cursed the whole world. "The US is finished, just like France. All Nazis should be castrated. The Russians are the only ones who are doing any fighting." Then he came back to me. "What do you care about the lies they're telling about you? All that's just chicken-shit!"

Only after long reflection did I succeed in setting my doubts at rest. Hemingway was a hunter. He had always had a natural taste for Kipling's jungle-laws. His books ended in death-tragedy; death had a mysterious attraction for him and always a meaning. It took longer for a man as unpolitical as he to understand that modern dictators had no respect even for the law of the pack, and that I could only have been one of their sub-chiefs for a very transitory period, while they were all going about clad in the sheep's clothing of liberalism. Hemingway thought too much in terms of black and white to be able to see through this masquerade. He mistrusted only one of my slanderers, a man who was hanged by his party in Prague in 1953, and he proposed to me that he should have him disposed of in Cuba. He saw nothing but the physical danger, and gave me money for a revolver. That the slanders wounded more than the body was something he could not understand, and he also misinterpreted Marie Louise's silent bitterness.

After his visit she shut herself off more implacably than ever from the friends of yesterday. It helped her that new friends appeared, unsummoned, who soon became an immeasurable new source of happiness in her life. I

mean the group of surrealist painters and poets who had withdrawn to
Mexico from Paris and London—Wolfgang Paalen, Alice Rohan, Onslow
Ford, Lenora Carrington, Benjamin Peret; and with them, at a distance that
was lessened by the common suffering of isolation, the Russian revolutionary
and novelist, Victor Serge, a survivor of the Moscow trials, who, even in our
first conversation, seemed to replace all my lost friends. Marie Louise regarded these new friends as a rediscovered family. What did the siege of
Leningrad matter, the threat to Moscow, the occupation of Kharkov?—the
wolves were quarreling among themselves. Her tears had been for Paris and
the tumult of victory that she had seen in her own country in 1934. In the
midst of the excitement of the slander-campaign she had a quite unpolitical
idea. The small house had a fairly big hall in the Spanish style. One morning
she started to hang her pictures in it. A defiance of all the baseness of the
time!

Here was a radiant stem of flowers, rising above scurrilous dead thistles,
which she had picked on Popocatepetl above the tree-line. Spring, high
above all earthly decay.

There glittered the constellation of the Swan, in which the astronomers
had discovered a hidden star. She held this discovery to be the event of the
year.

And there Don Quixote and Sancho Panza, wholly unpolitical pilgrims
into nothingness, trotted along a sky-line over which hung an enormous rose
like a rejoicing sun of petals.

All were painted with fine, Japanese brushes.

Paalen, the painter, appeared on the morning of the opening, bringing me a
majestic, terracotta god of one of the Guerrero tribes. He said with princely
irony, "In Polynesia when a woman bears a child the man receives presents.
Here is a present for the husband of the woman who has created this ex-
quisite display!"

It was the sort of language I had not heard for years. I read Paalen's manifesto on surrealism. The language was even more remarkable, even more
captivating. I went to his studio to look at his pictures. There was something
of *Moby Dick* in the lofty room of which one wall was entirely covered by a
panel of Eskimo culture; and beneath the ceiling hung the impressive, out-
outstretched phallus of a whale. As for the pictures—well, it looked as
though Captain Ahab had embarked with his ship on a happy voyage over
the ocean of the stars. Then, however, everything again assumed the dis-
quieting character of the prophetic. I remember one picture which had been
painted at the time of the Munich Pact in 1938. Paalen had called it *Combat
des Princes Saturnians*; it was an apocalyptic thunderstorm!

I stood in astonishment, feeling that I was undergoing a healing change.
What were the asthmatic leading-articles, the anaemic war-cries of the

politicians compared with visions such as these? A tree stood, rising out of chaotic cells, growing upon knees knocking with fear; it flung up witches' arms, trembling, hung with bats and fruit which were protesting skulls; it swallowed its own crest, shuddered and was itself defeated, was lashed by the storm of hatred which it had itself provoked, was senseless as all hatred, including the hatred of hatred.

The word "prophet" is as worn as a priest's stole; but through that picture I came to understand that one did not need to involve oneself in politics to discern the forces that were unleashed in that year of 1938. It was not the Brueghelian vision that took my breath away; it all went much deeper. My former friends had denied that anyone could grasp the significance of events without being an adept of the Marxist creed. Picasso had caused confusion in the minds of many when he saw fit to endorse Communism. Although his *Guernica* needed no party-permit, and his doves flew warningly, without membership-cards, over the first waters of the flood, the Catalonian master seemed nevertheless to want to prove that one needed to be a Marxist to understand the times.

Paalen refuted this superstition in that he showed himself to be bound up with the time in a more deeply tragic sense, and created pictures which were immeasurably superior to the simplicist world-philosophy of the materialists.

To me it was as though a prison-door had been opened for me which had never been locked. A painter who supposedly revelled in esotericism, who "cooked his stew in his ivory tower" and knew nothing of the real world (so the know-alls said), taught me that not only was this Church of dialectical materialism built upon sand, but that the god within it was made of straw. And men whom we had dismissed as merely frivolous had long known it! Now I made the same discovery everywhere: through Paalen's "starscapes," bold attempts to triumph over earth, through Alice Rohan's animation of the Indian temple-towns, through listening to the seasons of the year, through the irrational portrayals of human sacrifice by Benjamin Peret, through the pictures of the Spanish painter, Remedios, which were like magic mirrors, through the paint-poems of Lenora Carrington, through the entranced and never self-completing studies of this school which acknowledged no headmaster, I again became aware of the meaning of the decade.

It was the kind of thinking that still feels surprise. It was warm-hearted curiosity in place of class-awareness and permanent mistrust. It was a questioning that was not resolved when the answers were enclosed within a frame: on the contrary, every frame was a temptation to renew the questions. One no longer classified everything, as the intellectual poverty of the political fanatics ordained; one felt strong enough to let the wealth of ideas pour over one, and to find a resting place beneath this Niagara. One did not march with a parade-ground step, or, to put it better, towards an objective with a yoke about one's forehead; one was always prepared to break out towards new horizons, and in this readiness there was a greater fulfilment than Marxism had ever been able to afford.

Conversion was unaccompanied by penitence. I felt happy in my hair shirt, for I stood confronting myself alone with a new insight. Something more than a conversion took place: it was a return to individuality with all its lights and shades, its moods and inspirations, its vices and hopes. But it was also my return to Marie Louise, whose profound loneliness I now for the first time fully realised. Was it too late?

She had withdrawn into her painter's cell, knowing that in the same suburb in the southern district of Mexico City our new friends were working in a similar seclusion.

She painted the swaying forests of algae, those stair-houses stretching into endlessness through which the sea flows seeking; she painted tufts of grass as though she remembered when she had been a grasshopper, hopping through the meadows of Chapultec Park on armoured and clawed feet; she painted all the reincarnations that presented themselves to her on the sea-shores of Vera Cruz and Zihuatanejo. It was easy to see how readily she lost herself in them and yet never went astray. But I went astray. Delighted by so much painter's patience and so much tenderness towards the thousand forms of Nature, I thought it would be easy to find the bridge back into her world. Mexico helped.

Together we descended into the womb of time and reached the pre-Columbian races. Leaving Liberal and Christian prejudice behind us, we plunged deeper and deeper into the world of the Indios. At the Pyramid of the Moon we saw the first clay heads which pious faith had left there. In the primeval forest near Papantla we gained an inkling of the feverish splendour of the temple-towns; the lianas had not overgrown all traces of their holy remains. Near the capital, in the clay-diggings of Tlatilco, excavators had uncovered an old, gracious culture. We gleaned in the abandoned diggings and brought graceful dancers, large-eyed goddesses and smiling child-figures home with us.

In the middle of the plateau on which the capital was situated there was a hill called Estrella. We found flints and obsidian knives, and the splinters of thousands of jars. This was where the Aztecs had held their festivals at the turn of the centuries. Each time they had feared the end of the world, but, obedient to their priests, they had extinguished their hearth-fires and gathered round the hill to await the new fire that was lighted above them on the breast of a human sacrifice. This was Marie Louise's favourite excursion.

"What a tremendous task," she said, and gazed over the landscape, solemnly inhabited by extinct volcanoes, "to light the fire for a whole century!" She meant the man who was slain. It was the first time I heard how fascinated she was by the Mexican sacrifices; she applied no sentimental criticism.

During this year, which was not yet overshadowed by her own tragedy, we watched the hectic dance of children, near Teotihuacan, who scattered seed over the graves in a village churchyard to a tune played by an old fiddler. A Socialist friend who was with us talked mockingly about "foolish, exaggerated superstitions."

Her face closed at once. She never again spoke to him about the Indios. This scornful, quick rationalisation had been my former world. I was thankful that she passed it over in silence. "The atheist is still only a theologian," said Paalen and drew a smile from her. He had his greatest triumph with his Canadian Diary—the oaks, the beeches and the pines.

Marie Louise, when she read it, uttered a short cry of delight, as though she had let an awakening thrush escape from her throat. I do not know why I should have thought of Turksib, the Soviet train linking Turkmenistan and Siberia, of which the Russians were so proud about 1925. It was the train of the late technical century, the train whose whistle howled down all social problems, the triumphant pounding of cylinders, the victory of mechanical order. Paalen's voiceless Canadian train, which was swallowed up by the forest in its sleep and then became overgrown with moss, was the contradiction of all planned economy; it brought the great green fear back again, "the mother of fear" as Paalen called it; but also the healthy mockery of all planned economy.

In Paalen she read the words: "the steps of the pyramids, whose peaks rise above the emptiness of reason." "Bravo, bravo!" she said. "It is the only temple that has any link with the cosmos." She loved the Mexican pyramids because they were not graves but altars speaking to Heaven.

There was something in her emphasis that silenced me. Shortly after this we went with an American professor to Teotihuacan, to the silent, heathenish landscape of the Toltec priest-town. In the courtyard of the citadel there was room for a whole nation terrified by its faith. The Pyramid of the Sun rose on its broad base, defying all earthquakes.

"A solemn tribute to all our uncertainties," said the professor. Marie Louise looked gratefully at him. Soon after this she disappeared. I thought she had gone to dig in one of the excavations, but as we turned the corner of the museum I saw her broad-brimmed white hat on the second terrace of the great pyramid. I left our friend in a grotto restaurant and went after her. I found her stretched on the empty terrace with her arms outspread, her eyes closed, her blouse undone and her firm breast visible. I sat down silently beside her. We saw no land, but seemed to have been raised high into the realm

z

of the clouds; only the ants, dragging their crumbs, were a reminder of the earth and its labours.

After a long time Marie Louise said as though to herself: "One can feel the earth turning. It makes one giddy to think of the void into which it might shake one off." Her eyes were still closed and her fingers were scratching at the ground on which the altar had stood.

"One can rise up into it," I said, and she smiled.

"What they took out was the heart, and then everything was emptied out. It was a purification."

She's talking of herself, I thought; and I wished she would open her eyes and give me her hands.

I did not realise how much she was talking of herself.

Shortly after this I had a lapse into what I may call political goat-fever. News reached us from occupied Paris. Kurt and Jeanne, our best friends, wrote. The sight of the familiar handwriting on the envelope gave us a happy shock. It brought a flood of memories. The midnight suppers after the day's work in the editorial office. The shared work on *The Brown Book*. The shared struggle in Spain. Their sick child which Marie Louise had saved from death.

We had known the proud defiance of the persecuted; we had shared the bitter-sweet friendship of the defeated. I had been happy when I secured a Mexican visa for them. "What a consolation!" Jeanne wrote. "Just when one doesn't believe anything any more, when life has lost all meaning, a friend like you, a real friend, appears at the edge of the abyss . . ." In a postscript she said: "*Quant à vos affaires, les caisses et les 1800 livres, les dos verts ont tout pillé.*" (She meant my library in Paris: the *dos verts* were the Gestapo.)

The Gestapo had got on the trail. The collection of twenty years, irreplaceable first editions, Malraux's Burmese busts, Marie Louise's Callots, the two Franz Marcs, the Corinths and Meids, the Kokoschkas and Laurencins, the Beckmanns and Klees, all had been taken, lost for ever!

The young German officer who had found my Spanish uniform, stained with the blood of my wounds, had urinated on it—so Jeanne wrote. "What an unrestrainable hatred!" I said. Marie Louise smiled. "At least," she said, "I'm glad that I gave the Siamese cats to Jeanne in time. I wonder if she'll bring them with her."

We had sold pictures and furnished and decorated the house we rented in Coyoacan. A glow of homeliness filled the rooms. One evening when we returned from a visit to friends we found the outer door open. I thought of a political ambush. Marie Louise ran through the front garden into the house.

The rooms were empty, only her paint-boxes were undisturbed. All the cupboards had been cleared out, the beds had been stripped and my writing-desk had vanished. The thieves must have come with a furniture-van. We sat down on the floor. Suddenly Marie Louise said, "They've taken Walter's tuxedo." She meant the dinner-jacket which our friend, Walter, had given us to look after. "He hadn't worn it a single time," she went on. The house had suddenly developed an echo, so empty had it become. Marie Louise repeated the sentence, listened to the echo and laughed. Did she really take it so lightly?

The ships brought hundreds of threatened Jews and Communists from Marseilles. The *Liga pro Cultura Alemana*, of which I was on the committee, sent me constantly to Vera Cruz to receive these refugees. I saw Kurt and Jeanne standing above me on the deck. I waved but they did not recognise me. I looked for them on the ship, but they were not to be found. When the ship was emptied of its passengers I looked for them in the town, but they had already left for Mexico City. When I returned there I asked for their address, but I was informed by the Refugee Committee that they had been ordered to have nothing to do with me; they had asked that I should not be given their address.

Marie Louise stared at me with incredulous eyes. "But the cats!" she cried. "They should at least give us news of *them*! And of their daughter. Do you know, she couldn't lie in her bed. I had to nurse her in my arms and then she didn't feel the pain. But don't look so distressed. We shan't be staying here much longer!"

On the advice of our American friends we had applied for an entry-permit to the United States. Mrs Roosevelt had vouched for us, Hemingway, John Dos Passos and Jay Allen. The permit might arrive any day.

"I know," I said. "But I'm expecting another campaign of lies."

My expectation was realised. Further articles appeared. It was said that I had betrayed comrades in the concentration camp to the executioners, that I was living on money sent by Himmler, that I was living a life of luxury and dissipation in a villa in the south of the town—the exact number of the house was given.

New figures of remarkable aspect posted themselves outside our door, played with their revolvers and were relieved by other figures looking equally remarkable. A *cordon sanitaire* was set up round our life. The poet Pablo Neruda allowed us to be jeered at at his table. Groups of acquaintances turned ostentatiously away from us in the vestibule of the Opera, when I greeted them. The Spanish, grateful for my efforts in Madrid, maintained a painful neutrality. Mexico became as confined as a corral surrounded by wolves.

Our new friends helped Marie Louise, but neutrality was no longer possible for me. I kept the lies away from her, but she found a newspaper in which the Czech, Kisch, asserted that I had offered myself as an informer to the reactionary American Dies Committee, on condition that I should be allowed to enter the States. Lies which they themselves did not believe.

I saw the paper in Marie Louise's hand and was horrified by her look of sadness. For a second the thought flashed through my mind that she might believe this slander, but then she took my hand and kissed it. Then she locked herself in her room. Kisch had been a good friend of hers. That he should have invented this shameful story in obedience to Party orders was like a blow that passed into her blood.

On that day, of this I am sure, her illness began. She absorbed the poison of disgust into her system. The fragile body swallowed it greedily. On that invisible frontier of the genes, where everything is infinitesimal and at the dividing line between the psyche and biology, the process began. I am convinced today that all undefinable illnesses spring from this source. Evil comes only from evil; it is a hypothetical logic, but a terrible one. Some single cell, after such a blow, conceives the idea of making itself independent, and multiplies itself without heed for its organic place, multiplies itself a millionfold and kills itself, in that it kills the parent body.

At first I saw nothing but her mimosa-like fastidiousness towards other people. Only Wolfgang Paalen, Alice Rohan and a remarkably vital Dutch adventuress were allowed into her life. I told her that I intended to hit back, and I showed her the pamphlet I had written. She asked me to tear it up or put it on the fire. I explained to her, with fatherly superiority and in the tone of one who knows better, how the world has to be treated. Friends who were present, who had also been slandered, reasoned with her. I remember the look she gave us all, in the garden of our house, before she went to her room. I think she hated us. It was no ordinary hatred, but rather the welling-up of despair. She simply could not understand my inability to see the senselessness of the struggle. She wanted me to raise myself up from the ground. I gave permission for the pamphlet to be printed.

The answer was a string of even more grotesque lies and a particularly devilish war-stratagem. They conveyed a letter into the hands of the American police, in which a former friend of mine, now living in Mexico, told a friend in New York, accusingly and almost in tears, that I had, alas, become a Nazi. I was a very tragic case of aberration induced by exile. Perhaps I would come to recognise my error—"He was always such a gallant fighter!" —but at present I had slipped back so far that I was even seen with Franco's people. All this must be tactfully conveyed to our friends in New York, and, for Heaven's sake, nothing must be allowed to leak through to the authorities in Washington; it could only hurt the Movement as well as Regler, who might some day come to his senses.

The letter, which in its calculated anxiety completely convinced the primitive postal censors of the USA, was passed on to the Federal Bureau of Investigation.

And then came the day when all the demons flocked together, as though for a malicious Walpurgis night.

That morning I met one of the communists while I was on my way to the American consul, who, I imagined, was going to tell me that I might visit my publisher in New York, and, as I hoped, work there permanently. The States had become a matter of life and death. The German broadcasting station was there, to which I might offer my services. There were friends, such as Jay Allen and Michael Straight, and writers such as Dos Passos and Ralph Bates. There were libraries and liberal reviews, such as the *Nation* and the *New Republic*. There was wise, bountiful Eleanor Roosevelt, who in 1940 had welcomed us to the shores of the new world. There were the people of America, who had understood the Spanish war. So many irresponsible condemnations were uttered, so many foxes sneaked about Mexico, jeering at the sour grapes beyond their reach—but who had bought Paalen's paper, *Dyn?* People in the USA. Who hung Marie Louise's pictures? Who collected Max Ernst and Paul Klee? Who employed the great conductors driven out of Germany by the scoundrelly Goebbels? Who paid Heinrich Mann an honorary stipend and published Thomas Mann's trilogy on the life of Joseph? The USA! Even the enemies of all bourgeois morality, cynics and professional conspirators such as the known Communist, Eisler, had been admitted to the States as fugitives because in Europe their lives were in danger.

I had set Marie Louise's fears at rest with the news that I intended to keep out of politics and that I had offered myself to John Collier as a lecturer for his Indian Ministry. In a light-hearted mood I strolled towards the American Consulate, and, tolerant as only hope can make us, I greeted my former friend and invited him into a café. He looked hastily about him and then followed me. Skipping the preliminaries I said:

"Does a single one of you really believe that *I* am a Nazi agent, or ever was one, or, with sixteen Fascist shell-splinters in my body, could ever go over to Franco?"

"Of course not," he replied coolly and with a startling assurance. "But you have deserted us, and that is treachery. No pity can be shown to traitors. Your idealism is dangerous. It is not a matter of honesty or morality. In this battle all means are permitted. As a born Catholic you should know that. We bolster up inadequacy with our methods, and whoever interferes with this has to be eliminated. We made you a hero in Spain, but not so that you might work out a philosophy of your own. You should now of your own accord rejoin the lower ranks. Nobody stays long in the top rank with us, particularly when they have rebellious quirks. You have never grasped that. If you go on fighting against us we shall liquidate you—here in Mexico you're as good as liquidated already. I wonder how much you have ever really understood about dialectical materialism. Pay for my coffee and don't ever again speak to me in the street—understand? *Adios!*"

"You won't get a chance!" I was tempted to say, and a wave of happiness welled up in me. Soon I should be in the States! The peaks of Manhattan seemed already to surround me like a protective wall. There no slander went unpunished; there I would be sheltered by the phalanx of friends on whom dialectical cynicism had made no impression.

I watched my lost friend as he marched out into the street, strong in his borrowed brutality and yet comical, as he looked all round to make sure that no one was following him. (He fell into Khrushchev's trap in Europe in 1957 and lost his life.)

Half an hour later I was received by the American consul, who informed me that my application for an entry-permit had been refused. He could give me no explanation; he personally was very disappointed, because he had formed a good impression of me. Naturally I could try again after a certain interval. No, no appeal was possible, still less any discussion. "I'm sorry, that's all."

I went home by a roundabout route, turned back at the garden gate, because I was not yet sufficiently master of myself, walked through the nearby lava-field, staring at the high walls of split rock with their ugly invitation to fling oneself down; then blamed myself sharply for this cowardice and halted. I went smiling into the garden. Marie Louise was sitting under the yucca-tree, sketching. I did not at first know how to begin, but then I found the clumsy words, "We've no need to sell the furniture—the journey to Wonderland has been called off."

"That's the way it goes," she said, and went on to say that she had been to see a doctor about her right breast. He had spoken very bluntly to her and had wanted to keep her there for an immediate operation; but she preferred— oh, the smiling gesture with which she pointed to the geraniums rising beneath the window!—to die in this house. Quite right, it was hopeless, and really it was rather much, all that was being heaped upon us.

Only later, at nightfall, which comes so suddenly in the south, did the whole truth seize us by the throat. We cursed the gods. I smashed one of the clay masks that we had so carefully dug up, and flung the fragments against the blue-grey wall of lava-rock. The doves in the pepper-tree began their two-syllable cooing; it was like an invitation to the monotony that is called death. We resolved to make an end of ourselves in the dawn. We wrote farewell letters and tore them up—people should read in our yellow masks why we had gone. We drank burgundy; we danced to the music of a foreign broadcasting station that seemed at that late hour to be playing for us alone; we wept again, tears of defiance, tears of loathing. The poison-goblets, filled with slimy brown fluid, stood on the table. We told each other of our love, and recalled the pictures in the Louvre, and Montmartre where I had won sugar in the shooting-booths. We remembered the peasant-wedding on the moor and Cézanne's house in the park and an evening with André Malraux when for hours he had played like a schoolboy, shooting rubber-tipped arrows at a target. We remembered Hemingway's coloured servant at Key West, who after serving the fish had danced a step-dance in white shoes. We remembered beleaguered, sunny Madrid and the dead Werner Heilbrun; and we both suddenly thought of Kurt, the friend who, when I was wounded, had knelt beside the stretcher and kissed my bloodstained bandages, and who had now betrayed us for the sake of a party and who was not the only one. The world was filled with treachery—what was such a world worth?

We looked at the poison-goblets and felt their nearness. The bird outside counted the minutes of our last hours. Jasmine breathed its sickly-sweet breath through the windows and over our burning eyes. We fell asleep exhausted.

When the sun awoke us we looked at one another and said together, "Every minute is precious." Foaming tide of the blood—rose-red mouth—blue morning-light of her eyes—voice to which the birds answered—if we do it, then everything is washed out for ever, eyes, voice and colours—what is the sense?—if we are so denied then we have no more responsibility—we spring down from the anvil—what do we care for the paid writers of a distant State? Why should we travel northwards? This is our Egypt—Mexico has everything, unassailable mountains, impenetrable woods, cliffs with waving water-veils, bays which no warship has ever befouled, Indios who weave toys, orchids with tiny blossoms the size of bees, villages still at the beginning of all time—why run away and not know where one is running? Perhaps it is all nothing but a bad dream—perhaps tomorrow a different doctor will say something less brutal.

We tried many of these knowledgeable but still so shatteringly helpless doctors. Only when a homoeopath, who worked successfully on that infinitesimal secret frontier where everything begins, declared that the most drastic means, an operation, was necessary, did Marie Louise surrender to the threat.

She sought for a long time, and then met the Frenchman, Pierre Mabille, and decided upon him. She was travelling with him on a suburban bus when a pickpocket slid his hand into the pocket of Mabille's overcoat. Mabille unobtrusively but firmly seized the misguided hand, held it beneath his eyes, studied it carefully, then let it go with a shake of his head as though it were something no longer usable. The youth sprang screaming from the moving bus; this mute condemnation had shaken him more than any arrest could have done. Marie Louise was fascinated by the heavy, invariably cheerful man whose air of certainty made one think of a magician. She felt that he knew the "other side," and that not much harm could come to her if she trusted him.

She smiled at him before they put the mask over her face on which they dropped the anaesthetic; she followed his counting as though it were a priestly command.

She awoke still "on this side," but the magician was standing there. She whispered his name through the still-thick mist of unconsciousness, then she asked for Alice Paalen to visit her. She started to plan journeys at once, saying that everything was different, that a rebirth must have this effect and that she wanted to break out immediately. Soon afterwards she flew to the Pacific, swam in the sea where the dolphins tumbled, and pursued Indio boys who offered captured iguanas for killing. She bought all the animals she could find and set them free by the lagoon under the palm-trees, undisturbed by the laughter of the other visitors.

After several bright months of hope a doctor, using an X-ray apparatus which looked like a black fortress, found that the evil had returned and had begun to invade her right hip-bone. He was a doctor trained on Spanish lines who at once had a lie ready for her; but he sent for me in the afternoon and told me the true diagnosis, which amounted to a death-sentence without possibility of appeal.

I drove through the town with a friend, Peggy Paul. She had seen me come down the steps of the Röntgen Institute. I had nothing to hide; my gaze was directed at a land of destiny where politeness had no meaning. She saw this and proposed that we should drive out into the country. "Anywhere," she said in that casual tone which later she used even in the darkest hours.

Her calmness was now like a bridge back to healthy life. I simply nodded. I thought to myself that I did not know whether I would accept the bridge. Oedipus, I thought; as innocent as he, as helpless as he. Innocent? I looked at the woman beside me. She avoided my gaze, not wanting to appear in the role of a consoler. She turned into the Paseo de la Reforma. Garlands hung from tree to tree and lorries with laughing workmen roared past. "The contrast!" I thought, as I had done so often before—at the Paris Exhibition, with the children in Cerbère, at the World's Fair in New York.

We drove north and came to the region of the dried-out Lake Texcoco, where in 1519 Cuautemoc's treasure was sunk. We passed the house where in 1812 they stood the revolutionary priest, Morelos, up against the wall—he died quite alone in the dawn. We drove along the road where for hundreds of years the nobles welcomed the Spanish Viceroy, past the high wall surrounding the capital's mental asylum—hundreds of tormented solitudes in small cells!—to the deserted, mighty monastery of Acolman, in the building of which thousands of Indios had died—destiny, solitude, everywhere suffering that went disregarded, unrighteousness over which the cross was planted . . . but did this relationship relieve the smarting of my own distress? Comparisons did not help. Every suffering came home to oneself.

We drove in silence farther into the countryside. In the distance rose the pyramids. A burnt-out hacienda appeared, a village. Indios eating *tacos* stood at the edge of the street, a bugle sounded outside a barracks; a child was playing with a lively, tail-wagging dog, a guitarist played and strummed in a *pulquería*: peace, contentment, the living everyday.

But now the great pyramid appeared abruptly at the end of the road. I heard Marie Louise's words again, and saw her lying on the terrace as she talked about being shaken off into eternity and the cutting out of hearts. A knife of obsidian seemed to be plunged into my own breast. I could control myself no longer. I cried: "Turn back! This is all too much!"

From that time the pyramids were constantly in my thoughts, identified in my mind with what we had to expect. Each of us experienced it in the same way, but while she drew her loneliness about her, my knowledge of the inevitability of her fate made me aggressive and at the same time hungry for human company. In the background of every happening the knowledge lurked and challenged me. I never ceased to protest.

Every morning the threat was there; it was the shark in the turbulent waters of my dreams.

I saw Death gazing over her shoulder at her painting hands; saw him smile at me when I had arranged a little party and thought that I had succeeded in driving him out of the house as though in a dance. Then he pointed to the hour with an ironical jerk, and clutched at my own heart, it was all one.

But when the resemblance was too great, and I drew as close to Marie Louise as I had done on the night of our first despair, she sent me on expeditions. "One doesn't know anything for certain," she said. She cut herself off, turning me out of the realm which had been allotted to her; but then life again displayed its richness and she could not wholly resist its enchantments. So letters followed me upon my journeyings, containing advice designed to render my adventures more fruitful. She had carefully studied the archaeological atlas of the country. She sent word to me of unexcavated sites, led me from one excavated town to another, demanded telegrams about the discoveries I made, described the puzzling *monticuli* which I would encounter the next day, drove me on with the allurements of new Fata

Morganas, encouraged me to forget her illness. The *route imperiale* of marvellous discoveries seemed to have no end. They led me ever deeper into the land, and sometimes I was visited by the panic-stricken thought that she wanted to separate herself from me in this fashion, and in all secrecy depart; but then at the next post office there would be another letter with new, promising objectives, and these reassured me.

When I was in the State of Oaxaca she wrote to me about a cathedral which the conqueror, Cortez, had started to build and never finished. I rode for hours through the hot countryside searching the horizon for the building which she had described in detail, with its collapsed arches and the pillars that had never been given a roof. "It is an architectural *incompleteness*," she wrote, "like the deserted city in the sea in the *Arabian Nights*. Perhaps you will find a king there too, seated in the dark throne-room half turned to stone."

"This time someone has misled her," I thought at sundown, and rode dog-tired to the crest of a hill, and there lay the mighty fragment of a church below me in the valley! I galloped down, tied my horse to a pillar, and walked hesitatingly in. The ship of green sandstone lay open like a mussel that has been split by a giant hand. No town lay about it to give the building a meaning. It was like a half-prayer, exactly as Marie Louise had described it— an *incompleteness*.

I thought of her astonishing power of portrayal. She had never been here. I felt her at my side as I plunged in among the ruins; but the more I came to understand the building, the more insistent became the thought, "Broken as she is! Uncompleted, like herself!"

My footsteps became ever heavier. I was thinking of the paralysed king of that bewitched Oriental town as I came to a closed sacristy standing isolated in the shadows. Its grey outer walls were broken by small, barred window-holes.

I do not know what it was that prompted me to drag a big stone against the wall and peer into the dark holes; perhaps I was impelled by my melancholy and the oppressive silence of that godless house of God. I hoped at least to see, on the table inside, a forgotten jug to the rim of which some full-blooded priest had once pressed his lips. And then the pitch-black darkness lightened and the "crippled king" looked at me! I knew at once who he was; the crown of thorns on his forehead was but too clear. But at that moment he was something quite different; he was a dethroned monarch who wished to rule notwithstanding. The stained sceptre in his pale hand was like a magic wand to which the plague clung, the plague of suffering to which he had wanted to give a meaning.

I was struck by the relationship between him and the distant woman who had sent me here. I thought of Europe and of the war.

I got down from my stone. Everything had become a symbol of chaos—the Oriental fairy-tale, the crippled king, the amputated breast, the deserted Christ, the world war that would not end and this ruined church. I got on my horse and rode back to the nearest station.

Two days later I was with Marie Louise, whose goodness alone, as I knew, could rid me of the weight of a gathering despair; for naturally, as I sat with her under the yucca-tree in the garden, we talked only about the jade masks and the unexcavated *monticuli*, the fresco gods in the diggings at Monte Alban, the stone filigree-work in the temple at Mitla, and of how the old architects there had protected the coffins of the kings against the frequent earthquakes by means of movable flat stones.

As I sat talking I resolved that not for a single day more would I deprive myself of the quiet gaze of those blue eyes.

A short time after this it became known that a volcano had erupted in the centre of the country.

Peggy Paul suggested that we should drive there before it subsided. Marie Louise supported her—"A good idea, Peggy. It doesn't happen often in anyone's life. I'll go with Alice to the coast. You'll be able to tell me all about it."

As I contemplated the flame of the mountain and the roaring of the earth upwards into the deaf night-sky, something extraordinary happened: for hours this inconceivable, brutal beauty caused me to forget all the troubles that had tormented me for months. It was as though something of this power which had rent the earth asunder in a humble maize-field had been transferred to myself. I was dizzy with the rise and fall of my emotions. Before us the chunks of lava, big as coffins, dropped with a craftily soft "plop" into the grey carpet of ashes. A wild desire for self-destruction came over me, but after I had gone a few yards into the danger-zone it was transformed into an equally wild lust for life, simply life. At this moment I thought of Marie Louise. I looked at the waiting horses whose nostrils were quivering in their terror at the smoke. Beside them stood our guide, impartially wrapped in his *sarape*. I asked him if his village was still standing. "*Se fué*," he said, without raising his voice. *Se fué*—it vanished! They had tried everything. The entire population had made a pilgrimage on their knees to the growing mountain. Until the last minute they had left the Holy Image in the church. But every night the stream had drawn nearer, the houses had burnt like kindling, the church had been crushed like a hollow nut.

I put my arm under the neck of one of the horses and stroked it. Marie Louise would have done the same, I thought. As though it were a last gesture, before the stream swept us all away.

An earth-tremor shook the ground beneath us. A bird flew with a complaining cry out of the ghostly wood on our right. Everything seemed to be in motion, the earth might open anywhere, the broad landscape was the valley of helplessness. Overcome by giddiness, I seated myself in the ashes, which yielded with a treacherous softness. That was how Marie Louise would go, that was death, and it stood at my door! I asked my friends to come away. Lightnings were gleaming in the pillar of smoke above the volcano, but I could no longer take in the unearthly beauty. I could no longer face this cosmic force. I had been reminded too brutally of human nothingness and of my approaching, final loss.

When I returned home everything seemed to be in good order, but the next day the doctor told me that a metastasis had declared itself in the liver; the evil had not been driven out, it demanded its sacrifice.

I sat beside her bed and described the unreal, angry colours in the cloud of smoke above the red lips of the crater-mouth, the lumps of rock gaily rolling down the self-made mountain, the silent, leafless ghost-woods and the constant soft trembling of the earth beneath the hooves of the mules.

She listened as though it were a fairy-tale which I had invented for her. When I had finished she asked for her paint-box. After this she painted every day until she was tired.

It was as though she was defying the evil whose spreading no one disclosed to her. Every picture was a victory of colour over darkness, of tenderness over brutality, of harmony over the chaos of the cells. She painted for all our friends. For Eva, who loved cats, she painted the velvet of mossy branches; for Alice the maze of the meadows, where only butterflies could find their way; for Paalen a facsimile of an ancient Codex; for her doctor a sleeping snake-woman. She painted springs rising in triumph above the leaves of autumn; she painted the strange faces of the caterpillars who protect themselves against greedy birds with a human countenance.

It was a superhuman effort. The disease kept her awake, and also, despite all my precautions, war-news crept in and paralysed her for days. Then she began again, and her reds became more glowing, her yellows more alluring, her greens more hopeful.

I banned all our acquaintances who talked too readily about illness. I censored the American papers, which often went pretty far in their realism. Our little circle of friends joined devotedly in this *Eroica*. Alice cooked special French dishes, and every week brought a new picture to brighten her room. Her doctor talked effortlessly of miraculous cures, and she faithfully echoed these fairy-tales. I have never known how far the nearness of her end helped her to this faith, or whether it was a politeness of the heart which she practised towards us. Suddenly she would talk with peasant realism, saying that she would not take the pain-killing drugs, so as to have the full benefit of them if a major crisis came.

This smiling duel with death, that resembled a unique dance in its feints and stratagems, its advances and retreats, was interrupted on a day when I had expected resignation at the least.

It was August 1945. I had been into the town and had leaned out of my taxi to buy a special edition from one of the nimble newsboys in Bucarelli Street. Not until I stood at the door of my house, thrusting my key into the lock, did I glance over the headlines. Japan had surrendered! Excited by the sensational news I ran into the garden to her bedside. The whole madness of six ghastly years swept over us like a tide. But in spite of this I rejoiced. "Peace! Real peace! Final peace!" I stammered—who can find words adequate to such an occasion?

She read for a long time. Then she let the paper fall and said in a husky voice: "Have you read it carefully?"

I picked up the paper and read the details of the catastrophe of Hiroshima. I read the number of the dead who had been blotted out in a minute. I looked at Marie Louise's face, that yellow mask with a tint of greenish-blue, and realised what her horrified eyes were saying. It was a last protest. It was like a denial of everything which we had striven for together. I read the appalling justification appended to the report, which spoke of "preventing even worse blood-baths." I looked again at her face, from which all concern for her personal sufferings had vanished. I saw how she had withdrawn herself from everything that is called life as she said:

"In 1915, when I was a child, my governess once said to me, 'War? You want to know what war is? You must picture a man dying every minute.' I have never forgotten it, and I thought it terrible and abominable. And now it's 300,000 a minute!"

I only nodded. I was ashamed and wanted to crumple up the paper, but it seemed to me a too easy apology. I left the room.

That night she gave up. No diagnosis, not even the most positive banalities of official medicine, can persuade me that the progress of the disease enforcedly followed a biological law. I mistrust those who talk with so much certainty about the "course" when they know nothing about the origin. That life did not "run out" as science decreed. Marie Louise, though gnawed by doubts in her heart, had hitherto clung to her fairy-tale and believed in her home-coming, even though she was often the princess who saw the head of the martyred horse hanging over the doorway and cried plaintively to him, "Falada! Falada! How you hang there!"

On that August day she surrendered to the evil, just as the prisoners surrendered themselves on the summit of the pyramids. Only two days before the end she had thought that she must once again enact the fairy-tale before us all. She had allowed me to arrange a party that was to drive all shadows out of the house for a whole Sunday afternoon. Round the hall hung the last pictures she had painted. In the next room hung *The Coach*, which Alice had brought her: a dreaming picture with the questioning of the twilight and all the promises of a boulevard already stretched beneath the stars.

The string orchestra tuned its instruments. Walter Stein, from Vienna, conducted the concert.

Marie Louise lay in the next room talking to the four women-friends whom alone she had allowed to come to her bedside. She called them graciously her ladies-in-waiting. Our other friends, nearly forty in all, sat in the garden, or round the four musicians' stands or round the hearth, where a fire burned. The musicians had elected to play Mozart and Haydn. They ended with the *Kleine Nachtmusik*. I had never before so deeply felt the melancholy of the music.

It was as though one were standing in the park at Versailles, where it vanishes into the distance and where its artificial lakes become countrified. There were the cream-coloured horses, around whose hooves the leaves drifted. It was an *Adieu sans paroles* enveloped in a thin mist of autumn timelessness. An hour before sunset. At moments the dance-step became too distinct, wringing the heart of all those who did not want to let the woman go. But Marie Louise lay gazing with wide eyes at the landscape which Mozart unfolded.

Two days later she got up and insisted on going for her X-ray treatment. Her face was a deep yellow, she had a red rose in her hand. The next day she asked for an injection and slept. In the outer room our friends were again assembled, the fire burned, the doctors did not leave. Something bound them to that silent death. They talked of miraculous cures as though they wanted these fables of hope to penetrate the wall and accompany the sleeper on her journey. I looked at our friends one after another. They had been good friends, but at that moment of softly but unequivocally ordered accounting they were all a little more than themselves.

Serge sat by the window looking at a cluster of yellow orchids. Alice had brought the cluster, but Marie Louise had not looked at it. *"C'est la preuve,"* she whispered to me in the garden. *"Elle est déjà partie."* She said it softly, but the words were the more positive on that account. She went to the fireside, she did not want any words to be wasted, each of us has the right to our own death. She talked to none of the visitors, whose number steadily increased; she sat by the fire and stared at the ashes, which here and there breathed out a soft red.

In that hour Marie Louise departed. An emptiness ensued which had no bounds. The worlds mingled and overlaid one another. My desire for any kind of continuation in the familiar place was implacably denied. Even her pictures did not know me any more. The rainbows that had still stretched above that bed paled into a shark-grey sky; the guilt of survival flooded the day, whose silence was too unequivocal, for there was only this secret of the breath-stilled mouth—was there any other at all? Was it a beginning or an end? Heaven remained dumb.

Our ship's siren utters three short, dark cries. I jerk myself back into this lonely 28th of March 1957. I am still holding the Eskimo priest's glass of rum in my hand. A tender appears out of the mist, steering towards our high bows. The pilot is coming to guide me back into the old world. I look about me in my new reality.

Islands with crumbling fortress-towers rise above the waters. They have become a parody of security. Slate-grey destroyers lie pitching on the waves; they have been brought here to be broken up.

The mist hangs like a shroud over the town, where many gaps are to be seen. I can make out a church with its windows blown in. Is everything really waiting for another war?

Why am I thankful because Marie Louise is no longer here? A rampart of the fortress has collapsed as though in a ruthless earthquake and lies on the damp lawns, which are without colour. No one seems to think of rebuilding the look-out towers, nor has any pious subscriber come forward with money for the church windows.

The pilot-boat has come alongside and the gang-plank has been run out. I look for a last time at the throttled harbour—*is everything really beginning again?*

A jet-fighter swoops invisibly through the grey clouds like a too-near comet. I empty my glass of rum at a gulp, and as the drink runs down my throat I think of the scene with which my childhood began—a man in uniform dragging a grown-up, the tailor of Merzig, by the ears up the steps of the *Rathaus*. To what tribunal, and before what masters, I have never discovered. But even if I had discovered it, would I know who has the right to judge?